NEW TE

SANCTITY OF TIME AND SPACE
IN TRADITION AND MODERNITY

JEWISH AND CHRISTIAN PERSPECTIVES SERIES

VOLUME I

SANCTITY OF TIME AND SPACE IN TRADITION AND MODERNITY

EDITED BY

A. HOUTMAN

M.J.H.M. POORTHUIS

J. SCHWARTZ

BRILL

LEIDEN · BOSTON · KÖLN

1998

Bar-Ilan University, Israel

 Catholic University of Utrecht, The Netherlands

 This book is published with the financial support of
The Rennert Center for Jerusalem Studies,
Faculty of Jewish Studies, Bar-Ilan University, Israel

This book is printed on acid-free paper.

Die Deutsche Bibliothek - CIP-Einheitsaufnahme

Sanctity of time and space in tradition and modernity / ed. by A.
Houtman ... – Leiden ; Boston; Köln : Brill, 1998
(Jewish and Christian perspectives series ; Vol. 1)
ISBN 90–04–11233–2

Library of Congress Cataloging-in-Publication Data is also available

ISSN 1388-2074
ISBN 90 04 11233 2

PRINTED IN THE NETHERLANDS

CONTENTS

PART ONE

STUDIES IN THE HISTORY OF
SACRED TIME AND SPACE

PART TWO

POSTBIBLICAL PERIOD

PREFACE

In June of 1993, scholars from Israel, the United States and the Netherlands met at Bar-Ilan University in Ramat-Gan, Israel for a conference devoted to 'The Centrality of Jerusalem'. The conference was organized by the Department of Land of Israel Studies of Bar-Ilan University and the Catholic Theological University of Utrecht. This was the beginning of a fruitful discussion and exchange between these two institutions, a Jewish and a Catholic University, examining issues of supreme importance to each religion, searching for what unites them while at the same time pointing out what is unique to each. The results of that conference were published by M. Poorthuis and Ch. Safrai as *The Centrality of Jerusalem: Historical Perspectives* (Kampen, 1996).

Three years later, in August of 1996, a second conference was held once again at Bar-Ilan University, this time under the auspices of the Ingeborg Rennert Center for Jerusalem Studies at Bar-Ilan (founded in 1995) and the continued auspices of Catholic Theological University of Utrecht and its research project "Relatie Jodendom Christendom". This conference was devoted to the theme 'Sanctity of Time and Space in Tradition and Modernity', a direct outgrowth of the study of Jerusalem at the first conference and once again studied both that which unites as well as which divides Judaism and Christianity regarding issues of sanctity at the very core of their individual existences. The present volume represents the fruits of that conference and proves once again that peaceful scholarly discussion can well bridge gaps created by centuries of tension and often much worse. At the conclusion of the proceedings, an agreement of cooperation was signed between Bar-Ilan University and the Catholic Theological University expressing a desire for continued dialogue and exchange in order to tackle the study of even the thorniest of issues important to both religions. This discussion will be continued at the next conference to take place at the Catholic Theological University in Utrecht, June-July 1998, and will be devoted to the study of 'Purity and Holiness' in Judaism and Christianity.

The present volume, as well as the one to be published based on the proceedings of the 'Purity and Holiness' conference appear or will appear as part of a new series of E.J. Brill in Leyden entitled: *Jewish and Christian Perspectives* to be published in cooperation with the Ingeborg Rennert Center for Jerusalem Studies of Bar-Ilan University and the Catholic Theological University of Utrecht. The series in general will attempt to present findings relative to both Jewish and Christian tradition to a broad audience of scholars. It is our hope that this first volume of the new series will represent both increased dialogue and study.

Thanks are due to the editor, Mr. Freek van der Steen, whose indefatigable efforts were indispensable for the realization of this volume and of the series at large. Thanks are due also to our publisher Brill in Leiden for the confidence in this project.

Utrecht and Ramat-Gan, May 1998

Alberdina Houtman
Marcel Poorthuis
Joshua Schwartz

Dr Alberdina Houtman is research fellow at the Theological University of Kampen, The Netherlands.

Dr Marcel Poorthuis is Coordinator of the research project "Relatie Jodendom Christendom" (RJC) at the Catholic Theological University of Utrecht, The Netherlands.

Prof. Dr Joshua Schwartz is Director of the Ingeborg Rennert Center for Jerusalem Studies and Professor of Historical Geography of Ancient Israel at Bar-Ilan University, Ramat Gan, Israel.

PROLEGOMENA

The scientific transliteration of the Hebrew is according to the directives of the American Academy of Religion and the Society of Biblical Literature Membership Directory and Handbook. In cases where a scientific transliteration was not considered necessary, a simplified transliteration was used. Names of rabbis are anglicized according to G. Stemberger's Introduction to the Talmud and Midrash, Edinburgh 1996 (authorized English translation by M. Bockmuehl of Einleitung in Talmud und Midrasch, München 81992).

In the references to talmudic literature, the following abbreviations are used: T= Tosefta; M= Mishnah; BT= Babylonian Talmud and PT= Palestinian Talmud. The individual talmudic tractates, as well as the names of other rabbinic works, are abbreviated according to the list on pages 374-375 of the Introduction to the Talmud and Midrash. For references to the Mishnah or the Tosefta, the abbreviated names of the tractates immediately follow the designation of the work: for example, 'MBer' for 'Mishnah Berakhot' or 'TSheb' for 'Tosefta Shebiit'. For references to the Talmuds, the abbreviated name of the tractate is separated from the designation of the work by a space: for example, 'PT Shab' for 'Palestinian Talmud tractate Shabbat' For the BT, only the tractate and the folio number are given. The PT is cited by tractate, halakhah, folio number and column. The abbreviations of the names of biblical books are according to the directives of the AAR/SBL Membership Directory and Handbook. Other abbreviations used are according to general standards for academic journals. The translation of biblical passages is according to the preference of the individual authors.

EDITORIAL STATEMENT

Judaism and Christianity share much of a heritage. There has been a good deal of interest of late in this phenomenon, examining both this common heritage, as well as the elements unique to each religion. There has, however, been no systematic attempt to present findings relative to both Jewish and Christian tradition to a broad audience of scholars. It is the purpose of the proposed series to do just that.

Jewish and Christian Perspectives will publish studies that are relevant to both Christianity and Judaism. The series will include monographs and congress volumes relating to the Hebrew Bible and New Testament, the Second Temple period, the Judaeo-Christian polemic (from Ancient until Modern Times), Rabbinical literature relevant to Christianity, Patristics, Medieval Studies and the Modern Period. Special interest will be paid to the interaction between the religions throughout the ages. Historical, exegetical, philosophical, and theological studies are welcomed as well as studies focusing on sociological and anthropological issues common to both religions, including archaeology.

Detailed information can be obtained at:
http://www.biu.ac.il/js/rennert/jcp

INTRODUCTION

Alberdina Houtman, Marcel Poorthuis
& Joshua Schwartz

One of the first casualties of modern-day society has been religion in general and the sacred in particular. Sacred became passé; secular and the quest for universal became the religion of modern man and that 'religion' for the most part centered on the here and now. Both Judaism and Christianity, however, had and indeed still have a different perspective. For both religions the notion of sacredness of time and space still is central, be it interpreted in very different ways.

Thus, both religions are oriented towards some type of meta-historical time, created by an encounter with the Divine. Meta-historical time, however, should not be understood as a separate reality without any impact upon history. On the contrary; historical events receive their significance in connection with the Divine. History is shaped and determined by continued appearances or visitations of God, imparting a sacred nature to at least some privileged moments and places. Sacred time takes on characteristics of its own and should not be measured by quantitative standards. As an important element of human experience, sacred time is in that respect no less fundamental and 'real' than the more quantitative clock-time. Sacred time is a complex phenomenon: it can be linear and it can be cyclical and it can be traversed in different directions and through different dimensions. Nor should cyclical time be considered as the only form of sacred time-experience: the cyclical returning pattern of time may be integrated into a more linear pattern by which a spiral is formed. The yearly cycle of the liturgy itself is a contraction of the whole of history, but transcends the 'myth of eternal return'. Past, present and future, i.e. creation, revelation and redemption, are woven into a messianic pattern. Renewal is a key-word here, achieved by remembrance of the past and expectation of the future.

Past, present and future in this conception of sacred time are all in some way oriented to God. In this way, profane history is intrinsically connected to Divine meta-history. Prayer, liturgy and morality are the concrete means to establish and to live that connection. Historical events form the backbone of this liturgical experience of time. This holds good for Judaism as well as for Christianity. The fragmentary nature of sacredness of time – not the whole week is holy, but only one day – can be interpreted as a *pars pro toto*: the partial time set apart as a holy day, contains in itself the program for time as a whole.

A similar observation can be made about sacred space. Space also can take on a sacred nature in both Judaism and Christianity accompanied by a permanent critical attitude towards that sacred nature. There are numerous forms of spatial sacredness in both religions (in spite of claims to the contrary). Sacred space may be geographic territory such as the 'Holy Land' or it may be of a more limited nature such as a building: a synagogue, church, monastery or 'holy site'. What is common to all sacred space is again its fragmentary nature: it is set apart from space that is not sacred, whether this 'other' space is neutral or profane. Thus, boundaries and boundary markers are necessary and essential characteristics of any space that is holy. How does one get to this sacred space, however, and how does one act once there? Thus, there are often laws and restrictions regarding the types of behavior permitted within holy space. What happens, though, to those who do not conform to these requirements? Conceptions of sacredness imply a conception of community and of society at large.

Socialization is also of great importance for all levels of sacred space and raises many relevant issues. Are the characteristics of sacred space unifying or not within that sacred space or without? Does holy space impart membership in a 'holy society' and are there different pre-requisites and standards for different genders and do gender differences affect the process of socialization in sacred space? Do different groups within the sacred space have different definitions for this sacred space and are these different definitions sometimes mutually incompatible and exclusive? Does original sacred space develop or change in relation to

changes outside of it or perhaps even instigated by it? What is the
relation of sacred space and those within it to the profane?

The question of accessibility, though, is not just a matter of
physical characteristics, but also one of 'proper time' and of sacred time. There is a relationship of sacred space to sacred time.
Do they function in concert or are they occasionally in opposition
to one another? A specific problem is the attitude of both Christianity and Judaism toward 'pagan' sacred places. The reaction of
wholehearted rejection might be expected but is nevertheless exceptional: tacit integration into the own cult is more often the preferred strategy.

It is clear that exactly these issues have been a bone of conten-
tion between Judaism and Christianity for centuries. The interpretation of sacred space is strongly connected to the notion of
'people' in Judaism, while Christianity strove to lessen that tie.
And although Christianity and Judaism use a similar underlying
pattern of creation, revelation and redemption in their interpretation of sacred history, needless to say the concrete outcome of
this interpretation is widely divergent. The studies in this book do
not avoid these differences. It is precisely these differences that
offer a better understanding of one's own religion. The articles,
ranging from biblical until modern times, deal with a wide range
of matters related to sacred time and space in both Judaism and
Christianity.

Isaiah's vision of the Temple (2:1-4) is traditionally held by
scholars to be a vision of universal peace and of pilgrimage by all
nations to Jerusalem. Baruch Schwartz undertakes a fresh examination of the text by comparing it to Deuteronomistic ideas about
the High Court of Arbitration. Isaiah turns out to be an appeal to
Israel to restore the Mountain of the Lord as a place of Justice to
be appreciated by all nations. Rather than universal peace and a
widespread acknowledgment of Israel's God, an appeal to Israel
seems to be the key to this famous prophetic text.

Pancratius C. Beentjes presents an interesting interplay between time and space in the biblical period. In examining Nathan's Oracle and David's Prayer in 1 Chronicles 17 and in comparison with its parent text in 2 Samuel 7, Beentjes shows that the

category of time prominent in the parent text has been subordinated in Chronicles to the category of space and what remains of
time, the Davidic dynasty of 2 Samuel, has been transformed into
a text relating basically just to Solomon. These changes are the
result of 'historical' time and events with which the Chronicler
was familiar.

The biblical heroine Hanna confronted the Priest Eli at the cultic site of Siloh. Post-biblical Judaism developed this event by
portraying Hanna as a prophetess of no mean stature. Pseudo-
Philo is a valuable testimony to this phenomenon. Bart Koet
demonstrates how the evangelist Luke was inspired by these same
developments in his description of the infant Jesus in the Temple,
hereby shifting the scene from Siloh to Jerusalem.

Bethesda is known from the Gospel of John as a place of healing. Apparently, the site was known for its healing power within
Judaism well before the rise of Christianity, a fact that has been
corroborated by archaeological evidence. Archaeological discoveries have proven that at a certain time pagans also frequented
that place. How should Christian tradition explain the healing
power of a site that works for both Jews and Christians and pagans – and in later time for moslems? Martien Parmentier discusses mediaeval legends about the wood of the Cross being
hurled in the pond. This motif is shown to be related to the holy
character of Bethesda even in pre-Christian times.

Lawrence Schiffman debates Qumran's topographical purity
system. The sanctity of the City of Jerusalem was greater than
that of the rest of the Land of Israel. Yet the Temple precincts
with their three concentric courtyards were of even greater sanctity.

The realm of Jewish mysticism has received considerable attention in the scholarly world. Lieve Teugels demonstrates how
rabbinical traditions about the holiness of Mount Sinai can be
connected to mystical traditions about the vision of the Merkabah.
Even in early rabbinical Midrash, the *Mekhilta*'s preoccupation
with questions of God's presence on the Mountain can be detected, in spite of reservations regarding mystical tendencies.

Shmuel Safrai shows how the understanding of Jerusalem in
the tannaitic literature of the first generation after the destruction

of the Temple was to a great extent the continuation of views held at the end of the Second Temple period. Thus many of the testimonies centering on Jerusalem and its Temple before its destruction in the year 70 CE were transmitted by sages who lived after the destruction. Also many traditions and even chapters and tractates describe the Temple service resulting in a continuum of tradition and of veneration for the sanctity of the Temple.

By studying the references to Jerusalem in Mishnah and Tosefta *Berakhot*, Alberdina Houtman comes to a remarkable discovery: there are hardly any references to Jerusalem in Mishnah Berakhot, whereas in its toseftan counterpart, the City is mentioned numerous times. Even when one takes into consideration the Mishnah's brevity in comparison with the Tosefta, this phenomenon remains remarkable. At least part of the textual history of Tosefta Berakhot must be looked for in Babylonia which may account for this difference in orientation between Mishnah and Tosefta.

Joshua Schwartz shows how a particular type of behavior in a holy site, standing or sitting in the azarah, the internal courtyards of the Temple Mount, was not absolutely mandatory but determined by time. The realities of everyday life, i.e. historical time, dictated a more lenient approach allowing sitting in the azarah during non-cultic occasions. After the destruction of the Temple, when it was transferred to the realm of meta-history, a much more rigorous code of behavior was retroactively demanded.

After these Jewish testimonies of sanctity of time and space, the scene shifts to the Christian evidence. The picture of Christianity being attached to holy sites against a Judaism that rejected such practices should be strongly challenged. Ze'ev Safrai investigates the cult of holy sites in Christianity from its inception. It can be demonstrated that many places were not yet holy sites in the proper sense when they first made their appearance in Christian literature. The development from holy place to a cult site venerated by many believers could take several centuries and shows a consistent pattern.

Hillel Newman follows the tracks of the ascetic Church Father Jerome. Known for his radical tendencies and antagonistic attitude, Jerome's relation to holy places seems to be contradictory.

Ideas of Jerusalem being internalized in man appear next to traditions praising pilgrimage to the Holy City. On closer scrutiny, a
general abhorrence of the depravities of city life induced Jerome
to settle in the village of Bethlehem, considered by him the holy
place 'par excellence', more so even than Rome.

   Both Judaism and Christianity cannot be studied in isolation
from one another. The following studies aim at an explicit comparison between the two. Marcel Poorthuis studies the vicissi-
tudes of Moses' Rod in Jewish and in Christian traditions. The
Rod served as a crystallization for a wide range of traditions. By
reconnecting Moses' Rod to Paradise and to the Messiah's Rod,
midrashic traditions weave an underlying pattern of creation,
revelation and redemption. By doing so, these post-biblical Jewish texts completely transform biblical time and space. The
Christian identification of the Rod with the Tree of Life and the
Cross implies a no less dramatic transformation of time and
space. Here as well, creation, revelation and redemption are
strongly linked together. Both perspectives serve a similar goal,
but precisely because of that similarity, these texts are highly antagonistic.

   Gerard Rouwhorst notes the need for structuring and sanctifying time and space both in Judaism and Christianity. He examines
two essential elements of early Christian liturgy from the Syriac
realm that shared both geography and language with many elements of talmudic Judaism. The celebration of Passover / Easter
and the plans of Church buildings in which these Syriac Christians celebrated their liturgy, can be tied to Jewish customs and to
the plans of synagogues. He finds elements which both liturgical
traditions have in common as well as Jewish influences on Christian tradition and mutual influences between both.

   Aaron Demsky compares two outstanding archaeological finds
in order to clarify the Jewish and the Christian perspective of the
'Holy Land': the Reḥob mosaic containing a text from the Palestinian Talmud, and the Madaba Map, displaying a map of the
Holy Land in mosaic form. These two finds have much in common, dating roughly from the same period and located at a distance of only some 100 kms from one another. However, their
ideological outlook differs strongly: whereas for Christians the

concept of the holy places accounts for the holiness of the Land, the Jewish text expresses the sanctity of the Land abiding by talmudic laws pertaining to agriculture.

Traveling through history we finally arrive at the modern era. Paul Post examines how sacred space and time come together in the ritual of pilgrimage and particularly in terms of post-modern Christian pilgrimage. Processes of new sacralizing and liturgizing are developed. Often the tension between remembrance of the past, living in the present and looking forward to the future which had been a focal point of classical pilgrimage has been defused. Post-modern pilgrimage may develop into a type of 'living history' creating a pilgrimage process leading to pseudo-sacredness of commerce and decoration.

Ophir Yarden deals with a remarkable aspect of civil religion in modern Israel: the cult of Theodor Herzl at Mount Herzl. While abstaining from explicit religious symbols, state regulations about the customs to be observed at his tomb show a remarkable similarity with traditional Jewish customs. Even the date of commemoration itself can be related to religious issues. Without claiming to reduce 'civil religion' to pseudo-religion, the interaction between both is a surprising phenomenon.

The poetess Raḥel Bluwstein was a cult hero for a whole generation of pioneers in the Kibbutz. Amos Ron describes how in the eyes of her admirers, her free lifestyle as well as her tragic death heightened the need to create a special place of commemoration. By using sociological methods he studied the rituals and patterns that attached themselves to her tomb.

This survey of mythical, historical, modern and even post-modern approaches to sacred time and sacred place attests to the lasting significance of these categories for Judaism and for Christianity.

PART ONE

STUDIES IN THE HISTORY OF
SACRED TIME AND SPACE

TORAH FROM ZION
ISAIAH'S TEMPLE VISION (ISAIAH 2:1-4)

Baruch J. Schwartz

The concept of 'sacred' space in the biblical literature, whether in the strictly consistent terminology of the Priestly writings or in the less rigid popular and prophetic usage, is limited to those locations where the deity is believed to reside. His momentary presence is generally not sufficient to render a site sacred, even temporarily; much less so the thought that he may have appeared there at some time in the past. Nor is it enough that the deity may be invoked or worshipped in a particular spot, either in the present or the past. Rather, though all of these may contribute to the place's eventually acquiring the aura of sanctity, for the biblical tradition, the *sine qua non* for a location to be considered sacred is the abiding presence of the God of Israel there. In the great majority of biblical passages dealing with the monarchic period and beyond, therefore, 'sacred space' is restricted to the one and only site at which Israel's God ultimately established his permanent earthly abode, which the Bible invariably calls 'the House of the LORD' or one of its synonyms, its precincts and its environs, the Temple Mount, the City of Jerusalem.

The vision of the 'Mountain of the House of the LORD' in Isaiah 2:1-4, in which the earthly abode of the Deity becomes a lode stone, magnetically attracting peoples to it, has always intrigued commentators. It is taken to be a supreme expression of prophetic eschatology. For many modern scholars this means that it cannot possibly be an authentically Isian oracle, since, they feel, the prophetic vision of the 'end of days' properly belongs to the exilic period. Others reason differently, adducing the linguistic and literary evidence connecting this prophecy with the remainder of the authentically Isian material, and attribute the prophecy, and thus the beginnings of prophetic eschatology, to the eighth-century Isaiah, the son of Amoz of Jerusalem. Ac-

cording to both approaches, the aim of the prophecy is to predict
the conversion of the Gentiles: their mass pilgrimage to the House
of the LORD, their acceptance of His teachings and the ultimate
peace and tranquility which will ensue as a result. Commentators
believe that the prophet forecasts a time when Israel's privileged
position among the nations of the world will be abolished, since
the Teaching of God will henceforth become the property of all
nations. This 'teaching' is understood to be some new form of
'instruction in His ways', replacing the Law of Moses which was
given to Israel alone. This eventual end of divine favoritism is
somehow associated with the end of international strife, thus, in
the standard translations, 'no nation shall take up the sword
against another.' All of this is considered to be part and parcel of
prophetic messianism, traditionally characterized in scholarship
by the universal acknowledgment of the God of Israel and worldwide participation in His worship – called by one recent commentator 'the consummation of history'.[1]

   I believe that a closer reading of this brief oracle will enable us
to assess more precisely just what is envisioned in it and what is
not. I shall begin with a reevaluation of some philological points,
and then proceed to suggest a possible origin both for the imagery
employed in the vision and for its symbolic significance. I shall

---

[1]'Die Vollendung der Geschichte'; O. Kaiser, *Der Prophet Jesaja Kap. 1-12*, Göttingen 1963, 17-22 (ET: *Isaiah 1-12*, trans. R.A. Wilson, Philadelphia 1972, 24-30). See also the commentaries of H. Wildberger (*Jesaja 1-12*, Bib-lischer Kommentar Altes Testament 10/1, Neukirchen-Vluyn 1972-1980 [ET: *Isaiah 1-12 – A Commentary*, trans. T.H. Trapp, Minneapolis 1991]), J.N. Oswalt (*The Book of Isaiah Chapters 1-39*, Grand Rapids 1986), J.D.W. Watts (*Isaiah 1-33*, Waco, TX 1985), all of which refer to earlier commen-taries and studies. Particularly worthy of mention is G. von Rad's 1949 essay, 'Die Stadt auf dem Berge', which appears in his collected essays (*Gesam-melte Studien zum Alten Testament*, München [4]1971, 214-224 [ET: 'The City on the Hill', in: *The Problem of the Hexateuch and Other Studies*, trans. E.W. Trueman Dicken, London 1966, 232-242). For additional insights see J. Lindblom, *Prophecy in Ancient Israel*, Philadelphia 1967, 249, 282-283, 292, 384 n. 182, 390, 402 and C. Westermann, *Prophetic Oracles of Salvation in the Old Testament*, trans. K. Crim, Louisville KY 1991, 90-94, 125-126 (both of whom deny that the prophecy is authentically Isaian).

conclude with an attempt to account for the placement of the prophecy in Isaiah.

Isaiah 2:1-4

> [1.] The word that Isaiah the son of Amoz prophesied concerning Judah and Jerusalem: [2.] In the days to come, the mountain of the LORD's House shall stand firm above the mountains, and shall be higher than hills, so that all nations will see it. [3.] Then many peoples shall set out on the way, saying: "Come, and let us go up to the mountain of the LORD, to the House of the God of Jacob; that He may instruct us in His ways, and that we may walk in his paths." For instruction will come forth from Zion, and the word of the LORD from Jerusalem.
> [4.] He will decide between the nations, and arbitrate for many peoples. Then they shall beat their swords into plowshares, and their spears into pruning hooks; one nation shall not take up sword against the other, nor shall they know war any more.

Philological Notes

For full linguistic discussion, the lexica and critical commentaries should be consulted.[2] For purposes of this paper, the main linguistic points that need to be stressed are as follows:

v. 2 *In the days to come*: The Greek ἐν ταῖς ἐσχάταις ἡμέραις – 'in the end of days', reflected in the Aramaic Targums as well (בְּסוֹף יוֹמַיָּא), misses the mark. The prophet is indeed speaking about a better future time, but not of the eschaton. In prophetic usage, as in early poetry אַחֲרִית הַיָּמִים – just like Akkadian *ina aḥrât ūmī* – simply means 'later' or even 'next'[3]; it becomes a term for the end of days when that concept develops, and is used in this

---

[2]See the previous note. The translations of biblical passages here and below are based on NJPS (TANAKH – *A New Translation of the Holy Scriptures*, Philadelphia 1985), differing when necessary.

[3]See Gen 49:1; Num 24:14; Deut 4:30; 31:29; Hos 3:5; Jer 23:30; 30:34; 48:47; 49:39; Ezek 38:16, all of which bear the sense 'in the next phase; subsequently.' For thorough discussion of בְּאַחֲרִית הַיָּמִים see Wildberger.

sense no earlier than Daniel.[4] Why this interpretation fits best here
will become clear below.

above the mountains, and shall be higher than hills: The image
of the firmly standing mountain conjures up the more mythologi-
cal depictions of creation, of God's having set the earth and sky,
mountains and hills firmly in place, never to be moved (Ps 8:4;
24:2; 93:1; 96:10; 119:90, etc.), and this idea is elsewhere associated with the City of Jerusalem and the Temple Mount (Ps 46:6;
48:9; 87:5) The predicted lofty height of the Temple Mount, in
direct opposition to the geographical reality of Mount Zion, introduces the central motif of the chapter: the exaltation of all that is
lowly and the humiliation of all that stands aloft.[5] Yet in the vision, the mountain is elevated not spiritually but physically, so
that it can be seen from afar.

so that all nations will see it: For the peoples to embark on
their journey to the mountain of the house of the LORD, the towering mountain would have to be visible to them wherever they
are, its sight being what induces them to set off on their trip. As
correctly seen by R. Jonah ibn Janah almost 1000 years ago, the
verb וְנָהֲרוּ in v. 2b means precisely this: the nations will see the
lofty mountain from afar.[6] The standard translation 'stream/flow'[7]
is based on the noun נָהָר 'river, stream', but as a verb נהר (which,
as here, always takes the preposition אל) does not seem to bear
this sense in the Hebrew Bible. In all its occurrences it appears

---

[4]Dan 2:28 (in Aramaic: בְּאַחֲרִית יוֹמַיָּא); 10:14.

[5]See Isa 2:12-18.

[6]Abulwalîd Merwân Ibn Ganâh (R. Jonah), *Sefer Haschoraschim* (edn W.
Bacher), Berlin 1896, 289-290. In this derivation he was followed in the 12th
century, perhaps independently, by R. Eliezer of Beaugency (see J. W. Nutt,
Commentaries on the Latter Prophets by R. Eliezer of Beaugency: Isaiah,
London 1879, *ad loc.*), who suggested a sense of 'gain enlightenment, receive
illumination' (cf. Aram. נְהִירוּ , Dan 5:11,14). The etymology was to be forgotten thereafter by all but H.L. Ginsberg (see *The Supernatural in the
Prophets, With Special Reference to Isaiah*, Cincinatti 1979, 14), who preferred 'gaze with joy;' he was followed by NJPS (see note 2 above), *ad loc.*
and *ad* Mic 4:1; Jer 51:44.

[7]Rashi; Ibn Ezra; Radak; KJB, RSV, NEB, *et al.*

more likely that the meaning is 'see, view', from נְהָרָה 'light'.[8] The sequence of actions makes no sense if the peoples are said to 'stream' *prior* to saying to each other 'Come, and let us go' etc. Further, if וְנָהֲרוּ were indeed 'stream', the verse division would be incomprehensible, as the words וְהָלְכוּ עַמִּים רַבִּים should have been included in v. 2 together with the synonymously parallel to הַגּוֹיִם־ וְנָהֲרוּ אֵלָיו כָּל   Finally, it should be noted that streaming upwards is patently impossible, and is also a mixed metaphor.

Indeed, this motif may be an indication that the passage is authentically Isaian, reminiscent of the banner borne aloft upon the heights as a beacon for nations to see and to proceed in its direction, so characteristic of Isaiah (5:26; 11:12; 13:2; 18:3; 33:23). Here, however, the 'banner' is the mountain itself. A previously existing lowly hill is transformed into a tall mountain, visible unto all.

Once it is realized that the image of '*all* the nations' *streaming* to the Mountain of the House of the LORD is not portrayed here, and indeed that this notion derives from a mistranslation, the conventional interpretation which sees this prophecy as foretelling the pilgrimage of the peoples to Jerusalem and the conversion of the Gentiles becomes problematic. Accepting the Masoretic reading[9], Isaiah vv. 3-4 only says that *many* nations will then proceed to travel to Jerusalem, not all. Verse 4 says merely that He will adjudicate between '*the* nations' – presumably, the ones who have come for instruction. As a result, *one* nation shall not take up the sword against *the other*, and *they* shall not know war. No mention is made anywhere in this prophecy of all nations other than the fact that the Mountain of the LORD will be visible to them.

---

[8]Job 3:4 and in Aram. (cf. Dan 2:22 *qere* נְהוֹרָא ; Dan 5:11,14 נַהִירוּ). As a verb, besides here and Mic 4:1, only Isa 60:5 (‖ ראה); Ps 34:6 (‖ הביט); Jer 31:11 ('when they behold the LORD's bounty... they shall no longer languish'); Jer 51:44 ('nations shall no longer look to him [Bel]').

[9]See below for a possible emendation.

Another reason to cast doubt on the idea that the prophet predicts here a mass 'pilgrimage of nations'[10] to Jerusalem and their ultimate conversion to faith in Israel's God is that wherever this motif appears in biblical literature, as indeed whenever the pilgrimage to the abode of the Deity is mentioned in its original and primary context, the indispensable element is the *visit*. The pilgrim *appears before*, or in the more original phrase, *sees*,[11] the Deity in his earthly residence; he prostrates himself in his presence, he makes an offering of the gift-type; he partakes of the sacrificial flesh in the presence of the LORD; he participates in the observance of a clan or national festival. This is the essence of the biblical pilgrimage; without it, no visit has taken place.[12] This is just as true in the prophetic extension of this motif; for example, the peoples who Zechariah describes as converging on Jerusalem will do so 'to make the Sukkot pilgrimage' (Zech 14:16-19; cf. Isa 60:1-22; 66:18-23; Ps 76:12; 96:7-9 *et al.*). In the oracle we are considering, however, this element is absent entirely. The peoples that come to Jerusalem do so for instruction, not to do homage and certainly not in order to worship.

shall set out on the way, saying: וְהָלְכוּ and וְאָמְרוּ are evidently simultaneous predicates; otherwise the nations exhort each other to undertake the journey after having already set out upon it.

instruction: תּוֹרָה in this passage, as indicated by the parallelism with דְּבַר ה׳ and by all the remaining instances of תּוֹרָה in Isaiah as well as the rest of the Bible, refers not to the body of laws given to Moses or any other corpus of laws, rather, to the specific

---

[10]The phrase ('Die Völkerwallfahrt') is repeatedly used to denote the prophecy by commentators; cf., typically, Wildberger.

[11]The phrase 'appear before YHWH' (niphal of ראה followed by פְּנֵי ה׳) in Exod 23:17; 34:23-24; Deut 16:16; 31:11; 1 Sam 1:22; Isa 1:12; Ps 42:3 is generally believed to have resulted from emended vocalization of an original 'see the face of YHWH' (qal of ראה), as explained by S.D. Luzzatto in his commentary on Isa 1:12 (Padua 1845-97; edn P. Schlesinger, Jerusalem 1970, 18-19).

[12]See, for instance, M. Haran, *Temples and Temple Service in Ancient Israel*, Oxford 1978, 289-316; idem, 'Priesthood, Temple, Divine Service: Some Observations on Institutions and Practices of Worship', *Hebrew Annual Review* 7 (1983), esp. 131-134.

instructions received in a given context.[13] This sense is also mandated by the immediately preceding cognate verb וְיֹרֵנוּ 'so that He
may instruct us', and especially by what follows: the concrete,
specific description of the sort of instruction given. It consists of
administering a judicial verdict: שָׁפַט בֵּין – literally 'adjudicate
between' (there is no justification for translating 'among', as
though there were many parties at once); to rule on an issue
pending between two parties. The nations who sought the verdict,
after receiving it, will have thereby settled their dispute. They will
then be in a position to reverse the normal process required when
international disputes must be settled. When the population of the
countryside is called to arms, as evidenced in Joel 4:10, the vil-
lagers are told 'Beat your plowshares into swords, and your
pruning hooks into spears'. In Isaiah's vision, the belligerent peoples will reverse the process, turning implements of warfare back
into implements of agriculture, which is what they were originally.

know war: לָמַד מִלְחָמָה in the sense of 'gain expertise in the art
of warfare' is another possibility (cf. 2 Sam 1:18; 22:35; Ps
144:1), but 'know', i.e. 'experience war' is preferable here (cf.
Song 3:8; 1 Chr 5:18, and esp. Jud 3:2).

---

[13] תּוֹרָה is always 'teaching, instruction', even when the instruction referred
to, as in the rhetorical framework of Deuteronomy, includes an aggregate of
laws. The parallelism תּוֹרָה ‖ דָּבָר here, as in Deut 17:11, as well as the previous clause, indicates that the instruction intended is of the specific, not the
general, kind. A somewhat different view is held by B. Lindars, 'Torah in
Deuteronomy', in: P. Ackroyd & B. Lindars (eds) *Words and Meanings: Essays Presented to David Winton Thomas*, Cambridge 1968, 121, who argues
that 'oracular instruction' specifically is intended. His view has been challenged by J. Jenson, *The Use of tôrâ by Isaiah – His Debate with the Wisdom
Tradition*, Washington DC 1973, who, while agreeing that an aggregate laws
is not intended, prefers to interpret תּוֹרָה in Isaiah as *wisdom* instruction, but
this view is somewhat forced.

The Model

These points having been clarified, it seems likely that the model for the prophetic image employed here, in which a pair of disputing nations are attracted to seek a judicial ruling from a trusted, impartial judge, the God of Israel, in order to settle their dispute by binding arbitration, thus avoiding all need for the use of force, is not to be found in the cultic motif of the pilgrimage nor in the general eschatological hope for the conversion of the Gentiles, expressed in Psalm and prophecy. It is rather to be sought in the legal tradition. Even if we could not point to a specific legal text on which the prophet has drawn, we should probably have to posit its existence, indeed, we might perhaps even have reconstructed it. I refer, of course, to the Deuteronomic law of the centralized High Court of Arbitration.

A century ago it would have been unthinkable to suggest that the prophetic literature was influenced in any way by Israel's legal tradition, and even less than a century ago it would have been inadmissible to speak of the possibility that Isaiah of Jerusalem may have had access to the laws and ideology of Deuteronomy. Law was believed to be later than prophecy, and no pre-Josianic dating of Deuteronomy or its tradition would have gained any credence. The second part of this century has witnessed gradual but extreme change; the antiquity of the legal traditions of Israel, and of the Torah literature in general, is widely recognized, and though the publication of the book of Deuteronomy is still associated with the reforms of 622 BCE, the origins of the Deuteronomic work are often sought in the 8th century BCE, and the beginnings of centralization even earlier, in the reign of Jehoshaphat.[14] The time is therefore ripe for suggesting that Isaiah the son of Amoz may have had access to something resembling Deutero-

---

[14]See M. Weinfeld, *Deuteronomy and the Deuteronomic School*, Oxford 1972, 163-164 and *passim*; idem, *Deuteronomy 1-11*, New York 1991, 16-19, 65-84, and literature cited; J.H. Tigay, *Deuteronomy*, Philadelphia 1996, xix-xxvi.

nomic law and thought. The Deuteronomic law of the High Court of Arbitration reads as follows (Deut 17:8-11):

> [8.] If there arises a case too hard for you in judgment, be it a controversy over a capital crime, civil law, or assault – matters of local dispute – then you shall arise and go up to the place which the LORD your God will have chosen; [9.] And you shall present yourself before the levitical Priests, and to the judge serving at the time, and present your inquiry, so that they may declare to you the verdict in the case. [10.] You shall carry out the ruling that they have announced to you from that place which the LORD will have chosen; you shall observe scrupulously all that they instruct you. [11.] You shall act in accordance with the instruction that they give you and the verdict which they announce to you; you shall not deviate from the ruling which they announce to you, either to the right or to the left.

In this law, a unique, accessory function of the centralized House of the LORD, so important to Deuteronomic legislation, is introduced. All the other centralization laws in Deuteronomy pertain to ritual; they are all interested in the manner in which sacred acts of worship, especially sacrificial gifts and festival pilgrimages, may be performed in a system devoid of local shrines (Deut 12:5-28; 14:22-26; 15:19-23; 16:1-7, 10-11; 15-18; 18:6-8; 26:1-15; 31:10-13). Only here do we learn of an additional, ancillary role, having nothing to do with worship, but belonging solely to the sphere of civil and criminal court procedure. It is a reform made possible by the very existence of a single, central locale in which levitical Priests, which Deuteronomic thought apparently takes for granted to imply judges, were to be found. A single, central Temple presupposes a Temple-city, which takes on some of the character of a πόλις. The very location of the High Court of Arbitration, in the 'place which the LORD your God will choose', is what gives it its authority.

The stylistic and thematic parallels between the two passages are remarkable:

Isaiah 2:1-4	Deuteronomy 17:8-11
וְהָלְכוּ ... לְכוּ וְנַעֲלֶה	וְקַמְתָּ וְעָלִיתָ ... וּבָאתָ
shall set out on the way ... 'Come, and let us go up ...'	you shall arise and go up ... you shall present yourself
אֶל־הַר־יְהוָה אֶל־בֵּית אֱלֹהֵי יַעֲקֹב	אֶל־הַמָּקוֹם אֲשֶׁר יִבְחַר יְהוָה אֱלֹהֶיךָ בּוֹ
to the mountain of the LORD, to the House of the God of Jacob	to the place which the LORD your God will have chosen
וְיֹרֵנוּ מִדְּרָכָיו	כְּכֹל אֲשֶׁר יוֹרוּךָ ... עַל־פִּי הַתּוֹרָה אֲשֶׁר יוֹרוּךָ
that He may instruct us (wĕyōrēnū) in His ways	all that they instruct you (yōrūkā) ... the instruction that they give you (yōrūkā)
תּוֹרָה ... דְּבַר ה'	עַל־פִּי הַדָּבָר אֲשֶׁר יַגִּידוּ לְךָ ... עַל־פִּי הַתּוֹרָה אֲשֶׁר יוֹרוּךָ ... לֹא תָסוּר מִן־הַדָּבָר
instruction (tōrāh) ... the word of the LORD (dĕbār YHWH)	the ruling (dābār) that they have announced to you ... in accordance with the instruction (tōrāh) that they give you you shall not deviate from the ruling (dābār) ...
וְשָׁפַט ... וְהוֹכִיחַ	לַמִּשְׁפָּט ... דְּבַר הַמִּשְׁפָּט ... אֲשֶׁר־יֹאמְרוּ לְךָ
decide (špṭ) between ... arbitrate	in judgment (mišpāṭ) ... the verdict in the case ... the verdict which they announce to you

Particular mention should be made of the use of תּוֹרָה and the re-curring use of the verb הוֹרָה 'instruction; instruct', of the paral-lelism דָּבָר / תּוֹרָה 'instruction/word', and of the use of שָׁפַט 'judge' and מִשְׁפָּט 'judgment'.

These similarities prompt me tentatively to suggest yet another one, perhaps obscured by mistaken Masoretic vocalization, in place of the puzzling עַמִּים רַבִּים 'many' peoples, appearing twice in the passage in Isaiah. For if *all* nations behold the towering

Mount, why do only '*many*' peoples embark on a journey? And why should the LORD arbitrate for '*many* peoples' when He decides simply between 'the nations' (v. 4)? Deut 17:8 may provide the key. Perhaps the phrase in Isaiah should be read עַמִּים רָבִים '*disputing* peoples'. Not all peoples will travel to Jerusalem, only those which have disputes to settle. This would not only correspond with דִּבְרֵי רִיבֹת 'matters of dispute (*rîb*)' in Deut 17:8, it would also be in accord with Deuteronomic usage; cf. Deut 19:17; 25:1.[15]

The scene depicted is essentially the same in both passages, only the prophetic extension has moved from the private realm to the dimension of international relations. Earthly legal practice and custom, as envisioned and legislated by the Deuteronomic code with its central abode for the Deity, is reflected and magnified to produce the prophet's picture of the future of international relations. The disputing parties are no longer individual Israelites from the provinces but rather nations from afar; they appeal to the highest authority not to settle private disputes but because they are on the brink of war; the arbitration they seek prevents not civil strife but international conflict; the Judge to whom they appeal at the House of the LORD is none other than the LORD Himself.[16]

---

[15]The parallel text in Mic 4:1-3 is somewhat different. There עַמִּים 'peoples' (without '*all*') will see the mountain (v. 1), גּוֹיִם רַבִּים will set out on the way (v. 2); the LORD will decide between עַמִּים רָבִים and arbitrate לְגוֹיִם עֲצֻמִים 'for *mighty* peoples' (v. 3a). The parallelism רָבִּים || עֲצֻמִים in v. 3a probably indicates that the author of the Mican version read רָבִּים, but interpreted רַב to mean not 'many' but 'great' – perhaps because he was puzzled by the very question dealt with here.

[16]The parallel between the passages was pointed out by the 19th-century exegete Meir Loeb ben Yechiel Michael (Malbim) in his commentary on Isaiah, *Miqrā'ōt Gĕdōlōt*, edn Lublin (repr. New York 1974). It was noted in passing (though direct literary connection was not posited) by Y. Kaufmann, *Tōlĕdōt HaEmuna Hayisre'elit*, III, Jerusalem 1938 (repr. 1972), 205 n. 54, and developed by M. Weinfeld, 'Zion and Jerusalem as a Religious and Political Capital: Ideology and Utopia', in: R.E. Friedman (ed.), *The Poet and the Historian: Essays in Literary and Historical Biblical Criticism*, Harvard 1983, 113; idem, *From Joshua to Josiah – Turning Points in the History of Israel from the Conquest of the Land until the Fall of Judah* (Hebr.), Jerusalem 1992, 131-132. I am unable to share their view that this vision predicts

Parties to a dispute who cannot resolve it locally and who are therefore expected to repair to the central High Court of Arbitration are not pilgrims drawn to the House of the LORD to worship or pay Him homage. They do not come to celebrate an annual family pilgrimage, much less one of the three pilgrimage festivals. Their aim is not to offer a *zebah*; not to dwell in the LORD's house or to be inspired by the magnificence of His city. Rather they are perplexed and distraught individuals seeking the assistance of the judicial authorities. They are aggrieved citizens unable to find relief in a lower court. They are drawn to the central judiciary because of its status, because they are confident of its ability to arbitrate wisely and fairly. Similarly in this prophecy: the nations are not impelled to visit the Mountain of the House of the LORD because they wish to acknowledge His sovereignty and become a part of the community of His worshippers; rather, they are attracted by His reputation as a fair and equitable judge.

The imagery is drawn from the prosaic world of legal procedure, but the picture painted is anything but prosaic. It is in fact quite supernatural: a mountain suddenly rises to new heights, so that it is visible from abroad (it might even be claimed that Isaiah envisions a *floating* mountain, suspended miraculously in mid-air, high above the earth's surface). Nations – not their leaders or their representatives, but whole nations – journey to Jerusalem. God holds forth as a sitting judge and arbitrates disputes. Such a prophetic vision, remarkable in itself, takes on new significance once it is realized that it is actually a fantastic projection of the mundane.

The question is: what does the prophet mean by it? Does this oracle simply signify itself, or is it a poetic way of expressing a realistic hope? Is Isaiah fantasizing pure and simple, or is his vision the imaginative expression of a reasonable expectation?

---

the end of idolatry and the widespread acknowledgment of Yhwh as the only God. More direct connection between Isaiah 2 and Deuteronomy 17 was made by A. Hacohen, 'The Sequence of the Oracles in Isaiah 1-4' (Hebr.), *Megadim* 4 (1987) 58-59.

Might he be contemplating some development that may in fact be realized in the world of history?

In attempting to answer this, I turn my attention from the source of the vision to the idea contained in it, the surprising suggestion that there is some way for nations to resolve disputes without resorting to force, and the even more surprising idea that they need only turn toward the Temple city of the Israelite God in order for this to occur.[17] Is this anything but the inventive imaginings of the prophet, anything but the optimistic musings of a dreamer convinced that the national and natural order will someday be transformed beyond recognition?

I refer once again to Deuteronomy. The rhetorical framework for the Deuteronomic laws includes the following passage from Deuteronomy 4:

> [5.] See, I impart to you laws and statutes, as the LORD my God has commanded me, for you to observe in the land that you are about to enter and occupy. [6.] Observe them faithfully, for this is your wisdom and discernment in the sight of other peoples, who, when they hear of all these statutes, will say, "Surely, that great nation is a wise and discerning people". [7.] For what great nation is there that has a god so close at hand as is the LORD our God whenever we call upon Him? [8.] And what great nation has laws and statutes so righteous as all this Teaching that I set before you this day?

The motif which attracts my interest here is the glowing praise heaped by the speaker on the laws themselves. Later biblical literature, particularly late Psalms, and post-biblical literature as well, speak of the individual's love for the Torah, for study and contemplation of God's commands. But only in Deuteronomy do we find admiration for the intrinsic worth of the laws and statutes of God, and the idea that they are destined to become the envy of

---

[17]On the motif of the Temple-city as a source of royal or divine justice in Israel and the ancient Near East, see M. Weinfeld, *Justice and Righteousness in Israel and the Nations* (Hebr.), Jerusalem 1985, esp. 40-44 (ET: *Social Justice in Ancient Israel and in the Ancient Near East*, Jerusalem & Minneapolis 1995, esp. 67-74); idem, 'Zion and Jerusalem', 88-114; idem, *From Joshua to Josiah*, 119-132.

other peoples. The Deuteronomic idea is that the laws are to be kept – among other reasons – because they are good and just laws, wise and perfect teaching, the observance of which will improve Israel's reputation for wisdom and discernment and merit the admiration of other peoples. Deuteronomy asserts that the fairness and equity of Israel's laws will make them the envy of all who hear of them.

Isaiah's Temple Mount prophecy may have been occasioned by this Deuteronomic motif. Perhaps Isaiah too is expressing, in exaggerated, supernatural terms, the idea that the social and legal system of the Israelites, based on wise and equitable civil laws, is worthy of admiration and of imitation. When the peoples of the world follow Israel's social example, they too will enjoy, on the international level, the tranquility that the Israelite population has been blessed with in the domestic sphere thanks to its perfect, divinely revealed, system of justice.

When does Isaiah imagine this can take place? It may indeed be a dream of the far-off future, 'the end of days', requiring the miraculous transformation of nature. Perhaps direct, oracular judgment issued in person by the Deity is the only way for the prophet's vision to materialize. On the other hand, the prophet may be speaking metaphorically. The towering Mountain of the House of the LORD and the scene of the High Court of Arbitration in which God and His teachings occupy center stage may be a symbol of something realizable in the existing world. Not now, says the prophet; now Israel's conduct is anything but worthy of emulation. But when Zion once again becomes the seat of righteousness, when justice and equity again dwell there, when the ways and paths of the God of Jacob become the hallmark of Jerusalem, the peoples will be inspired to follow the example of Israelite behavior.

Support for this can be drawn from this prophecy's placement in the book of Isaiah. In the great denunciations of Chapter 1, immediately preceding our prophecy, Isaiah castigates Zion and Jerusalem for the injustice, inequity and corruption which contaminate the city that was once filled with justice, where righteousness once dwelt (Isa 1:21-23). He calls upon the people of Zion and Jerusalem to cleanse themselves, to put away their evil

doings from God's sight, to learn to do good and to practice justice (Isa 1:16-17). He then goes on to speak of the restoration of
Zion's judges as of old, her counselors as of yore, promising that
Zion shall be redeemed in justice. Then Jerusalem will again be
called the 'City of Justice, Faithful City' (Isa 1:24-27). The vision
of the Temple Mount follows naturally upon this. The Jerusalem
of his own day is no example for the peoples of the world – as he
says in Chapter 2, they have become just like the other peoples!
But if the call to repentance is heeded, Zion will become God's
flagship city.[18]

If this reading is correct, then the vision of the exalted Mountain, and the image of the High Court of Arbitration to which disputing parties can appeal, is part of Isaiah's fully realistic call to
his own people, as the very next verse reads, 'O House of Jacob!
Come let us walk in the light of the LORD' (Isa 2:5). The plea to
establish justice and righteousness would then be reinforced, just
as the call to heed the commands of the LORD is reinforced in
Deuteronomy, by appeal to reputation. If the call is heeded, Israel
will become the parade example of peace and domestic tranquility, an inspiration for the peoples of the earth as soon as they hear
of it.

While Deuteronomy simply neglects to provide any realistic
theory as to how the peoples of the world will become aware of
Israel's marvelous legal system, Isaiah attributes the spreading of
the fame of Israel's High Court to the miraculous elevation of the
Temple Mount, so that peoples will be able to see it from afar. In
both cases, realism is sacrificed for hortatory effect, because in
both cases the primary concern is to elicit a practical, behavioral
response on the part of the Israelites. Thus the art of persuasion,
which is the primary tool of the trade of prophet and lawgiver
alike, capitalizes on the attraction of fame and repute, assuring the
listeners that if they will heed the call to follow the ways of the
LORD, their society will be the envy of all the surrounding nations.

---

[18]See H.L. Ginsberg, 'The Supernatural' (note 6, above), 15-18.

Of course, I do not mean to suggest that there are no prophetic visions of universal peace and the widespread acknowledgment of Israel's God. But on closer examination, the Temple Mount vision of Isaiah does not seem to be one of them.

TRANSFORMATIONS OF SPACE AND TIME
NATHAN'S ORACLE AND DAVID'S PRAYER IN 1 CHRONICLES 17

Pancratius C. Beentjes

Introduction [1]

I n a brand-new monograph dealing with the Book of Chronicles
published some months ago, Brian Kelly says: 'Most recently,
it has been argued that the Chronicler understood the Davidic
kingship to be transmuted into and in some sense exercised
through the temple'.[2] He is explicitly referring here to the publications of Rex Mason and the late William Riley. The former
suggests '... that the Chronicler's main interest was not so much
the Davidic dynasty *in itself*, but the temple, for the sake of which
the dynasty was called into being and in which it found its fulfilment'.[3] And Riley states: 'The Chronicler's interest in the Davidic
dynasty can therefore be seen as more concerned with the role of
the dynasty in relation to the Temple than with the dynasty's un-
ending rule over Israel ... For the Chronicler, the centre of the
covenant with David is not formed by the dynastic promise, but
by the task of temple-building, and the fulfilment of the covenant
is to be sought in the completed Temple rather than in an unend-
ing Davidic rule'.[4] In fact, however, both Mason and Riley are

---

[1]After completion of this article, the monograph of W.M. Schniewind, *The
Word of God in Transition: From Prophet to Exegete in the Seond Temple
Period*, Sheffield 1995, came to my attention. He deals with 'The Dynastic
Oracle' on 143-160.

[2]B.E. Kelly, *Retribution and Eschatology in Chronicles*, Sheffield 1996,
158.

[3]R. Mason, *Preaching the Tradition: Homily and Hermeneutics after the
Exile*, Cambridge 1990, 32.

[4]W. Riley, *King and Cultus in Chronicles. Worship and the Reinterpreta-

elaborating upon some observations which were already published *in nuce* three decades ago by A. Caquot.[5]

This paper will deal with 1 Chronicles 17, one of the Chronicler's clue-texts dealing with dynasty and temple. In a number of
details, some of which have never been commented upon, this
narrative indeed will prove to be a major gateway to the Chronicler's point of view relating to these crucial theological issues.

Text and context

At first glance, one might think that the author of 1 Chronicles 17
adopted the text of his *Vorlage* (2 Samuel 7) without substantial
alterations. Initial appearances, however, are deceptive.[6] The
omissions and changes which the Chronicler on several points has
introduced into his own composition create a complete new text
with its own dynamics and meaning.[7] However, before starting
our analysis of 1 Chronicles 17, we should pay attention to its
context; this narrative should, of course, not be studied in splen-
did isolation. Thus, the Chronicler appears to have repeatedly
woven thematic strings, or even incorporated complete semantic
networks, throughout his book. Investigating a pericope too
restrictedly could unwittingly obscure or even sever such thematic or theological strings. Therefore, it is necessary now to pay

---

tion of History, Sheffield 1993, 75.

[5]A. Caquot, 'Peut-on parler de messianisme dans l'oeuvre du Chroniste?',
Revue de Théologie et de Philosophie 16 (1966) 110-120.

[6]It is rather strange that L. Eslinger, *House of God or House of David: The
Rhetoric of 2 Samuel 7*, Sheffield 1994, in Chapter 4 , entitled 'Biblical Echoes of 2 Samuel 7' (88-102), does not even mention 1 Chronicles 17!

[7]An almost complete survey of all textual differences between 2 Samuel 7
and 1 Chronicles 17 is found in: R. Braun, *1 Chronicles*, Waco 1986, 196-
197; H. Van den Bussche, 'Le texte de la prophétie de Nathan sur la dynastie
davidique (II Sam. VII - I Chron. XVII)', *ETL* 24 (1948) 354-394. The latter
takes the rather unusual position that the Masoretic text of 2 Samuel 7 has
been corrected on the principle that 1 Chronicles 17 is the more authentic
Hebrew text.

some attention to the context of 1 Chronicles 17 in comparison with the structure of its parent text, 2 Samuel 5-8.

1 Chr 13	2 Sam 6:1-11
1 Chr 14	2 Sam 5:11-25
1 Chr 15, 1-24	. . .
1 Chr 15:25-16:3	2 Sam 6:12-19a
1 Chr 16:4-6	. . .
1 Chr 16:7-22 (Ps 105:1-15)	. . .
1 Chr 16:23-33 (Ps 96:1-13)	. . .
1 Chr 16:34-36 (Ps 106:1,47-48)	. . .
1 Chr 16:37-42	. . .
1 Chr 16:43	2 Sam 6:19b-20a
. . .	2 Sam 6:20b-23
1 Chr 17	2 Sam 7
1 Chr 18	2 Sam 8

In 2 Sam 6:1-11, the *unsuccessful* transfer of the Ark is recorded. Within the context of 2 Samuel, this episode is immediately followed by a narrative dealing with the *successful* transfer (2 Sam 6:12-20). The Chronicler, however, has separated these two episodes. In 1 Chr 13:1-14, he describes the unsuccessful transfer. Then, in 1 Chronicles 14, he links together a number of episodes that in 2 Samuel appear *prior* to the report of the unsuccessful transfer of the Ark (2 Sam 5:11-25). Strikingly, these narratives have been compressed into a period of 'three months' (1 Chr 13:14). This brief time frame not only limits the possibility of *two* campaigns against the Philistines (1 Chr 14:8-12; 14:13-16), but is also insufficient to produce the large family which the Chronicler attribute to David! It is likely, therefore, that the insertion of 1 Chronicles 14 at this particular point was done for a specific purpose. A clue appears in the opening line of Chapter 14. Thus, it is rather intriguing that at the very start (1 Chr 14:1) of this 'inserted' text, the wording לבנות לו בית ('to build him a house') is used, a phrase which reappears in 1 Chr 17:25 (and 2 Chr 36:23).

Every single pericope in 1 Chronicles 14 serves as proof that it is not David who is to blame for the unsuccessful transfer of the Ark. One should be aware that in the Chronicler's composition, a number of 'markers' has been explicitly put into 1 Chronicles 13-

15 to emphasize this point of view. Thus, in the first campaign against the Philistines (1 Chr 14:8-12), the Chronicler uses the verb פרץ ('to break through'; 1 Chr 14:11) which also played an important role in the report of the unsuccessful transfer of the Ark (1 Chr 13:11). The same verb will recur in 1 Chr 15:13 where it occurs in combination with the verb דרש ('to seek'), which is one of the Chronicler's most favorite and crucial motifs.[8] It can hardly be a coincidence that precisely this verb played such an important role in the narrative reporting David's second campaign against the Philistines (1 Chr 14:13-16).[9]

Once the Chronicler with the help of 1 Chronicles 14 has stated that David in no way is to blame for the failure of bringing the Ark to Jerusalem, he begins his report of the *successful* transfer of the Ark (1 Chr 15:1-16:43). This is described not only in much more detail than the parallel description in 2 Samuel 6, but has also included *extra* material. Thus, no less than three Psalms have been inserted (1 Chr 16:7-36)[10] and a number of liturgical pre-scriptions are expressly mentioned as well (1 Chr 16:37-42). None of them are to be found in the parallel account in 2 Samuel.

From 1 Chr 16:43 onwards, the narrative keeps pace with 2 Samuel 6, albeit that the negative scene between Michal and David as reported in 2 Sam 6:20-23 is completely *absent* in the Chronicler's presentation. Only the positive opening of 2 Sam 6:20a (וישב דוד לברך את־ביתו; 'And David returned to bless his house')[11] has been adopted into 1 Chr 16:43b, although with a small alteration (ויסב). I should like to stress that (1) the theme of

---

[8]1 Chr 10:13-14 is to be considered a key passage. See C. Begg, '"Seeking Yahweh" and the Purpose of Chronicles', *Louvain Studies* 9 (1982) 128-141.

[9]R. Mosis, *Untersuchungen zur Theologie des Chronistischen Geschichts-werkes*, Freiburg 1973, 55-84, esp. 55-61.

[10]1 Chr 16:8-22 = Ps 105:1-15; 1 Chr 16:23-33 = Ps 96:1-13; 1 Chr 16:34-36 = Ps 106:1,35-36.

[11]Translating these words as 'David returned to *greet* his household' (NEB; REB) of course can be considered an adequate equivalent of the He-brew words. At the same time, however, such a translation blurs the vital and crucial semantic motif ברך ('to bless') which plays such an importan role within the entire context!

'blessing the house of David' will again be a crucial item at the conclusion of 1 Chronicles 17, and (2) that one should pay attention to the fact that the formula 'to bless his house' in its new context (1 Chr 16:43) not only functions as the conclusion of the Chronicler's Ark-narrative, but at the same time lays also the groundwork for the theme of 1 Chronicles 17. It must be considered, therefore, a crucial link between these two narratives.

Whereas in the study of the Book of Chronicles it is always important to be fully cognizant of the need to consider a synoptic comparison with the Books of Samuel and the Books of Kings as far as the *context* is concerned, it is necessary to proceed with caution when the *texts* themselves are discussed. Differences between the masoretic text of 2 Samuel 7 and 1 Chronicles 17 are not intrinsically related to the Chronicler's intervention. Hebrew fragments of the Book of Samuel found at Qumran have made it absolutely clear that text traditions are much more complex than has been assumed for a long time.[12] Thus, it is crucial to be awake of it, that the Hebrew text of Chronicles bears a great resemblance to these Hebrew fragments of Samuel from Qumran, and that both texts are also closer to the Septuagint version of Samuel and Kings.[13] Once therefore should always try to determine whether a textual variant originates from a different *Vorlage* or could be the result of theological considerations by the Chronicler.

---

[12] See e.g. A. van der Kooij, 'De tekst van Samuel en het tekstkritisch onderzoek', *NTT* 36 (1982) 177-204. W.E. Lemke, 'The Synoptic Problem in the Chronicler's History', *HThR* 58 (1965) 349-363.

[13] See the comment of J.M. Myers, *I Chronicles*, New York 1965, 130: '...Qumran evidence renders it imperative to take into account the fact that Chronicles reflects a somewhat different Vorlage (archetype) than MT and conforms more closely to the Samuel MSS found at Qumran which are more Septuagintal in character... Care must be taken not to attribute variants to the deliberate purpose of the Chronicler, who may simply have been following a different text, which may be attested by LXX of Samuel or the Qumran MSS, especially 4QSam[a]...'.

1. The Introduction to Nathan's Oracle

Drawing up an inventory of the main *theological (or ideological)* differences between 2 Samuel 7 and 1 Chronicles 17, it strikes one that they are to be found both at the *opening* (1 Chr 17:1) and at the *end* (1 Chr 17:13-14) of Nathan's Oracle, and at the *conclusion* of David's prayer (1 Chr 17:24-27). What do they contribute to the message of 1 Chronicles 17? A brief discussion of these differences follows.

1.1 נוח – 'to rest'

Reading 1 Chr 17:1 in a direct synoptic connection with 2 Sam 7:1, a complete line is *missing* in the Chronicler's version: ויהוה הניח־לו מסביב מכל־איביו ('and YHWH had given him rest from all his enemies round about'). This suppression is caused by the fact that 'to rest / rest' is treated by the Chronicler as one of his very special motifs. This is proven beyond any doubt somewhat further in the Book of Chronicles, when the author makes David recapitulate Nathan's Oracle in front of Solomon, whom is called to him in a private audience (1 Chr 22:6-13). It must be kept in mind that this pericope belongs to the so-called *Chronistisches Sondergut*.[14] The thematic issue that 'YHWH had given him rest ...', which is missing in 1 Chr 17:1, will explicitly function within 1 Chronicles 22, where it has been included in a very important context:

> 6. He sent for Solomon his son and charged him with building a house for YHWH, the God of Israel. 7. "Solomon, my son", he said, "it was my intention to build a house for the name of YHWH my God; 8. but YHWH forbade me and said:
> "You have shed much blood in my sight and waged great wars; for this reason you are not to build a house for my name. 9. But you will have a son who will be a *man of rest*; I shall *give him rest from all his enemies on every side*; his name will be Solomon, and

---

[14]This is a technical term to mark those sections that are only found in the Book of Chronicles.

I shall grant peace and quiet to Israel in his days. [10.] It is he who will build a house for my name; he will be my son and I shall be a father to him, and I shall establish his royal throne over Israel for ever" (1 Chr 22:6-10).[15]

Here we find the reason why the theological motif 'to rest' is so notably absent in 1 Chr 17:1. For throughout the Book of Chronicles, this motif is explicitly connected with *Solomon*.

That this is a conscious strategy indeed is confirmed by another passage that has directly to do with 1 Chronicles 17. This time it is not a private audience by Solomon at his father David's court, but an official meeting of all possible functionaries and the people of Jerusalem during which David again summarizes Nathan's Oracle. This narrative is to be found in 1 Chronicles 28, which is *Chronistisches Sondergut* as well. Here the נוח-motif is given a further dimension:

> [2.] King David stood up and addressed them: "Hear me, my kinsmen and my people. I had it in mind to build *a house of rest* for the Ark of the Covenant of YHWH which might serve as a footstool for our God, and I made preparations to build it" (1 Chr 28:2).[16]

That the Chronicler has taken great pains over the 'rest'-motif,[17] and has consistently carried it through, is not only obvious by its special appearance in 1 Chronicles 22, and 28, but also by the way in which the author of the Book of Chronicles has modified the text of his *Vorlage*:

---

[15]Translation according to the *Revised English Bible* with occasional revision.

[16]In the next line (1 Chr 28:3), these words are also followed by a mentioning of איש מלחמות ('a man of wars'), which is an important theme of 1 Chr 22:8.

[17]In the book of Chronicles the verb נוח ('to rest') is *only* used in *Chronistisches Sondergut*! An extensive analysis of the 'rest'-motif is found in R. Braun, 'Solomon, the Chosen Temple Builder: The Significance of 1 Chronicles 22, 28, and 29 for the Theology of Chronicles', *JBL* 95 (1976) 581-590, esp. 582-586.

| 2 Sam 7:11 | והניחתי לך מכל־איביך | I shall give you peace from all your enemies |
| 1 Chr 17:10 | והכנעתי את־כל־אויביך | I shall subdue all your enemies |

It is not David, but *Solomon* who has to be connected with the important theological concept of 'rest'. In order not to complicate matters, we shall not discuss here whether or not the Chronicler developed this line of thought from 1 Kgs 5:18[18]: ועתה הניח יהוה אלהי לי מסביב אין שטן ואין פגע רע ('But now on every side the Lord my God has given me rest; there is no one to oppose me, I fear no attack'). It is remarkable, anyhow, that just this sentence has been left out in 2 Chron 2:2, the instance to be considered the parallel of 1 Kgs 5:18. By explicitly linking up the 'rest-motif' with 1 Chr 22, and 1 Chr 28, being literary creations of his own, the Chronicler has marked this theological motif as a very special one: only a situation of rest which has been realized *by God* can provide all conditions necessary to start building the Temple.[19]

1.2 בנה הבית / בנה בית – *'to build a/the house'*

The Hebrew text of 1 Chr 17:4b is not only different from the wording of 2 Sam 7:5b, since the *rhetorical question* of the *Vorlage* has been changed into an apodictic statement, but also be-

---

[18] REB 5:4.

[19] Another important theological motif which places emphasis on Solomon is the verb בחר ('to choose'). See V. Peterca, 'Die Verwendung des Verbs BHR für Salomo in den Büchern der Chronik', *BZ* 29 (1985) 94-96. Peterca's view that 1 Chr 28:5b-10 should be considered a Chronistic revision of 2 Sam 7:12-13, by which the verb בחר brings about a 'midraschartige Betrachtung', in my opinion is robbing the Chronicler. For a question which in this connection is not answered by Peterca is why the verb בחר ('to choose') in that case should not occur in such a key text as 1 Chronicles 17. See also R. Braun, 'Solomon ...', 588-590.

cause the noun בית has a definite article. Both changes have important consequences with regard to the structure and the coherence of 1 Chronicles 17.

Since 1 Chr 17:4b is no longer presented as a rhetorical question, but has been remolded into an apodictic statement: לא אתה תבנה־לי הבית ('it is not you who will build the house for me'), a more explicit link has been created between this statement and the communication of 1 Chr 17:10b: ובית יבנה־לך יהוה ('YHWH will build a house for you'). In order to emphasize this link between 1 Chr 17:4b and 17:10b the verbal form יעשׂה ,which is found in the *Vorlage* (2 Sam 7:11b), has been changed[20] into יבנה (1 Chr 17:10b).[21] It is important to notice that by this slight verbal alteration, not only has a perfectly *chiastic structure* between 1 Chr 17:4b and 17:10b been created, but also a more solid coherence between 1 Chr 17:4b ('It is not you who are to build me the house') and 1 Chr 17:12b ('It is he who will build me a house') has been introduced at the same time.

The other difference between 1 Chr 17:4b and 2 Sam 7:5b mentioned above refers to the definite article of בית. The fact that the text in 2 Samuel has an indefinite noun ('a house'), whereas in 1 Chr 17:4b it is accompanied with the definite article[22] means that for the Chronicler it is not the construction of the Temple as such that is under discussion, but only that it will *not* be David who is the one to realize this project. In a way, the definite article ('*the* house') in 1 Chr 17:4b could even be considered to have a *proleptic* function: foreshadowing 1 Chronicles 22-27, being the most extensive section of *Chronistisches Sondergut* within the entire Book of Chronicles. In these chapters David will undertake all possible preliminary steps for building the Temple.[23]

---

[20] This important alteration, however, has *not* been listed by Braun, *I Chronicles*, 197.

[21] The explanation by S. Japhet relating to this verbal alteration, that the wording עשׂה בית is to be considered a special idiom 'denoting the establishing of family and progeny' is, in my opinion, untenable in light of 1 Chr 15:1 (ויעש־לו בתים). See S. Japhet, *I & II Chronicles*, London 1993, 333.

[22] A distinction that is not observed by S. Japhet, *I & II Chronicles*, 333.

[23] Without going further into the scholarly debate relating to the final two

2. The End of Nathan's Oracle

In 1 Chr 17:13-14 the reader meets a series of very substantial alterations with regard to 2 Samuel 7. The most striking transformation is undeniably to be found in 1 Chr 17:14, which is different in at least three major cases in respect of 2 Sam 7:16:

2 Sam 7:16

ונאמן ביתך וממלכתך עד־עולם לפניך כסאך יהיה נכון עד־עולם

Your house and your kingdom will be established for ever in your sight; your throne will endure for all time

1 Chr 17:14

והעמדתיהו בביתי ובמלכותי עד־העולם וכסאו יהיה נכון עד־עולם

I shall give him a sure place in my house and kingdom for ever; and his throne will endure for all time

Whereas God's promise in 2 Sam 7:16 refers to *David* in *all* aspects, in 1 Chr 17:14 this has been radically changed. Thus, 1 Chr 17:14b does not use the verb אמן ('to establish'), which in 2 Sam 7:16a refers to the stability of the Davidic dynasty. By introducing the verb עמד ('to give place') instead of אמן, 1 Chr 17:14b has been radically transformed. The verb עמד in hiph'il, accompanied by a preposition, indicates the appointment of an official to his new position.[24] In fact Solomon is successively described by the Chronicler as a Temple official and a governor. In 1 Chr 17:14a, therefore, the issue at stake is no longer '*your* house', the house of David as the royal *dynasty*, or '*your* kingdom', the kingdom of *David*. By changing possessive suffixes, the Chronicler's text is emphasizing '*My* house', i.e. God's house as the *Temple*, and '*My*

---

verses of 2 Chronicles 36, I want to stress the wording of the final verse of the book (2 Chr 36:23a). It refers to God's order to Cyrus 'to build him a house at Jerusalem in Judah'. Here too, it is *God* who takes the initiative!

   [24]*THAT* II, 330; see BDB, 764: 'station, set for duty'.

kingdom', i.e. the kingdom of *God*. Only the *final* element, 'throne', is applied to *Solomon*.

Later on in his book, in 1 Chr 28:5, when the Chronicler makes David recall this final line from Nathan's Oracle, it becomes clear beyond doubt that the author has entirely incorporated this theological concept into David's address to Solomon in the presence of a huge crowd of Jerusalem functionaries:

> [5.] Out of all my sons – for YHWH gave me many sons – he has chosen Solomon to sit on *the throne of YHWH's kingdom* over Israel.[25]

I feel confident that this specific theological concept is the reason why the Chronicler has suppressed the word המלך ('the king') from his *Vorlage* and replaced it by 'David' in 1 Chr 17:1-3. It is a small, but functional alteration which has escaped the attention of commentators. It cannot be accidental, however, that in 2 Sam 7:1-3, the phrase 'the king' has been used consistently, whereas the text of 1 Chr 17:1 ff. systematically refrains from using this. On the other hand, the Chronicler's text has preserved the title הנביא ('the prophet') for Nathan. Isaac Kalimi, who has recently published a very extensive monograph dealing with textual differences between the Book of Chronicles and Samuel-Kings, is of the opinion that in 1 Chr 17:1-2 the name of 'David' is used on purpose instead of the functional designation 'the king' to create an atmosphere of private conversation.[26] Although this view should not immediately be rejected, we feel confident that since the 'kingdom of YHWH' is a dominant theological issue of 1-2 Chronicles, a more *formal* reason can be adduced for the alteration of 'the king' into 'David'. This scenario is more likely since one can ascertain that elsewhere in his book, the Chronicler uses the formula 'David, the King' several times, and most of these

---

[25]This notion is also found in 1 Chr 29:23 (MT; not in LXX); 2 Chr 9:8; 13:8.

[26]I. Kalimi, *Zur Geschichtsschreibung des Chronisten: Literarisch-historiographische Abweichungen der Chronik von ihren Paralleltexten in den Samuel- und Königsbüchern*, Berlin 1995, 159-160.

usages are to be found in *Chronistisches Sondergut*![27] Since the
expression 'the king' is not found in 1 Chr 17:1ff, this suppression should be considered, therefore, to have a special *function*.
The same theological background makes it clear why regarding
Solomon in 1 Chr 17:12, reference is made to 'his throne',
whereas 2 Sam 7:13 uses 'the throne of his kingdom'.[28]

Let us now return to the *conclusion* of Nathan's Oracle. The
wording 'my house' (1 Chr 17:14) compels the reader to at least
consider the possibility of whether the noun 'house' in 1 Chr
17:10b ('I have declared to you that YHWH will build you a
house')[29] could mean 'temple' instead of 'dynasty'.[30] But even in
addition to this point of view, the special wording of 1 Chr 17:14
proves that *within the setting of 1 Chronicles,* the promise to
David is almost exclusively focused on Solomon as the builder of
the Temple.

This could also be one of the reasons, or maybe even the reason, why only the *positive* elements from 2 Sam 7:14-15a have
been transferred into 1 Chr 17:13. For in the Chronicler's version,
a rather remarkable phrase is missing: 'When he commits iniquity, I will chasten him with the rod of men, with the stripes of the
sons of men' (2 Sam 7:14b; RSV). Within the context of 2 Samuel 7, this phrase reflects an *unconditional* promise to the Davidic
dynasty; God promises that He will call to order every king who
commits iniquity. The Chronicler has dropped this negative

---

[27] 1 Chr 21:24; 26:26,32; 27:31; 28:2; 29:1,9; 2 Chr 7:6. Only in 1 Chr
18:10,11; 2 Chr 2:12; 23:9 this formula has been adopted from the *Vorlage*.

[28] The Greek text of 2 Sam 7:13, however, reads: τὸν θρόνον αὐτοῦ ('his
throne').

[29] I feel confident that 1 Chr 17:8-10 should be rendered in the *perfect
tense*. See R. Mosis, *Untersuchungen*, 82-87; S.J. De Vries, *1 and 2 Chronicles*, Grand Rapids 1989, 154; J. Becker, *1 Chronik*, Würzburg 1986, 76; O.
Loretz, 'The perfectum copulativum in 2 Sm 7:9-11', *CBQ* 23 (1961) 294-
296.

[30] See W. Riley, *King and Cultus*, 183: 'There is perhaps a fuller connection between Temple and security in Nathan's oracle if the possibility is en-
tertained that the Chronicler saw בית in 1 Chron. 17.10 to pertain to the Temple even more than to the dynasty'.

phrase since all his narratives on David and Solomon deal with a *conditional* promise relating to the royal dynasty:[31]

> [11.] Now, my son, may YHWH be with you! May you prosper and build the house of YHWH your God as he promised you would. [12.] May YHWH grant you insight and understanding, so that when he gives you authority in Israel you may keep the law of YHWH your God. [13.] You will prosper *only if* you are careful to observe the decrees and ordinances which YHWH enjoined upon Moses for Israel; be strong and resolute, neither faint-hearted nor dismayed (1 Chr 22:11-13).

> [9.] And you, Solomon, my son, acknowledge your father's God and serve him with whole heart and willing mind, for YHWH searches all hearts and discerns whatever plan may be devised. *If* you search for him, he will let you find him, *but if* you forsake him, he will cast you off for ever (1 Chr 28:9).

> [17.] *If* you, for your part, live in my sight as your father David lived, doing all I command you, and observe my statutes and my judgements, [18.] *then* I shall establish the throne of your kingdom, as I promised by a covenant granted to your father David when I said, "You will never want for a man to rule Israel" (2 Chr. 7:17-18).

I fully agree with H. Williamson that the Chronicler's focussing of Nathan's oracle upon Solomon made the inclusion of 2 Sam 7:14b quite irrelevant: 'In the Samuel text, it refers to the whole future line of Davidic kings, to many of whom the saying could have applied, whereas for Solomon in the Chronicler's scheme it could have no application whatever. Either he was going to obey, in which case the dynasty would be established, or he would fail, and his house with him; the possibility was not foreseen that he would fail personally, but the dynasty nevertheless endure.'[32]

---

[31]The next three quotations are from REB; italics mine.

[32]H.G.M. Williamson, 'The Dynastic Oracle in the Books of Chronicles', in: A. Rofé (ed.), *Essays on the Bible and the Ancient World*, Vol. III Non-Hebrew-Section, Jerusalem 1983, 305-318, at 318. A less detailed version of this article has been published as part of: H.G.M. Williamson, 'Eschatology in Chronicles', *Tyndale Bulletin* 28 (1977) 115-154, at 142.

It is intriguing to see that during the period in which Solomon
will build the Temple he, in any case, will be safe from negative
influences:

> [20.] Be steadfast and resolute and carry it out; be neither faint-
> hearted nor dismayed, for YHWH God, my God, will be with you;
> he will neither fail you nor forsake you, *until you have finished all
> the work needed for the service of the house of YHWH* (1 Chr
> 28:20).

It is inconceivable why commentators systematically pass this
aspect. Since, on the one hand, Solomon in the Chronicler's presentation is heavily idealized and, on the other hand, he is the chosen Temple-builder, the insertion of the negative phrase from 2
Sam 7:14b into the Chronicler's version of Nathan's Oracle
would have run counter to the Chronicler's general picture of
Solomon and would have nullified the special aspects of the conditional dynastic promise.

3. David's Prayer and Blessing

If the interpretation of 1 Chr 17:1-15 presented so far is plausible,
that there is no question of an unconditional promise of a Davidic
dynasty, but rather of a conditional promise which is almost exclusively concentrated in Solomon as the Temple builder, then the
prayer of David as reflected in 1 Chr 17:16-27 needs to be carefully studied and compared with its parallel text (2 Sam 7:18-29).
Such an investigation is not so much needed because of the textual differences – they have expertly been listed by Braun[33] – but
because of the *function* that David's prayer is now performing in
light of the oracle in which Solomon has been designated to build
the Temple.

   As should be clear, nowhere in David's prayer (1 Chr 17:16-
27) is there to be found a single reference to Solomon, as was the

---

[33] R. Braun, *1 Chronicles*, 196-197.

case in the first part of 1 Chronicles 17. In this way the Chronicler is able to emphasize his 'David-programme' in the second part of 1 Chronicles 17.[34] That a 'David-programme' has actually been woven into the Chronicler's version of David's prayer is proved by the application of the verb אמן ('to establish'). While this verb in 2 Sam 7:16a plays an important role with respect to the *Davidic dynasty*, in 1 Chr 17:14 – where only Solomon is explicitly meant – this verb is absent and its place taken by the hiph'il of עמד. It is remarkable then, and it can hardly be accidental, that the verb אמן ('to establish') appears suddenly in 1 Chr 17:23 and 17:24, resulting in wordings with a completely new theological bent with regard to the parallel texts of 2 Samuel 7:

2 Sam 7:25

הדבר אשר דברת על־עבדך ועל־ביתו הקם עד־עולם

Perform for all time what you have promised for your servant and his house

1 Chr 17:23

הדבר אשר דברת על־עבדך ועל־ביתו יאמן עד־עולם

Let what you have promised for your servant and his house stand fast for all time

2 Sam 7:26

ויגדל שמך עד־עולם

May your name be great for ever

---

[34] I therefore am very surprised that Williamson, who explicitly wants to emphasize that 1 Chronicles 17 preserves God's promise with respect of the Davidic dynasty, nowhere refers to David's prayer as such in his important article on this subject. His only reference to this is a footnote: 'It should be noted that David's prayer is apparently adopted by the Chronicler *without any significant or tendentious alteration*'. H.G.M. Williamson, 'The Dynastic Oracle', 310 note 14 (italics mine).

1 Chr 17:24

ויאמן ויגדל שמך עד־עולם

Let it stand fast, that you name may be great for ever

The verb אמן ('to establish') has been removed by the Chronicler
from its parent text (2 Sam 7:16a), in which it refers to the Davidic dynasty. The verb has been transferred to *other* motifs from
that same parent text that deal *exclusively* with *YHWH*. In this
new context, the verb אמן ('to establish') relates to God's word
and name. It is no longer David and his dynasty who are in the
centre of the Chronicler's attention, but YHWH Himself. This
pattern is also seen in 2 Chr 1:9 and 6:17, where the Chronicler
diverts from its parent texts with the help of the verb אמן ('to establish').[35] For more than one reason, the *final* line of David's
prayer is particularly fascinating:

2 Sam 7:29a

ועתה הואל וברך את־בית עבדך להיות לעולם לפניך

Be pleased now to bless your servant's house so that it may continue before you for ever

1 Chr 17:27a

ועתה הואלה לברך את־בית עבדך להיות לעולם לפניך

Now it has pleased you to bless your servant's house so that it
may continue before you for ever

---

[35]The only text within the entire Book of Chronicles where YHWH is *not*
the subject or agent of אמן ('to establish') is to be found in 2 Chr 20:20,
which is a transformation of a *quotation* from Isa 7:9. See P.C. Beentjes,
'Tradition and Transformation: Aspects of Innerbiblical Interpretation in 2
Chronicles 20', *Biblica* 74 (1993) 258-268, esp. 266-268.

2 Sam 7:29b

כי־אתה אדני יהוה דברת ומברכתך יברך בית־עבדך לעולם

for you, Lord YHWH, have spoken, and from your blessing may your servant's house be blessed for ever

1 Chr 17:27b

כי־אתה יהוה ברכת ומברך לעולם

for you, YHWH, have blessed and will be blessed for ever

1 Chr 17:27 brings to light a much more permanent situation as is the case in 2 Sam 7:29. While the latter has been modeled as a *supplication* for blessing in the future, 1 Chr 17:27 should be characterized as a *panegyric* establishing that God's blessing on the house of David has already been realized. As a result, the second half of 1 Chr 17:27 is significantly different from its parent text. Whereas the final line of 2 Sam 7:29b refers to the *Davidic dynasty*, the wording of 1 Chr 17:27b can only bear upon *YHWH Himself.*

Almost all authoritative Bible translations add here the object 'it', the Davidic dynasty[36] that is absent in the Hebrew text. In my opinion, based on theological grounds, such a rendering is a misconception. For it is *God* who is exalted here by the Chronicler: 'For you, YHWH, have blessed and will be blessed for ever'.

Summary

The promise addressed to David by the intermediary of Nathan as reflected in 2 Sam 7:1-16 almost exclusively deals with the Davidic dynasty. As a result of a number of textual interventions,

---

[36]NEB: 'Thou it is who has blessed *it*, and *it* shall be blessed for ever'; REB: 'You it is who have blessed *it*, and *it* shall be blessed for ever' (italics mine). The same kind of rendering is found in, for example, *Bible de Jérusalem; Die Bibel, Einheitsübersetzung; Bible in Dutch* (NBG, 1951); *Statenvertaling* (1637).

this promise in 1 Chr 17:1-14 has been transformed into a new kind of text referring basically just to Solomon, since, after all, it is he who is predestined to build the Temple. For the Chronicler, dynasty is important as far as it has a positive bearing upon the Temple. It is also within this new concept that David's prayer (1 Chr 17:16-27) is presented in a different way. Whereas in 2 Samuel 7, David entreats for God's future blessing, in the Chronicler's context, the divine blessing has already been realized. The category of time has been subordinated to the category of space.

HOLY PLACE AND HANNAH'S PRAYER:
A COMPARISON OF LAB 50-51 AND LUKE 2:22-39
À PROPOS 1 SAMUEL 1-2[1]

Bart J. Koet

Introduction

T his article intends to investigate to what extent material peculiar to Luke preserves a strand of Judaism which can be
found in Jewish literature, originating in the second half of the 1st
century CE. Two texts from this period which both use the biblical story of the child Samuel as a model and an inspiration, although in different ways, will be compared.

The first text is from Pseudo-Philo's *Liber Antiquitatum Biblicarum* (LAB), the second is Luke 2:22-39. LAB survived only in
a Latin translation from the 4th century. It is generally assumed
that the Latin text is a translation of a Greek text, which in turn is
a translation of a Hebrew text from the 1st century.[2] The text we

---

[1]I want to thank C. O'Reilly and my cousin A. Koet for their corrections of
the English, J. van der Meij and Dr J. Schwartz for their lucid comments on
earlier drafts of this paper and Dr Ch. Safrai for her encouragement to write
it.

[2]There has been much discussion about the exact date of LAB and whether
it should be dated before or after the destruction of the Temple. I follow the
arguments of P.-M. Bogaert, 'Luc et les Écritures dans l'Évangile de
l'Enfance à lumière des Antiquités Bibliques', in: C.M. Tuckett (ed.), *The
Scriptures in the Gospels,* Leuven 1997, 243-270, esp. 246-250. But even if a
date before the destruction is too early, there seems to be nearly a *communis
opinio* about dating LAB to the latter part of the 1st century. A convenient
edition is D.J. Harrington & J. Cazeaux, *Pseudo-Philon Les Antiquités Bibliques; T. I, Introduction et Texte Critique - Traduction,* Paris 1976; C. Perrot
& P.-M. Bogaert, *Pseudo-Philon Les Antiquités Bibliques; T. II, Introduction
littéraire, Commentaire et Index,* Paris 1976. An important translation is
M.R. James, *The Biblical Antiquities of Philo,* London 1917, especially in the

shall study is LAB 49-51, and especially chapter 51 which is a paraphrase of 1 Sam 1:20-2:11 (§1-2). In LAB 50-51 Anna, the mother of Samuel, is depicted as a paragon. Adopting the framework of 1 Sam 1-3, Ps-Philo interprets the story of Anna and her son in its own way. A remarkable addition is Anna's use of the metaphor of 'light for the nations' (LAB 51:6; see 51:3).

This motif concurs to a certain extent with the second text, a key-text within Luke-Acts. In Luke 2:22-39 Simeon announces that Jesus will be a light for the Gentiles (2:32). Simeon is joined by Hanna (Luke 2:36-38). She is an elderly widow who never leaves the Temple and who fasts and prays (§3). The theme of the presentation of the boy Jesus provides the context for a Samuel-like story involving parents, child and an elderly man at the Temple. Because LAB 50-51 and Luke 2:22-39 have several elements in common such as 'light of the Gentiles', the Sanctuary, prominent women, both praying and both named {H}anna{h}[3]; and a prophetic canticle is uttered regarding a very young boy of great promises, it seems worthwhile to compare them in more detail (§4-5).[4]

---

reprint by L.H. Feldman with an excellent prolegomenon, New York 1971. A modern English translation is to be found in: J.H. Charlesworth (ed.), *The Old Testament Pseudepigrapha,* New York 1985, II.297-377. Recently some important studies have appeared: F.J. Murphy, *Pseudo-Philo. Rewriting the Bible*, Oxford [etc.] 1993; E. Reinmuth, *Pseudo-Philo und Lukas. Studien zum Liber Antiquitatum Biblicarum und seiner Bedeutung für die Interpretation des lukanischen Doppelwerks*, Tübingen 1994; H. Jacobson, *A Commentary on Pseudo-Philo's Liber Antiquitatum Biblicarum,* Leiden 1996. For a discussion of the genre of LAB, see E. Reinmuth, *Ps-Philo und Lukas*, 14-17.

[3]Although in English the translation of all the forms are the same, for the sake of convenience I will use Hannah for Samuel's mother in the Bible (including LXX and Tg), Anna referring to her in LAB and Hanna for the woman in Luke 2.

[4]A more general connection between the story of Samuel's birth in LAB and the whole of Luke 1-2 has already been suggested by P. Winter, 'The Proto-Source of Luke 1', *NT* 1 (1956) 184-199, at 193. See also P.-M. Bogaert, 'Pour une phénoménologie de l'appropriation de la prière. Le cantique d'Anne dans le Ier livre de Samuel, dans Les Antiquités Bibliques et dans le Nouveau Testament', in: H. Limet & J. Ries (eds), *L'expérience de la prière*

It should be stressed from the beginning that we are not suggesting any literary dependence between LAB and Luke. Rather,
this comparison is important because it may reveal that a device
which is very important in Luke-Acts, is not unknown in a 1st
century Jewish version of biblical stories.[5] It can also contribute
to a better understanding of the way Scripture was interpreted
around 70 CE. Hopefully, this investigation can also shed some
light on the issue of to what extent Luke's exegesis is part and
parcel of contemporary Jewish interpretations of Scripture. The
role that the biblical story of the events surrounding the birth of
Samuel plays in LAB and in Luke respectively will become apparent.

1. The Role of Anna within the Story of Samuel in LAB

LAB tells the story of Israel, adopting the framework of the Bible,
while selectively abbreviating or expanding passages and even
adding new material. One particular feature of its style is its inclination to elaborate or reshuffle speeches and prayers. Ps-Philo
attributes speeches to some people, among them quite a few
women, who do not have speeches or prayers attributed to them in
the Bible.[6]

---

dans les grandes religions. Actes du colloque de Louvain-la-Neuve et Liège
(22-23 nov 1978), Louvain-la-Neuve 1980, 246-259, 256-259; and K. Berger,
'Das Canticum Simeonis (Luke 2:29-32)', NT 27 (1985) 27-39, 35, n. 15.

[5]See D.J. Harrington, 'Birth Narratives in Pseudo-Philo's Biblical Antiq-
uities and the Gospels', in: M.P. Horgan & P.J. Kobelski (eds), To Touch the
Text. Biblical and Related Studies in Honour of Joseph A. Fitzmyer, S.J.,
New York 1989, 316-324, esp. 317.

[6]See e.g. R.J. Bauckham, 'The Liber Antiquitatum Biblicarum of Pseudo-
Philo and the Gospels as 'Midrash'', in: R.T. France & D. Wenham (eds),
Gospel Perspectives. Studies in Midrash and Historiography, Sheffield 1983,
III.33-76, 38-39. Ps-Philo elaborates upon and extends speeches by women
and thus attributes greater prominence to some women far beyond the biblical
stories: see Deborah (LAB 30:5-7); Jael (31:5) Seila, the daughter of Jephta
(40:5-7) and Samson's mother Eluma (42:2). For the descriptions of some
examples, see P.W. van der Horst, 'Portraits of Biblical Women in Pseudo-

As mentioned above, the first text we study is chapter 50-51 of Biblical Antiquities, Samuel's birth narrative.[7] The basic framework of LAB 50-51 is more or less the same as 1 Sam 1-2: a man has two wives and the beloved one is 'barren'. In LAB Samuel's birth is also the result of the process initiated by the quarrels between the two wives of Elkanah, as it is in 1 Sam. After this quarrel the childless woman prays to God in a holy place, becomes pregnant and gives birth to a son. After going to the sanctuary with her son she offers prayers by singing a song.[8]

Besides the similarities there are also many variations. Ps-Philo's version of Samuel's birth is introduced by different elements mentioned in LAB 49.[9] In this chapter it is said that the children of Israel ask God for a new leader like Kenaz, because there were no suitable leaders in those days (48:4). Who is Kenaz? Although Kenaz in the Bible is only mentioned in passing (Judg 3:9,11), Ps-Philo presents him in LAB 25 as the first important leader (*dux*) after Joshua (instead of biblical Othniel; Judg 3:9). He is chosen at God's command by casting lots (LAB 25). Ps-Philo inserts a comparable procedure as an introduction to Samuel's birth (49:4). This recalls also the selection by lot of Saul as the Lord's elect in 1 Sam 10:20-26. This is a first indication that LAB intends to give Samuel royal features. When the lot falls on Elkanah, he declines to become their leader (again *dux*; 49:5).

Philo's *Liber Antiquitatum Biblicarum', JSP* 5 (1989) 29-46. For a comparison between Ps-Philo's Anna and Josephus' Hanna, see C.A. Brown, *No Longer be Silent: First Century Jewish Portraits of Bibical Women*, Louisville 1992.

[7]On LAB 51, see J.E. Cook, 'Pseudo-Philo's Song of Hanna: Testament of a Mother in Israel', *JSP* 9 (1991) 103-114; M. Philonenko, 'Une paraphrase du cantique d'Anne', *RHPhR* 42 (1962) 157-158.

[8]For a description of this and similar patterns within the Scriptures, see S. Ketelaar, 'De 'Onvruchtbare' Moeders in de Hebreeuwse Bijbel', *Amsterdamse Cahiers* 12 (1993) 7-19 and the literature cited there.

[9]For some differences between 1 Sam 1-2 MT and LXX, see P.-M. Bogaert, 'Le cantique d'Anne', 247-252 and E. Tov (ed.), *The Hebrew and Greeks Texts of Samuel*, Jerusalem 1980. See also L. Warren, 'A Trisagion Inserted in the 4QSam a Version of the Song of Hannah, 1 Sam 2,1-10', *JJS* 45 (1994) 278-285.

After that it is announced that not Elkanah but his son, (who will be born from Elkanah's beloved infertile wife) will be the new leader (now: *princeps*). Because in LAB the title *princeps* is often used for a king, this attributes royal features to Samuel.[10] LAB 49 is entirely an addition to the biblical narrative and is an example of the phenomenon that Ps-Philo introduces a prophecy as a disclosure of the future of Israel's new leader more often than in the biblical narrative. À propos the birth narratives in Luke 1-2, Tannehill uses the technical term 'disclosure' and argues that this is an eye-opener for the reader. It can be a preview of the future task of an important person. This is highlighted by a quotation, a song, a special person as a kind of godfather or a special place. He claims that disclosures are clues for the readers, establishing a set of expectations about the course of the story.[11] This is also the case in LAB 49-51. In these chapters the author discloses to the readers that Samuel, the boy whose appearance is announced in 49 and 50, who is born and presented in a holy place, will be a prophetic leader with even universal impact. Thus, in this case it creates an atmosphere of expectation.[12]

In LAB 50 we find Ps-Philo's version of 1 Sam 1:2-19: the quarrels between Anna and Penninah (Latin: *Fenenna*) as well as Anna's visit to Shiloh, where she asks for a son and where Eli prophesies that her wish will be fulfilled (1 Sam 1:17; LAB 50:7). Here Ps-Philo returns to the framework of 1 Sam 1:1-19, using words or phrases from the biblical text.[13] In 1 Sam 1 the quarrel begins after Elkanah gives his wives portions of his sacrifice. In

---

[10]See LAB 56:1,5; see also 6:6,8; 21:5 and 25:3, but for a slightly different use see 9:12. Kenaz is characterised as *dux* (LAB 25:2) Although Moses (LAB 19:3; unlike the biblical text!), Abdon (41:1) and Elon (42:2) do get the title *iudex*, Ps-Philo does *not* mention Samuel as a judge. This also shows that in Ps-Philo Samuel acquires different features than in the biblical text.

[11]R.C. Tannehill, *The Narrative Unity of Luke-Acts. A Literary Interpretation. 1: The Gospel according to Luke*, Philadelphia 1986, 20-23.

[12]R.J. Bauckham, 'Ps-Philo and the Gospels', 57.

[13]H. Jacobson, *Ps-Philo*, 1084, observes that "in his close adherence here to the biblical narrative, he [ps-Philo] uses elements of the story that jibe poorly or not at all with the background he has created in ch. 49".

LAB 50 this element of the story vanishes and thus Elkanah's role becomes less relevant. The interaction starts immediately with Penninah's daily taunting of Anna about her not having children.[14] While in 1 Sam 1:6 we do not hear what Penninah says, in LAB 50:1 she says explicitly that Anna is a dry tree and that a husband only loves a wife with sons.[15] The remark that Penninah taunts Anna, which makes her very sad, is combined with the statement that Anna has been God fearing from her youth.[16] The taunting becomes explicit again when Elkanah leaves the house to sacrifice (LAB 50:2). Unlike the biblical story, Ps-Philo specifies this as a Passover sacrifice.[17] When Elkanah leaves, Penninah insults Anna. After being consoled by her husband, Anna goes to the House of the Lord in Shiloh and there prays for a child (although less explicitly than in 1 Sam). In contrast with the biblical story Ps-Philo does not mention a vow.

LAB 50:4-7 reflects Ps-Philo's tendency to enhance God's role: it is God who closed Anna's womb.[18] In 1 Sam 1:13 we hear that Hannah is praying silently, her lips were moving although her voice could not be heard. This behavior causes Eli to think that Hannah is drunk (1:14). LAB 50:5 explains this remarkable element of the biblical text: Anna prays in silence because she is

---

[14]The element of taunting disappears in Josephus' *Jewish Antiquities* V.341-347. Only the barrenness as it is causes Hanna's pain.

[15]See B. Halpern-Amaru, 'Portraits of Women in Pseudo-Philo's Biblical Antiquities' in: A.-J. Levine, (ed.) *Women like This. New Perspectives on Jewish Women in the Greco-Roman World*, Atlanta 1991, 83-106, at 97: "... Hannah – taunted and tormented by Penninah well beyond the biblical account ...".

[16]According to F.J. Murphy, *Ps-Philo*, 189, this concurs with Elkanah's remark in 50:3, where he asks whether her ways of behaving are not better than sons (*Nonne meliores sunt mores tui super decem filios Fenenne?*).

[17]This passage is important as an early testimony to later (rabbinic) developments. The expression *bono die* seems to be a translation of יום טוב the statement that the festival is a Passover festival seems to be the result of using a hermeneutic rule of analogy, known in rabbinic literature as 'gezerah shavah'. The analogy is מימים ימימה in 1 Sam 1:3 and in Ex 13:10. See L. Ginzberg, *The Legends of the Jews*, Philadelphia ⁴1954, VI.213, n. 135.

[18]F.J. Murphy, 'God in Pseudo-Philo', *JSJ* 19 (1988) 1-18, esp. 5.

afraid that if she is not worthy of being heard, Penninah will be even more eager to taunt her.

Although Eli and the reader of LAB know that the boy will be special, the Priest does not tell Anna that it has been foreordained that she would give birth to a prophet (LAB 50:8). After her visit to Shiloh and her encounter with Eli, Anna goes home consoled. Following the announcement of a new leader in LAB 49 this is the second time that it is disclosed to the reader that Anna's child will be special. The House of the Lord is a perfect place to make such a disclosure. While in the Bible there is stress on Hannah's personal need for a child, in Ps-Philo there is the need for a leader. The boy Samuel is promised to the tribes (51:3). The new title *princeps* even suggests a new era.

In LAB 51, we find Ps-Philo's paraphrase of the birth and dedication of Samuel, including the crucial hymn of Anna after the boy's presentation to Eli (51:2). In the beginning of 51, it is described that Anna conceived and bore a son (see 1 Sam 1:20). A remarkable detail is that in 1 Sam 1:20 Hannah names Samuel, while in LAB 51:1 Anna gives him the name as God named him when He prophesied about him. It is not mentioned in this story how Anna knew this. After two years Anna 'went up'. On the basis of the use of *ascendit cum eo* (51:1) as a technical term for going up to the Sanctuary and because Anna meets Eli the Priest (see 50:6 and 51:2), it may be assumed that she, as she did in 1 Sam 1:24, goes to the house of the Lord, a perfect place for making a disclosure.[19] Anna explicitly mentions the fulfillment of the 'word and prophecy about the new leader for Israel' (51:6: *Ecce perfectum est verbum et convenit prophetia*). By speaking of fulfillment of a prophecy Ps-Philo depicts the birth of Samuel as the

---

[19]According to R.D. Aus, 'The Child Jesus in the Temple (Luke 2:41-51a), and Judaic Traditions on the Child Samuel in the Temple (1 Samuel 1-3)' in: idem, *Samuel, Saul and Jesus. Three Early Palestinian Jewish Christian Gospel Haggadoth*, Atlanta Georgia 1994, 19, in Judaic tradition the only site anyway comparable to Jerusalem, is Shiloh, because the ark was there for 369 years.

beginning of a new era for the tribes to which the boy is promised (51:2).

In LAB Samuel's presentation is described in less detail than in 1 Sam. While in 1 Sam 1:24-25 a sacrifice is mentioned, in LAB 51:2 Anna brings only gifts.[20] She places the boy before Eli, who at that moment finally discloses to Anna that her son is not only an answer to her request, but also to the people's prayer for a leader of Israel. Anna reacts by praying.[21] This prayer in particular is important for the comparison with Luke 2:22-39

In the first part of the song in LAB 51:3 there are only slight allusions to 1 Sam 2. For the rest Ps-Philo follows his own way (among others using biblical images resembling sentences of Isaiah). After a remarkable appeal to all the nations to listen ('Come to my voice, all you nations and pay attention to my

---

[20]The omission of the sacrifice concurs with that of the vow. In the LXX and QSam this vow is interpreted as a vow to make Samuel a Nazir. In the LXX a reference to the vow seems to be added to Hannah's prayer in LXX 2:9 "granting the vow to the person who vows". The biblical Hannah had promised to give her son to God at the time of her request for a son. Such a promise does not occur in LAB. B. Halpern-Ameru, 'Women in Pseudo-Philo's Antiquities', 96, suggests that Ps-Philo by omitting the vow removes the female initiative in dedicating Samuel to God. For a more appropriate reason for these omissions, see L. Cohn, 'An Apocryphal Work Ascribed to Philo of Alexandria', *JQR* 10 (1897/98) 277-332, 326, who observed that in LAB little is said of the Temple service and of the offerings and that the priestly laws are omitted.

[21]LAB 51:3: *oravit et dixit*; like 1 Sam 2:1 MT; but unlike in 1 Sam 2:1 LXX. There Hannah starts immediately with her song. Her song is introduced in LXX 1:28 only with 'she said'. J.E. Cook, 'Pseudo-Philo's Song of Hannah', 103-114 argues that this 'song' is a testament. This genre includes a narrative with autobiographical episodes, combined with an ethical section. In my opinion she focuses too much on her idea of the genre of the testament (even overstressing its forms, see 105) and neglects the content of the speech. Anna's autobiographical description in LAB 51 covers only a very limited part of her life, deals with the birth of her son and is not very apt to a death-bed. More important is the fact that in 51 there is no real transition of power or the retirement of a leader. Although Anna has prophetic features, she is not in charge in Israel (and thus there is no retirement). Moreover, when the song is finished Samuel is far too young to be a leader. Thus, Anna's prayer is not a testament but a disclosure about the future of her son.

speech, all you kingdoms'; see Isa 49:1) Anna says that her mouth is opened to speak (LAB 51:3). After another appeal, this time to her own breasts to witness, Anna moves to the description of the boy who is sucking her breasts (51:3b). With three complementary phrases (and the people will be enlightened by his words and he will show to the nations the statutes and his horn will be exalted very high) the twofold programme of Samuel's ministry to the world is described: he will be a teacher both for Israel and for the nations. In the next sentence there is a small transition; Anna goes back to her own position (51:4). From her shall arise the *constitutio Dei* and all men will find the truth.[22] In the following sections (51:4-5) we see more correspondences with 1 Sam 2: the language (some phrases and some words) as well as the theme of this part are clearly more reminiscent of Hannah's song in 1 Sam 2 than in the previous parts. Anna describes the changes that accompany Samuel's being a light. The theme of an infertile woman giving birth fits the setting of the story in 1 Sam as well in LAB 51. It is clear that here the author had the biblical text in his mind when composing this song. In 51:6 a new section starts in which first Anna is addressed. She is the mother of – and source of nourishment for – the new leader of Israel and this new leader has a twofold programme: to be a prophet (to Israel of course; as is clear from LAB 49 and 50) and to be a light to the nations. After the appeal to Anna, Elkanah is addressed. Anna appeals to him to join in a hymn about God's wonders by giving Israel a new leader, a Priest like Moses and Aaron.

In the following paragraph some of the features with which Ps-Philo promotes Samuel in Anna's song are described. A first indication of Ps-Philo's esteem for Samuel is his use of Ps 99:6 (51:6). There is a discussion about the implication of this quotation. Although not all manuscripts present Samuel as a Priest, it is

---

[22]M. Philonenko, 'Une paraphrase du cantique d'Anna', 165 argues that *constitutio* is a possible translation of Torah. In this context this is not impossible. The Torah is in LAB often considered as a light and in LAB 51 *constitutio* is parallel to light and the *terminos* shown to the 'nations'.

safe to say that Ps-Philo does associate Samuel with Moses and
Aaron as Priests.[23]

2. The Role of Samuel in LAB

In 1 Sam 2:10 Hannah says that God will endow his king with
strength and exalt the horn of his anointed It is clear that the
whole verse refers to a king like Saul. In the tradition of exegesis
of this verse this clear-cut interpretation is not followed. An example is LXX 1 Sam 2:10: "He will give strength to our kings
and will exalt the horn of his anointed (χριστος)"; thus, the LXX
does make a difference between the kings of Israel and the
anointed of the Lord. In LAB the identification of 'king' with
Saul is not clear at all. Although in LAB a part of 1 Sam 2:10 is
retained (until [*quousque*] give a horn to his anointed),[24] this sentence and the following 'until (again: *quousque*) he/there will be
(*fiat*) a light for this nation' are open at least to two interpretations. It is clear that there is a connection between these sentences, both introduced by 'until'. The use of *quousque* in the first
sentence suggests that the fulfillment of Asaph's prophecy is only
temporary and that it will be followed by another period: 'until
they give the horn to his christ/anointed one'. In the last phrase
we find a parallel to this sentence: Samuel will serve until he *fiat*
a light for this nation. Who is the subject of '*fiat*'? If *fiat* in the
last sentence is understood as 'there will be', it can refer to a king

---

[23]M. Philonenko, 'Une paraphrase du cantique d'Anna', 168 and Perrot-
Bogaert, *Ps-Philo II*, 220 understand this quotation as a characterisation of
Samuel as a Priest; but see Jacobson, *Ps-Philo*, 1107: 'Et Samuel inter eos' is
left out by the important manuscript π. This can indicate that the entire verse
is intended by Ps.-Philo and that thus Samuel is not among the Priests but
among those, who invoked his (God's) name.

[24]It is remarkable that in this Latin translation a graecism is used:
"*christo*". We find this Greek word in Latin characters also in LAB 57:3
(*christi*) and in LAB 59:2,4 (*christus*). Elsewhere in Latin versions of Pseu-
depigraphs only 4 times: *Adam and Eve* 1:42 (2x); 4 Ese 7:29 and in a Latin
fragment of a Slavic Henoch Z 2.

who is mentioned in the first sentence as *christus*/anointed one (either Saul or David or maybe even both).[25] If *fiat* is taken as 'he will be' or 'he will be made', it can be Elkanah's son about whom Asaph prophesied. It is possible to suppose that this new light will be the new 'messiah'. The Latin, however, is ambivalent. The word *fiat* can also refer to Samuel. After serving in the sanctuary Samuel will be the light for his people. This last interpretation seems to be confirmed by 51:7. As a conclusion the collective response in 51:7 reaffirms Anna's emphasis on Samuel being a light for the people (singular). But there is more. Samuel is even depicted in Anna's song with messianic features. This is suggested by the connection between the description of Samuel in 51:3 'his (here quite clearly Samuel's) horn will be greatly exalted' and the phrase 'until they give a horn to his anointed' (51:6). Another indication is Samuel's being anointed immediately after this presentation. This seems to be a special feature of Ps-Philo (LAB 51:7).[26] Also the language in which Samuel and his task are described endows him with features of the coming 'anointed one'. We can conclude that by Ps-Philo's adaptations Samuel, as a prophet, a *princeps* and a light for his people, acquires messianic features.[27] His task resembles that of a messiah

---

[25]For Saul as Gods anointed one, see LAB 57:3. David is anointed in LAB 59:1-3; see the use of *christus Domini* in 59:2,4.

[26]R.D. Aus, 'The Child Jesus', 32-33 argues that the phrase "until they give the horn to his anointed one and power be present at the throne of his king" is certainly meant here for Samuel, for in 51:7 the people festivally present him to Eli and anoint him, praying that the prophet 'may be a light to this nation for a long time'. That Samuel is the anointed king of 1 Sam 2:10, who in fact is anointed at this point, is peculiar to Ps-Philo. For another opinion, see Jacobson, *Ps-Philo*, 1107: "LAB ... is apparently referring to Saul though David is possible". Although in Perrot-Bogaert, *Ps Philo II*, 220, it is argued that in 61:6 *christo suo* refers to David, we find in Bogaert, 'Le cantique d'Anne', 256: "Le oint du cantique biblique était le roi, dans les Antiquiétes Bibliques, c'est Samuel". Aus seems to me to be overstressing the evidence (anointed *king*). I agree with the last quotation of Bogaert.

[27]In this context it is impossible to discuss any further the extent to which Samuel fits in with messianic patterns of that era as manifested in other literature. For the diversity of messianic expectations (a king from the Davidic line, two Messiahs or the messianic teacher, Priest and prophet), see now the

of God as described in the LXX addition that characterizes Saul as king of Israel and anointed one in LXX 1 Sam 10:1: 'and you shall rule among the people of the Lord and you shall save them out of the hand of their enemies and this shall be the sign to you that the Lord has anointed you to be a ruler over his inheritance'. Samuel's task is announced in LAB 49:8 in the same vein: 'By giving to Israel a new *princeps* (Samuel), God will deliver Israel from the hand of them that hate it'. From LAB 57:3 we learn that for Ps-Philo, the transfer of Samuel's rule to a king is due to Israel's unworthiness to be ruled by him. Samuel as prophet is thus presented as more important than the king.

In addition to the atmosphere of anticipation and fulfillment, Anna's song in LAB adds several aspects to its biblical counterpart. In LAB Anna's hymn deals with the special future of the boy: it is the boy who inspires this song. The explicit mention of Samuel's task is a clear-cut adaptation in LAB's version of Anna's song. This task, however, is also extended: instead of his task being reserved for Israel only, now he is given a double task relating also to the nations. A most remarkable feature of Samuel's future role and thus of this new version is its application to a programme both for Israel *and* the nations. Samuel's task as a new leader has an impact on the Gentiles; he will show to the Gentiles the statutes (*terminos*); from Anna will arise the *constitutio Dei* and *all* men will find the truth. Through Samuel Anna will bear a light to the peoples (nations).[28] This task reminds us of the task of the Servant in Isaiah and has an eschatological flavor.[29] In Isa 42:6 and 49:6 it is announced that the Servant has not only a task for Israel, but also for the Gentiles (see also Isa 51:4). In Isa

---

overview of J.J. Collins, *The Scepter and the Star. The Messiahs of the Dead Sea Scrolls and Other Ancient Literature*, New York 1995.

[28]In the quite elaborate version of Hannah's song in *Tg Sam* 2:2-5 the relation of Israel with the Gentiles/nations is also at stake but in a way quite opposite to Ps-Philo: enemies like the Assyrians (2:2), the Chaldeans (2:3), the Greeks (2:4), the sons of Haman and the Romans (2:5) will be defeated.

[29]See Perrot-Bogaert, *Ps-Philo II*, 58: "Dans LAB 51:3.6.7, le rôle de Samuel est fortement souligné à l'aide des traits «messianiques»: tel le Serviteur d' Isaïe, Samuel doit apporter la lumière à Israel et aux Nations."

49:1, a quite unique address, the Gentiles are themselves directly addressed in an elaborated form and invited to listen to the Servant.[30] The use of this theme of light for the Gentiles in this form is quite unique in Jewish traditions.[31] In sum: Samuel's being anointed (51:7) to deliver Israel and to be a light for the Gentiles makes him a prophetic *princeps* with messianic features and at the very least comparable to Priests.[32]

The literary history of Hannah's hymn in 1 Sam 2 is not unlike that of its interpretation in LAB: 1 Sam 2:1b-10 is a song of a more general nature which has been secondarily inserted into the story about Hannah and adapted to her situation. An (existing?) song is used as a hymn on the occasion of the presentation of the boy Samuel. In a sense, the literary history of Anna's hymn in LAB is a repetition of this procedure: Hannah's song is adapted to a new situation and seems now more suited to the situation of Anna and Samuel than in the biblical text.[33] The theme of change and reversal is now more attuned to the theme of motherhood for the infertile beloved (e.g. the introduction of breasts in 51:1 and

---

[30]For the importance of the position of the nations in relation with God's dealing with Israel, see G.I. Davies, 'The Destiny of the Nations in the Book of Isaiah' in: J. Vermeylen (ed.), *Le Livre d'Isaïe. Les oracles et leurs relectures. Unité et complexité de l'ouvrage,* Leuven 1989, 93-120.

[31]See already H.L. Strack & P. Billerbeck, Kommentar zum Neuen Testament aus Talmud und Midrasch, 6 vols., München 1922-56, II.139: "Die zugrunde liegenden Stellen Jes 42,6 u. 49,6 werden in der rabbin. Literatur so gut wie gar nicht erwähnt; doch hat der Targum Jes 42 auf den Messias gedeutet". Using concordances and computer data no other relevant parallels are found in the Greek and Latin Pseudepigrapha and in rabbinic literature. Similar use of the theme of light of the Law in relation with the position of the Gentiles in T.Levi 14:3 is quite probably a Christian element. Within LAB this usage is also particular: Ps-Philo constantly associates light with the Torah and the gift of it to Israel (LAB 33:3: *lumen legis*; see also LAB 9:8; 11:1; 12:1). See also LAB 12:2: *et legem illuminabit nobis* (see LAB 19:6; 23:10; 28:3). For God as light, see LAB 12:1,9.

[32]For the tendency to combine offices as a significant factor in the revival of messianic expectations in the last centuries BCE, see Collins, *The Scepter and the Star*, 194.

[33]See Bogaert, 'Le cantique d'Anna', 256.

the phrase: 'nor those who have borne in abundance will be called mother' in 51:4).[34]

In LAB not only Samuel but also Anna acquires special qualities. Already at the beginning of the story she is typified as: God-fearing from her youth (see Jdt 8:29). This is probably confirmed by the statement about her good behaviour in 50:3. In LAB her position is described as far more important than in 1 Sam. She opens her mouth and that may be interpreted as an indication of prophetic language (see Isa 6:7 and Jer 1:9). She declares: "from me will arise the ordinance of the Lord". From this we learn that as a mother and a pious women Anna has an important say in the new leader's future.[35] In this way the figure of Anna is a special religious woman who attains prophetic features.

3. Hanna in Luke 2:22-39

In this section we will discuss another Hanna with prophetic features, namely the prophetess in Luke 2:36-38. We will also deal with context of her appearance, the story of Jesus' presentation in Luke 2:22-39. There is a mass of literature on Luke 1-2.[36] Until recently, however, the figure of Hanna and her role in the story

---

[34]Apropos LAB 50:5, Perrot-Bogaert, *Ps-Philo II*, 215 refers to Isa 54:1. Isa 54:1 and 66:9-11 are a possible background to the description of Anna in 51:3-7. Thus, Anna acquires features of Sion. By *Tg Sam* 2:5 Hannah is associated with Jerusalem: "they returned to Jerusalem, which was like a barren woman".

[35]See Brown, *No Longer Be Silent*, 144: "It (LAB 49) is not one woman's story, but one nation's story".

[36]For literature about the origin of Luke 1-2 and related problems, see my 'Simeons Worte (Lk 2,29-32.34c-35) und Israels Geschick', in: F. van Segbroeck e.a. (eds) *The Four Gospels*, Leuven 1992, 1549-1569, esp. 1549, n.3. For studies dealing with the OT background of Luke 1-2, see R.E. Brown, *The Birth of the Messiah. A Commentary on the Infancy Narratives in Matthew and Luke*, London 1977; R.D. Aus, 'The Child Jesus'; S. Farris, *The Hymns of Luke's Infancy Narratives Their Origin, Meaning and Significance*, Sheffield 1985.

have been dealt with only to a limited extent.[37] In exegetical literature we find that Simeon and Hanna are modeled after OT persons. They recall biblical figures and fit very well the other reminiscences of the OT in Luke 1-2.[38] A great part of this literature refers to 1 Sam as a possible background to Luke 1-2.[39] An example of this dependence on Samuel is that quite often it is argued that the author of Luke-Acts used 1 Sam 2:1-10 as a background for the Magnificat.[40] But also the situation of Zechariah and Elisabeth is compared with that of Elkanah and Hannah.[41] Finally the story of Jesus' presentation in Luke 2:22-39 and his stay in Jerusalem at the age of twelve (2:41-52) are likewise connected with 1 Sam 1-2.[42]

---

[37]For the figure of Anna, see M. Wilcox, 'Luke 2,36-38 "Anna Bat Phanuel, of the Tribe of Asher, a Prophetess...". A Study in Midrash in Material Special to Luke', in: F. van Segbroeck e.a (eds), *The Four Gospels,* 1571-1579. Cf. N. Visser, 'Hier is meer dan Jozua. Over de opdracht van Jezus in de tempel en zijn ontmoeting met Simeon en Hanna', *Benedictijns Tijdschrift* 47 (1986) 139-154; and idem, 'Laatsten die eersten zullen zijn', *Benedictijns Tijdschrift* 48 (1987) 130-137 and esp. idem, 'De veertig voldragen. Waarom Hanna trekken van Judit meekreeg' *Benedictijns Tijdschrift* 53 (1992) 165-184.

[38]The annunciations are comparable to OT scenes; Zechariah and Elisabeth are like Abraham and Sarah. John the Baptist is explicitly compared with Elijah (Luke 1:16-17; see Mal 4:4-6). Luke 1:32-33 seems to refer to 2 Sam 7:8-16. This is merely the tip of the ice-berg, see e.g. M. Miyoshi, 'Jesu Darstellung oder Reinigung im Tempel unter Berücksichtigung von "Nunc Dimittis" Luke II 22-38', *Annual of the Japanese Biblical Institute* 4 (1978) 85-115.

[39]An interesting study is E. Burrows, 'The Gospel of Infancy: The Form of Luke Chapters 1 and 2', in: E.F. Sutcliffe (ed.) *The Gospel of the Infancy and Other Biblical Essays*, London 1940. Burrows argues that the author of Luke 1-2 composed a narrative in the style of the Old Testament using for his principal model the history of the child Samuel in Hebrew.

[40]See J.A. Fitzmyer, *The Gospel according to Luke I-IX*, New York 1981, 359-362.

[41]R.E. Brown, *The Birth of the Messiah*, 268-269.

[42]R.E. Brown, *The Birth of the Messiah,* 357. Brown (450-451) observes that while the conception of John the Baptist was patterned on the conception of Samuel, Luke now shifts the Samuel-imagery over to Jesus and patterns Joseph and Mary on Elkanah and Hannah just as he modelled earlier Zechariah and Elisabeth on Samuel's parents. This is a fine example of a Lucan artistic inclusion: an infancy narrative that began with an upright and

How is it possible that in these two chapters we see so many references to Samuel and Hannah? Is it probable that Elisabeth as well as Mary and Hanna have features in common with Hannah? Suffice to refer here to Brown who made a thorough study of the OT background of Luke 1-2. He argues that "Luke's method is not one of identifying figures in the infancy narrative with OT characters; rather he uses pigments taken from OT narratives to color in the infancy narrative."[43]

This article deals with only a small part of this complex of references, comparing LAB 49-51 – and especially 51 – with Luke 2:22-39. Investigating those developments of Jewish tradition as witnessed by LAB 49-51 in Luke 2:22-39, Hannah, as Samuel's mother, is the most important focus.[44] It is the thesis of this article that the author of Luke-Acts uses themes of the Hannah-tradition not only from the Bible but even from the Anna traditions such as those in LAB as a background to Luke 2:22-39. Therefore I will now first sketch the structure of Luke 2:22-39 and its context (Luke 1-2). Subsequently I will discuss in Luke the same elements dealt with above concerning LAB, namely: (a) the prophetic figures in the Temple and (b) the birth of a messianic savior as a disclosure of a new Era.

Structure of Luke 2:22-39 and its context.

---

law-abiding man and woman and a Temple scene ends with an upright and law-abiding man and woman and a Temple scene. For the connection between 1-2 Samuel and Luke 2:41-52, see especially R.D. Aus, 'The Child Jesus'. In his article R.D. Aus lists fifteen biblical and Judaic traditions regarding the presentation of their firstborn son Samuel in the Temple, who also partially shape Jesus' visit to the Temple at the age of twelve.

[43]*Birth of the Messiah*, 451; See R.C. Tannehill, *The Narrative Unity* 18-19. Tannehill argues (20) that the multiple possibilities of comparison suggested by the use of Samuel material and other OT material and by the parallel between John and Jesus, promote a complex interaction of narrative elements with an enriching background.

[44]The similarities between LAB 49-51 and Luke 1-2 are not exhausted: cf. LAB 51:1 with Luke 2:21 and 1:31, see Reinmuth, *Ps-Philo*, 166. See also Luke 1:9 and LAB 49:5-8; Reinmuth, *Ps-Philo*, 157-158.

Even after a first superficial reading of Luke 1-2, it is clear that there is a carefully composed parallel between Jesus and John the Baptist.[45] Here only the parallel structure of these stories is sketched:

A   Annunciation of the birth of John the Baptist (Luke 1:5-25)
A' Annunciation of the birth of Jesus (Luke 1:26-38)
        Mary's visit to Elisabeth (including *Magnificat*;
        Luke 1:39-56)
B   Birth of John the Baptist, circumcision / presentation
    / conclusion
        (including Zechariah's *Benedictus;* Luke 1:57-80)
B' Birth of Jesus, circumcision/ presentation/conclusion
        (including Simeon's *Nunc dimittis;* Luke 2:1-40)
        Jesus' stay in Jerusalem (Luke 2:41-52)

This scheme is an outline for a series of poetic 'disclosures': the annunciation of Gabriel to Zechariah's and to Mary are a key for understanding their future mission. Mary's *Magnificat*, Zechariah's *Benedictus* and Simeon's *Nunc dimittis* are also 'disclosures'. By these utterings, the author indicates how to understand Luke-Acts. It is in this context that Simeon and Hanna are mentioned during Jesus' presentation in the Temple (Luke 2:22-39).[46] I propose the following structure for this pericope.

A   2:22-24   Joseph and Mary [in this sequence] go to
                      Jerusalem to fulfill the Law

---

[45]See, for example J.A. Fitzmyer, *Luke 1-IX*, 313-316; E. Schweizer, 'Zum Aufbau von Lukas 1 und 2', in: D.Y. Hadidian (ed.), *Intergerini Parietis Septum (Eph 2:14),* Pittsburgh 1981, 309-335, also in: idem, *Neues Testament und Christologie im Werden*, Göttingen 1982, 11-32.

[46]The unity of this passage is clear from the unity of time, place and action. The indication of time in Luke 2:22a corresponds with Luke 2:39a. Unity of place is clear from Luke 2:22b and Luke 2:39b. While the main event takes place in Luke 2:25-38, the introduction in Luke 2:22-24 indicates that this encounter is made possible by the lawabiding nature of Jesus' parents and this is exactly the background (and reason) for Jesus' presentation in the Temple. For the position of Luke 2:40, see Brown, *The Birth of the Messiah*, 468.

B	2:25-28a	Characterization and action of Simeon (referring three times to the Spirit)
C	2:28b-32	First blessing and first pronouncement by Simeon
D	2:33	Reaction of the parents
C'	2:34-35	Second blessing and second pronouncement by Simeon
B'	2:36-38	Characterization and action of Hanna, the prophetess
A'	2:39	After fulfilling the Law Mary and Joseph [now in this sequence] go back to Galilee.

Within Luke 1-2, Simeon and Hanna's appearances are quite clearly a literary unit. Because in A as well as in A' the law-abiding nature is stressed, this framework is the setting for Hanna and Simeon. The observation that Simeon is expecting the consolation of Israel (2:25) is paralleled by Hanna's speech to all who expect the redemption of Jerusalem. The salvation of Israel/Jerusalem is another framework for the pronouncements by Simeon and Hanna.[47]

3.1 Simeon and Hanna as prophetic figures in the Temple

In Luke 2:22-24 and 2:39 Jesus' parents are presented as law-abiding, making them reliable to the readers. Their observance of the law brings them to the Temple in Jerusalem, a place that is central and holy for Jews.[48] Within this framework of law-abidingness Simeon and Hanna come to the fore.

Luke characterizes Simeon as upright and devout man. By these qualities the author presents Simeon as a reliable witness. His uprightness brings to mind that of Zechariah and Elizabeth (1:6) and of Joseph of Arimathaea (23:50). The centurion calls Jesus 'upright' (23:47). Simeon's devoutness is another positive

---

[47]For Simeon's pronouncements as disclosures of Jesus' mission as a light to the Gentiles and as Israel's glory, see my 'Simeons Worte'.

[48]See S. Safrai, 'Jerusalem in the Halacha of the Second Temple Period', in: M. Poorthuis & Ch. Safrai (eds), *The Centrality of Jerusalem. Historical Perspectives*, Kampen 1996, 94-113, 112.

quality (see Acts 2:5; 8:2; 22:12) and fits with the law-abidingness of Jesus' parents.

That the Holy Ghost was upon him, is a further indication that Simeon is reliable in every way (2:25,27). At first glance it is remarkable that Simeon is not typified as a prophet while this is said explicitly about Hanna. But although he is not called prophet, the reference to the Holy Spirit does describe him as a prophetic figure (see Num 11:29 and 11:17,25). He resembles other prophetic figures in Luke-Acts: Elizabeth (1:41), Zechariah (1:67), John the Baptist (1:80; see 1:16-17), Jesus (e.g. 3:22; 4:1,14,18; 10:21; Acts 1:2; 10:38) and Stephen (Acts 6:8,10; 7:55). A special prophetic feature of Simeon is the fact that it was revealed to him by the Holy Spirit that he should not see death before he had seen the Lord's Christ (2:26).[49] A sign of Simeon's devoutness is the fact that he was expecting the consolation of Israel (see Hanna in 2:38). He knows about God's promises to Israel (see Isa 40 and 66:10-13) and longs not for fulfillment of a personal wish, but for salvation for his people.

Hanna completes Simeon's testimony and stresses the importance of his pronouncements.[50] In the composition of Luke 2:22-

---

[49]P. Figueras, 'Syméon et Anne, ou le témoignage de la Loi et des Prophètes', *NT* 20 (1978) 84-99, argues that there is a parallel between Simeon in the Temple, who is prepared for death because he has seen God's salvation, and Moses on the Mount Nebo, who only dies after seeing the promised land. Figueras argues that this parallel characterises Simeon as a personification of the Law (91). Hanna personifies the prophets. On this basis he supposes that after the coming of Jesus as the Christ, the Law personified in Simeon, can abide with him (90,91,92,93,98). This reminds me of the old Christian model of Christ versus the Law, but seems to me to be an oversimplification. It is against the tendency of the pericope in which fulfilling the Law is stressed in a positive way. The Law of Moses is the Law of the Lord (2:22,23,24). The division between Hanna and Simeon as personifications of Law and Prophets is quite improbable while Simeon is also described as prophetic. While Figueras neglects these elements of the text, he demonstrates that his remarks about the end of the Law and Prophets are more based on his own theological concepts than on the text.

[50]For Luke's tendency to use men-women parallels, see T. Karlsen Seim, *The Double Message. Patterns of Gender in Luke-Acts,* Edinburgh 1994, 11-25.

39 the figure of Simeon is inseparable from that of Hanna. There is a certain balance between the descriptions of Hanna and Simeon. What is said about Simeon (that he is upright, devout and waiting for the consolation of Israel, and that the Holy Spirit is resting upon him), is not said about Hanna. Conversely, details of Hanna (her descent, her civil status, her age and the fact that she acquires the title 'prophetess') are missing in the description of Simeon. In concurrence with the fact that Simeon is associated with the Holy Spirit three times and thus gets prophetic features, Hanna is described as a prophetess. While Simeon's prophetic features are implied, Hanna gets the title, and while we hear about Simeon that he is upright and devout, the law-abiding attitude and piety of Hanna are concrete: as a widow she lived an exemplary life of piety. Both descriptions serve to suggest to the reader that both persons belong to the same group of people who love God, are beloved by God and are present within a holy place, God's Court.

A difference between Simeon and Hanna is that we are told what Simeon says and not what Hanna says. The audiences are also different. Simeon speaks only to Jesus' parents, especially to Mary, while Hanna talks to all (!) who are looking forward to the redemption of Jerusalem. This wider audience makes Hanna's characterization as a prophetess all the more plausible.

The way Simeon and Hanna are described here show that they are complementary. Although they are different, they match as pious prophetic figures, who thank God (2:28,38) before speaking their message to fellow human beings (2:34-35,38).[51]

3.2 A new Era as fulfillment of the expectation of the people for a savior

---

[51]For 2:33,38, see, J. Jaschke, 'Lalein bei Lukas. Ein Beitrag zur lukanis-chen Theologie', *BZ* NF 15 (1971) 104-114, at 111: "... indem sie (Maria) sich einreiht, wie Zacharias, Simeon (Luke 2,33), Hannah (2,38), in den Kreis der Propheten, durch die Gott schon vorher sprach (Luke 1,55; 1,70; Apg 2,31; 3,21; 26,22)."

We referred above to a number of similarities in expressions and motifs which exist between the narratives of 1 Sam 1-2 and Luke 1-2. A fine example are the verses Luke 1:80; 2:40,52 describing as a conclusion to the preceding narratives, the growing up of the boys John and Jesus. These verses are clearly reminiscent of the description of the boy Samuel in 1 Sam 2:21b,26; 3:19a. However, C. Perrot argues that in the OT there are not so many stories concerning the birth and infancy of important persons.[52] He states that since the 2nd century BCE, oral tradition has created a new framework for the heroes of the OT such as stories about the birth and infancy of Noah, Abraham, Isaac, Jacob, Moses, Samson, Samuel and Elijah. Perrot shows that although there are a lot of differences between these stories there is also quite a number of similarities. He roughly outlines this pattern. In the beginning there is a difficult situation for Israel. God intervenes. He sends a savior. The birth of this savior is announced, frequently together with his task and name. This birth has special aspects: the parents are too old and/or the mother is barren. Quite often the child born is only seven months old and frequently it is the first-born. The child is beautiful and dedicated to God from conception.[53] In our analysis, the elements which are specific to Luke and LAB are focused on .

In the biblical story Samuel is God's answer to Hannah's prayer. In LAB Samuel is no longer just the fulfillment of a personal request from Anna, but he is also the answer to the people's prayer for a leader. In LAB, the story of Anna and Elkanah becomes even more a prologue to the Samuel stories. In this prologue, Samuel's significance is already summarized. Anna's song in LAB becomes a programmatic introduction to Samuel's prophetic life. According to Luke 2:25, Simeon is waiting for the

---

[52]Birth: Moses in Ex 1-2; Isaac in Gen 21 and Jacob in Gen 25:19-27; annunciation: Isaac (Gen 17-18) Samuel (1 Sam 1), Samson (Jud 13). Cf. C. Perrot, 'Les récits d'enfance dans la haggada antérieure au IIe siècle de notre ère', RSR 55 (1967) 481-518, 481-482, for his dealing with Samuel, see 496-497. See also Bauckham, 'Ps-Philo and the Gospels', 57 and Harrington, 'Birth Narratives'.

[53]See Perrot, 'Les récits d'enfance', 505-506.

consolation of Israel. In Luke 2:22-39, we find that Jesus is an
answer to the expectation of the people for redemption: for
Simeon (2:25) as well as for other people (2:38; cf. Luke 1:69-
72). In Luke 1-2 it is stated *explicitly* that Jesus is born for the
sake of the people – unlike Samuel in 1 Sam 1-2, but like Samuel
in LAB 49-51. In LAB, the announcement of the birth of Samuel
is elaborated upon and his special place for Israel is known to Eli.
His name is, unlike in 1 Sam, made known by God. Likewise in
Luke 1-2, Jesus' birth is announced and his name is made known
by God.

Luke 1-2 appear to be a prologue to the stories about Jesus in
the Gospel. In this prologue, Jesus' significance – like Samuel's
in LAB – is already summarized. Like Anna's song in LAB,
Simeon's song is a programmatic introduction to Jesus' life as a
prophet and an anointed one.

4. Samuel in LAB and Jesus in Luke: anointed with a special task

In Ps-Philo's version of Anna's song she describes Samuel's task
in terms alluding to a concept from Deutero-Isaiah (Isa 51:4; see
Isa 42:6; 49:6.9). The allusion in LAB 51 outlines the effect of
Samuel's appearance. Two important new elements in LAB are
that Samuel is an anointed one and that his special task will affect
not only Israel but also the nations in a *positive* way. While it is
said that Samuel will be a light to the peoples (51:6; see 51:3), he
himself deals only with Israel.

In Luke 2:25, it is said that Simeon is awaiting the anointed
one. The twofold programme of this anointed one, Jesus, as
sketched in Luke 2:32, strongly resembles Samuel's task.[54] These

---

[54] It is remarkable that Jesus, as well as Samuel, does not realize his task to
the Gentiles. Only the first half of Jesus' mission, his mission to Israel, is
realized in the Gospel, whereas the second part comes to the fore as the main
subject of Acts. In LAB 51 as well as in Luke 2, the concept of light for the
Gentiles is brought to the fore in the context of people who fulfill the Torah:
Elkanah (by going to the house of the Lord each year doing the Passover sacrifices; LAB 50:2) and Anna (fearing God from her youth; LAB 50:2 see

similarities are specific. As far as could be determined, 'being a light for Gentiles' as a task for a prophet comes only to the fore in Luke-Acts and LAB as an interpretation of Isa 49:6,9. During the presentation in the Temple, Simeon describes Jesus in terms that are taken from the Servant songs in Deutero-Isaiah (Luke 2:32; see Isa 42:6; 49:6,9). The allusion in 2:32 outlines the effect of Jesus' appearance: "a light for revelation to the Gentiles and glory to your people Israel". It is quite usual for a person's programme to be sketched during the presentation of such a person. The importance of Jesus' presentation is underlined by Simeon's prophetic stature and by Anna's being explicitly named 'a prophetess' and by the place of the presentation, the Temple. What will happen in Luke-Acts is described in this verse and it is a good characterization of both the Gospel and Acts. The programmatic nature of the presentation is confirmed by the fact that the texts alluded to in Luke 2:32 will reappear at several points in Luke-Acts. As argued elsewhere, Luke outlines the ministry of Jesus and that of the disciples, and that of Paul in particular, by means of quotations from or allusions to Isaiah, especially in terms reminding us of the figure of the Servant.[55] In this way, Luke uses ideas from Isaiah as a framework, illustrating at crucial points the ministries of his protagonists. Isaiah's songs of the Servant proclaim both the restoration of the twelve tribes of Jacob and the salvation for the Gentiles.

The twofold programme of Jesus' ministry, as sketched in Luke 2:32, is realized – according to Luke – in the two separate parts of his work, which was drafted as a unit. Only the first half of Jesus' mission is realized in the Gospel: his mission within the land of Israel, practically restricting itself to the Jewish people. The second part of this programme forms the main subject of Acts: the mission to the Jews in the Diaspora goes hand in hand with a mission to the Gentiles. After Luke 2:29-32 Jesus' relation to the people of Israel is further specified in Luke 3:21-22 (with an allu-

---

50:4,5 and 51:4 'for from me shall arise the ordinance of the Lord') and Mary and Joseph (Luke 2:22-24,39).

[55]See my 'Simeons Worte', 1553-1557.

sion to Isa 42:1) and especially in the quotation from Isaiah in
Luke 4:18-19. Although the salvation for the Gentiles is already
announced in Luke 2:32 and alluded to in 3:6, its proclamation is
only appropriate after, and as a consequence of, Jesus' mission to
Israel. Therefore the salvation for the Gentiles does not reoccur
until the end of the Gospel (Luke 24:47) and in the beginning of
Acts (1:8). Luke conveys the message that the Gentile mission
was transferred to his disciples as part and parcel of Jesus' mission by writing Acts as a sequel to his Gospel. Paul is a protago-
nist in it. It is only after several chapters of Acts that the proclamation of Jesus is extended beyond the circle of the Jews (see
Acts 8:26-40; Acts 10:1-11:18 and Acts 11:20-21). In Acts Isaiah
texts are used to describe and to legitimize the Gentile mission as
a consequence of Jesus' programme (see Acts 13:47).

5. The biblical Hannah as a role model in LAB and in Luke

A new element in LAB is that Anna is more explicitly described
as a God-fearing woman. Her religiosity, however, is connected
to her motherhood. Although she is already depicted as being pious when she is barren, her being a mother gives her the possibility to share in God's dealings with Israel.[56] Although there is in
LAB a tendency to stress stories about women and to reconstruct
them in an even better shape, this mostly concerns mothers.

Hanna in Luke 2 is God-fearing, like Samuel's mother in LAB.
She prays and fasts, she is old and a widow and she is a prophetess.[57] While in biblical stories and LAB, religious women are married and mothers, widowhood (next to virginity) is in Luke-Acts

---

[56]Halpern-Amaru, 'Women in Ps-Philo's Biblical Antiquities', 98 referring
to LAB 51:3-4, says: "The personal exaltation of motherhood, a departure
from the biblical text is striking". She argues that the maternal role is a major
theme in Ps-Philo's depiction of women.

[57]For a lengthy description of the similarities between Judith and Anna, see
Visser, 'De veertig voldragen', but see also Wilcox, 'Anna Bat Phanuel',
1572-1573.

one of the more appropriate characteristics of religious women.[58] We can find the phenomenon of remaining a widow as an important feature of religiosity also in other Jewish literature, for example in the book of Judith.[59]

There is another important element in common to Anna in LAB and to Hanna in Luke. In LAB 51 Anna gives a speech in a Sanctuary. In 51:3 all the nations and kingdoms are addressed. Her audience is hardly mentioned. We hear only Eli's and Elkanah's names and Samuel will also be there. The audience to whom she addresses her speech gives it quite a public character, which is appropriate for a setting in or near a Sanctuary. LAB 51:7 confirms the fact that Anna's message became public.

Simeon's pronouncements are directed to God (2:28-29). Although these words are clearly audible to the parents (see 2:33), they are not meant for them, let alone for a larger audience. His words in 2:34-35 are addressed only to the parents, especially to Mary. Regarding content, his words deal with Israel and the nations, but within the narrative this is only an eye-opener for his parents and thus a disclosure to Luke's own audience.

Although we do not hear what Hanna is saying, we do hear to whom she is speaking: to all who were seeking the redemption of Jerusalem. Although Luke honors Simeon by quoting his message, the content of this message is apparently not very different from that of Hanna's (see the parallel between 2:25 and 2:38). Hanna's appearance in the Temple is clearly more public than Simeon's.[60] In a certain sense, the combined role of Hanna-

---

[58]In NT exegesis there has been ample discussion about Luke's attitude towards women: see Seim, *The Double Message* and the literature mentioned there. Not mentioned e.g. J.M. van Cangh, 'La femme dans l'Évangile de Luc. Comparaison des passages narratifs propres à Luc avec la situation de la femme dans le judaïsme', *RTL* 24 (1993) 297-324 and R.J. Karris, 'Women and Discipleship in Luke', *CBQ* 56 (1994) 1-20.

[59]See Seim, *The Double Message*, 229-248, esp. 235.

[60]Rightly observed by Seim, *The Double Message*, 131. Seim argues that in those days the public sphere was the forum for men, while the home was the action base for women. Seim also argues that for Luke the mother as such is not that important, but that women who are free from man are more destined for an attachment to God than married women. Although Anna (a

Simeon of Luke 2 is analogous to the single role of Anna in LAB
51. Reinmuth argues that Simeon's *Nunc Dimittis* formally corresponds to Hanna's song in LAB.[61] Although this is true, it is important to note that the public character of Anna's speech also occurs in Hanna's performance. Thus, not only do the descriptions
of Hanna and Simeon match perfectly, but also their different
tasks do. Simeon gives the content of the message, while from
Hanna's action we learn that this message is addressed to all who
were looking for the liberation of Jerusalem. This leads us to the
conclusion that Anna in LAB as well as Hanna in Luke acts as a
prophetic speaker in the most important and most sacred of public
places, the Sanctuary.

However, the religious prototypes are different: mother or a
woman unattached to a man (virgin or widow). Like the rabbinic
literature Ps-Philo in LAB 51 and elsewhere stresses that the
mother, who as a mother is the bearer of salvation, is a religious
prototype. Here and elsewhere Luke uses the other category
'woman unattached to a man' as a religious prototype. But both
use Hannah as a model of female religiosity. This concurs with
later rabbinic and Christian tradition to attach female religiosity
to women called Hanna.[62]

---

widow!) and the daughters of Philip (virgins!; Acts 21:9) are qualified as
prophetesses and likewise Mary and Elisabeth have prophetic features, they
proclaim their messages in private circles and are deprived of prophesying in
public (see e.g. pp. 164-184). Seim observes that Hanna is an exception to the
rule that, although women may be important disciples of Jesus and even teach
in private circles, they are not allowed to preach in the public sphere, the
world of men.

[61]*Ps-Philo und Lukas*, 166.

[62]In the rabbinic tradition Hannah was—like Moses—a prototype. There is
a tendency in Jewish literature to combine different 'religious' women. See
for example Anna in Tob 1:9. In later rabbinic tradition (Midr Samuel 4:1)
the mother of Samuel is also old, like Sara, like Judith and like Anna in Luke
2. In later Jewish tradition the nameless mother in 2 Macc 7 is given – because of the obvious association with 1 Sam 2:5 – the name of Hannah. In a
late midrash, Judith is apparently replaced by a Hannah, daughter of the
Hasmonean dynasty, see Chanukah-midrash III in A. Jellinek (ed.), *Beth
Hamidrasch* VI, Jerusalem 1967, 2. See also Y. Adler, 'Midrash le-
Chanukah' (Hebr.), in: *Studies in Jewish Bibliography, History and Litera-*

6. Conclusions

Both Luke and LAB use elements of 1 Sam 1-2 for their stories. LAB gives a new version of this biblical text, adapting the story with themes important for the author and presumably also for his audience. In Ps-Philo's version of Samuel's birth, Samuel is promoted as an expected, promised and anointed prophet. The expectation of a new and special leader with messianic features and a special task as a new element shows that this is an issue of importance for him and his audience. Luke goes even further in his free use of patterns and models of the Bible and biblical interpretations. Luke 1-2 uses several biblical models to depict the story of John and Jesus. In this way Luke's new story is presented as a worthy successor of the older biblical stories. But although the working methods are different, it is remarkable that those elements of the LAB version which are new in comparison to 1 Sam are also used in Luke 2: the expectation of a new leader with messianic features. A remarkable and exceptional similarity between both texts is that the new leader has a task both for Israel and for the nations. This double task is linked to motifs found in Isaiah.

From the comparison of Luke and LAB 50-51, we learned that the figure of Hanna inspired both writers as a type of a religious woman. Ps-Philo stresses the motherhood of Hanna in her contribution to God's dealings with his people.[63] This concurs with his picture of women elsewhere in LAB. Luke depicts Anna as a widow. This fits his tendency to depict religious women as being free from domestic responsibilities and oriented to the word of God. The comparison with LAB teaches us that Hanna in Luke 2 has a very special place next to Simeon. In LAB, Anna acquires prophetic features. Influenced by the biblical story of Hannah Luke seems to give Hanna in Luke 2:35-38 an important role in

---

ture, New York 1971, 1-6. For the Christian tradition see e.g. Mary's mother Anna in the Protevangelium of James.

[63] By contrast, Josephus diminishes Hannah's role significantly. See Brown, *No Longer Be Silent,* 163-173, esp. 170. Josephus presents Hannah's story as Elkanah's story.

the opening chapters of his work. Luke 2 is, as such, a witness of the same interpretative tendency as LAB. The biblical Hannah, Samuel's mother, is a model for both Anna and Hanna. She acquires prophetic features and proclaims in a holy place to a wider audience. Because Hanna, daughter of Phanuel, has such a ancestor, she is at least on a par with Simeon, but because of her public appearance may be even more important.

THE LASTING SANCTITY OF BETHESDA

Martien Parmentier

1. Introduction

One of the most pleasant and picturesque walks in Jerusalem is round the city, within the walls, especially on the southern side of the town. Any self-respecting dragoman, however, does not encourage this kind of desultory ramble, for the strict ritual of a visit to Jerusalem enforces – after the churches have been 'done' – an inspection of certain tombs and pools. These are not pleasant places, and the viewing of the same in many instances suggests such a visit as a sanitary inspector would be called upon to pay.

In the Gospel according to St. John it is written: 'Now there is at Jerusalem by the sheep market a pool, which is called in the Hebrew tongue Bethesda, having five porches. In these lay a great multitude of impotent folk, halt, withered, waiting for the moving of the water.' This account suggests a wide sheet of limpid water surrounded by a cloister of some magnitude, for it will be noted that the multitude that came to the pool was 'great'. The pool of today is far down in the earth at the bottom of a pit delved out of a deposit of vague ruins. At the summit of the excavation, in place of a sheep market, is a modern laundry with a corrugated iron roof, and around it a quite extraordinary number of stockings hanging out to dry. A stone stair, very steep and narrow, leads down to the side of the pit and finally ends before a small cistern or reservoir cut out of the rock and arched over by ancient vaulting. In the cistern, which could not accommodate a larger multitude than five or six, is water that would probably be condemned by any medical officer of health. This is the pool of Bethesda.

Among the debris through which the shaft leading to the 'Pool' has pierced are the ruins of two churches. The present church that stands upon the spot is the ancient and interesting Church of St. Anne. It is dedicated to the mother of the Virgin Mary, who is stated to have lived in a cave that is still shown to believers. In this cave the Virgin Mary was born. It is very noteworthy that many of the sacred sights in the Holy Land are in or about caves, and, were these sites genuine, one could only conclude that the humbler folk at the time of Christ were all cave-dwellers.

This is the description of the site of Bethesda as it presented itself before the excavations of the 20th century, published by the British medical officer Sir Frederick Treves just before World War I.[1] In the years to follow, Bethesda received quite a new look. In 1981, a survey of the excavations at the site of Bethesda was published in *Proche Orient Chrétien* by M.-J. Pierre and J.-M. Rousée.[2] The results of earlier excavations were published before World War II by H. Vincent and F.-M. Abel in their large work *Jérusalem; Recherches de topographie, d'archéologie et d'histoire,*[3] and by N. van der Vliet.[4] After the war, J. Jeremias wrote his brief but important study *Die Wiederentdeckung von Bethesda.*[5] In 1957 the excavations were taken up again. The results for the ancient period were published by A. Duprez in his *Jésus et les dieux guérisseurs. A propos de Jean V,*[6] and for the Christian edifices by J.-M. Rousée.[7] For our survey, the article by Pierre and Rousée offers a ready framework. We follow it here, and supplement it by other relevant information.

---

[1] F. Treves, *The Land that is Desolate; An Account of a Tour in Palestine,* London 1913, 108-109.

[2] M.-J. Pierre & J.-M. Rousée, 'Sainte Marie de la Probatique, état et orientation des recherches', *POC* 31 (1981) 23-42.

[3] Vol. II, *Jérusalem nouvelle,* Fascicule IV, Paris 1926.

[4] N. van der Vliet, *Sainte Marie où elle est née et la Piscine Probatique* Paris 1938.

[5] J. Jeremias, *Die Wiederentdeckung von Bethesda,* Göttingen 1949.

[6] A. Duprez, *Jésus et les dieux guérisseurs. A propos de Jean V,* Paris 1970.

[7] 'L'Eglise Sainte Marie de la Probatique; Chronologies des sanctuaires à Sainte-Anne de Jérusalem d'après les fouilles récentes', in: *Atti del VI Congresso Internazionale di Archeologia Cristiana; Ravenna 23-30 settembre 1962,* Città del Vaticano 1965, 169-176.

2. The Archeology of Bethesda

Pierre and Rousée begin by pointing out that Bethesda was located at the north edge of the early city of Jerusalem, at the side
where it could best be accessed. It is by this spot, that all conquests and invasions of the city took place. It is also a place
where the winter rain is concentrated into waterfalls, and ends up
in natural reservoirs. There are also natural caves in the area. Until the latest excavations, begun in 1957, the two reservoirs present at the site were considered to be contemporary. The recent
study disclosed that the northern reservoir, created by the central
dam, is older than the southern one. Three meters below, in front
of the dam, was an open conduit that possibly supplied water to
the Temple. The southern reservoir, which operated independently from the northern one, was dated to the time of Simon, son
of Onias (220-195 BCE), on the basis of Sirach 50:3, which
states: "In his (i.e. Simon's) day a cistern for water was quarried
out, a reservoir like the sea in circumference". Pierre and Rousée
argue that, therefore, the older northern reservoir must date back
to pre-exilic times.

A very important new insight gained through the latest excavations, is that we can discern three independent and well-dated levels of occupation at the site. First, there was an installation which
lasted from the 2nd century BCE until 70 CE. Then there was another installation in the time of the pagan city of Aelia Capitolina.
The third and last installation was comprised of a Byzantine basilica built in the 5th century and was destroyed not long before
the Crusades.

The Gospel of John in Chapter 5 refers to the first installation
and a number of remains belong to it. It seems likely that it must
have been of religious importance, since this was definitely the
case during the next period of its existence. It was then, in the 3rd
or 4th century CE, that buildings were erected on the ruins of the
preceding installation. The new buildings were adorned with
paintings and mosaics. It is to this period that a votive offering
dedicated to Sarapis belongs. This ex-voto was discovered a long
time before the latest excavations, which excavations indeed have
yielded some additional sculptures. There was a temple dedicated

to Asclepius/Sarapis, which was razed to the ground by the next builders, who were Christians. They built the basilica that was depicted in the famous Madaba map.[8] Pierre and Rousée note, that no traces of this basilica had been discovered until the recent excavations. Its existence is however attested to by a number of texts that we shall examine below. The church was most probably not destroyed altogether by the Persians in 614, but remained largely intact until the beginning of the 11th century, when Hakim destroyed it.

The mediaeval churches of St. Anne and of the monastery are not immediate successors to preceding Christian churches. Rather, they are built on Hellenistic and Roman remains.[9]

3. Bethesda in the Second Temple Period

3.1 'The Valley of the Healers' connected with Bethesda?

Pierre and Rousée search the Bible and popular traditions for references to our site. The first toponym they connect with it, is 'the Valley of the Rephaim'. The sole reason for a connection between the Valley of the Rephaim (as a pre-Israelite toponym) and Bethesda however seems to be the (possible) association of both places with healing.[10] Scholars through the centuries have located the Valley of the Rephaim in different spots in and around Jerusalem. The name has also been explained differently. The references in the Bible are sometimes interpreted as references to giants who used to inhabit the land[11] of which breed Og, the king of Bashan was the last representative.[12] In the time of David, the giants returned with Goliath.

---

[8]See the contribution of Aaron Demsky in this book (285-296).
[9]Pierre & Rousée, *POC* 31 (1981) 28.
[10]Pierre & Rousée, *POC* 31 (1981) 29.
[11]See Gen 14:5 etc.
[12]Deut 3:11.

Another meaning of the name as cited by Pierre and Rousée, is 'the (shades of the) dead' and since the word appears in this sense in both Ugarit[13] and in poetic texts in the Bible[14], this second meaning may be the more important one. Here the word is derived from רפה. It is in the so-called historical books of the Bible that the notion 'giants', i.e. the early inhabitants of Palestine, appears.[15] Yet another meaning of the word derives from the verb רפא, 'to heal'. The Rephaim are then 'healers' or 'hale ones'.[16] Indeed, in Ugaritic texts the royal dead were in a sense 'healers', because they watched over the fertility of the dynasty. Then 'healers' would be the root meaning of the word (cf. Isa 26:14 and Ps 88:11) and since it was the dead who healed, the association with 'the weak ones, the dead' (from רפה) seems likely. The connection with the giants is made by the fact that in several writings the giants are said to have been cast into the netherworld.[17]

In the ancient Greek and Latin versions of the Hebrew Bible, the Rephaim designate either giants or the spirits of the dead, if the word is not simply transliterated.[18] In Latin patristic literature, the transliteration is either 'rafaim' or 'raphaim'. The word is connected with healing by Ambrose, who in a discussion of Gen 15:20 speaks of the Rephaim as someone "who claims to bring medicine to others, although he cannot cure his own wounds".[19] Jerome identifies the Rephaim as giants[20] or as either giants or healers.[21]

---

[13]H. Rouillard, 'Rephaim', in: K. van der Toorn, B. Becking & P.W. van der Horst (eds), *Dictionary of Demons and Deities in the Bible* (henceforward DDD), Leiden 1995, col.1308 ff.

[14]Ibid. col.1314 ff.

[15]Ibid. col.1317 ff.

[16]Ibid. col.1321 ff.

[17]Ibid. col.1321.

[18]Ibid. col.1320 ff.

[19]*Raphaim, qui profitetur aliis se ferre medicinam, cum uulnera sua curare non possit*, "Raphaim, he who is said to bring medicine to others, although he cannot cure his own wounds", in: *Explanatio psalmorum xii*, CPL 140 , psalmus 43, cap. 10, par. 2, pag. 267, linea 12.

[20]*Liber quaestionum hebraicarum in Genesim*, CPL 580, pag. 22 (edn La-

Although modern authors often connect the Valley of the
Rephaim and Bethesda, in ancient literature there is evidence only
to prove that this valley was somewhere in the vicinity of the city
of Jerusalem.[22] Pierre and Rousée suggest[23] that the valley can be
associated with Bethesda on the basis of a passage in the Onomasticon of Eusebius and the Latin translation of Jerome.[24] However, in this passage we merely find the observation that the Valley of the Rephaim, as mentioned in Josh 18:16, lies in the land of
the tribe of Benjamin. Eusebius writes: "Emekraphaeim. A(quila),
S(ymmachus): 'in the Valley (of) Raphaeim', of the tribe Benjamin".[25] The Septuagint reads Emekraphaïn, but apparently Aquila
and Symmachus in their versions translated 'in the Valley (of)
Raphaeim'.[26] This only implies that it was located in the northern
area of Jerusalem, but there is no explicit identification with Bethesda. So it seems to us that there is no direct evidence to con-

---

garde), linea 19; *Liber interpretationis hebraicorum nominum*; CPL 581, pag.
9 (edn Lagarde), linea 23; 29, linea 28; *Commentarii in Isaiam*, CPL 584,
CCSL 73, lib. 7, cap. (s.s.) 17, par. 4+, linea 20; lib. 8, cap. (s.s.) 26, par. 14,
linea 42 here an explicit equation of the giants with the *'nephilim'* or 'fallen
ones' of Gen 6: *et gigantes, id est raphaim, non suscitabunt alios, qui ipsi
iuxta geneseos librum appellantur cadentes*, "and the giants, that is the
Rephaim, will not raise others, as according to the book of Genesis they
themselves are called 'fallen ones'"; lib. 8, cap. (s.s.) 26, par. 19, linea 28 –
here the bodies of the raphaim are called 'earth', on the basis of Isa 26:19
(LXX); *Commentarii in prophetas minores*, CPL 589 , CCSL 76, In Amos,
lib. 2, cap. (s.s.) 5, linea 283.

[21]*Liber interpretationis hebraicorum nominum*; CPL 581, p. 23 (edn Lagarde), linea 6; 59, linea 29; *Commentarioli in psalmos*; CPL 582 , psalmus
87, linea 7. Jerome discusses different meanings in his *Commentarii in
Isaiam*, CPL 584 , CCSL 73, lib. 8, cap. (s.s.) 26, par. 19.

[22]Cf. the references to ancient and modern authors in H. Rouillard,
'Rephaim', *DDD*, col. 1319 and M. Avi-Yonah, *Encyclopedia of Archaeological Excavations in the Holy Land* II, London 1976, 579-580.

[23]*POC* 31 (1981) 31.

[24]GCS 11,1 (edn Klostermann) Leipzig 1904, 86 line 22.

[25]Jerome translates: *Emecrafaim, id est uallis Rafaim, in tribu Beniamin.*

[26]Strangely enough this reading of Aquila and Symmachus is not recorded
in Field's edition of Origen's Hexapla, in which he otherwise makes good use
of the Onomasticon. But Field published his work before Klostermann edited
his. Cf. F. Field, *Origenis Hexaplorum quae supersunt* I, Oxford 1875, 377.

nect this Valley of the Rephaim with Bethesda as Pierre and
Rousée speculatively do, but if there were, it would be very attractive to associate the 'Valley of the Healers' with Bethesda as a
place of healing. Unfortunately, this must remain unclear until
specific evidence connecting the two, and more especially evidence firmly locating the Valley of the Rephaim, is found.

Another biblical citation speaks of an 'upper pool' with a 'conduit', located 'on the highway to the Fuller's Field'.[27] Pierre and
Rousée remark that nearly all historians and exegetes locate this
reservoir in the valley of Siloam. However, based on Josephus[28]
who speaks of a 'camp of the Assyrians' on the north side, they
locate it on the northern side of Jerusalem. According to these
authors, it must have been the pool mentioned in reference to the
events of 736-735 BCE by Isaiah Chapter 7 and in reference to
701 by Isaiah Chapter 36. The next piece of literary evidence is
Sirach 50:1-3, quoted above, which may refer to the construction
of the southern reservoir.[29]

3.2 Documentation of the Name "Bethesda"

The actual name Bethesda first appears in Hebrew in the Qumran
Copper Scroll (3Q15, xi 12, 57) as בית אשדתין. In the New Testament in the Gospel of John, Chapter 5, Bethesda is the place
where one Sabbath day Jesus heals the man who had been ill for
38 years. However, as Raymond Brown remarks the name appears in the manuscripts in various forms:

a) 'Bethsaida' has the strongest attestation, but this may be the
result of a confusion with the town of Bethsaida on the Sea of
Galilee. There is also a number of Church Fathers who confuse
the issue in this way (see below).

b) The name "Be(t)zatha" is found in Codices Sinaiticus and
Bezae. Josephus speaks of a quarter of the city of Jerusalem

---

[27]Isa 7:3 and Isa 36:2 (= 2 Kgs 18:17).
[28]*War* 5, 303, 504-507.
[29]Pierre & Rousée, *POC* 31 (1981) 25-26.

called Bezetha, near the Northeast corner of the Temple area. [30]
Eusebius in his Onomasticon speaks of 'Bezatha' when he describes Bethesda.[31]

c) 'Bethesda', found in Codex Alexandrinus, has the weakest
attestation. The entry in the Qumran Copper Scroll, however,
supports this third reading. In the Syriac speaking church, the
form 'Bethesda' could have been preferred, since it was possible
to associate it with the symbolic 'house of mercy': בית חסדא
which Barrett finds 'a name evidently suitable for the place in
which Jesus cured the lame man'.[32] This is in fact the reading in
the Curetonianus and the Peshitta; only the Harklean version
(early 7th century, a 'slavish adaptation to the Greek'[33]) reads בית
צידא. However, the root is probably אשד and therefore the most
likely interpretation is 'house of the flowing', as this root implies.
The Greek 'Bethesda' is then a rendition of the singular. J.T.
Milik suggests that 'Bezatha' renders the Aramaic emphatic plural בית אשדתא.[34]

There is some specific information about Bethesda found in the
Gospel account in John Chapter 5. Thus, verse 2, seems to have a
word missing. The Greek reads either: "In Jerusalem next to the
Sheep …. there is a pool called Bethesda in Hebrew" or: "In Jerusalem next to the Sheep Pool, there is a …. called Bethesda in
Hebrew". Authors favoring the first reading inserted 'Gate'. In
the second format, we could insert 'place' or 'pool' or, without
any addition, we could read the sentence as: "… there is that
which is called Bethesda in Hebrew".

Bethesda had five porticoes. They have been explained as a
symbolic reference to the alleged deficiency of the Pentateuch,
forming the Law,[35] but since the actual remains between the two
pools have been excavated, there need not be any symbolic

---

[30] *War* 2, 328.

[31] GCS 11,1, 58, line 21-26.

[32] C.K. Barrett, *The Gospel according to St. John*, London 1958, 210.

[33] S. Brock, in: B.M. Metzger, *The Early Versions of the New Testament;
Their Origin, Transmission and Limitations*, Oxford 1977, 69.

[34] DJD III, 271.

[35] Pierre & Rousée, *POC* 31 (1981) 34.

meaning.[36] Cyril of Jerusalem (†386) in his Homily on the Paralytic mentions the five porticoes and states specifically: "four surrounding, the fifth one in the middle".[37] This information is confirmed (or copied? from Cyril?) by Theodore of Mopsuestia (5th century, see below). This must have meant that four porticoes surrounded the pools and one divided them. According to Cyril, the sick used to lie waiting in that fifth portico. This must have been the physical arrangement of the pagan sanctuary, which may not have been replaced by a Christian building but put to Christian use for some time (see below).

Pierre and Rousée note that the 38 years of sickness of the paralytic healed at Bethesda may refer to Deut 2:14, the time that the Israelites spent in the desert. The meaning of this 'polemic' referred to in John would then be: the Law could not save the people who spent 38 years in the desert and only had to wait until the coming of Jesus before their 'sickness' could be cured. However, this exegesis, found for example in Apollinaris of Laodicaea in the 4th century[38] seems for good reason to find little support in the modern commentaries. Returning to the text of John, some manuscripts extend verse 3 with the phrase: "...waiting for the moving of the water (4) for an angel of the Lord went down at certain seasons into the pool, stirring up the water: whoever stepped in first after the stirring up of the water was healed of whatever disease he had". Duprez notes that the angel of John 5:4 might be related to 'the angels of the waters' and 'the angels of the rivers' who occupy an important place in Jewish literature.[39]

---

[36] C.K. Barrett, *The Gospel*, 211.

[37] Edn J. Rupp (1860), 407. The importance of this text is underlined by J. Jeremias, *Die Wiederentdeckung*, 13.

[38] J. Reuss, *Johannes-Kommentare aus der griechischen Kirche*, in: *Texte und Untersuchungen* 89, Berlin 1966, 10-11.

[39] A. Duprez, *Jésus et les dieux guérisseurs* 86, referring to L. Ginzberg, *The Legends of the Jews*, Philadelphia 1909, I.83; IV.302 and J.Z. Lauterbach, "Tashlik, A Study in Jewish Ceremonies", *HUCA* 11 (1936) 207-340.

4. A Pagan Sanctuary at Bethesda

After 135 CE, Jerusalem was rebuilt as the pagan city of Aelia
Capitolina. Since his pilgrimage to Alexandria in 131, the emperor Hadrian had developed a special reverence for the Egyptian
god of healing Sarapis. There is quite a bit of evidence that his
cult was well established in the city. A. Duprez has studied the
evidence and argues that the layout of the site from the second
period identifies it as a site where Sarapis, the Egyptian healing
god equated with the Greek Asclepius, was worshipped and
where incubation took place:[40] it was a temple where the faithful
could lie down to sleep and wait for healing dreams sent by the
god.[41] The votive offerings found on the spot confirm the argument of Duprez. The incubations took place in the subterranean
rooms and pools excavated in the rock.[42]

It is unclear when the Asclepius/Sarapis temple was demol-
ished. If the Byzantine basilica was built in the early 5th century,
then there is almost a century in which the change must have
taken place. It may not seem unreasonable to suppose that
Constantine's building programme in Jerusalem might have also
involved Bethesda, but in fact there is no evidence that this first
Christian emperor did indeed include Bethesda in his programme.
Was this because he left the Temple area as it was and concentrated on other places like the Church of the Holy Sepulchre?[43] All
in all, it is possible that the old pagan shrine was left standing and
converted into a church before the Byzantines razed it to the
ground in order to build their own .

---

[40]A. Duprez, *Jésus et les dieux guérisseurs* 89-95.

[41]Cf. E.J. Edelstein & L. Edelstein, *Asclepius; Collection and Interpretation of the Testimonies*, 2 vols., Baltimore 1945, esp. the chapter 'Temple
Medicine', II.139 ff.

[42]D. Bahat, *The Illustrated Atlas of Jerusalem,* New York 1990, 66.

[43]On Constantine's building programme in Jerusalem, see R.L. Wilken in:
H.W. Attridge & G. Hata, *Eusebius, Christianity & Judaism,* Leiden 1992,
741 ff. and R.L. Wilken, *The Land Called Holy; Palestine in Christian History and Thought*, New Haven/London 1992, 93 ff.

In the *Onomasticon* by Eusebius (4th century), the entry for Bethesda follows Bethsaida (the town in Galilee), Bethphage, Bethany and Bethabara, and reads as follows: "Bezatha, a reservoir in Jerusalem, which is 'the Probatica' [= of the sheep], once having (had) five porticoes. In that place two pools are shown even today, each of which is filled by the annual rains, whereas one of them strangely shows reddish water, which is a trace, as they say, that it bears of the sacrifices which were once killed in it. So it is called 'probatica' because of the sacrifices." Jerome in his Latin adaptation of Eusebius' work does not write quite the same.[44] In his text, it is 'Bethsaida' that follows after the town of Bethsaida, Bethphage and Bethabara. He continues: "a reservoir in Jerusalem which was called 'Probatica'", which we can translate as 'of the sheep'. This once had five porticoes, and a couple of pools are shown, one of which[45] is usually filled by the winter rains, whereas the other, being colored red in a miraculous way as if by bloody waters, testifies in itself to a sign of something done in the past. For they say that the sacrifices were always washed in it by the Priests, from which it took its name".[46] Jerome confuses Eusebius' καθαιρεω (to kill) with καθαιρω (to cleanse), but Eusebius tries to explain the red color of the water by suggesting that the sheep were slaughtered in the pool of Bethesda, whereas these sheep did in fact just enter Jerusalem at Bethesda and were of course killed in the forecourt of the Temple.[47] However, is Jerome perhaps correct after all in thinking that the sheep were washed first at Bethesda before they were brought into the Temple? A number of later authors also tries to explain the reddish waters of Bethesda by connecting them with some activity having to do with the blood of sacrifices, but this cannot be verified. Yet perhaps this explanation of the red waters may contain a reminiscence of a certain pagan practice (see below).

---

[44]GCS 11,1, 59.

[45]Eusebius: 'each one'. Jerome is misled by 'the other' which follows.

[46]J. Jeremias, *Die Wiederentdeckung*, 11 ff.

[47]J. Jeremias, *Die Wiederentdeckung,* 8.

What references are there to Bethesda in post New Testament literature? The text of Eusebius quoted above is generally taken to be the oldest we have after the Gospel of John. After this reference comes that of the pilgrim of Bordeaux who came to Jerusalem on pilgrimage in 333: "There are in Jerusalem two large pools on the side of the Temple, that is one on the right and one on the left, which Solomon made, but more inside the city are twin pools, which have five porticoes, which they call Bethsaida. There, those who had been sick for many years were cured. These pools however have water which is stirred up scarlet in colour".[48] Next we have the homily of Cyril of Jerusalem mentioned above, in which the five porticoes are described as four surrounding and one in the middle.

In *De situ Hierosolimae*, written by an anonymous author, we read: "Near the temple is the pool of Bethsaida, clearly distinguished by a twin lake. One of them is usually filled by the winter rains and the other has a different colour because of its red waters".[49] This work was formerly ascribed to Eucherius, bishop of Lyon in the middle of the 5th century. Today, this work is dated to a period two centuries later. We note however that it makes no mention of the 6th century church.

There seem to be no other geographical descriptions of Bethesda in the 2nd through 5th centuries. We do however have a number of patristic commentaries on the Gospel of John. We shall now attempt to determine if these add new information.

Unfortunately, Origen's commentary on John 5 has not been preserved, so he can be of no help.[50] There are 88 homilies on John by John Chrysostom († 407).[51] Homily 36-39 are about John Chapter 5, but they do not seem to contain any concrete information about Bethesda. The same is true of the commentary by Cyril of Alexandria († 444).[52]

---

[48] *Itinerarium Burdigalense* 7-11, CCSL 175, 14-15.
[49] *De situ Hierosolymae* 8, CCSL 175, 238 lin.40-42. ET: JP 53 (altered).
[50] CPG 1453.
[51] CPG 4425.
[52] CPG 5208.

The commentary of Theodore of Mopsuestia († 428) is more interesting for our purpose.[53] Fragments of this commentary exist in the original Greek; there is a complete Syriac translation of the work. He writes: "He did not judge it necessary to go around and heal the sick anywhere, in order not to get the reputation of love of self, but by healing one he makes himself manifest to all through him. For this reason he goes to the Sheep Pool[54] with its five porticoes – for besides the four around it, it had one in the middle. [It was called the Sheep Pool on account of the fact that the sheep brought for the feasts were assembled there and that the entrails of the sheep that were sacrificed were washed in the water.[55]] Here on this spot a great crowd of people, suffering of various illnesses, gathered in hope of healing, as if the very water had a certain power, because in it the entrails of the animals offered to God and sacrificed were thrown.[56] God co-operated with this idea of theirs sometimes by causing a movement of the water. And since they believed that this was accomplished by some divine operation, they went down and secured their cure. Yet not many were cured at the same time, only the first who went down received this grace, in order that the ease of the cure would not diminish the miracle. But by having to be vigilant for a longer time and by having to await the movement of the water with much eagerness, they are taught to have fitting thoughts after their cure also." Theodore bases himself on a text that contained the extended version of verse 3 and 4 of John 5. Like Eusebius, he refers to a practice of throwing animal sacrifices or parts of them into the pool. If this information does not constitute an attempt to explain the reddish color of the waters, then does it perhaps reflect the custom of throwing sacrifices into the pool of Bethesda during the period of Aelia Capitolina? A near parallel might be

---

[53]R. Devreesse, *Essai sur Théodore de Mopsueste*, Città del Vaticano 1948, 324 ff. (Fragments of the Greek text); cf. CSCO 115 (Syriac text) 98 ff. and CSCO 116 (Latin translation) 69 ff.

[54]Syriac: בית חסדא

[55]Not in the Syriac; probably a later addition to the Greek, from an epitome.

[56]Syriac: 'were washed'.

the custom of throwing human sacrifices into the sources of the river Jordan near Banias, as recorded by Eusebius. This practice was stopped by the Christian holy man Astyrius in about 265 CE.[57] In addition to this possible reference by Eusebius to the pagan cult at Bethesda between 135 CE and the 5th century, we have some archaeological evidence in the form of votive offerings and a number of statues. They confirm that in the period of Aelia Capitolina, there was, close to the present church of St. Anne, a sanctuary of the healing god Sarapis. [58]

5. A Byzantine Church at Bethesda

It was probably when Juvenal was bishop of Jerusalem (422-458), and specifically before the council of Chalcedon (451), that a three-aisled church, dedicated to St. Mary, was built at Bethesda.[59] The basilica was built on the dam dividing the two pools, i.e. on the site of the fifth portico, mentioned by Cyril of Jerusalem, as we saw above. The side aisles were erected above the pools and were supported by arches. The church was reached by way of the dam itself.[60] Many Byzantine churches continued the pagan practice of incubation (temple sleep) under the patronate of their saint. Possibly this was also the case at Bethesda.[61] This church is also visible on the famous Madaba map. This map has been regarded as a cartographic representation of the 6th century pilgrims' itineraries of a number of pilgrims such as the archdeacon Theodosius, the anonymous pilgrim of Piacenza and the so-called *Breviarius de Hierosolyma*.[62] Theodosius notes: "From the house of Pilate it is about 100 paces until the Sheep Pool. There the Lord

---

[57]*Church History* VII,17.
[58]A. Duprez, *Jésus et les dieux guérisseurs,* 46 ff., 94.
[59]John Rufus, *Plérophories* XVIII, in: PO VIII, 35-37. ET: JP 58.
[60]D. Bahat, *The Illustrated Atlas of Jerusalem,* 72-73 (reconstruction).
[61]Cf. M. Parmentier, 'Incubatie in de antieke hagiografie', in: A. Hilhorst (ed.), *De heiligenverering in de eerste eeuwen van het christendom,* Assen 1988, 27-40.
[62]H. Donner, *The Mosaic Map of Madaba,* Kampen 1992, 14.

Christ cured the paralytic, whose bed is still there. Beside the Sheep Pool is the church of the Lady Mary". [63] The pilgrim of Piacenza writes: "Having returned to the city, we went to the swimming pool that has five porticoes, one of which has the basilica of St. Mary, in which many miracles take place. But the pool itself has become mucky, because all the city's laundry is done there. In a dark corner we also saw the iron chain with which the unhappy Judas hanged himself. And on the way out towards the main gate, we came to Saint Isicius[64], who lies there in the body, where bread is being distributed at the orders of Helena[65] to poor people and pilgrims".[66] In the *Breviarius de Hierosolyma*, we read a more vague description: "And there is a basilica where at one time the sick used to wash and be healed." [67]

It is difficult to believe that the connection to the Virgin Mary is authentic. There is no evidence of any such local tradition until after the establishment of the basilica. Only then, Marian traditions blossom. Bethesda is seen as the place where Mary was born, where her parents Joachim and Anna lived[68] and where they were buried.[69] Other features are added: the chain with which Judas hanged himself, the tomb of St. Hesychius.

Pierre and Rousée claim that there is no evidence that this church was razed at the time of the Persian conquest in 614 and they point to certain repairs that were probably made in the 9th century.[70] Jeremias however refers to two pieces of evidence regarding events at Bethesda in the year 614: the list of the dead

---

[63]*De situ terrae sanctae* 8, CCSL 175, 118 lin. 2 etc. ET: JP 66 (altered).

[64]Hesychius of Jerusalem, a 5th century theologian.

[65]Constantine's mother.

[66]*Itinerarium* 27, CCSL 175, 143 lin.14 etc. ET: JP 84 (altered).

[67]*Breviarius de Hierosolyma* 7, CCSL 75, 112b, lin.109 etc. ET: JP 61 (altered).

[68]Cf. Sophronius of Jerusalem (7th century) and John Damascene (8th century), Pierre & Rousée, *POC* 31 (1981) p. 40 and H. Vincent, *Jérusalem nouvelle,* 680 nrs. VIII & IX.

[69]Since the report of the Russian pilgrim Daniel in 1107 (N. van der Vliet, *Sainte Marie où elle est née,* 114; H. Vincent, *Jérusalem nouvelle,* 681 nr.XIV).

[70]*POC* 31 (1981) 28.

compiled by Antiochus Strategius, which indicates that there were 2107 victims at the Probatica, and a calendar in Georgian, dating back to 670, which gives the 9th of June as the date of the rededication of the church after its northern aisle had been repaired. [71]

6. The Crusader Churches of St. Anne and of St. Mary at Bethesda

The church of St. Anne is mentioned for the first time (as being the house of Joachim and Anna) in 1102 by the Scandinavian pilgrim Saewulf: "From the temple of the Lord you go to the church of St. Anne, the mother of blessed Mary, on the side of the north, where she lived with her husband. This is where she gave birth to her most beloved daughter Mary, the redeemer of all believers. Close by is the Sheep Pool which is called Bethsayda in Hebrew and has five porticoes."[72] Other authors specify that it is the crypt under the church, which was the actual house of Mary's parents and also her birthplace.

St. Anne's church was built next to the site where the Byzantine church of St. Mary had been. This church had probably been destroyed in 1009, a century before St. Anne's was built.[73] Old St. Mary's was last mentioned by the *Commemoratorium de casis Dei*[74] (a short notice on the monasteries in the Holy Land of about 808[75]), so that it may have ceased to exist earlier. In the Crusader period, there was a monastery dedicated to St. Mary which is hardly mentioned in historical sources and which was built on the

[71] *POC* 31 (1981) 15.

[72] Text: H. Vincent, *Jérusalem nouvelle* ,681 nr. XIII; English translation also in Th. Wright, *Early Travels in Palestine*, London 1848, 41.

[73] N. van der Vliet, *Sainte Marie où elle est née,* 27; Pierre & Rousée, *POC* 31 (1981) 28; Rousée, 'L'Eglise Sainte Marie de la Probatique', 173.

[74] H. Vincent, *Jérusalem nouvelle,* 680-681 nr. XI.

[75] N. van der Vliet, *Sainte Marie*, 24-25.

ruins of the Byzantine church.[76] This monastery is first mentioned in 1231.[77] The time of its destruction is unknown.[78]

One of the objects associated with St. Anne's church is a tree in the forecourt which according to the poet Perdikas of Ephesus (14th century[79]) is said to have healed barren women. Perdikas also mentions the Crusader church of St. Mary:[80]

> You will find lofty buildings, a royal hearth,
> and the divine and all delightful house of Joachim and Anna,
> where the tomb of both ancestors of God is,
> and a tree standing in the forecourt well provided with leaves
>   affording shade,
> which, having sprung up at the birth of the wholly undefiled
>   maiden,
> grants fruit to the barren, who partake of the fruit of the tree.
> Near to these is also the Sheep Pool with five porticoes,
> where once the healing of the paralytic took place,
> underground, on the stairs by which all go down
> to be washed, trembling after he had been submerged in
>   unfathomable depths.
> Above ground is a splendid temple,
> belonging to him who grants healing to all who come forward.[81]

The Franciscan brother Odorico wrote his *Liber de terra sancta* in 1320. He connects the pool adjacent to the church with the wood of the Cross: "...next to the wall of the Temple is the Sheep Pool of which the Gospel speaks, in which it is said that the wood of the holy Cross was thrown for a long time".[82]

In James of Verona (1335), who gives an elaborate description of Bethesda, we find the idea that the wood of the Cross was cut

---

[76]D. Bahat, *Atlas*, 98-99.

[77]H. Vincent, *Jérusalem nouvelle*, 681 nr. XX.

[78]J. Jeremias, *Die Wiederentdeckung*, 15.

[79]K. Krumbacher, *Geschichte der byzantinischen Literatur*, [2]1897, 420. Van der Vliet (XIV) gives the date of 1250.

[80]H. Vincent, *Jérusalem nouvelle*, 681-682 nr. XXIV; PG 133, 964AB.

[81]Tentative translation: the text is very obscure in places.

[82]N. van der Vliet, *Sainte Marie*, XIV. Text: H. Vincent, *Jérusalem nouvelle*, 682 nr. XXIX.

from a tree which stood by the pool: "This pool is next to the
Temple plateau, and in it the animals which were offered in the
Temple were washed in the past. Over this pool that tree was
placed from which the holy wood of the holy Cross was made.
The builders of the Temple did not know how to use this tree and
therefore it stayed until the times of Christ. The queen of Saba
saw this tree and knew by the Holy Spirit that this was the wood
by which the human race was to be saved and she adored it..."
James of Verona then describes "a beautiful church of St. Anne,
which now is a mosque of the Saracens. This is where St. Anne
lived and where the most blessed Virgin Mary was born from
Joachim and Anna".[83]

In the late 15th century, the Dominican Fabri also claims that
the sheep to be sacrificed were washed first in the Sheep Pool.
Then he adds a history of the wood of the Cross retrojected into
Old Testament times: "Solomon ordered that the wood which the
Sibyl[84] had shown to him, and on which she had predicted that
Christ would suffer, should be immersed by the insides of this
pool. It was hidden there until the time of Christ's passion and
then drifted on top and it was taken to be made into the Cross of
Christ. It is believed that an angel came down from heaven and
moved the water on account of the dignity of this wood". After
describing St. Anne's church, he says: "Furthermore before the
church stands a large and very old tree, which they say was
planted by the most blessed Virgin Mary, when she was still a
little child, in the care of her parents who are believed to have
lived here on this spot; although Joachim and Anna spent many
years in Nazareth, nevertheless at the instigation of the Holy
Spirit they traveled from Galilee to Jerusalem when it was time to
conceive and give birth to the most blessed Virgin Mary... They

---

[83]H. Vincent, *Jérusalem nouvelle,* 682 nr. XXXII, cf. Pierre & Rousée,
POC 31 (1981) 41.

[84]Jews and Christians wrote 'Sibylline oracles' in imitation of Roman prophetic books, said to have been composed of sayings of inspired women
called Sibyls. The Jewish and Christian versions did of course contain
prophecies which suited the Jewish and Christian faith.

came and bought a house near the Temple at the Sheep Pool, in which the Virgin Mary was conceived and born, according to the testimony of John Damascene… In the course of time, however, on the site of that holy home, the Christians built a church with an attached monastery… and there were some very rich women there right up until the capture of the city by the Saracens in AD 1187".[85]

7. The Development of the Legend of the Wood of the Cross

From the 12th century onwards, there seems to have developed a whole tradition which connects the wood of the Cross with Bethesda.[86] Was there a link between this developing tradition and an actual trunk in the forecourt of St. Anne's church, close to the pool? The Latin texts reflecting the growing legend have been examined by W. Meyer.[87] The oldest relevant text, the *Historia*, otherwise called *De ligno crucis*, tells the following story: In the time of David a certain Jew found in the forest a kind of tree which has three different types of leaves. He cut the tree down because he admired it, and he brought it to king David. When the king saw it himself, he immediately understood what this tree would be in the future and he adored it as long as he lived. His son Solomon also adored it, and not just because his father did. He also gilded the whole tree. Then the Queen of the South, when she came to listen to the wisdom of Solomon, prophesied about it, saying: 'If Solomon knew what the tree signifies, he would certainly not adore it any longer'. A philosopher (or: adviser) of the king who heard this reported to his lord what he had heard. The king then sent him after the queen, who had already left, with many precious gifts, to give them to the philosopher (or: secre-

---

[85]H. Vincent, *Jérusalem nouvelle,* 683 nr. XXXVII.

[86]W. Meyer, 'Die Geschichte des Kreuzholzes vor Christus', AKBAW, philos.-philol. Kl., München XVI (1892), 105 ff. See also the contribution of Marcel Poorthuis in this book, esp. 240.

[87]W. Meyer, 'Die Geschichte des Kreuzholzes', 105 ff.

tary) of the queen who did not know about these things, until he had asked his lady to tell what the tree signified. When he had received the gifts he told him not to show himself to the queen. Then he secretly asked his lady concerning the matter. She answered and said that a man would hang on it by whom the whole kingdom of the Jews would be destroyed. When king Solomon heard this he scraped the gold off the tree and threw the tree in the depth of a pool. This is why later an angel of the Lord descended daily into the pool, in which not because of the water, but because of the tree, the sick were saved through the descent of the angel. This pool had dried up at the time of the passion of our Lord and the Cross which was extracted out of it, Christ carried on his shoulders until the gate.

There are also Greek, Slavonic and English versions of the legend. The Bethesda episode is however restricted to the Latin version, related above. Further developments of the legend are recorded by Honorius of Autun (early 12th century), Petrus Comestor (late 12th century) and a number of later authors, some of which we have discussed above.[88] In these other versions many different motifs appear, connecting the tree with the Tree of Life in Paradise, with Solomon's construction of the Temple and similar motifs.

8. Conclusion

Throughout the history of Jerusalem, Bethesda has been a holy place, and especially a place of healing for the sick. First, it was an Israelite, possibly even a pre-Israelite sanctuary, perhaps connected with the 'Valley of the Rephaim', where the sick waited to be healed by the waters. This was the situation when Jesus was there, according to the witness of John Chapter 5. When after 135 CE the Romans had rebuilt Jerusalem as the pagan city Aelia Capitolina, Bethesda became a pagan healing shrine, dedicated to

---

[88]Cf. E.C. Quinn, *The Quest of Seth for the Oil of Life*, Chicago/London, 1962, 151 note 47.

Asclepius/Sarapis. This temple was razed to the ground by the Byzantines in the early 5th century. However, it is possible that the pagan practice of incubation continued to exist in the Byzantine basilica of St. Mary. This church was completely destroyed in 1009. About a century later, the church of St. Anne was built at a short distance from the ruins of the first church. A monastery was later built on the site of the old basilica.

The legend of the wood of the Cross, developing since the 12th century, was at some point associated with the pool of Bethesda. The earliest witness to this connection is the *Historia*. In the meantime, at an earlier date, but not before the Byzantine basilica of St. Mary had been built, legends surrounding the birth of the Virgin Mary and relating to her parents Joachim and Anna had also begun to take root in Bethesda. The Muslims continued to revere the sanctity of Bethesda in their own way by using St. Anne's church either as a mosque or as a centre of learning. In 1856, after the Crimean war, the Pasha of Jerusalem, on behalf of Sultan 'Abdul Mejîd, gave the site to the French consul on behalf of the emperor Napoleon III. In 1866, when St. Anne's church was restored, the first pagan votive offering was found. It was in that century that the excavations began, which would necessitate a thorough study of the site to differentiate between the mediaeval legends about the place and its actual history.[89]

---

[89]J. Jeremias, *Die Wiederentdeckung*, 17-18; K. Baedeker, *Jerusalem and its Surroundings; Handbook for Travellers*, Leipzig/London 1876, 91.

IR HA-MIQDASH AND ITS MEANING IN THE TEMPLE SCROLL AND OTHER QUMRAN TEXTS

Lawrence H. Schiffman

In my presentation at our first conference, on the topic 'Jerusalem in the Dead Sea Scrolls', I touched on a controversy that has now been debated for almost one hundred years regarding the meaning of עיר המקדש, translated as either 'the City of the Sanctuary' or 'Temple-City'.[1] I took the view in that study that this term referred to the *temenos*, the Temple area itself, as opposed to referring to the entire City of Jerusalem as some other scholars have observed. It was noted there that the matter was also connected with a passage in 4QMMT which required detailed investigation. Since then, the release of the full corpus of Judean Desert manuscripts, including most notably the Qumran scrolls, has made available another example of this usage as well, in addition to those already known from the *Zadokite Fragments* (also known as the *Damascus Document)* and the *Temple Scroll.* Accordingly, it is time for a new and complete study of this term.

1. The Zadokite Fragments

The starting point for our investigation must be the first passage to come to light, that in CD 12:1-2:

אל ישכב איש עם אשה בעיר המקדש לטמא את עיר המקדש בנדתם:

---

[1]L.H. Schiffman, 'Jerusalem in the Dead Sea Scrolls', in: M. Poorthuis & Ch. Safrai (eds), *The Centrality of Jerusalem,* Kampen 1996, 82-3.

> Let no man have sexual relations with a woman in the City of the Sanctuary so as to make impure the City of the Sanctuary with their impurity.[2]

That this reading is correct is confirmed by the presence of this same text in the Qumran fragments of the *Zadokite Fragments* (4Q 271 frg. 5 i 17-18).[3] Already in his pioneering study, L. Ginzberg set out both of the possible interpretations.[4] Ginzberg first argues in favor of seeing this as a law prohibiting sexual relations in the entire city of Jerusalem, understanding עיר המקדש to refer to the entire city. He understood the מקדש to be the Temple in Jerusalem, and the 'city' to be the city as a whole. He suggested that the text had widened the prohibition known from rabbinic literature (MKel 1:8[5]) which forbids one who had a seminal emission from entering the Temple Mount. Here the prohibition, he said, had been widened to include the entire city of Jerusalem which was now endowed with a higher status of sanctity. He suggested that this law would have made life in the city of Jerusalem impossible for the sectarians of this document and that it would have led to their departure from the city – all this he suggested with no knowledge of the Dead Sea Scrolls.

But after setting down this proposal, he immediately backtracked. "Probably, however" the true meaning of the city of the sanctuary was just the Temple Mount, in the same way that עיר דוד 'City of David', had this meaning as well. He then asserted that accordingly this text was in complete agreement with rabbinic *halakhah* which likewise forbids one who had a seminal

---

[2]All translations presented in this paper are by the author.

[3]J.M. Baumgarten, *Qumran Cave 4.XIII, The Damascus Document (4Q266-273)* (= *Discoveries in the Judaean Desert 18)*, Oxford 1996, 181.

[4]L. Ginzberg, *Eine unbekannte jüdische Sekte*, New York 1922, *ad loc.*; English translation: *An Unknown Jewish Sect*, New York 1976, 73-4. The entire issue is ignored by the first editor of the text, S. Schechter, *Documents of Jewish Sectaries*, Volume I. *Fragments of a Zadokite Work* (originally published in 1910, reprint New York 1970), p. L.

[5]Cf. BT Pes 67b.

emission from entering the Temple Mount. He saw our law as derived in this way from 2 Chron 8:11.[6]

In his commentary on this passage,[7] C. Rabin refers to Lev
15:18 as the basis of this law, but there it only says that a man and
a woman who have had sexual relations become impure until the
evening, and are required to wash. Interesting is his not-so-precise
reference to Josephus, War, V, v, 6 (227) which says that those
afflicted with gonorrhea or leprosy (the skin disease ṣara'at) were
excluded from 'the entire city.' But contrary to the general reference of Rabin to 'one affected with flux', Josephus is clearly referring only to specific impurities of more serious nature. His
comment is noncommittal on the meaning of עיר ('îr) here – temenos or, literally, city.

The recent commentary of J.M. Baumgarten and D.R.
Schwartz[8] appears to follow the views that were developed by Y.
Yadin based on the Temple Scroll (on which see below) and to
interpret the 'City of the Sanctuary' as referring to the entire City
of Jerusalem. In view of the common halakhic substratum of
these documents it is certainly not unreasonable to expect the
term to have a similar meaning in both texts. But the problem before us is actually to determine the meaning of this expression in
the Temple Scroll, and we will see that there it remains ambiguous as well.

One point is clear from the investigation of this text. It seeks to
avoid the rendering of the עיר impure 'with their impurity', that
is, with the impurity of the man and woman who have sexual relations in the city. This means that they become impure through
sexual relations and as a result the impurity is transmitted to the

---

[6]The text states there לא תשב אשה לי בבית דויד ... כי קדש המה אשר באה אליהם
ארון ה' which he understands to mean: 'A woman may not dwell (i.e. sexual
relations are prohibited) in the House of David (i.e., the Temple Mount), for
that area is sanctified as the ark of the covenant has been brought there.' Cf.
Rashi and Radak ad loc.

[7]C. Rabin, The Zadokite Documents, Oxford 1954, 59.

[8]'Damascus Document', in: J.H. Charlesworth (ed.) The Dead Sea Scrolls,
Hebrew, Aramaic, and Greek Texts with English Translations, vol. 2, Tübingen / Louisville 1995, 51.

עיר המקדש (*'îr hamiqdāš*). In this respect, Rabin appears to be correct. The Bible tells us that sexual relations result in ritual impurity and this text goes one step further saying that if done in certain holy precincts, the impurity which results will render the area
impure. Further, we should note that in this passage, as elsewhere
in Qumran texts, נדה (*nidâ*) appears as a general term for impurity.
It is not a reference to menstrual impurity as is most usual in the
Bible and as is virtually the exclusive usage in rabbinic literature.

2. The Temple Scroll

The question of the meaning of the expression עיר המקדש (*'îr
hamiqdāš*) was again raised with the discovery and publication of
Temple Scroll, where this expression occurs several times. One
can summarize the argument as follows: Y. Yadin[9], followed by J.
Milgrom[10], took the view that this term refers to the City of Jerusalem (the city in which there is a Temple), and B.A. Levine[11],
followed by this author and recently S. Japeth[12], took the view that
it referred only to the *temenos,* the Temple precincts.

---

[9]*The Temple Scroll*, Jerusalem 1983, I.277-307. His views had already appeared in a number of preliminary articles and in his Hebrew edition,
המקדש מגילת, Jerusalem 1977, I.215-38. See also Yadin's 'Addenda et Corri-
genda' to the English edition, I.415-6.

[10]'Sabbath' and 'Temple City' in the Temple Scroll, *BASOR* 232 (1978)
25-7 (a response to Levine, see below); idem, 'The City of the Temple, A
Response to Lawrence H. Schiffman', *Qumran Studies, JQR N.S.* 85 (1994)
125-8.

[11]'The Temple Scroll: Aspects of its Historical Provenance and Literary
Character', *BASOR* 232 (1978) 5-23. Yadin responded to this article in 'Is the
Temple Scroll a Sectarian Document?', in: G.M. Tucker & D.A. Knight
(eds), *Humanizing America's Iconic Book, SBL Centennial Addresses 1980,*
Chico California 1980, 153-69.

[12]'The Prohibition of the Habitation of Women: The Temple Scroll's Attitude Toward Sexual Impurity and its Biblical Precedents', *JANES* 22 (1993)
69-88.

It is most logical to begin with the parallel to CD 12:1-2 which appears in 11QT 45:11-12 and then to study the remaining occurrences of this term in the *Temple Scroll:*

ואיש כיא ישכב עם אשתו שכבת זרע לוא יבוא אל כל עיר המקדש אשר
אשכין שמי בה שלושת ימים:[13]

> And if a man has sexual relations with his wife[14] he may not enter any part of the City of the Sanctuary in which I cause My name to dwell[15] (for) three days.

This passage is also based on Lev 15:18.[16] But the wording of the first part of the sentence is taken from Lev 19:20, ואיש כי ישכב את אשה שכבת זרע [17] While there is no question that this passage is in agreement with CD 12:1-2 quoted above, some of the conclusions that have been reached on this basis are unproven.

Yadin interpreted this passage according to his two basic assumptions, that the City of the Sanctuary is the entire City of Jerusalem, and that the scroll is the product of a celibate Essene community.[18] The second assumption is beyond the scope of our paper, except to observe that in our view, the sect of Qumran was not celibate.[19] This paper concerns the other issue on which we hope to show that Yadin was not correct.

---

[13]The text is also preserved partly in 11QT^b. Cf. Yadin II.188-9 and E. Qimron, *The Temple Scroll, A Critical Edition with Extensive Reconstructions*, Beer Sheva /Jerusalem 1996, 63.

[14]Or more literally, 'And if a man lies with his wife so as to have a seminal emission.'

[15]For the use of this expression and its significance in the scroll, see L.H. Schiffman, 'The Theology of the Temple Scroll', *JQR* 85 (1994) 119-21. Unfortunately, the two excellent responses to my paper published there by J. Milgrom and J.C. VanderKam (pp. 125-35) do not take up this particular issue.

[16]For MT איש, 'man', the Samaritan reads, אישה, 'her husband'.

[17]Yadin II.193 who also compares Num 5:12-13.

[18]See his analysis in II.285-9.

[19]L.H. Schiffman, *Reclaiming the Dead Sea Scrolls*, Philadelphia 1994, 127-43; contrast J.M. Baumgarten, 'The Qumran-Essene Restraints on Marriage', in: L.H. Schiffman (ed.), *Archaeology and History in the Dead Sea*

Two particular problems with this view must be raised. The first is the matter of the opening of this passage with 'And'. It implies strongly that this law is closely connected to what has gone before. In this case, the preceding law is that of 11QT 45:7-10 which concerns one who has had a seminal emission. That this previous law is connected to that under discussion here (lines 11-12) is also clear because there are paragraphing spaces in line 7 and 12, before and after this unit of two laws. We must therefore briefly examine that passage.

There the text is based on Deut 23:11 and accordingly refers to someone who has had a 'nocturnal emission', although it clearly refers to anyone who has a seminal emission regardless of when. Such a person is excluded from 'the entire Temple' (כול המקדש) until he completes a three-day purification period, washes his clothes and immerses.[20] The three-day period is clearly based on the scroll's understanding of the purification period observed by Israel before receiving the Torah at Sinai. But what concerns us here is the specific restriction. The one who has had a seminal emission, what the Rabbis called the בעל קרי (ba'al qĕrî), may not enter the entire Temple. But immediately afterwards we learn that one who has had sexual relations (hence a seminal emission) may not enter the City of the Sanctuary for three days. There appears to be a direct parallel between these two terms and it seems from this passage, when viewed as a totality, that the 'City of the Sanctuary' and the 'Sanctuary' are one and the same thing – the *temenos* or Temple area, not the entire City of Jerusalem.[21] An-

---

Scrolls, The New York University Conference in Memory of Yigael Yadin, Sheffield 1990, 13-24; E. Qimron, 'Celibacy in the Dead Sea Scrolls and the Two Kinds of Sectarians', in: J. Trebolle Barrera & L. Vegas Montaner (eds), *The Madrid Qumran Congress, Proceedings of the International Congress on the Dead Sea Scrolls,* Madrid, 18-21 March 1991, Leiden 1992, I.287-94.

[20]On the rejection of the concept of the טבול יום by this passage, see L.H. Schiffman, 'Pharisaic and Sadducean Halakhah in Light of the Dead Sea Scrolls, The Case of the *Tevul Yom*', *DSD* 1 (1994), 291-93.

[21]This argument is heightened by the parallel use of the term נדה in CD 12:1-2 and in our passage. One contrast between these passages must be noted. As opposed to the parallel from CD 12:1-2 quoted above, this text only speaks of the male and says that he may not enter the City of the Sanctuary

other passage with similar significance to our study is 11QT
45:15-17:

וכול איש אשר יטהר מזובו, וספר לו שבעת ימים לטהרתו:
וכבס ביום השביעי בגדיו ורחץ את כול בשרו במים חיים:
אחר יבוא אל עיר המקדש:
וכול טמא לנפש²² לוא יבואו לה עד אשר יטהרו:

> And any man who becomes pure of his gonorrheic flow shall
> count seven days for his purification (period). On the seventh day
> he shall wash his clothes and bathe his entire body in living wa-
> ters. Afterwards, he may enter the City of the Sanctuary. And
> anyone who is impure with impurity of the dead may not enter it
> (the city) until they (sic!) have been purified.

This passage makes clear that until purification, a gonorrheic or
one who became impure through contact with the dead[23] may not
enter the City of the Sanctuary. Now the *Temple Scroll* specifically sets up areas outside of the city, to the east, for those afflicted with the disease of צרעת (ṣaraʿat) those who have had gon-
norheic discharges, and those who have a seminal emission. Despite the claims that have been made, these laws refer to the City
of the Sanctuary, not to the entire city of Jerusalem. Before offering their purification offerings, these people had to wait outside the Temple during the period of purification.

The next passage to be considered is 11QT 47:7-15. This text
forbids bringing into the City of the Sanctuary, even to serve as
storage containers, the skins of animals which were not slaughtered sacrificially within the Temple. The details of this law,
which also appears in 4QMMT, have been explicated by us previously[24], so that we need only to present a summary and an

---

for three days after sexual relations.
   [22]The פ is written above the line.
   [23]Cf. L.H. Schiffman, 'The Impurity of the Dead in the *Temple Scroll*', in:
idem (ed.), *Archaeology and History*, 135-56.
   [24]L.H. Schiffman, '*Miqsat Maʿaseh ha-Torah* and the *Temple Scroll*', *RQ*
14 (1990) 442-8. Cf. E. Qimron & J. Strugnell, *Qumran Cave 4.V, Miqsat
Maʿaseh ha-Torah* (= *Discoveries in the Judaean Desert* 10), Oxford 1994,

analysis of the specific Temple terminology. The preserved portion of the column begins with a general statement that 'the city
(עיר) which I sanctify so as to cause My Name and My Sanctuary
(מקדש) to dwell in its midst' must be kept holy and pure[25] and that
all food brought into it must be pure. Then we encounter the prohibition of bringing in skins of animals slaughtered elsewhere
(בתוך עריהמה, 'in their cities'). The fundamental command is
stated as follows in 11QT 47:9-11:

ואל עיר מקדשי לוא יבואו[26] ... ולוא תטמאו את העיר אשר אנוכי משכן
את שמי ומקדשי בתוכה:

> And they may not enter into the city of My Sanctuary ... so as not
> to render impure the city in which I cause to dwell My Name and
> My Sanctuary.

Rather, the scroll rules (lines 11-14):

כי בעורות אשר יזבחו במקדש בהמה יהיו מביאים ... לעיר מקדשי ולוא
יגאלו את מקדשי בעורות זבחי פגוליהמה ...

> Rather, in skins which have been slaughtered sacrificially in the
> Temple shall they bring ... to the City of the Sanctuary, so that
> they not defile My Temple with the hides of their disgusting sacri-
> fices ...

From this passage, it is clear that if improperly slaughtered hides
are brought into the City of the Sanctuary the result is that the
Temple is rendered impure. This only makes sense if the City of
the Sanctuary is the Temple precincts which are required to
maintain Temple standards of purity. In this case, therefore, there
would be a slight technical difference between the terms מקדש and
עיר המקדש. The former would refer to the Temple building proper,
while the latter refers to the *temenos* – the Temple complex which

---

154-6.
    [25]11QT 47:3-6. Qimron, 68 has restored considerably more than Yadin
II.202.
    [26]Following the reading of Qimron, p. 68. Yadin reads יביא.

in our scroll is the entire structure of three concentric courtyards and the Temple within. But in no way can the City of the Sanctuary here be a reference to the entire City of Jerusalem.[27]

An important passage to consider in this context is that which requires that a barrier, termed חיל (*ḥêl*), be erected around the three courts of the Temple (11QT 46:9-10):

ועשיתה חיל סביב למקדש רחב מאה באמה אשר יהיה מבדיל בין
מקדש הקודש לעיר:

> And you must make a barrier around the Temple at a distance of 100 cubits which shall separate between the holy Temple[28] and the city.

This text shows that the term עיר could be used in the sense of the city, that is, the area of residence. In this case, the barrier is designed to separate the sanctified *temenos*, which we have argued is termed עיר המקדש, from the city of Jerusalem which was intended by the author to surround the Temple complex.[29]

3. The Parallel Evidence of 4QMMT

When the text of 4QMMT, the so-called 'Halakhic Letter', became known, it was immediately cited as evidence for the notion that the City of the Sanctuary was indeed the entire City of Jerusalem, including the residence areas.[30] But we will see that this

---

[27]Cf. Yadin I.308-311. Several passages not examined here use מקדש in an unambiguous manner to refer to the Temple precincts or to the Temple building itself: 11QT 3:11, 29:8-9, 35:7, 43:12, 46:2, 3, 8, 11 (twice), 52:14, 15, 17, 18, 20. Yadin also restores עיר המקדש tentatively in 11QT 16:11, but apparently influenced by 4QMMT Qimron restores מחנה הקודש.

[28]Note also line 11 in which the Temple is referred to twice as המקדש.

[29]On this passage cf. Yadin I.274-5; II.198 and Qimron & Strugnell, 145 n. 70.

[30]A parallel discussion of this material by the editors of MMT may be found in Qimron and Strugnell, 143-6. On p. 144 they identify the camp with the City of the Sanctuary which in their view is the entire city of Jerusalem.

conclusion was highly questionable. In providing the justification
for a law prohibiting dogs in the 'holy camp'[31], because they
might eat of the flesh remaining on bones of sacrificial offerings,
the text states (B 59-62):

כי ירושלים היאה מחנה הקדש והיא המקום שבחר בו מכל שבטי
ישראל, כי ירושלים היא ראש מחנות ישראל:

> For Jerusalem is the holy camp and it is the place which He (God)
> chose from among all the (territory of the) tribes of Israel, for it is
> the chief of the camps of Israel.[32]

The second passage, occurring earlier in 4QMMT, comes in connection with a section that requires that within a certain distance
of the sanctuary, all slaughter take place in sacrificial fashion and
in the north of 'the camp' (B 27-28).[33] The text of 4QMMT then
continues (B 29-33):

ואנחנו חושבים שהמקדש [משכן אוהל מועד הוא וי]רושלי[ם] מחנה היא
וחוצה למחנה [הוא חוצה לירושלים ו]הוא מחנה ער[י]הם ... [כי ירושלים]
היא המקום אשר [בחר בו] מכול שב[טי ישראל]:

> But we are of the opinion that the sanctuary [is (equivalent to) 'the
> Tabernacle, the Tent of Meeting', and Je]rusale[m] is (equivalent
> to) 'the camp'. And 'outside of the camp' [is (equivalent to) out-
> side of Jerusalem, and] that is the camp of their cities[34]... [for Jeru-
> salem] is the place [which He (God) chose] from all the (territory
> of the) tri[bes of Israel].

This text sets up a simple set of equivalencies between the various
boundaries of sanctity which were in effect in the desert period in
Israel's history with the boundaries in the Land of Israel in the

---

[31]Literally, 'the camp of holiness'.
[32]See the edition and commentary in Qimron & Strugnell, 52-3.
[33]See the detailed analysis in Qimron & Strugnell, 156-7.
[34]This is the only use of the word עיר in 4QMMT, Qimron and Strugnell,
222 [Concordance]).

author's own day. We may summarize the equivalencies in a simple table:

present-day:	*desert period:*
sanctuary	Tent of Meeting
Jerusalem	camp
outside of Jerusalem	outside of the camp
(camp of their cities)	

Qimron and Strugnell have argued that the presentation of these equivalencies is intended to argue for the position of this text that the entire city of Jerusalem is 'the chosen place', as opposed to the view of the opponents of the sect that only the Temple precincts are equivalent in sanctity to the chosen place.[35]

It seems that they have noticed the discrepancy between their interpretation of this text and Yadin's claim that the City of the Sanctuary is the Temple as a whole, although they never state it directly. They note that in their opinion Yadin was correct in saying that in the view of the *Temple Scroll* the City of Jerusalem was more sacred than other settlements. But they also say that the sanctuary must still be seen as a separate area more sacred than the City of Jerusalem, as can be seen in 4QMMT B 24. This separation, in their view, is the purpose of the rampart (חיל) required in 11QT 46:9-11.[36]

In order to evaluate properly these terms and their equivalencies, and then to compare them to similar or parallel expressions in the *Temple Scroll,* we must first establish the biblical background of these terms. The restored phrase משכן אהל מועד occurs in Exod 39:32, 40:2, 40:6 and 29, and 1 Chron 6:17. In Exod 39:32 and 40:2 it clearly refers to the entire complex of the Tent of Meeting and the various furnishings and ritual objects fashioned for it (cf. v. 33). But in Exod 40:6 and 29 it is differentiated from the attendant furnishings and refers only to the Tabernacle structure itself. In 1 Chron 6:17 it seems to be used in the same

---

[35]Qimron & Strugnell, 144 paragraph C.
[36]Qimron & Strugnell, 144-5 paragraph D.

way since it is set opposite the 'House of the Lord' which Solomon built in Jerusalem. From these descriptions it appears that the term applies in both Exodus and in our text to the entire Temple complex, including the courtyards surrounding the sanctuary.

That Jerusalem is equal to the desert camp (מחנה) is a statement that raises the question of the meaning of the term 'camp' (מחנה) in the Bible. This constitutes a difficult problem since the term is used in various ways. To solve the ambiguity of this term in the Bible, tannaitic opinion determined that there were three 'camps': The camp of the divine presence was the actual Tabernacle area itself, in which the rituals were performed. The second camp, located concentrically around it, was known as the 'camp of the Levites', since the Aaronide Priests and the Levites were said to have actually lived in the immediate area surrounding the Tabernacle. Finally, the entire camp of the rest of the tribes was termed the 'camp of Israel'. This was the residence of the tribes which was also arranged concentrically around the Tabernacle and the camp of the Levites.

The Tannaim then transfered this assumed pattern of ritual and residence from the desert camp to the Land of Israel in order to make possible following the sacrificial laws originally set in the Tabernacle and desert camp. The Temple building and the courts of the Priesthood and Israel were equivalent to the 'camp of the Divine Presence'. The court of women and the rest of the Temple Mount area were taken as equivalent to the 'camp of the Levites'. The City of Jerusalem was equivalent to the 'camp of Israel'.[37]

This system corresponds to that adopted in the MMT text. The present Temple is in the eyes of the authors of MMT equivalent to the Tabernacle of the Tent of Meeting which in tannaitic terms is the camp of the Divine Presence and the camp of the Levites. The City of Jerusalem is 'the camp' of the Bible which for the Tannaim is 'the camp of Israel'. But MMT adds a discussion of the area outside of the camp. This area is known as 'outside of the camp' in their terminology. This term occurs numerous times in

---

[37] Cf L.H. Schiffman, 'Exclusion from the Sanctuary and the City of he Sanctuary in the Temple Scroll', *HAR* 9 (1985) 308.

the Bible in the form of מחוץ למחנה and refers to the area outside of the camp of Israel. This camp, we have just seen, is equivalent to the City of Jerusalem in the rabbinic view as it is according to MMT. The area outside, described as 'the camp of their cites' in MMT, refers to the residence of the Jewish people who dwell outside of Jerusalem.

The above discussion shows that the notion in MMT, as correctly realized by the editors, is not that proposed by Yadin for the *Temple Scroll.* In MMT there is an established boundary between the *temenos* and the city of Jerusalem, where people actually lived. The laws of Temple purity applied to the *temenos* – the equivalent of the Temple Mount – and not to the entire city of Jerusalem, which was one step below in its purity status.

We would argue that the same is the case with the *Temple Scroll.* The so-called City of the Sanctuary is in fact the *temenos* and the surrounding sanctified precincts. Its purity laws were observed only in its own boundaries. Outside, the rest of the city had a special status above that of other cities, but it was still not equivalent to the Temple. Outside of Jerusalem were the cities of Israel in which in the ideal view of *Temple Scroll* lived the twelve tribes.

4. 4Q Historical Text (4Q248)

One final text (4Q248) preserves usage of the term City of the Sanctuary. This manuscript, 4Q *Historical Text,* used to be known as 'Acts of a Greek King' or 'Pseudo-History'. It is an account of the conquest of Judea and some neighboring countries by a Hellenistic king. The text is only a fragment, but the lower right and bottom margins are preserved. Essentially, then, we have the right part of the last few lines of a text at the bottom of a column.[38]

---

[38]See the edition, commentary and analysis of M. Broshi & E. Eshel, 'The Greek King is Antiochus IV (4QHistorical Text = 4Q248)', *JJS* 48 (1997) 120-29.

The editors, M. Broshi and E. Eshel, have been able to locate the historical details presented in this text. It describes a series of events in the reign of Antiochus IV Epiphanes (ruled 175-164 BCE), including his first invasion of Egypt in 169 BCE,[39] the subsequent sale of Egyptian land, his capture of Jerusalem soon afterwards (also in 169), probably his conquest of Cyprus, and his second campaign against Egypt in 168 CE – all in the form of *ex eventu* prophecy.[40] Then our reference appears (lines 6-7):

ואת]ה] אל עיר המקדש תפשה עם כ]ל אוצרותיה] :

Then he shall com[e] to the City of the Sanctuary and seize it with al[l its treasures].[41]

Our interest in this passage in the present context is in regard to the meaning of the designation 'City of the Sanctuary'. The fragmentary nature of the passage makes it difficult to be certain of all its details. The editors propose to understand this phrase as referring to the entire City of Jerusalem, comparing its use in the *Zadokite Fragments* and *Temple Scroll*. Regardless of its meaning in other sources, it would seem at first glance that the entire City of Jerusalem is referred to here. But detailed analysis of the passage in 1 Maccabees describing this invasion raises serious doubt about this interpretation, especially in light of the attractive restoration of Broshi and Eshel. 1 Macc 1:20 tells us that Antiochus came to Jerusalem where he apparently met with no resistance. But verses 21-24 describe his entering the Temple where he helped himself to the golden altar, the menorah and its utensils, the table of the showbread, other sacrificial vessels, censers, the curtain (פרוכת), and gold decorations. Further, he took the hidden treasure kept there as well, probably a reference to public funds collected for financing the sacrificial offerings. All this indicates that the 'treasures' described in our text – as restored by the edi-

---

[39]See 1 Macc 20:24 and cf. 2 Macc 5:1, 11-16.
[40]For bibliography, see Broshi and Eshel, 128 n. 28.
[41]My translations according to the restorations of Broshi and Eshel, 125.

tors – are Temple treasures only, and, therefore, it is quite probably that the City of the Sanctuary in this text is the Temple from
which Antiochus expropriated the various treasures. In this case,
the City of the Sanctuary would be the *temenos*, as we have
claimed.

Conclusion

The term City of the Sanctuary denoted the *temenos* or Temple
precincts in the legal terminology of the Zadokite Fragments and
the Temple Scroll. This expression was used in the same way in
4Q *Historical Text*. The authors of the Qumran texts we have
studied did indeed believe that the Sanctity of Jerusalem, God's
chosen City, was greater than that of the rest of the Land of Israel.
Yet the Temple precincts, in the view of the *Temple Scroll* con-
stituted of three concentric courtyards, were themselves of even
greater sanctity. In the view of these authors, God was truly thrice
sanctified. Holy, Holy, Holy was the Lord of Hosts: Holy in His
Temple, Holy in His city Jerusalem, and Holy in His land, the
Land of Israel.

PART TWO

POSTBIBLICAL PERIOD:

1. Judaism

HOLINESS AND MYSTICISM AT SINAI ACCORDING TO THE MEKHILTA DE RABBI ISHMAEL

Lieve Teugels

1. Introduction

Mount Sinai is a holy place. It is holy because the major event in Jewish history occurred there, namely the giving of the Torah *(matan Torah)*. The primary factor that contributed to the holiness of this event was the proximity of the human and the Divine. Related to this, the events on Mount Sinai are suitable subjects for mystical interpretations.

This study deals with mystical interpretations of the *matan Torah*, and in particular with the question of whether such interpretations are present in the *Mekhilta de Rabbi Ishmael*. Three preliminary questions need to be asked: (1) Why and when is a rabbinic interpretation called 'mystical'?; (2) Why does this study concentrate on the *Mekhilta*?; and (3) How did the biblical narrative of the Revelation at Sinai generate mystical interpretations?

1.1 What is mystical?

Next to the Story of Creation (*ma'aseh bereshit*) and Ezekiel's Vision of the Chariot (*ma'aseh merkabah*), the Giving of the Torah (*matan Torah*) is one of the major themes in Jewish mysticism. The use of the term 'mystical' when interpreting rabbinic texts (3rd - 8th century CE) implies a different meaning than the one that is current in the psychology or philosophy of religion. There, one thinks of union with the divine by means of contemplation and self-surrender, whereby religious experience is a central element. With respect to rabbinic mysticism, there is much discussion and uncertainty about the element of experience. It is not at all clear whether, behind the texts, there was an actual mystical practice, such as meditation, which was intended to effect a special union with the Deity.[1] However that may be, rabbinic mystical experience as such is not the subject of this study.

What is commonly accepted, is that certain biblical *texts*, and in particular those mentioned at the beginning of this section, are the subject of rabbinic mystical interpretation. In other words, rabbinic mysticism is primarily of a 'midrashic nature'.[2] In such interpretations, a special relationship or union between the human and the deity, which is not, or only obliquely, present in the biblical text, is accentuated and expanded. The characteristic elements of Jewish mystical interpretations are: (1) heavenly ascensions of human beings; and (2) visions in which God descends upon earth, often accompanied by angels.[3] Since it is assumed that a human being enters the divine domain and vice versa, the borders between the sacred and the profane become blurred. The particular focus of this study is the exchange of domains between the human and the divine on Sinai as represented in the *Mekhilta.*

1.2 Why the Mekhilta?

My choice of the *Mekhilta de Rabbi Ishmael* has two reasons: (1) it is considered old, that is tannaitic; and (2) it is midrash.

1. Gershom Scholem claimed that Jewish mysticism could be found as early as the tannaitic literature. With a different purpose

---

[1] See E.E. Urbach, 'The Traditions about Merkabah Mysticism in the Tannaitic Period' (Hebr.), in: idem (ed.), *Studies in Mysticism and Religion Presented to G.G. Scholem*, Jerusalem 1967, 1-28; contra G. Scholem, *Jewish Gnosticism, Merkabah Mysticism and Talmudic Tradition*, New York 1965, who, here and elsewhere, claims that the rabbinic texts testify to real ecstatic ascents by the mystics. Against Scholem, see also I. Gruenwald, *Apocalyptic and Merkavah Mysticism*, Leiden 1980, 73-97.
[2] Gruenwald, *Apocalyptic*, 77
[3] These are not restricted to rabbinic literature, but also apply to both the earlier Jewish apocalyptic works and the later Hekhalot literature. Antecedents of these elements can be found in certain biblical texts, e.g. 1 Kgs 12:19; Isa 6; and in the book of Ezekiel. See Gruenwald, *Apocalyptic* 29-30.

– he did not want to prove that the tannaitic texts refer to mystical ecstatic *experience*, to the contrary – David Halperin has again tried to demonstrate that mystical interpretations of the *matan Torah* go back to the tannaitic period.[4]

Halperin's main evidence comes from works which are generally considered rather late, i.e., *Pesiqta de Rab Kahana* (PRK) and *Exodus Rabbah*. However, he demonstrates that the relevant passages do contain tannaitic material. This gave me the idea of systematically examining the alleged oldest midrash that covers the *matan Torah*, namely *Mekhilta de Rabbi Ishmael, parashah Baḥodesh ha-shlishi*. If the *Mekhilta* contained mystical midrash, then this would support the antiquity of the rabbinic mystical interpretation of Sinai.[5] To anticipate the details of this study: My findings support the existence of mystical interpretations of the *matan Torah* in tannaitic times, but in a rather unexpected way. The *Mekhilta* seems to contain a polemical exegesis against mystical interpretations known to its author.

2. The second reason for my choice of the *Mekhilta* is that it is midrash. The most important characteristic of midrash is that it is 'encoded as biblical interpretation'.[6] This distinguishes midrash from other rabbinic genres which do not explicitly present themselves as interpretations of Scripture. In the past, mystical elements in the halakhic tannaitic sources, namely *Mishnah* and *Tosefta,* have received considerable attention.[7] Well-known is the so-

---

[4]D. Halperin, *The Faces of the Chariot. Early Jewish Responses to Ezekiel's Vision*, Tübingen 1988.

[5]It has been shown elsewhere that mystical, *merkabah*-like associations were already present in pre-tannaitic, non-rabbinic sources, such as Philo of Alexandria, or a passage in Ezekiel the Dramatist's *Exagoge*, which is dated in the second century BCE. See P.W. van der Horst, 'Moses' Throne Vision in Ezekiel the Dramatist', *JJS* 34 (1983) 21-30; L Teugels, 'Did Moses see the Chariot?' in M.Vervenne (ed.), *Studies in the Book of Exodus*, Leuven 1996, 595-602.

[6]D. Boyarin, *Intertextuality and the Reading of Midrash*, Bloomington /Indianapolis 1991, 3.

[7]See, e.g., Gruenwald, *Apocalyptic*; Halperin, *The Faces*; I. Chernus, *Mysticism in Rabbinic Judaism. Studies in the History of Midrash*, Berlin/New York 1982

called 'Pardes-episode', where we are told how Rabbi Aqiba and
his three students made a mystical journey and only Aqiba
emerged safely;[8] the regulations in the *Mishnah* on the subject of
the 'forbidden expositions';[9] the story about Rabbi Yoḥanan and
Rabbi Eleazar ben Arakh that follows this regulation in the *Tosefta*;[10] and the discussion on whether the *merkabah* may be read as
a prophetic reading in the synagogue (*haftarah*), probably for Shavuot.[11]

The use of the verbs 'to discourse' (דרש) and 'to open' (פתח) in
these passages – two technical terms that refer to the interpretation
of the Bible – already demonstrates that rabbinic mystical speculations are connected with study or midrash.[12] However, the contents
of the study, the midrash itself, are not related in these texts. They
could be found in tannaitic midrashic works, especially in the *Mekhilta* which deals with the book of Exodus. Since tannaitic midrash
is less frequently dealt with in this connection than the halakhic
sources, it now deserves special attention.

*1.3 How did the biblical narrative generate mystical interpreta-
tions?*

The account of the Revelation on Sinai with the Giving of the Torah (*matan Torah*), can be found in Exodus 19-20. The regulations surrounding the communication and contact between Moses
and the People, on the one hand, and God, on the other hand,
evokes a feeling of 'holiness'. It is not surprising that the word
'holy' (קדוש) and its corresponding verb are repeatedly found in the
text. It is applied to the mountain (Exod 19:23) and to the people
(Exod 19: 6,10,14,22). The holiness of the mountain, however, is
related to the events that took place: the encounter between the

---

[8]THag 2:3-4
[9]MHag 2:1
[10]THag 2:1
[11]MMeg 4:10
[12]E.g. MHag 2:1: דורשין בעריות בשלשה ... ולא במרכבה ביחיד ; THag 2:1:
פתח רבי אלעזר בן ערך ודרש במעשה מרכבה. See Gruenwald, *Apocalyptic*, 82.

human and the divine. As is stated explicitly (Exod 19:12-13, 21-24; 20:18,21), the holiness of the events and the mountain, ultimately entail the setting of limits. Because of the 'holy' events taking place, the people may not climb the mountain nor even touch it. The people have to take special precautions to sanctify themselves.

The fact that the event is situated on a mountain enhances this effect. More particularly, the description of Moses' repeated ascents towards God and descents towards the people, suggests that he visited the realm between the sacred and the profane. Of God it is said that he descended on the mountain. Keywords or -roots in the account that express this movement from both sides are 'to ascend' (עלה) and 'to descend' (ירד): Moses has to climb up the mountain (Exod 19:3,20,24) and God has to come down upon the mountain (Exod 19:11,18,20). Each has his own domain: God has the heaven and the human has the earth; the mountain is their meeting point. When Moses mediates between God and the people, this is also expressed by the verb ירד (Exod 19:14,21,24,25).

However, 'holy' is not the same as 'mystical'. On the contrary, holiness is a function of the strict preservation of the borders between the human and the divine domains. In the biblical narrative, it is not said that Moses crossed over the border towards the divine and entered heaven. Conversely certain rabbinic and other interpretations of the story do claim that Moses entered heaven on this particular occasion. These interpretations can be called mystical, because they assume a crossing of the border between the human and the divine. The same can be said of interpretations that focus on God's physical descent upon the earth.

With regard to the study of midrash, it is always important to realize what exactly is stated in the Bible and what is not. Midrash always has a starting point in the text. Exod 20:21, e.g., might be a starting point for a mystical midrashic interpretation. Even though it is not said that Moses ascended into heaven, it is said that Moses drew near the cloud where God was. The supernatural effects related in Exod 19:16-19 and 20:18: the smoke, the shaking of the earth, the trumpet and the lightning, could also evoke mystical interpretations. The text itself, however, does not automatically suggest such interpretations. On the contrary, the thunder, lightning etc. serve in their own way to frighten the people and thus to keep them away from the Divine; just as the smoke and the clouds serve, as it were, as a smoke-screen to prevent them from seeing the Deity. For a mystical interpretation of Exod 19-20, much expansion was required.

2. A Study of Mekhilta Baḥodesh

Halperin, among others, points out that the Sinai-pericope in Exodus and the throne-vision described in Ezek 1 were read in the light of each other in rabbinic midrash. That is, elements of both accounts were conflated. The vision of Ezekiel was presented as a repetition of the miracles that occurred on Sinai, and the revelation on Sinai was described in terms of the vision of Ezekiel. This connection certainly enhanced, and perhaps even gave rise to, the mystical interpretation of the Sinai-experience. The connection, however, was established by a third text that is often found in midrashic interpretations of the *matan Torah*, namely Ps 68:18-19. These verses are known to contain some difficulties, but, in the light of rabbinic interpretation, they can be rendered as follows: (18) The chariots of God: two myriads and two thousand angels (שנאן)[13]; the Lord is among them: it is Sinai in holiness. (19) You ascended on high, you took captivity captive, you took gifts for humanity.

The relevance of Ps 68:18 is clear at first sight: it deals with the Chariot and with Sinai. Yet, both verses are paradigmatic for two significant aspects of the rabbinic interpretation of the Sinai-pericope: (1) The Divine chariot (*merkabah*) was seen both in the vision of Ezekiel and on Sinai; (2) Moses ascended, not only onto the mountain, but also into heaven. Thus, Ps 68:18-19 served to combine the motif of God's descent onto Sinai with the Chariot of Ezekiel.

---

[13]The meaning of this word is much debated in rabbinic midrash, and gave rise to different interpretations that will be discussed later (note 33).

Halperin's discussion of the combination of Sinai and the Chariot concentrates on PRK 12:22 (*Bahodesh*) and its parallels.[14] Even though PRK is usally considered a relatively late work,[15] Halperin claims that this particular passage contains traditions that date back to at least the 3rd century CE. The second element in the mystical interpretation of Sinai, the ascent of Moses to heaven, is found, among others, in *Exodus Rabbah* (ExodR) 28:1.[16] This text is also said by Halperin to contain tannaitic material.[17]

Now it is possible to proceed to the study of the relevant chapters in the *Mekhilta*. As a working definition of mystical midrash on the Sinai pericope, I will treat those interpretations as mystical that contain either one of the two elements which Halperin recognized, or both: (1) the combination of the Sinai-event with Ezekiel's Chariot; and (2) the ascent of Moses into heaven. These two elements correspond to those mentioned in the introduction of this article as characteristic for rabbinic mysticism. The appearance of Ezek 1 and/or Ps 68:18-19 as proof-texts can be treated as a sign that a mystical interpretation might be at hand. I will compare *Mekhilta Bahodesh* with passages from PRK 12 and ExodR 28-29. The question of whether the latter do indeed contain tannaitic material is not of primary importance for this discussion. It can only be said that, if the *Mekhilta* does contain clear parallels to interpretations found in PRK or ExodR, we would have more certainty about the antiquity of such interpretations.

2.1 The Vision of God on Sinai and by Ezekiel

In *Mekhilta Shirata* 3:28-32, which does not deal with Sinai but with the Song at the Sea (Exod 15), Ezekiel's vision of the Chariot

---

[14]Halperin, *The Faces*, 141-149. See par. II.1

[15]5th-6th century, see G. Stemberger, *Introduction to Talmud and Midrash*, Edinburgh 1991, 321

[16]See par II.2

[17]For the classification of PRK 12: 2-25 and ExodR, Chapter 15 to the end as 'Tanhuma-midrashim', and arguments that these passages preserve material from the 3rd century CE, see Halperin, *The Faces*, 142.

is used in a midrash on what the Israelites saw at the Sea. Ezek 1:1
is explicitly cited as a proof-text.[18]

> 'This is my God and I will glorify him' (Exod 15:2). R. Eliezer
> says: Whence can you say that a maidservant saw at the sea what
> Isaiah and Ezekiel and all the prophets never saw? It says about
> them 'And by the ministry of the prophets have I used similitudes'
> (Hos 12:11). And it is also written: 'The heavens were opened and
> I saw visions of God' (Ezek 1:1).

The 'peg' in the text on which this interpretation is hung, is the
word 'this' (זה). It is a standard rabbinic hermeneutic device to read
'this' in a deictic way, i.e. as if a real pointing (with the finger) occurred when someone said 'this'.[19] With the citation of the verses
from Hosea and Ezekiel, the author of the midrash demonstrates
that, opposed to the people at the Sea, who saw God in His real appearance, the prophets only could see Him indirectly: in similitudes
or in a vision.[20] It is remarkable that we do not find Ezek 1:1 quoted
in the following parallel in *Mekhilta Bahodesh* 3:37-40, which
comments on the events at Sinai.

> *In the sight of all the people* (Exod 19:11). This teaches that at
> that moment the people saw what Isaiah and Ezekiel never saw.
> For it said: 'And by the ministry of the prophets have I used
> similitudes' (Hos 12:11).

There are several arguments for the originality of the version in
Shirata.[21] When *Shirata* has the original version, the absence of

---

[18]Translation from the *Mekhilta* by J.Z. Lauterbach, *Mekilta de-Rabbi Ishmael*, Vol II, Philadelphia 1933. The citations from Scripture are, where necessary, adapted.

[19]See Boyarin, *Intertextuality*, 119-121; H. Fox, 'As if by Finger – The
History of an Anti-Anthropomorphic Figure' (Hebr.), *Tarbiz* 49 (1980) 278-
291.

[20]See also LevR 1:14

[21]The relationship between the Sea and Sinai, exegetically linked through
the *merkabah*, is developed by Halperin, *The Faces*, 211-249. He argues that
the midrash was transferred from the Sea to Sinai (215). See also Chernus,
Mysticism, 21.

Ezek 1 in *Baḥodesh* is probably deliberate. The reason for the omission could be that the vision of Ezekiel was no longer considered a veiled view by many contemporary readers, but a clear vision of God in his Chariot. A proof that this was at least so in later rabbinic midrash can be found in PRK 12:22.[22]

> *I am the Lord your God, who brought you out of the Land of Egypt* (Exod 20:2). These words are to be considered in the light of the verse 'The chariots of God: two myriads and two thousand angels; the Lord is among them: it is Sinai in holiness' (Ps 68:18). R. Abdima of Haifa said: In the study of a *mishnah* which is in my possession, I learned that twenty-two thousand [chariots of][23] ministering angels came down with the Holy One on Mount Sinai, as many, so said R. Berekhya the Priest Berabbi, as there were males in the camp of the Levites. (...) Another comment: 'The chariots of God: two myriads and two thousand angels'. With the Holy One there came down twenty-two thousand chariots, and each and every chariot was like the chariot which Ezekiel saw.

This text contains an obvious mystical interpretation of God's descent at Sinai, whereby Ps 68:18 is cited as a so-called prooftext.[24] Ezek 1 is not cited, it is implicitly present in the last sentence: it is stated that Ezekiel did see the chariot.

---

[22]Translations according to W.G. Braude & I.J.Kapstein, *Pesikta de Rab-Kahana*, Philadelphia 1975. The citations from Scripture are, where necessary, adapted.

[23]Not in Braude. Some sources have a reference to the chariots and others omit it. See Halperin, *The Faces*, 530, note n, for arguments that the version with the chariots is the original one.

[24]More correctly, as a *petiḥta*-verse. I agree with Halperin that PRK 12:22 has the form of a *petiḥta*. Halperin, however, follows Joseph Heinemann, who holds that a *petiḥta* – in its original, liturgical form – was a small introductory homily that preceded the reading of the *parashah*. According to Halperin, this *petiḥta* was used as an introduction to the reading of Exod 20 in the synagogue. He says that this verse "is so perfectly suited to be the starting point of a *petiḥta* for Shavuot that it would be astonishing if it were not" (p. 147). Even though I am not convinced by Heinemann's and Halperin's theory about the liturgical function of the *petiḥta*, it is clear that, in its literary form, PRK 12:22 serves as a *petiḥta* to the exposition of Exod 20:2, to which it is connected at the beginning and at the end of the *pisqa*. It should be mentioned that parallels to this

Two reasons why the author of *Mekhilta Baḥodesh* 3:37-40 could have omitted the quotation of Ezek 1, can be suggested.

1. Because he knew that the vision of Ezekiel was considered to be a clear vision of God already in his time, the citation of Ezek 1:1 lost its function. It was not meaningful anymore as a proof that 'the prophets never saw what the people saw'. According to many of his contemporaries, Ezekiel saw the same! The fact that the name Ezekiel remained in the text, is a residue of the original version of the midrash which the author, so to say, 'forgot' to remove. This residue is another indication that the version in *Baḥodesh* is secondary with respect to the version in *Shirata.*

2. He did not want the explicit conflation of Exod 19 and Ezek 1 in his midrash to encourage further mystical speculations about the Sinai event. A combination of the two reasons is very probable as well.

2.2 Ps 68:19 and the Ascent of Moses

In PRK 12:22, which has just been cited, Ps 68:18, serves as the 'clip' (Halperin) that connects the vision of God by the people at Sinai and Ezekiel's vision, and thus introduces the first mystical element, i.e. God's descent. In other midrashim, Moses ascent into heaven is introduced by the combination of Exod 19 and Ps 68:19. An example of this can be found in ExodR 28:1.[25]

> 'And Moses went up unto God' (Exod 19:3). It is written, 'You ascended on high, you took captivity captive' (Ps 68:19). What is the meaning of 'You ascended'? You have been exalted, because you have wrestled with angels on high. Another explanation of 'You ascended on high': No creature on high has prevailed as Moses did. R. Berekhya said: The length of the Tablets was six handbreadths; two were – could we but speak thus! – in the hands

---

passage occur in other collections; but without the clear *petiḥta*-structure (TanB *Yitro* 14; ExodR, 29:2; MidrPss 68:10).

[25]Translation of H. Freedman & M. Simon (eds), *The Midrash Rabbah. Volume 2: Exodus*, London/Jerusalem/New York ³1961, where necessary adapted in more modern language.

of Him who called the world into being; two handbreadths were in the hands of Moses, and two handbreadths separated the two pairs of hands.

According to this midrash, Ps 68:19 proves that Moses, while ascending Mount Sinai, actually ascended into heaven. This view is explicitly rejected in *Mekhilta Baḥodesh* 4:53-58.

> R. Yose says: Behold, it says: 'The heavens are the heavens of the Lord, but the earth he has given to the human beings' (Ps 115:16). Neither Moses nor Elijah ever went to heaven, nor did the Glory ever come down to earth. Scripture merely teaches that God said to Moses: Behold I am going to call you through the top of the mount and you come up, as it says: 'And the Lord called Moses to the top of the mount' (Exod 19:20).

This interpretation in the name of Rabbi Yose is clearly anti-mystical. Ps 115:16 is cited as a proof that Moses and Elijah never went to heaven; and even that God never came down to earth. Rabbi Yose's interpretation of Ps 115:16 is all the more noteworthy when it is compared with the following *mashal* in PRK 12:11. This *mashal* is told at the end of an exposition on Exod 19:1.

> R. Abba bar Yudan said: Listen to a story of a king who was about to give his daughter in marriage. Now this king had issued a decree forbidding marriages with people from across the sea, specifying that Romans should not go and marry in Syria and that Syrians should not go up to Rome. But when he himself gave his daughter in marriage, he withdrew the decree. So, before the Torah was given: 'The heavens are the heavens of the Lord, but the earth He hath given to the children of men' (Ps 115:16). But after the Torah was given from heaven: 'And Moses went up unto God' (Exod 19:3), 'And the Lord came down upon Mount Sinai' (Exod 19:20)

In the *nimshal*,[26] Ps 115:16 refers to the pre-Sinai reality, which differed from the post-Sinai reality represented by Exod 19:3 and

---

[26]Following D. Stern, *Parables in Midrash*, Cambridge (Mass)/London

Exod 19:20. Since the events on Sinai, the borders between the two domains were removed. According to R. Yose in the *Mekhilta*, however, the situation never changed: heaven and earth remained two different domains, even on Sinai. It is obvious that Rabbi Yose reacted to the opinion represented in the *mashal*, and thus that this view was already current in his time.

An illuminating parallel to the above statement of Rabbi Yose can be found in a *baraita* in BT Suk 5a. [27]

> *And there I will meet with you and I will speak with you from the ark-cover* (Exod 25:22). And it has been taught, R. Yose stated: Neither did the Shekhinah ever descend to earth, nor did Moses or Elijah ever ascend to heaven, as it is written, 'The heavens are the heavens of the Lord, but the earth he has given to the human beings' (Ps 115:16). But did not the Shekhinah descend on earth? Is it not in fact written, 'And the Lord came down upon Mount Sinai?' (Exod 19:20). That was above ten handbreadths from the summit. But is it not written, 'And his feet shall stand in that day upon the Mount of Olives' (Zech 14:4). That will be above ten handbreadths. But did not Moses and Elijah ascend to heaven? Is it not in fact written, 'And Moses went up unto God' (Exod 19:3). That was to a level lower than ten handbreadths. But is it not written, 'And Elijah went up in a whirlwind into heaven' (2 Kgs 2:11). That was to a level lower than ten handbreadths. But is it not written, 'He[28] seized hold of the face of his throne, and He spread His cloud upon him' (Job 26:9), and R. Tanḥum said: 'This teaches that the Almighty spread some of the radiance of his Shekhinah and his cloud upon him'? – That was at a level lower than ten handbreadths. But in any case is it not written, 'He seized hold of the face of his throne' – The throne was well lowered for his sake until it reached a level lower than ten handbreadths and he seizeth hold of it.

This passage deals with the size of a *sukkah*: according to the Mishnah, it should be higher than ten handbreadths, the same as the

---

1991, 8, I distinguish between the narrative or '*mashal-proper*' and the narrative's application, the *nimshal*.

[27]Translation in M. Simon & I. Epstein, London 1935-1952.

[28]In this interpretation Moses is meant.

total height of the Ark of the Covenant. A distance of ten handbreadths on both sides, it is said, maintains the strict separation
between heaven and earth, or the human and the divine. Rabbi
Yose's remarks all confirm the same basic message: a human never
ascended to heaven and God, or the Shekhinah, never descended to
earth. There was always a minimal distance of ten handbreadths
between them. These remarks about the handbreadths contrast
sharply with the statement in ExodR 28:1, cited in the beginning of
this paragraph, that only two handbreadths separated Moses and
God.

To conclude: the *baraita* in BT Suk 5a and the sayings attributed
to Rabbi Yose in *Mekhilta Baḥodesh* 4:53-58, demonstrate that
there was a reaction to (1) the interpretation of Ps 115:16 as a removal of the borders between the human and the divine on Sinai,
as found in PRK 12:11; and (2) the view that only 'two handbreadths' separated God and Moses, as is found in ExodR 28. The
traditions preserved in these two amoraitic works seem therefore to
have been already known in tannaitic times. The fact that the
baraita has preserved the name of Rabbi Yose probably indicates
that the separation between the human and the divine was a main
preoccupation of this *Tanna*.[29]

2.3 God's descent on Mount Sinai

Just before the statement of rabbi Yose in the *Mekhilta*, the following midrash is found.[30]

> 'And the Lord came down upon Mount Sinai' (Exod 19:20). I
> might understand this to mean upon the entire mountain, but it
> says: 'To the top of the mount' (ibid.). One might think (יכול) that
> the Glory actually descended from heaven and was transferred to
> Mount Sinai, but Scripture says: 'That I have talked with you
> from heaven' (Exod 20:19). Scripture thus teaches that the Holy
> One, blessed be He, bent down the lower heavens and the upper

---

[29]See Gruenwald, *Apocalyptic*, 93. He says that Rabbi Yose was an exception among the *tannaim* by not accepting the possibility of heavenly ascents.
[30]*Mek Baḥodesh* 4:45-53.

heavens of heaven, lowering them to the top of the mountain, and
thus the Glory descended. He spread them upon Mount Sinai as a
man who spreads the mattress upon the bed and speaks from the
mattress. (...).

Ira Chernus claimed that this midrash is mystical.[31] However, his
opinion is based upon an incorrect understanding of the יכול –
phrase. He translates this phrase as: 'Is it possible that the Glory
actually descended upon Mount Sinai? That is why Scripture says
etc.'. In his view, the quotation from Scripture confirms the fact
that God actually descended upon Mount Sinai. However, יכול
regularly introduces a false hypothesis, which is then refuted by a
citation from Scripture which gives the correct interpretation.[32] The
way Exod 20:19 is interpreted here, as God lowering the heavens
as a mattress on the mount, does not ignore the separation between
heaven and earth; but, on the contrary, is a solution to the problem
of God being present on the mountain but still not being present in
the earthly domain. This interpretation has a parallel in *Mekhilta
Baḥodesh* 9:134-136, where it is attributed to Rabbi Aqiba:

> *That I have talked with you from heaven* (Exod 20:19) (...) R.
> Aqiba says: Scripture teaches that the Holy One, blessed be He,
> lowered the upper heavens of heaven down to the top of the
> mountain and thus actually still spoke to them from the heavens.

Because of the attribution to Rabbi Aqiba, who is, among other
things, known for his experiences in the 'Pardes' (see above), this
midrash had to be mystical for Chernus. However, the saying in the
last sentence of this midrash clearly demonstrates his anti-mystical
stance on this matter.

---

[31] Chernus, *Mysticism*, 5.
[32] See W. Bacher, *Die exegetische Terminologie der Jüdischen Traditions-
literatur. Part 1,* Leipzig 1899, 72.

2.4 Ps 68:17

It has already been said that the quotation of Ezek 1 was probably deliberately omitted in one crucial midrash on Exod 19:11 in the *Mekhilta* (see 2.1). It has not yet been noted, however, that *nowhere* in *Mekhilta Baḥodesh is* any verse of Ezek 1 or Ps 68:18-19 actually cited. Since these texts are regularly found in mystical interpretations of the Sinai pericope, as we have seen, their absence could point to a deliberate negative reading of a known exegesis where the three texts are combined. The following text from *Mekhilta Baḥodesh* 4:17-25 could support this argument.

> *And the whole mountain quaked* (Exod 19:18). And was not Sinai in one class with all other mountains? For it is said: 'The mountains quaked before the Lord, that is Sinai, before the Lord the God of Israel' (Judg 5:5). And it also says: 'Why do you look with envy, O many-peaked mountain' (Ps 68:17) (...)
> But even though this be so, it [Sinai] was: 'the mountain which God desired for his abode' (Ps 68:17)

Here, Ps 68:17 is cited, but not vss. 18 or 19, the known 'mystical' verses. Ps 68:17 is neither found in PRK 12, nor in ExodR 28-29. It is not a verse that is frequently used in the interpretation of the Sinai pericope, even though, due to its position in the Psalm, one need not look far to find the connection. Taken on its own, the presence of v. 17 in this midrash may not be very conclusive. However, when taken together with the fact that v. 18 and v. 19 are *not* quoted, it could indicate two things: (1) The use of Ps 68:18-19 in this context was known to the composer of the midrash. He did not want to cite these verses; however, because Ps 68 was known to him in the general Sinai context, he decided to use v. 17, i.e. the immediately preceding verse. (2) Vss. 16-17 connect Mount Sinai with other mountains, particularly the mountains of Basan. Moreover, in the midrash, the fact is stressed that Sinai, apart from its special position, was 'in one class' with all other mountains. In this midrash, so it seems, the physical, terrestrial nature of Mount Sinai is stressed, as opposed to the interpretation of Sinai as the threshold of heaven; or even heaven itself.

2.5 'Twenty two thousand' angels or humans?

A second indication that the application of Ps 68:18-19 to the revelation at Sinai, and especially v. 18, was known to (but not used by) the composers of the *Mekhilta* can be found in the *Mekhilta Baḥodesh* 3:41-43. Another interpretation:

> *In the sight of all the people* (Exod 19:11). This teaches that if only one of them had been missing they would not have been worthy of receiving the Torah. R. Yose says: Even if there had been only two and twenty thousand (שני אלפים ושני רבבות) of them they would have been considered worthy of receiving the Torah. For it said: 'And when it rested, he said: 'Return, O Lord, unto the ten thousands (רבבות אלפי) of the families of Israel'' (Num 10:36).

By itself, this indication may seem at first sight to be even less obvious than the previous one. However, when construed together with PRK 12:22 (cited in 2.1) the connection becomes clear. According to PRK, Ps 68:18 teaches that the number of angels, or chariots of angels, descending upon Sinai, was twenty-two thousand (רבתים אלפי), and this is mentioned repeatedly in the sources.[33] The fact that the number twenty-two thousand was applied in the *Mekhilta* to humans and not to angels, could point towards a delib-

---

[33]See E.E. Urbach, *The Sages. Their Concepts and Beliefs*, Jerusalem 1987, Vol 1., 148; Vol 2., 746-748. The number twenty-two thousand is arrived at by a literal understanding of the phrase רבתים אלפי in Ps 68:18 רבתים with a dual suffix, is taken as two myriads, that is twenty thousand, and אלפי, the plural of אלף, thousand, is taken as another two thousand. The interpretation of שנאן as 'angels', as found here and elsewhere, is based on the fact that this is a *hapax* in the Bible, and thus open to different interpretations. In the Bible it probably means 'repetition'; so, combined with אלפי (thousands), it could mean 'two-thousand'. In different midrashic works, however, רבתים אלפי by itself is construed as two thousand, and שנאן is interpreted in several ways: as שנאים (that are friendly), שאנאן (quiet) and שנונים (sharply intended), all applied to angels (see e.g. ExodR 29). On Ps 68:18 and its angelic interpretation, see S.M. Olyan, *A Thousand Thousands Served Him. Exegesis and the Naming of Angels in Ancient Judaism,* Tübingen 1993, 50-51.

erate negative reading of a widely known midrash. The proof-text cited in *Mekhilta*, Num 10:36, renders 'twenty two thousand' in a similar way as Ps 68:18, i.e. רבבות . Even though the scene in Num 10:36 is also set at Sinai, it would not be surprising if this proof-text, explicitly referring to human beings, was adduced *instead of* Ps 68:18, traditionally interpreted as a reference to angels.

Admittedly, the number twenty-two thousand is known as the number of the male Levites at Sinai as stated in Num 3:39, and this verse probably underlies all the other interpretations; in PRK 12:22 however, the Levites are only mentioned in order to prove that the angels were the same in number; whereas in the *Mekhilta,* the number is explicitly construed as a certain number of Israelites: that is human beings.[34] This negative exegesis of the *Mekhilta* seems to contain a deliberate reaction to an assumed presence of angels (or chariots of angels) at Sinai; and thus an anti-mystical polemic.

2.6 *The Song of Songs and Sinai: mystical traces in Mekhilta Baḥodesh?*

Rabbi Yose, whose anti-mystical stance has been developed above (2.2), has lent his name also to the following midrash in *Mekhilta Baḥodesh* 3:115-119. The stance of this midrash is less clear.

> And Moses brought forth the people out of the camp to meet God (Exod 19:17). Said R. Yose: Judah used to expound: 'The Lord came from Sinai' (Deut 33:2). Do not read it thus, but: 'The Lord came to Sinai', to give the Torah to Israel. I, however, do not interpret it thus, but: 'The Lord came from Sinai', to receive Israel as a bridegroom comes forth to meet the bride.

This midrash could be treated as anti-mystical by virtue of the fact that it spiritualizes God's coming from/to Sinai: it is merely a metaphor to denote God's 'marriage' with Israel. However, the reference to a marriage might also point in the opposite direction. It is

---

[34]Urbach, *The Sages*, 148.

an intertextual link to the Song of Songs, which plays an important role in the mystical interpretation of Sinai.[35]

An important feature of this particular interpretation is that the Song of Songs was given at Sinai, and that the descriptions of the lover in the Song of Songs refer to God as he appeared on Mount Sinai. This explains why the Jews, according to Origen, were not allowed to teach the Song of Songs to the young: a rule similar to the one that was applied to parts of the book of Ezekiel and the Creation Story. [36] In this regard, another passage in this tractate in the *Mekhilta*, and a parallel in *Song of Songs Rabbah* (CantR), need to be cited. In the former text, the Song of Songs is used in a midrash on the Sinai account according to the book of Exodus, and in the latter text, a verse from Exodus is inserted into a midrash on a verse from Song of Songs.

> *And it came to pass on the third day, when it was morning* (Exod 19:16). This teaches that God had come there before Moses. Thus it is confirmed what has been said: 'While the king was still at his table, my spikenard sent forth its fragrance' (Cant 1:12).[37]

> *While the king was still at his table...* R. Aqiba says: While the King of Kings, the Holy One blessed be He, was still at his table in the firmament, already, 'And the glory of the Lord dwelt upon Mount Sinai' (Exod 24:16).[38]

Elswhere in *Mekhilta Baḥodesh*, the identification of the People of Israel with the beloved of the Song of Songs is also made. [39] The presence of the Song of Songs in the interpretation of the *matan Torah* in the *Mekhilta* should prevent us from concluding too quickly that *Mekhilta Baḥodesh* is anti-mystical as a whole, as e.g.

---

[35] See S. Lieberman, 'Mishnat Shir ha-Shirim' in G. Scholem, *Jewish Gnosticism*, 118-126.

[36] The reference is to Origen's *Commentary on the Song of Songs*, see Lieberman, 'Mishnat', 126; Halperin, *The Faces*, 26-27.

[37] Mek Baḥodesh 3:100-103

[38] CantR 1:12,1

[39] Mek Baḥodesh 2:58 (Cant 6:9); 3:125-130 (Cant 2:14).

Meeks would have it.[40] Some passages, such as the ones already cited, could even be construed as a confirmation of its mystical implications. Also the following interpretations cannot be called anti-mystical.[41] Another interpretation:

> They said: It is our wish to see the King. For hearing is not like seeing. God then said: Give them what they ask for: *In the third day the Lord will come down in the sight of all the people upon mount Sinai* (Exod 19:11).

> *For the third day the Lord will come down etc.* (Exod 19:11). This is one of the ten descents mentioned in the Torah.

> *And all the people saw the thunderings* (Exod 20:15). 'They saw what was visible and heard what was audible' – These are the words of R. Ishmael. R. Aqiba says: 'They saw and heard that which was visible. They saw the fiery word coming out of the mouth of the Almighty as it was struck upon the tablets, as it is said: 'The voice of the Lord hewed out flames of fire'' (Ps 29:7).

These three texts deal with the manner in which God presented himself at Sinai and the way in which the people perceived it. The interpretations that deal with the Song of Songs, which were cited before, are also concerned with this aspect of the events at Sinai. At the beginning of this article, a distinction was made between two elements of the mystical interpretation of the *matan Torah*: God's descent and Moses' ascent. We have called such interpretations 'mystical' which eliminate the borders between human and divine domains. It might seem now that God's descent to earth caused fewer problems in the *Mekhilta* than Moses' ascent into heaven. Perhaps it can be said that, apart from some exceptions, such as rabbi Yose's teaching about 'the Shekhinah that never descended to earth', descriptions of God's descent, or, rather, of visions of it, were not considered by the tannaitic authors of *Mekhilta Bahodesh* to be as dangerous as descriptions of human ascents into heaven.

---

[40]W.A. Meeks, *The Prophet-King. Moses Traditions and the Johannite Christology*, Leiden 1967, 205.

[41]Mek Baḥodesh 2:122, 3:35 and 9:1-5

This could be explained by the fact that precisely these mystical ascents are at stake in tannaitic stories about heavenly journeys such as the 'pardes' episodes. Even earlier sources (such as the *Exagoge* of Ezekiel the Dramatist which has already been mentioned)[42] relate Moses' ascent into heaven, on which occasion he is even allowed to sit upon God's throne. Such divinization of a human being was severely rejected in some rabbinic sources, where it is treated as the heresy of 'two powers in heaven'.[43] It is, therefore, likely that this was also the main concern in *Mekhilta Baḥodesh.*

3. Conclusions

It is now possible to formulate some conclusions about the *Mekhilta*'s rendering of the events on Mount Sinai. The fact that Ezek 1 and Ps 68:18-19 are not cited, and even avoided, in *Mekhilta Baḥodesh* is significant. It has already been shown that men's, and in particular Moses' ascent, seemed to be more problematic than God's descent. Descriptions of God's descent, in terms that allude to the Song of Songs, can be found. That not only Ps 68:19, but also Ps 68:18 and Ezek 1, which refer more to the divine than to the human side of the 'crossing of the domains', are avoided could be explained by the fact that the specific features described in these texts – the angels, the chariots etc... – were also used in stories about the mystical heavenly journeys of human beings, traces of which can already be found in tannaitic and even earlier sources.

Rabbi Yose is a special case. In his dicta in *Mekhilta Baḥodesh* and in the parallel *baraita* in BTSuk, not only the description of Moses' (or any human's) ascent into heaven is unacceptable, but also the fact that God descended to the earthly domain. The fact that Rabbi Aqiba would be his mystical opponent, as Chernus

---

[42]See note 5.

[43]See A.F. Segal, *Two Powers in Heaven; Early Rabbinic Reports about Christianity and Gnosticism*, Leiden 1977. In the Mekhilta, the danger of saying that there are שתי רשויות (two powers) is mentioned in *Shirata* 4:26 and *Baḥodesh* 5:27.

claims, is not obvious: The midrash of the 'mattress', which is considered mystical by Chernus, has, rather, been shown to involve a strict separation of the domains.

To conclude: this survey of *Mekhilta Baḥodesh* offers enough indications for the presence of a deliberate reaction to a known exegesis of the Sinai pericope. Characteristic for such exegesis, as is found in PRK 12 and ExodR 28-29, is the intertextual reading of Exod 19-20, Ezek 1 and Ps 68:18-19. The latter texts are avoided in *Mekhilta Baḥodesh*. The fact that very specific scriptural texts are banned is very indicative of the role of midrash in the generation of ideas. Even though other texts, e.g. from Song of Songs, might give rise to similar associations, only Ezek 1 and Ps 68:18-19 were known to give rise to unacceptable mystical speculations, when combined with the pericope of the Revelation at Sinai. This is an example of how midrash, that is the exegesis of specific scriptural verses, could be at the root of the development of ideas. Of course we know from Mishnah, Tosefta and *beraitot* that mystical ideas were a highly contentious issue in tannaitic times. However, these sources do not generally refer to specific verses from Scripture. Midrash, however, does do so, and therefore the study of tannaitic midrash demonstrates more clearly how the interpretation and combination of texts could generate mystical speculations.

JERUSALEM AND THE TEMPLE IN THE TANNAITIC LITERATURE OF THE FIRST GENERATION AFTER THE DESTRUCTION OF THE TEMPLE

Shmuel Safrai

Introduction

J erusalem and the Temple are mentioned frequently in talmudic literature as an interchangeable entity. A list of ten 'miracles that happened to our fathers in the Temple' includes among them 'things that happened in Jerusalem'.[1] Elsewhere the Mishnah discusses the sounding of the Shofar in 'the Temple', but speaks only about Jerusalem.[2] One can find expansive descriptions of the heavenly Temple and discover that they actually describe the heavenly Jerusalem.[3]

Both Jerusalem and the Temple are mentioned numerous times in talmudic literature. Traditions about Jerusalem of the past and traditions about hopes for the future fill talmudic literature. Many traditions are devoted to halakhot pertaining to the Temple and Jerusalem; many details are reported regarding life in that city and the Temple. Various legendary descriptions stress the central role of Jerusalem and the Temple in the life of the people and in its thoughts and aspirations. Every generation of Tannaim and Amoraim passed on traditions and produced new ideas relating to

---

[1] Abot 5:5; cf. ARN A, Ch. 35; ARN B, Ch. 39.

[2] MRH 4:1. Cf. the commentary of Maimonides *ad loc*. See also the comment of Ch. Albeck in his 'Additional Notes and Commentary', in: Ch. Albeck, *Shishah sidre Mishnah; Seder Moed* (Hebr.), Jerusalem/Tel Aviv 1958, 489-490.

[3] See in particular GenR on Genesis 28, 17 (edn Ch. Albeck), Jerusalem 1967, 136-137. See also S. Safrai, 'The Heavenly Jerusalem', *Ariel* 23 (1969) 11-15.

Jerusalem. They report traditions about Sages who went on pilgrimage to Jerusalem and what happened to them there. Jerusalem and the Temple are mentioned in every prayer for weekdays, Sabbaths and festivals, and on various occasions, such as at the Grace after Meals and in the Blessing for Mourners. There is virtually no event for which the accompanying blessings do not mention Jerusalem.

It is not always possible to determine precisely when and how the references to the Temple and Jerusalem were composed. However, there are specific chapters in the Mishnah for which the time of composition may be determined fairly accurately. One may also establish what sort of reality these chapters reflect. In certain cases, it is even possible to ascertain who actually composed them. In this article, we will systematically investigate these chapters and their tradents in order to discover the motifs underlying their transmission.

Organization of the Material

Some chapters in the Mishnah are organized along numerical divisions. The opening line determines the structure of the whole chapter. Thus, for example: 'There are two exits on the Sabbath which are four' (MShab 1:1); 'A woman may be wed in three ways' (MQid 1:1); 'Three times a year the Priests raise their hands four times [in one day]' (MTaan 4:1).

Other chapters are not arranged numerically, but deal clearly with definite actions: 'From what time do we read Shema in the evening?' (MBer 1:1); 'The morning prayer until noon' (MBer 4:1); and the like.

There is a third kind of chapter in the Mishnah which is not organized as a group of related *halakhot*, but rather as a group of *stories*. These stories describe life in the Temple and the City of Jerusalem. MBik Chapter 3 relates the entire process of presenting the first fruits, from setting them aside until putting them down next to the altar. MPes Chapter 5 describes in detail how the Paschal lamb was sacrificed in the Temple courts. The same narrative phenomenon occurs in MSuk. MSuk 1-2 provides all the halakhot of the Sukkah and MSuk 3 mentions the laws pertaining to the four species. In Msuk 4 the Mishnah deals again with the order of the four species, but specifically in describing how relevant ceremonies were observed in the Temple. MSuk 5 describes the water drawing celebrations on the nights of the Festival.

Some descriptive passages do not encompass entire chapters, but appear only in one or two mishnayot that describe a particular event. For example MSot 7:7-8 describes how the High Priest read the Torah on the Day of Atonement and how the Torah was read by the king.

There are some tractates in which all or most of the tractate is descriptive, such as all of the tractate Tamid and the first seven chapters of Yoma. Admittedly they also contain halakhot, but they are composed primarily of descriptions of daily life in the Temple. Similarly, tractate Middot has a good deal of non-halakhic descriptions of life in the Temple. To a lesser degree, this also is true of tractate Sheqalim.

Mishnah Tractate Yoma

Tractate Yoma contains eight chapters. The eighth chapter is written and edited in the form of a standard chapter of the Mishnah, setting out the halakhot of the Day of Atonement and concluding with an aggadic passage, as is commonly the case at the end of tractates or groups of halakhot within the Mishnah. The first seven chapters of the tractate contain a great number of halakhot about the service of the High Priest in the Temple on the Day of Atonement. These halakhot are written in the form of describing what took place in the Temple. Thus, the Mishnah opens with a description of the preparation of the High Priest for that great day. It describes how he separated himself from normal everyday life for seven days before the Day of Atonement and where he spent that week; how he was prepared to perform the service; how he was kept occupied during the night that preceded the Day of Atonement, since he was not allowed to fall asleep during the night before he performed the sacred service. The descriptions of the Mishnah follow him throughout the day until the conclusion

of the service, 'And they would escort him to his home and he
would make a holiday for his friends when he came out safely
from the sanctuary' (MYoma 7:4). The entire description depicts
the reality of the Temple in the last generation of its existence.
MYoma 2:1-2 reports that the Priests would draw lots to see
which one would have the honour of cleaning the altar of ashes in
the morning. This was a privilege for which they had not previously drawn lots, but after the competition to participate in this
cultic action engendered episodes of violence it was determined
that a lottery would be the fairest way to determine who would
enjoy this honour. When a violent incident took place surrounding this task, it was Rabbi Ṣadoq who chastised the participants.[4]
Rabbi Ṣadoq was active at the end of the Second Temple period
as well as just after the destruction of the Temple and was a contemporary of Rabban Gamaliel of Yabneh.[5] Obviously such a tradition helps us in dating the events.

Mishnah Tractate Tamid

The tractate that stands out in its descriptive character is that of
Tamid, which describes the daily routine of the Temple. It starts
with the description of the night watch; sleeping arrangements of
the Priests; the elder Priests and the Priests in training; what a
Priest would do if he experienced a nocturnal emission; how the
Priests were awakened; the procedure of offering the daily sacrifice; the gathering of the Priests to read the Shema and recite
prayers, until the conclusion of the ceremony with the recitation
of the Psalm for the particular day of the week. Of course, this
tractate contains halakhot, some of which do not appear elsewhere, but the reader notices immediately that these chapters do

---

[4] 'Rabbi Ṣadoq came and stood on the steps of the Hall [and] said to them:
Hear me my brothers of the House of Israel'. TYoma 1:12 and SifreNum (end
of Masʿê).
[5] TSanh 8:1 *et al.*

not form primarily a compilation of halakhot, but rather a lively description of the activities of Priests and Levites in the Temple.

Several scholars in recent generations have pointed out the unique character of the tractates which concern Temple issues. They have established their antiquity and demonstrated how they were preserved as entire blocks of text in the Mishnah. L. Ginzberg pointed out the unique character of Tamid[6] and J.N. Epstein that of the other tractates.[7] Our aim here is to try and ascertain the precise period from which the descriptive chapters stem. Although the redaction of the Mishnah probably took place in the early 3rd century CE, it can be demonstrated that these descriptive chapters of the Mishnah reflect the reality of Temple life during the last generation – even the very last years – of the Second Temple. We wish to attempt to prove that they were composed by Tannaim who witnessed the Temple in operation and survived the period of its destruction. By recalling the reality of the Temple and Jerusalem, they strove to preserve these precious traditions, as is stated in TEduy 1:1: 'When the Sages gathered in the vineyard at Yabneh, they said: there will be a time when a man will seek some words of Torah, but he will be unable to locate them, some words of the scribes and be unable to locate them ... they said: let us start from Hillel and Shammai'. They not only collected the teachings of Hillel and Shammai but also preserved for posterity a description of the reality of Temple and City, a reality that ceased to exist when the Temple was burned and Jerusalem destroyed.

Tractate Tamid describes the entire daily routine of the Temple, as opposed to chapters in other tractates that describe only one specific ceremony, such as the bringing of first fruits, the slaughter of the Paschal lamb or the bringing of the *Omer*. Both Talmuds state that the mishnaic tractate of Tamid was the teaching of Rabbi Simeon of Miṣpah. Thus, it is stated in the name of Rabbi

---

[6]L. Ginzberg, 'Tamid, The Oldest Treatise of the Mishnah', *Journal of Jewish Law and Philosophy* I (1919) 33-44, 197-209, 265-295.

[7]J.N. Epstein, *Introduction to Tannaitic Literature* (Hebr.), Jerusalem 1957, 25-58.

Yoḥanan: 'Tamid is the way of Rabbi Simeon of Miṣpah' (PT Yoma 2:3,39d). And in the name of Rabbi Huna it is stated: 'Whatever is taught in Tamid [is the teaching of] Rabbi Simeon of Miṣpah' (BT Yoma 14b). This testimony is endorsed by TYoma 1:13. The Tosefta quotes the Mishnah (MYoma 2:3), that describes the manner in which the second lots were drawn for the daily sacrifice. Yoma as a whole deals of course with the special service of the Day of Atonement, but first it prescribes the normal procedure of the daily sacrifice. The mishnah in Yoma is a citation from MTam.[8] In the same mishnah in Yoma and in MTam 3:1 we read: 'The appointed [Priest] says to them: Come draw lots to see who will slaughter, etc.' On this passage the Tosefta adds: 'These are the words of Rabbi Simeon of Miṣpah'. An even more explicit testimony may be found regarding MTam 4:1. The Mishnah determines where the daily sacrifice was to be slaughtered: 'The morning [sacrifice] was slaughtered in the northwestern corner ... the evening [sacrifice] was slaughtered in the northeastern corner ... He came to the northeastern corner and tossed to the north [and] east; to the southwestern [corner] and tossed to the south [and] west'. And in TZeb 6:13: 'Rabbi Simeon of Miṣpah taught in Tamid: He came to the northeastern corner, he tossed to the north [and] east; western he tossed to the west, southwestern tossed to the south'.[9]

Rabbi Simeon of Miṣpah lived during the time of the Second Temple as we may conclude from an explicit reference in MPeah 2:6 'It happened that Rabbi Simeon of Miṣpah planted [his field and came] before Rabban Gamaliel, and they went to the Chamber of Hewn Stone and asked.[10] Naḥum the Scribe said:[11] I re-

---

[8]J.N. Epstein, *Introduction to Tannaitic Literature*, 29.

[9]See D. Pardo, ספר חסדי דוד , in his commentary on TZeb, Jerusalem 1971 (repr.), 129.

[10]The Chamber of Hewn Stone was the seat of the Great Sanhedrin. His question regarded the laws of the corner of a field to be left for the poor (the so-called Peah).

[11]That is the version found in manuscripts of the Mishnah, including Genizah fragments and the quotation from the Mishnah in BT Naz 56b, and in Tan Bemidbar §22 (edn Buber §27 (11a). Ginzberg (above, 139 n.6) suggests that

ceived from Rabbi Measha, who received from his father, who received from the pairs, who received from the prophets, a halakhah from Moses at Sinai ...'.

We cannot presume that the Rabban Gamaliel in this mishnah is Rabban Gamaliel the Elder since he appears with Rabbi Simeon of Miṣpah before the Sanhedrin as a petitioner with a question to be resolved. Rabban Gamaliel the Elder was a member of the Sanhedrin, either as its head or as a distinguished member (Acts 5:34). The Rabban Gamaliel in this mishnah reached adulthood during the time of the Temple,[12] and as a property owner leased his field to Rabbi Simeon of Miṣpah, or hired him as a worker. Rabbi Simeon of Miṣpah survived after the destruction of the Temple as we know from the fact that in all the parallel passages he is referred to as 'Rabbi', a title that was used only after the destruction of the Temple. Hence Rabbi Simeon was a contemporary of Rabban Gamaliel of Yabneh, or a younger member of the same generation. Both of them were adults in the last years that the Second Temple stood and were active in the period after its destruction.

Mishnah Tractate Middot

We find a similar case in Mishnah tractate Middot, which is devoted entirely to a description of the structure of the Temple and its courts. The tractate, according to the testimony of both Talmuds, reflects the teaching of Rabbi Eliezer ben Jacob. That is the opinion of Rabbi Abahu in the Palestinian Talmud and of Rab Huna in the Babylonian Talmud.[13] These testimonies may be en-

---

the aforementioned Nahum was a scholar from the end of the Temple Period and relies on the text in Ms Munich that reads Nahum the Mede. However Ms Munich does not read the Mede, but בבלי – the Babylonian, no doubt a copyist's error for לבלר – the scribe.

[12] He transmits an applied halakha that was practiced by his grandfather Rabban Gamaliel the Elder in Temple times, who permitted the widows of those killed in Tel Arza near Jerusalem to remarry (MYeb 16:7).

[13] PT Yoma 2:3,39d; BT Yoma 16a.

dorsed by internal testimony within the tractate. MMid 2:5 describes in detail the functions of the four chambers in the corners of the Women's Court. The Mishnah tells about three of them and regarding the fourth it says: 'The southwestern — Rabbi Eliezer ben Jacob said: I forgot for what it was used'. Interpreters of the Mishnah, both ancient and modern, commented correctly that everything up to that passage was the teaching of Rabbi Eliezer ben Jacob, but that regarding this matter he had to admit 'I forgot'. To this a later Tanna added the opinion of Abba Shaul regarding its use. The later Tanna, who edited the mishnah, added 'Rabbi Eliezer ben Jacob said', making it parallel to the quote from Abba Shaul. This form appears again in MMid 5:4 regarding the use of the Chamber of Wood: 'The Chamber of Wood, Rabbi Eliezer ben Jacob said: I forgot for what it was used. Abba Shaul said: the Chamber of the High Priest'. In MMid 1:2 the Mishnah reports how 'the chief [of the guard] of the Temple Mount' would make the rounds of every watch at night to check if the guards were sleeping and if he found one sleeping he 'had the right to burn his garment'. To this Rabbi Eliezer ben Jacob adds: 'Once they found my mother's brother sleeping and set fire to his garment'. Eliezer ben Jacob's uncle was a Priest or Levite serving in the Temple.[14] This is further evidence that Rabbi Eliezer ben Jacob lived during the generation of the destruction and relates various testimonies to Temple reality elsewhere in the Mishnah and in rabbinic literature.[15] One may presume that a significant part of the tractate Middot is based on literary traditions and various lists, but as we can see in the teachings of Rabbi Eliezer ben Jacob, at least part of what he said is based upon his own memories. It is not unlikely that Rabbi Eliezer ben Jacob, whose maternal uncle was a Priest or a Levite, was a Priest or Levite himself,

---

[14]Historians of the tannaitic period have concluded from this passage that he was a Priest, however the night watchmen in the Temple were primarily Levites and not Priests. The Priests kept watch over three sites and the Levites over twenty-one (MTam 1:1). From this we may presume that Rabbi Eliezer ben Jacob was a Levite.

[15]MSheq 6:3; MMen 5:6; BT Yoma 69b; BT Suk 54a et al.

since we know that during Temple times priestly and levitical families practised endogamy to a degree.

Mishnah Tractate Sheqalim

Our next tractate is Sheqalim, which deals with Temple tax. The form of this tractate is like that of most other tractates in the Mishnah. It provides the halakhot regarding the half-sheqel donation and the regulations of the Temple and the city. However, throughout the tractate one finds mishnayot that are descriptive in character, detailing life in the Temple and Jerusalem, rather than prescriptive. For example MSheq 8:4 tells what was done with a curtain that became ritually impure: how it was spread 'on the roof of a balcony for the people to admire its beautiful workmanship'. Among the many details from Temple life, Msheq 5:1 provides a list: 'These were the officers of the Temple'. Commentators of the Mishnah, since talmudic times, have long debated the meaning of this title. Does the Mishnah here mean that pious and worthy individuals should always be appointed,[16] or were all the appointees in the Temple throughout the generations called by these names?[17] It is more likely that the second interpretation, which may be found in PT 5:1,48c is the correct one:[18] 'Whoever was in that generation reported what took place in his generation'. As we shall see later, Josephus and tannaitic sources prove conclusively that the list reflects the officials appointed in the last generation of the Temple period. The supplementary list found in

---

[16]Thus in the Palestinian Talmud at the beginning of the chapter (PT Sheq 5:1,48c). Many commentators on the Mishnah have followed this interpretation.

[17]Thus Ch. Albeck in his commentary on the Mishnah. This interpretation may also be found in the Talmud commentary of Rabbenu Meshullam on Sheqalim, 55, and other mediaeval commentators, and in the commentary of Obadiah of Bertinoro who quotes his teachers on this point. Cf. *Tosafot Yom Tob, ad loc.*

[18]This is the understanding of J.N. Epstein, *Introduction to Tannaitic Literature*, 25.

TSheq 2:14, which provides the minor officials, is also from the same time. We do not have sources whereby we can prove precisely when all fifteen officials mentioned in the Mishnah and Tosefta lived, but we can demonstrate that at least some of them lived in the last generation of the Second Temple period.

The list of officials concludes with 'Eleazar over hangings and Pinḥas in charge of dressing the Priests'.[19] There was an official who was responsible for the treasury and the Temple curtains named Eleazar (in the time of Hyrcanus II and Crassus and the war against the Parthians in 53 BCE), but Eleazar was a most common name in the priestly circles of the last generations of the Second Temple, and it is difficult to draw conclusions from this fact. Josephus mentions this Pinḥas in *The Jewish War* 6:390: 'The guardian of the Temple treasury, Pinḥas, was also captured [by the Romans], who showed them the tunics of the Priests and their girdles and much purple cloth and satin for making curtains and also much cinnamon and cassia and other spices which they used to mix and offer as incense to the Lord every day, were delivered up by him and other valuables and many ornaments for holy things'. Thus we may conclude that the Pinḥas referred to in the Mishnah was the last official with this appointment in the period before the destruction of the Temple.

Our mishnah also lists: 'Gabini the public crier', which was interpreted in the Palestinian Talmud as he 'who would cry out in the Temple. What did he say? The Priests to their service and the Levites to the podium and Israel to its station'.[20] In both Talmuds the continuation tells how 'Agrippas heard his voice eight parasangs away and gave him many gifts'. MTam 3:8 tells about various voices that were heard all the way to Jericho and among them 'the voice of Gabini the public crier'.[21] Agrippas, the king men-

---

[19] In the accepted versions of the Mishnah the text says על המלבוש – on the vestments, but the version of the Mishnah in the Palestinian Talmud and in many manuscripts says: פנחס המלביש – Pinḥas in charge of dressing the Priests. That is also the text of all versions of MMid 1:4.

[20] Cf. a *baraita* in BT Yoma 20b.

[21] This legend may be found in expanded form in PT Suk 5:3,55b and in Eccl Zutta 9:18 (edn Buber, Vilna 1925, 76a).

tioned here, is no doubt Agrippas II who ruled over other parts of the Land of Israel, but not over Jerusalem. Nevertheless the Temple was under his supervision. As we shall see below, the King Agrippas mentioned several times in tannaitic literature in reference to the Temple is Agrippas II.

The list of officials in the Tosefta opens with 'Yoḥanan ben Gudgada on closing the gates'.[22] Rabbi Yoḥanan ben Gudgada, a tannaitic sage quoted several times in tannaitic literature,[23] was a contemporary of Rabbi Yehoshua ben Ḥananyah, who served with him as a Levite in the Temple.[24]

Epstein demonstrates that MSheq 6 is the teaching of Abba Yose ben Ḥanin since he taught that there were thirteen gates to the Temple and thirteen corresponding genuflections.[25] That is also the opinion of Abba Yose ben Ḥanin in MMid 2:6. The Palestinian Talmud on our mishnah says: 'It is the mishnah of Abba Yose ben Ḥanin (PT Sheq 2:6,49d). The entire chapter is built around the principle of 'thirteen things' that were in the Temple.

Abba Yose ben Ḥanin lived at the end of the Second Temple period and was a contemporary of Abba Shaul ben Batnit. A poetic diatribe against the High Priestly families was recorded in their name.[26] Abba Shaul ben Batnit was a colleague of Rabbi Eliezer ben Ṣadoq, both of whom sold oil in Jerusalem.[27] Rabbi Eliezer ben Ṣadoq also lived in and was active in the Yabneh period after the destruction of the Temple and passed on various

---

[22]Commentators have struggled to resolve the contradiction between this tradition and the words of the Mishnah: 'Ben Gever on closing the gates'. A number of explanations have been offered. The most likely is that Ben Gever who is mentioned in the Mishnah was responsible for the gates of the Sanctuary itself (היכל) and Yoḥanan ben Gudgada, who was a Levite as we shall see below, was responsible for the outer gates, since a Levite would not have been permitted to approach the Sanctuary gates. Cf. Epstein, *Introduction to Tannaitic Literature*, 27.

[23]MGit 5:5; TTer 1:1 *et al.*

[24]SifreNum §116, 132.

[25]J.N. Epstein, *Introduction to Tannaitic Literature*, 26 and 339.

[26]TMen 13:21; BT Pes 57a.

[27]PT Beṣah 3:9,62b.

traditions from that time.[28] We do not have explicit evidence regarding Abba Yose ben Ḥanin from the period immediately after
the destruction of the Temple, but it is likely that he too was active then, since we find him disputing with sages from the Yabneh generation[29] and even transmitting a legend in the name of
Samuel the Small, one of the sages of Yabneh.[30]

There is further evidence that MSheq 6 describes the Temple
reality in the last generation of the Temple. MSheq 6:1 relates
'that the house of Rabban Gamaliel and the house of Rabbi Ḥananyah the Deputy High Priest would bow down fourteen times,
and which was the extra [in addition to the accepted thirteen]?
Opposite the Wood Store — since they had a tradition from their
ancestors that the Ark [of the Covenant] was hidden there'. 'Of
the house of Rabban Gamaliel' clearly means from the time of
Rabban Gamaliel and afterwards, which is the last generation of
the Second Temple period. But this is even clearer from the case
of Rabbi Ḥananyah the Deputy High Priest. We invariably find
the title 'Rabbi' added to the name of Ḥananyah the Deputy High
Priest — which in itself indicates that he also lived after the destruction of the Temple. Even more edifying is his teaching that
one may not immerse oneself on the Ninth of Ab 'because the
House of our God deserves missing one immersion a year'.[31] This
of course means that as a sign of mourning over the destruction of
the Temple, one should not immerse oneself on the Ninth of Ab.

In summary: Mishnah Sheqalim Chapter 6, and perhaps even
the preceding chapter which describes Temple life and its officials, is the teaching of Abba Yose ben Ḥanin. The chapter has
one late addition by Ben Azzai, a younger member of the generation of Yabneh, stating that the Temple seals were in Aramaic,
but the entire description of daily life in the Temple in Chapter 5
is ancient, as we have seen, and should be attributed to the same
Tanna as Chapter 6.

[28]TSanh 8:1 *et al.*
[29]SifreNum §8, 15.
[30]Derekh Ereṣ Zutta (end).
[31]BT Taanit 13a; PT Beṣah 2:2,61b.

King Agrippas in Tannaitic Literature

The last issue we shall discuss is the identification of the King Agrippas mentioned in a number of mishnayot and other tannaitic traditions in relation to the Temple.[32] As is well known, Agrippas I, Herod's grandson, reigned between 37 and 41 CE over part of the Land of Israel and between 41 and 44 over the entire country. His son Agrippas II reigned from 50 to about 100 CE. According to Josephus, when Agrippas I was in Jerusalem, he observed commandments, even practised ritual purity and was loyal to the Temple.[33] Agrippas II did not rule over Jerusalem, but the Roman authorities entrusted him with responsibility over the Temple.[34]

Both places in the Mishnah mentioning Agrippas the King stress the king's noble behaviour towards the Temple. In MBik 3:4, which describes the bringing of the first fruits to the Temple it says: 'Even Agrippas the King takes the basket on his shoulder and enters until he reaches the Court'. This is clearly a gesture of respect for the Temple, but we have no way to discern to which of the two kings the name Agrippas refers. In MSot 7:7-8 there is a detailed description of the assembly that was held at the end of the Sabbatical year, the so-called *haqhēl*. In this ceremony the High Priest or the King read several chapters from Deuteronomy. The second part of MSot 7:8 says: 'The King stood and received [the Torah scroll] and read and sat down. Agrippas the King stood and received and read standing, and the sages praised him and when he reached the passage 'You may not put a foreigner over you' (Deut 17:15) his eyes welled up with tears. They said to him "Fear not Agrippas, you are our brother, you are our brother, you are our brother"'.

---

[32]MBik 3:4 and parallel passages, MSot 7:8; TPes 4:15 (edn Lieberman, 94-95) and parallel passages; BT Pes 107b; PT Sheq 5:1,48d and parallel pasages; LevR 3:5 (edn Margulies, 66-67) and parallel passages.

[33]Antiquities, XIX:331.

[34]Antiquities XX:222.

Some hundred years ago David Hoffmann, in his book *Die Erste Mischna,* identified the Agrippas of this mishnah as Agrippas
I, who was faithful to the Torah of Moses and to the Jewish people.[35] For some reason, this opinion has been widely accepted in
historical research to this day. On the other hand, some outstanding scholars have pointed out that the tradition could only refer to
Agrippas II.[36] We shall briefly repeat their arguments with a few
additions. It appears that in the fall of 42 CE, when the Sabbatical
year ended, Agrippas I was in Rome.[37] TBik 7:16 on the mishnah
just cited above states: 'On account of this Rabbi Nathan said:
Israel was obliged to be decimated because they flattered King
Agrippas'. The parallel passage in BT Sot 41b even adds 'at that
time'. Such a statement can only refer to Agrippas II who participated in the War of Destruction. There would be no reason to
condemn flattery towards Agrippas I. After all, he had a perfectly
good Jewish lineage, was devoted to Jewish affairs in Jerusalem
and the Temple and clearly deserved to be hailed with the expression 'you are our brother'. On the other hand, Rabbi Nathan's argument regarding Agrippas II would be quite understandable.
Moreover, shortly after the incident of *haqhēl*, war broke out, and
it would have been reasonable to link the destruction that fell
upon Israel with flattery towards a king who supported the enemies of Israel. The Tosefta in this passage adds: 'On the very
same day Rabbi Tarfon saw a cripple standing and sounding the
trumpet'. Rabbi Tarfon was a young boy when the Temple was
destroyed.[38] If we presume that he refers to the same incident of

---

[35]D.Z. Hoffmann, *Die Erste Mischna und die Controversen der Tannaim,*
Berlin 1882, 15-20.

[36]For a list of references to criticism of Hoffmann's interpretation, see S.
Safrai, *Pilgrimage at the Time of the Second Temple* (Hebr.), Tel Aviv 1965,
214, notes 209-210.

[37]See A. Büchler, *Die Priester und den Cultus im letzten Jahrzehnt der
Jerusalemischen Temple,* Vienna 1895, 9-16. Cf. parallel passages to this
mishnah in the first chapter of SifreNum §75 (p. 70); and in the Palestinian
Talmud: PT Yoma 1:1,38d; PT Meg 1:12,72b; PT Hor 3:15,47d.

[38]He belonged to the second generation of Yabneh sages and according to
the Palestinian tradition was one of the ten martyrs executed during the suppression of the Bar Kokhba Revolt (LamR Ch. 2, edn Berlin 1938, 375 *et al.*).

haqhēl ceremony, we may conclude that the Agrippas in the incident is Agrippas II.[39] Although Agrippas I was more sympathetic to Pharisaic Judaism than his son, this does not mean that every act of respect towards the Temple should be assigned to him and that his son Agrippas II could not have treated the Temple with honour. Roman rulers in general behaved respectfully towards the Temple, and one should keep in mind that Agrippas II was responsible for the Temple and appointed and deposed High Priests. It is therefore perfectly reasonable to assume that Agrippas II would have shown respect for the Temple in a public ceremony attended by great numbers of people, even if only as an outward gesture.

The tradition in TPes 4:15 reports that Agrippas the King wanted to know how many groups offered the Passover sacrifice and demanded that the Priests set aside one kidney from every offering.[40] This tradition no doubt refers to Agrippas II since Josephus tells about Gallus, the Procurator of Syria during the Great War, who wanted to know how many Jews there were and demanded that the Priest count the number of people making sacrifices.[41] It is possible that the two stories are one: Gallus demanded the census from Agrippas and Agrippas from the Priests. Josephus reports Gallus' request while the Talmud reports Agrippas' orders. But even if that is not the case, both stories reflect events from the last years of the Second Temple, and the Agrippas referred to here is Agrippas II.

Our conclusion that the *haqhēl* ceremony described in the Mishnah is the one in which Agrippas II took part, leads us to conclude that it describes the last observance of *haqhēl* before the

---

Regarding Rabbi Tarfon's memories of the Second Temple, see BT Qid 71a *et al.*

[39]Rabbi Tarfon may possibly be referring to the practice that during *haqhēl* even a blemished Priest, who could not normally take part in the Temple service, was allowed to sound the trumpet. However, from the expression 'on the same day' it appears that he was talking about the same incident or that mentioned above.

[40]See parallel passages in BT Pes 74b; LamR Ch. 1 (edn Buber, 45).

[41]The Jewish War 6:423.

destruction of the Second Temple, i.e. in 63 CE. The year 70, in which the Temple was destroyed, was also a Sabbatical year, but no ceremony was observed that year. *Haqhēl* could have been observed only during the Sukkot festival following the end of the Sabbatical year, i.e. in Tishri, but the Temple had already been destroyed in the month of Ab.

There is another tradition regarding Agrippas, but unrelated to the Temple. No doubt this tradition refers to Agrippas II as well. In Midrash Tanḥuma, Agrippas the King asks Rabbi Eliezer why the important commandment of circumcision is not mentioned in the Ten Commandments.[42] Rabbi Eliezer is Rabbi Eliezer ben Hyrcanus, a contemporary of Agrippas II. He was born before the destruction of the Second Temple and even studied under Rabban Yoḥanan ben Zakkai in Jerusalem. He survived the destruction and lived afterwards a rather long time. The rest of the references to Agrippas the King in talmudic literature, whether in relation to the Temple or not, provide no definitive clue as to which Agrippas they refer.

Summary and Conclusion

Our purpose in this article has been to stress two issues in particular:

1. The testimonies regarding Jerusalem and the Temple in the last generation of the Second Temple period were transmitted by sages who lived and flourished after the destruction of the Temple as well.

2. In tannaitic literature, there are not only individual testimonies on particular practices or ceremonies from Temple times, but also entire chapters and even tractates that describe the daily service in the Temple on ordinary weekdays, on the Day of Atonement and during the Sukkot festival. One tractate – Middot – was devoted

---

[42]Tan Lekh Lekha, §20. A different version of this legend appears in Aggadat Bereshit, §17 (edn Buber, 36). Cf. Buber's note *ad loc.*

to a description of the structure of the Temple and the practices related to it.

It is not easy to determine whether sages as Rabbi Simeon of Mişpah, Rabbi Eliezer ben Jacob and Abba Yose ben Ḥanin set down their teachings on their own initiative to preserve the memory of Temple and Jerusalem life that had been tragically interrupted, or whether it was done on the initiative of the leaders of the Yabneh generation in order to reconstruct and preserve the Oral Law. The last possibility might be reflected in TEduy 1:1, as we saw in our discussion above. As we have also seen above, the descriptions that have been preserved in the Mishnah are realistic, without miraculous stories, and generally without exaggerations. We find here accounts based on recollections and on lists (as in the case of tractate Tamid) without any supernatural descriptions. Admittedly, the case of MTam 3:8 about the acts in the Temple which could be heard as far as Jericho, is an exception to this rule.[43] The Mishnah goes on to count seven more miraculous phenomena connected to Temple practice, However, this entire section is an addition based on *beraitot* and *amoraic* sayings and is not an integral part of the Mishnah.[44]

The concluding passage in MTam says: 'This is the order of the daily sacrifice in the service of the house of our God, May it be His will to rebuild it speedily in our days, amen'.[45] This closing passage may provide an explanation for the editing of the tractate — to provide information on how to act when the Temple will be rebuilt in the near future. However, this concluding sentence was also added from a *baraita*, as we read in BT Sanh 49b: 'As we taught about it this is the order of the daily sacrifice etc.', i.e. a

---

[43]See above, 144.

[44]See J. Schwartz, 'Mishnah Tamid and Jericho', in: Z. Safrai, Y. Friedman & J. Schwartz (eds), *Hikrei Eretz* (Hebr.), Ramat Gan 1997, 247-257.

[45]The subsequent mishnah reports which chapter of Psalms was recited every day in the Temple: 'The Psalm that the Levites recited in the Temple — on Sunday they would say etc.'. However that is a late addition taken from a *baraita* in BT RH 31a: 'Rabbi Yehudah said in the name of Rabbi Aqiba: On Sunday what would they say etc.'.

baraita appended to the Mishnah. The Palestinian Talmud says:[46] 'Rabbi Ḥiyya bar Ada taught: This is the order of the daily sacrifice in the service of the House of our God both on weekdays and on the Sabbath'. This then was a *baraita* of Rabbi Ḥiyya bar Ada. One may presume that Simeon of Miṣpah and the other sages who set down elements of Jerusalem and Temple life also regarded what they did as a basis for practice when they would return to Jerusalem, but that was not their primary purpose. First and foremost they wished to preserve for perpetuity the description of Temple and Jerusalem life.

---

[46]PT RH 1:10,57c; PT Meg 2:7,73c.

'THEY DIRECT THEIR HEART TO JERUSALEM'
REFERENCES TO JERUSALEM AND TEMPLE IN MISHNAH AND TOSEFTA BERAKHOT

Alberdina Houtman

1. Introduction

In the discussion about Sanctity of Place in Judaism, the unique position of the Temple is unchallenged; the sanctity of this building and surrounding courts being so great that it emanates to the whole City of Jerusalem. It is to be expected that this special status of Jerusalem and Temple will be reflected in tannaitic literature just as it is in the Hebrew Bible.[1] Elsewhere in this book Shmuel Safrai expounds upon the status of Jerusalem and Temple in the literature of the Tannaim in general.[2] The present paper focuses upon this status in one specific tractate of Mishnah and Tosefta, namely tractate Berakhot.

A few years ago, while working on my dissertation about the relationship between Mishnah and Tosefta, I chanced upon an odd phenomenon in Mishnah and Tosefta Berakhot. It appeared that while in Tosefta Berakhot the word Jerusalem occurs ten times, in Mishnah Berakhot it is totally absent.[3] A cursory check of the vocabulary of the complete corpora of Mishnah and Tosefta confirmed that this phenomenon was contrary to what was to be

---

[1]For the sanctity of the Temple in biblical literature, see e.g. the contributions of P.C. Beentjes and B.J. Schwarz in this book. See also K. Seybold, 'Jerusalem in the View of the Psalms' and P.C. Beentjes 'Jerusalem in the Book of the Chronicles', in: M. Poorthuis & Ch. Safrai (eds), *The Centrality of Jerusalem*, Kampen 1996, 7-14, 15-28.

[2]S. Safrai, 'Jerusalem and the Temple in the Tannaitic Literature of the First Generation after the Destruction of the Temple'.

[3]See A. Houtman, *Mishnah and Tosefta; A Synoptic Comparison of the Tractates Berakhot and Shebiit*, Tübingen 1996, 122.

expected.[4] As it happens, there are 119 occurrences of Jerusalem in the Mishnah, as against 149 in the Tosefta. Taking into account that the Tosefta is about four times as large as the Mishnah, the Mishnah has, therefore, relatively more references. Furthermore it turned out that the distribution of the references between Mishnah and Tosefta is in general rather even, except for the case of tractate Berakhot under consideration and for the three Baba-tractates, Baba Qamma, Baba Meṣia and Baba Batra, where the Mishnah has only one reference to Jerusalem as opposed to fifteen references to it in the Tosefta.

The present paper will examine in detail the specific case of references to Jerusalem in Mishnah and Tosefta Berakhot.[5] This investigation will consist of three parts:

1. Analysis and classification of the references to Jerusalem in order to determine their relevance for the issue of Sanctity of Place.
2. The tracing of parallels of the toseftan traditions to see where and how they are used in other rabbinic literature.
3. Engaging in similar word counts relating to the Sanctity of the Temple, in order to check whether the disproportion regarding Mishnah and Tosefta Berakhot is incidental or part of a pattern.

2. References to Jerusalem in Tosefta Berakhot[6]

In Ms Vienna of TBer, the word Jerusalem occurs ten times.[7] Moreover, in one of the passages involved, T1:15, other names of Jerusalem, Salem and Zion, are also mentioned, as well as the ab-

---

[4]The check was carried out by means of the third edition of the CD ROM *Judaic Classics Library*.

[5]At another occasion the references to Jerusalem in the Baba-tractates should be studied in the same manner as these references in Berakhot are studied in this paper, in order to compare the evidences.

[6]The basis for our study is Ms Vienna for the Tosefta and Ms Kaufmann for the Mishnah.

[7]i.e. T1:15, T3:15, T3:16, T3:25, T4:9, T4:10, T5:22 (twice), T5:24 and T6:1.

stract designation of the city העיר (hā ʿîr). Examination of the other textual traditions shows that the *editio princeps* of the Tosefta has still another reference to Jerusalem in T3:6. By contrast, neither the name Jerusalem nor any of the other designations occurs in the extant text traditions of MBer.

In order to assess the toseftan traditions in their contexts, it is first necessary to briefly describe and categorize them. The first occurrence of Jerusalem is in T1:15, in a homiletic discourse about the significance of different designations for the same person or place. In Ps 76:3 it says, "His abode has been established in Salem, his dwelling place in Zion." According to the Tosefta, Scripture reverts to using Jerusalem's former name, because it says in Jer 32:31, "This city has aroused my anger and my wrath." Since from this verse one might erroneously assume that even now it is regarded by God with vexation, the Psalmist preferred to use the emotionally uncharged name Salem.[8] The Tosefta argues that Jerusalem's destruction atoned for its sin and that, therefore, it is now again regarded by God with loving desire. The argument is then supported by various scriptural passages.

In T3:6 according to the *editio princeps,* there is an interesting tradition about Jerusalem that does not occur in the extant manuscripts.[9] In all the textual traditions, this pericope supplies scriptural passages as proof that one must pray at specific times of the day; that one must pray both in Israel and in the diaspora; that one may pray silently; that one must recite the three daily prayers at fixed times; and that one must praise God along with making requests in prayer. The *editio princeps* extends this series with yet

---

[8] According to K. Seybold, this was also the original context of the Psalm. The psalmist grappled with the question of whether after the catastrophe of the destruction of the Temple, Zion could still be regarded as God's dwelling place. He stressed the principle of sacral continuity. Salem remains Jerusalem, the Mount of the Lord remains Mount Zion, the place of the Temple, even in ruins. K. Seybold, 'Jerusalem in the View of the Psalms', 11.

[9] The *editio princeps,* which was first published in Venice 1521/22 as an addendum to the second edition of Isaac Alfasi's *sēp̱er hā-hălāḵôṯ,* is based on a manuscript now lost and therefore a valuable witness.

another aspect. It raises the question of whether one may pray in any desired direction. The answer is negative; one must pray in the direction of Jerusalem. Scriptural support is given from Dan 6:10, where it says, "and his windows being open in his chamber toward Jerusalem, he kneeled upon his knees three times a day."

In T3:15-16, precepts are given for the required prayer direction. The argument develops from general to precise. Scriptural passages from Kings and Chronicles are quoted as proof for the required direction of prayer:[10]

> if people are outside of the Land of Israel,
> *they direct their hearts to the Land of Israel* (2 Chr 6:38);
> if people are in the Land of Israel,
> *they direct their hearts to Jerusalem* (2 Chr 6:34);
> if people are in Jerusalem,
> *they direct their hearts to the Temple* (2 Chr 6:32);
> if people are in the Temple,
> *they direct their hearts to the Holy of Holies* (1 Kgs 8:30).

The scriptural citations are all from the prayer of Solomon which occurs in two versions, in 1 Kgs 8:23-53 and 2 Chron 6:14-42. In two of the four quoted passages of this well-known prayer, Solomon prays for soldiers who must go abroad to fight their war and for people who are banished to exile, 2 Chr 6:38 and 2 Chr 6:34.

T3:25 discusses the composition of the eighteen benedictions of the set prayer, which is generally called the Tefillah. It says that the reference to the restoration of the monarchy of David may be inserted in the benediction concerning the rebuilding of Jerusalem, i.e. the fourteenth benediction. Joseph Heinemann argued with reason that this is an instance of a Palestinian rite which fell into disuse in Palestine proper but was preserved in Babylonia.[11] T4:9 and T4:10 recount two social customs of Jerusalem:

---

[10]Though in none of the versions the quotations are verbatim, there is no doubt as to which scriptural passages they refer.

[11]See J. Heinemann, *Prayer in the Talmud*, Berlin/New York 1977, 66-67, and the literature cited there.

9. Rabbi Simeon ben Gamaliel said, "This was a fine custom in Jerusalem: A cloth was spread over the doorway. So long as the cloth was spread, guests entered. When the cloth was removed, no guests entered." 10. And another fine custom there was in Jerusalem: They entrusted [the preparations of] a banquet to a chef. If anything went amiss during the meal, they punished the chef. [The degree of the punishment] was wholly dependent on the honour of the guests as well as on the honour of the host.

T5:22 relates which benedictions ought to be said when sacrifices were brought in the Temple. Mss Vienna and Erfurt relate the benedictions for animal sacrifices and for meal offerings. The *editio princeps* only relates the benedictions for animal sacrifices.[12]

T5:24 discusses how domestic labourers should say Grace after Meal. Two benedictions are prescribed for them, whereas normally four benedictions are said.[13] The first benediction is said as usual, but the second one is a combination of the originally second and third benedictions, which concerns the restoration of the Temple in Jerusalem. Obviously the plea for God's mercy upon Jerusalem was something that could not be omitted even in an abridged prayer.[14]

T6:1 gives the aetiology of the four regular benedictions after the meal from Deut 8:10.

---

[12] The order of the traditions concerning meal offerings and animal sacrifices is in reverse order in Mss Vienna and Erfurt. Ms Vienna first describes the meal offerings and then the animal sacrifices; Ms Erfurt first describes the animal sacrifices. Within the prescriptions for the meal offerings, there are some additional differences between Ms Vienna and Ms Erfurt. According to Ms Vienna, one who was about to offer meal offerings in Jerusalem should say, "Blessed is He who has brought us to this time". According to Ms Erfurt he should say, "Blessed is He who *let us live* and brought us to this time". The blessing to be said with the actual offering is lacking in Ms Erfurt.

[13] i.e. according to this tradition, see also T6:1.

[14] For a comparison of the versions, see J. Heinemann, *Prayer in the Talmud*, 70-72.

The references to Jerusalem in Tosefta Berakhot just described can be divided into four categories:
1. An abstract use of the name Jerusalem in a long homiletic discourse with emphasis put on God's returned favour towards Jerusalem (T1:15).
2. Jerusalem in the benedictions of the Tefillah and Grace after Meal (T3:25, T5:24, T6:1).
3. Historical situations in Jerusalem (T4:9-10, T5:22).
4. The required prayer direction towards Jerusalem (T3:6, T3:15-16).

Of these categories, the second is the least interesting for the present investigation, because it deals with fixed benedictions that, though they do not occur verbatim in the Mishnah, are obviously presupposed there. After all, a definite structure for the public prayers had emerged already before 70 CE,[15] whereas the custom of recitation of grace after a communal meal may even be older.[16] Moreover, it is also clear from the corresponding Mishnah text that these traditions were known in that literature. MBer 4:3, for instance, mentions the obligation to recite the eighteen benedictions of the Tefillah, which includes the Prayer for Jerusalem, and MBer 3:3 includes women, slaves and minors in the obligation to recite the Grace after Meal. Therefore, I have excluded these traditions from the comparison with other rabbinic literature.

3. Parallel Traditions in Other Rabbinic Literature

In accordance with the decision to exclude the traditions where Jerusalem occurs in the framework of fixed benedictions, I traced parallels for the following eight traditional units:

---

[15]See S. Safrai, 'The Synagogue', in: S. Safrai & M. Stern (eds), *The Jewish People in the First Century*, CRINT I.2, Assen/Amsterdam 1976, 908-944, at 922-923 and the literature cited there.
[16]See J. Heinemann, *Prayer in the Talmud*, 115-116; idem, 'Birkath Ha-Zimmun and Ḥavurah-meals', *JJS* 13 (1962) 23-29, at 25-26.

Tosefta	Babylonian Talmud	Palestinian Talmud	Midrashim
TBer 1:15			
TBer 3:6	BT Ber 31a	PT Ber 4:1,7a	MidrSam 2:10
TBer 3:15	BT Ber 30a	PT Ber 4:5,8b-c	TanB *wa-yišlaḥ* 21; SifreDeut *wa-ethanān* Pisqa 29; PesR 33; CantR 4:4; Yelam Ginze Schechter I:99
TBer 3:16	BT Ber 30a	PT Ber 4:5,8b-c	TanB *wa-yišlaḥ* 21; SifreDeut *wa-ethanān* Pisqa 29; PesR 33; CantR 4:4; Yelam Ginze Schechter I:99
TBer 4:9	BT BB 93b		LamR 4:2
TBer 4:10	BT BB 93b		LamR 4:2
TBer 5:22a (meal offerings)	BT Ber 37b; BT Men 75b		
TBer 5:22b (animal sacrifices)			

This table[17] indicates the following facts:

1. The homiletic discourse about the renewed love of God for Jerusalem is unique for the Tosefta.

2. The tradition about the required prayer direction in T3:6 has parallels in the Talmuds and in MidrSam. The parallel in MidrSam is not surprising, because the list of which this tradition is part, contains a reference to the prayer of Hannah in 1 Sam 1:13. This reference obviously presented a fitting opportunity to insert the material.

3. The traditions about the required prayer direction in T3:15-16 have parallels in the two Talmuds and in a number of Midrash collections. However, there are some differences to be noted. In TBer 3:15-16, the verb used for the prayer direction is the *pi'el* of כון (to direct) in a combination with לב (heart). The same combination is found in BT Ber 30a. On the other hand in PT 4:5,8b-c, a combination of the *qal* of הפך (to turn) and פנים (face) is used.[18] According to Louis Ginzberg, in his commentary on the Palestinian Talmud, the version as found in the Tosefta and the Babylonian Talmud is the original, whereas the

---

[17]Some remarks about the context of the parallels: BT Ber 31a is the Gemara to MBer 5:1. BT Ber 30a is the Gemara to MBer 4:5, this unit of tradition is more extensive than in the Tosefta. After the four cases mentioned in TBer 3:15-16, BT Ber 30a continues: if people are in the Holy of Holies, *they direct their hearts to the mercy-seat,* if people are standing behind the mercy-seat, *they should imagine themselves in front of the mercy-seat.* The tradition in TanB *wa-yišlaḥ* occurs in the context of Gen 35:1, where God asks Jacob to return to Bethel, to the place where He revealed Himself when Jacob fled for his brother. BT BB 93b is the Gemara to MBB 6:1, about someone who sells seed to his neighbour and the seed does not sprout. If it was edible seed the seller is not responsible, but if the seed is not edible, the seller is responsible. LamR 4:2 is a midrash on Lam 4:2, about Zion's precious sons. It occurs in both textual recensions, i.e. the Vilna edition and the Buber edition. BT Ber 37b is the Gemara to MBer 6:1. BT Men 75b is the Gemara to MMen 6:4.

[18]In SifreDeut 29 and CantR 4:4 the combination הפך and פנים is used; in TanB 21 and PesR 33 the combination כון and לב. For further treatment of these cases, see S. Lieberman, *Tosefta Ki-Fshuta; A Comprehensive Commentary on the Tosefta* (Hebr.), 10 vols. and supplement to Moed, New York 1955, I.44.

reading of the Palestinian Talmud is a later reworking.[19] Note that all the Midrash collections have a supposedly Palestinian origin. Only the passage from SifreDeut possibly stems from the school of Rabbi Ishmael in Babylonia.[20]

4. The last category, of traditions that recount historical situations in Jerusalem, has parallels in LamR and in the Babylonian Talmud, but not in the Palestinian Talmud. The absence in the Palestinian Talmud is somewhat unexpected, because generally the Palestinian Talmud is closer to the Tosefta than the Babylonian Talmud.[21] The parallel in LamR fits the general tendency of this Midrash collection to glorify Jerusalem's past.[22]

4. Related Vocabulary

Now that we have seen that Tosefta Berakhot pays more attention to Jerusalem than Mishnah Berakhot, we will broaden our view to check whether this phenomenon is incidental or part of a larger pattern. Two steps are necessary for this investigation. Firstly, we will examine whether the noticed difference between Mishnah and Tosefta Berakhot concerning references to Jerusalem also pertains to related vocabulary, such as the Land of Israel, Temple Mount, Temple and Holy of Holies. Secondly, we will engage in a quantitative examination of these same words in tractate Berakhot of the Talmuds, to see how the relative frequency is

---

[19]See L. Ginzberg, *A Commentary on the Palestinian Talmud* (Hebr.), 4 Vols., New York 1941-1961, III.378-379, 381.

[20]See G. Stemberger, *Introduction to the Talmud and Midrash*, Edinburgh [2]1996, 272-273 and the literature cited there.

[21]See, for example, J.N. Epstein, *Introduction to Tannaitic Literature; Mishna, Tosephta and Halakhic Midrashim* (Hebr.), edited by E.Z. Melamed, Jerusalem 1957, 245-246; A. Goldberg, 'The Tosefta – Companion to the Mishna', in: S. Safrai (ed.), *The Literature of the Sages*, CRINT II.3.1, Assen/Maastricht 1987, 283-302, at 292; idem, 'The Palestinian Talmud', in: S. Safrai (ed.), *The Literature of the Sages*, 303-322, at 307.

[22]See e.g. S.J.D. Cohen, 'The Destruction; From Scripture to Midrash', *Prooftexts* 2 (1982) 18-39, at 22-25.

there. The results for Mishnah and Tosefta Berakhot are as follows.

Land of Israel[23]	T3:15 (twice), T6:2 (twice)	M9:1
Jerusalem	T1:15, T3:6, T3:15, T3:16, T3:25, T4:9, T4:10, T5:22 (twice), T5:24, T6:1	
Temple Mount	T1:15 (three times), T6:2 T6:19	M9:5
Temple	T3:16 (twice), T6:21, T6:22 (twice)	M9:5
Holy of Holies	T3:16	M4:5, M4:6, M9:5

Except for the case of the Holy of Holies, Tosefta Berakhot pays
again more attention to notions concerning Sanctity of Place than
Mishnah Berakhot. So the noticed phenomenon seems more
likely to be part of a pattern than to be coincidental.

If we now broaden our view to the Talmuds, we see that a
rough count of the same vocabulary shows an interesting picture.[24]

---

[23] ʾereṣ yiśrāʾēl and ʾarṣēnû, which means our land, i.e. the promised land.

[24] I used again the 3rd edition of the CD-ROM Judaic Classics Library.
However the texts on this CD-ROM are not 100% reliable. I discovered quite
a few typing errors. Besides I may have overlooked some deviant spellings in
my search. I did not investigate and categorize the finds as I did with the occurrences of Jerusalem in Tosefta Berakhot, which may also cause a certain
degree of inaccuracy. Some concepts were difficult to trace. For example, in
T1:15 it is clear that the simple designation הר (mount) denotes the Temple
Mount. When I would have included this simple designation in my search,
instead of the complex (and by far more regular) designation הר הבית (Temple
Mount), it would have led to too much confusion. Therefore I took the risk of
skipping one or two occurrences by restricting my count to הר הבית. Nevertheless I am sure that the overall picture is reliable enough.

Land of Israel	**TBer 4**	MBer 1	**BT Ber 18**	PT Ber 4
Jerusalem	**TBer 10 (11)**		**BT Ber 41**	PT Ber 19
Temple Mount	**TBer 5**	MBer 1	**BT Ber 9**	PT Ber 4
Temple	**TBer 5**	MBer 1	**BT Ber 35**	PT Ber 15
Holy of Holies	TBer 1	**MBer 3**	BT Ber 7	**PT Ber 11**

There is a remarkable pattern in the frequency of the references. In the cases where Tosefta has more occurrences than Mishnah, the Babylonian Talmud has more than the Palestinian Talmud. But in the single case where Mishnah has more occurrences than Tosefta, namely the case of the Holy of Holies, the Palestinian Talmud has more occurrences than the Babylonian Talmud. This complex of data suggests that the interest of Tosefta Berakhot in the religious centre of Judaism is not coincidental. The question whether this may have something to do with its cultural setting seems therefore legitimate.

5. Interpretation of the Data

We have attempted to shed light on the references to Jerusalem in Tosefta Berakhot. On the one hand we have compared parallels and on the other hand we have expanded the investigation to vocabulary related to the Sanctity of Place. These investigations have presented a new problem. As has become clear, in matters pertaining to the religious centre of Judaism, Tosefta Berakhot shows a greater affinity to the Babylonian Talmud than to the Palestinian Talmud. This is rather surprising, because in most respects the reverse is true.[25] The fact that for this specific issue Tosefta is quantitatively and qualitatively closer to the Babylonian

---

[25]See above, note 21.

Talmud,[26] therefore requires an explanation. Let us sum up the main points up to now:

1. TBer pays more attention to Jerusalem and cognate issues than MBer.
2. BT Ber pays more attention to the same issues than PT Ber.
3. In T3:15-16 the wording of the toseftan halakhot is closer to the Babylonian Talmud than to the Palestinian Talmud. According to Louis Ginzberg, the version of TBer T3:15-16 and BT Ber 30a is original.
4. The tradition that is handed down in T3:25 is, according to Joseph Heinemann, an instance of a Palestinian rite which fell into disuse in Palestine, but was preserved in Babylonia.

The textual resemblance between TBer 3:15-16 and BT Ber 30a might be explained as a later adjustment of the Tosefta text to the text of the Babylonian Talmud. In the introduction to his commentary to the Palestinian Talmud, Ginzberg noticed already that there are clear indications of such an influence of the BT on the Tosefta.[27] However, these later adaptations are always recognizable in language and style. In my opinion, the case in TBer does not belong to this category, for besides the points of agreement between BT Ber 30a and TBer 3:15-16, there are also remarkable differences. It so happens that BT Ber 30a uses consistently the imperfect form of the *pi'el* of כון, whereas T3:15-16 use a present participle in all the versions. If there had been an adaptation to the BT, one would have expected an adaptation of the conjugation as well.

Another possible explanation for the resemblance would be that at least part of the material of TBer has come down to us through Babylonia. The advantage of this option is that it also explains the other points mentioned above. A Babylonian back-

---

[26]For the qualitative resemblances see Heinemann's remark on T3:25 (above, 156) and Ginzberg's remark on T3:15-16 (above, 160-161).
[27]L. Ginzberg, *A Commentary on the Palestinian Talmud* (Hebr.), Vol. 1, New York 1941, Hebrew introduction, נו.

ground might explain both the conservative character[28] of the material and the way it relates to Jerusalem. One might argue that tradition in exile is not only more conservative, as a defense mechanism against assimilation, but also that it is more Zion-oriented than Palestinian tradition. Not necessarily because the people who lived in exile were expressed Zionists, if one uses an anachronistic term. Many cases are known of people who will-ingly remained in exile even when there was ample opportunity to return to the Land of Israel.[29] The feelings expressed in the dias-pora may be no more than a nostalgic longing for a utopia, an ideal vision of the Land of Israel. Perhaps we have to read the tra-ditions about the fine customs in Jerusalem (T4:9-10) in that light. That would account for their occurrence in the BT and in the Midrash collection on Lamentation. For although LamR originates in Palestine, as regards it subject matter it is the book of exile par excellence.[30] The tradition in T3:25 about the inser-tion of the reference to the restoration of the monarchy of David in the blessing concerning the rebuilding of Jerusalem, would fit in this picture as well, since it refers to the ideal vision of Jerusa-lem as the residence of the Davidic dynasty.

Incidental evidence for a Babylonian role in the transmission of (part of) the material of TBer can be adduced from TBer 2:10,

---

[28]In my book on the relation between Mishnah and Tosefta, I argued that one of the aims of the compilers of the tosefta-collections was the preserva-tion of traditions in their original wording. See A. Houtman, *Mishnah and Tosefta*, 234-235.

[29]Palestinian Jewish leaders tried to counteract the large scale emigration and to stimulate remigration by means of legal measures and moral pressure. See e.g. M. Avi-Yonah, *The Jews of Palestine*, Oxford 1976, 26-27. For an account of the motives for remigration, see J. Schwartz, 'Aliya From Babylo-nia During the Amoraic Period', *The Jerusalem Cathedra* 3 (1983) 58-69.

[30]As a matter of fact, probably all the Jerusalem traditions we have been talking about in this exposition originate in Palestine and spread from there to the centres of Jewish learning in exile. This explains their occurrence in Pal-estinian Midrash collections. But whereas in Palestine the traditions con-cerned went gradually out of vogue, in exile they remained popular for the reasons mentioned.

where a Babylonian Amora of the first generation is cited, namely Rab Shêla from the Academy of Nehardea.

Among modern scholars, it is generally acknowledged that it is impossible to treat the Mishnah and the Tosefta as complete literary works. One has to reckon with several editorial stages and with the possibility that some of the tractates had a history of their own before becoming part of the corpus in question.[31] Therefore, the general assumption that the Tosefta as a whole is a Palestinian compilation that was put together some decennia after the Mishnah,[32] does not exclude a prehistory of TBer in another setting. On the basis of the material studied is this paper, one might conclude that at least part of the history of TBer must be looked for in Babylonia. The textual data, combined with the historical setting of the formative period of the tannaitic literature, certainly allow for such a model.

---

[31]See e.g. J.N. Epstein, *Introduction to Tannaitic Literature*, 25-58; P. Schäfer, 'Research into Rabbinic Literature; An Attempt to Define the Status Quaestionis', *JJS* 37 (1986) 139-152, at 147-149.

[32]See e.g. A. Goldberg, 'The Tosefta - Companion to the Mishnah', in: S. Safrai (ed.), *The Literature of the Sages*, 293-295.

'TO STAND – PERHAPS TO SIT' SITTING AND STANDING IN THE AZARAH IN THE SECOND TEMPLE PERIOD

Joshua Schwartz

The Biblical Period

In the biblical period, the accepted posture on the Temple Mount for both Priest and layman was standing upright.[1] Thus, for example, after the seven Days of Consecration, 'the congregation drew near and stood before the Lord' (Lev 9:5). Likewise, the Priests of the tribe of Levi were chosen 'to stand before the Lord to minister unto Him, and to bless in His Name' (Deut 10:8) and 'to stand to minister in the name of the Lord' (Deut 18:5).[2] Standing was considered the proper normative position of respect for God and His cult, although bending over, bowing or prostration might be the proper response in the face of Divine awe or the common position for worship both within and outside of sacred precincts.[3] Sitting was for the most part not considered an appropriate posture for cultic acts or worship and the few times that 'sitting before the Lord' is mentioned in the Bible, the root *yāšab*

---

[1] On Temple and Temple Mount during the biblical period see Th.A. Busink, *Der Tempel von Jerusalem von Salomo bis Herodes, I, Der Tempel Salomos*, Leiden 1970, *passim*.

[2] Although the biblical Hebrew verb *'āmad* a cultic or prayer sense can also be understood in a *sensus technicus*, this does not preclude the plain meaning of the verb in the physical sense of standing. See in detail M.I. Gruber, *Aspects of Nonverbal Communication in the Ancient Near East*, Rome 1980, I-II and particularly I.145 ff. As we shall see below, when the Rabbis had to determine the boundaries of permitted postures and sought the aid of biblical verses, they tended to understand the verb in the plain physical sense.

[3] Gruber, *Nonverbal Communication*, 90-120

probably refers to sitting back on one's heels in a kneeling position and not to actual sitting.[4]

The only apparent exception to all this in biblical literature is found in the dedication ceremony of the Temple. 1 Kgs 8:14 states that Solomon 'turned his face about, and blessed all the congregation of Israel.' The verse continues to state that 'all the congregation of Israel stood', but does not tell us what Solomon was doing. However, since 1 Kgs 8:22 tells us that 'Solomon stood before the altar of the Lord', it is assumed that before-hand he had been sitting and indeed this is exactly how Josephus interpreted these verses.[5] Solomon apparently then kneeled and only stood up again after completing his prayer (1 Kgs 8:54). In 2 Chr 6:12-13, Solomon stood up and addressed the people standing on a brazen *kîyôr*, some type of podium or scaffold. This version also seems to imply that he had been sitting before.

It is important to remember, however, that all of the verses above refer in some form or another to some type of cultic action. What, however, was accepted practice when cult was not involved? If Solomon could sit and bless the people, it is possible that kings could sit in more casual circumstances? Was this also the case regarding everyone else? It is probably impossible to answer these questions regarding the biblical period. Our task will be to try and answer them regarding the period of the Second Temple.

---

[4]See, for instance, 1 Chr 17:16: 'Then David the king went in, and sat before the Lord.' 'Before the Lord' refers to the ark and the sitting is interpreted as kneeling in a manner similar to that common in Islamic ritual. See A.A. Anderson, *Word Biblical Commentary 11: 2 Samuel*, Waco, Texas 1989, 126. The verb, however, might also simply mean 'to tarry' (Gen 24:55).

[5]See *Ant.* 8.107: 'And while they were occupied with this thought, Solomon arose – for he chanced to be seated – and addressed God'.

No Sitting in the Azarah

Much of talmudic literature takes it for granted that only kings of the House of David could sit in the azarah (= ʿăzārâ)⁶, and there were views that even they could not do so.⁷ Since there were no kings from the House of David during the Second Temple period, this would mean that no one could sit in these sacred precincts. We shall first examine those traditions which prohibited sitting in the azarah and then the other traditions dealing with sitting, standing and other related gestures there in order to determine exactly what was the correct and permitted posture in the internal precincts of the Temple Mount.

The basis for the general prohibition against sitting in the azarah is found in relation to the ceremony of *haqhēl* which took place every seven years, at the end of the sabbatical year and during the Sukkot Festival, or afterwards, when the people of Israel assembled in Jerusalem to hear portions of the Torah read to them.⁸ According to MSot 7:8, the portions were read by the king, while according to Josephus (*Ant.* 4.208-210), it was the High

---

⁶The phrase azarah usually refers to the area from the Court of Israelites and beyond, including that court, the Court of Priests and the area immediately adjacent to the Temple and surrounding it. See J. Schwartz, 'Once More on the Nicanor Gate', *HUCA* 62 (1991) 250-251.

⁷See TSanh 4:4 (420, edn Zuckermandel). The prohibition appears as a *baraita* in the name of R. Ḥiyya. See PT Sot 7:7,22a; PT Yoma 3:2,40b; PT Pes 5:10,32d; MidrPss 1:2 (1-2a, edn Buber) and MidrSam 27:1 (64a-b, edn Buber). These traditions also add a statement of R. Ammi, quoting Resh Laqish that even kings of the House of David could not sit there. BT Sot 40b, 41b; BT Yoma 25a, 69a-b; BT Tam 27a; BT Qid 78b and BT Sanh 101b do not mention the additional prohibition.

⁸There are problems regarding the exact time that the ceremony took place, but since our concern is where the king stood and not when he stood there, all this is beyond the purview of our discussion. On the date and time of the ceremony see D. Henshke, 'When is the Time of *Hakhēl*?' (Hebr.), *Tarbiz* 61 (1992) 177-194. For a more historical discussion of the issues involved see D. Trifon, 'A Mishnah Fragment as Evidence of the Status of King Agrippa II' (Hebr.), *The Jerusalem Cathedra* 53 (1989) 27-48.

Priest who read them.[9] After establishing the date of the ceremony, the Mishnah states that:

> They make for him in the azarah a wooden platform *(= bîmâ)* and
> he sat on it as it is written, 'at the end of seven years on the ap-
> pointed time etc.' (Deut 31:10). The *'ḥazān* of the synagogue'[10]
> takes a Scroll of the Law and gives it to the 'head of the syna-
> gogue'. And the 'head of the synagogue' gives it to the deputy and
> the deputy gives it to the High Priest and the High Priest gives it
> to the King. And the King stands and receives it and reads it sit-
> ting. King Agrippa[11] stood and received it and read it standing and
> the Sages praised him.

We have already mentioned above that there was some sort of
platform, scaffold or podium on the Temple Mount somewhere
which served the king, although in the case of Solomon it was
bronze.[12] The Mishnah, as we just saw, locates the platform in the
azarah. R. Eliezer b. Jacob, commonly identified as the late first
and early second century CE Rabbi credited with the authorship
of tractate Middot, disagreed and placed the platform in the

---

[9]See Trifon, 'A Mishnah Fragment', 30 n.12. Our concern here is also
where the High Priest stood and not necessarily who read the portion. In any
case, as Trifon points out, during the Second Temple period there were only
three kings who were not Priests: Herod, Agrippa I and Agrippa II and it is
possible, therefore, to understand the confusion that might have arisen regarding who was to read these portions.

[10]The titles are somewhat problematical and are found much more commonly and later on in relation to synagogues. There were, however, synagogues in Second Temple period Jerusalem and perhaps even on the Temple
Mount. See Trifon, 'A Mishnah Fragment', 27-28 n.6.

[11]There is a good deal of scholarly discussion as to whether this was Agrippa I or II. This question is not important for our purposes. See Trifon, *op.
cit.* who seeks to prove that it was Agrippa II. See also D.R. Schwartz, *Agrippa I: The Last King of Judaea*, Tübingen 1990, 159 ff. and D. Goodblatt,
'Agrippa I and Palestinian Judaism in the First Century', *Jewish History* 2
(1987) 7-32. See in this book S. Safrai, 'Jerusalem and the Temple', 147-150.

[12]See also 2 Chr 23:13 which mentions a platform without stating the material from which it was made. Josephus (*Ant.* 4.209) states that the High
Priest read from a raised platform, but, likewise, does not tell us from what it
was made.

'Temple Mount', i.e. either in the Court of Women or outside of it.[13] R. Eliezer's view is based on Neh 8:3-5 which states that Ezra read the Torah on a wooden platform in the 'broad place before the Water Gate'. Although it is hard to superimpose the Temple Mount geography of the end of the Second Temple period on that of the Persian period, it would seem clear that Ezra was not within the internal precincts of the azarah.[14] Of course the Rabbis could claim there is no proof that the platform of the Mishnah should be located in the same place as that used by Ezra and, indeed, the respective sources seem to indicate that both were constructed for those particular ceremonies described in the sources. In any case, the issue did not seem to be a matter of posture. Rather, R. Eliezer apparently was concerned by the fact that the platform was made of wood, and this he claimed was forbidden in the azarah. The Sages apparently did not seem to think that a wooden platform should be included in this prohibition.[15] For our purposes, however, it is the location of the platform on which the king could theoretically sit which will prove to be of great importance.

The king, however, was not the only one engaging in ceremonial reading somewhere on the Temple Mount or in the azarah. The High Priest also read from the Law on the Day of Atonement and received it from the same functionaries mentioned regarding the *haqhēl* ceremony.[16] The High Priest like the king, received the Torah while standing, but unlike the king, continued to stand while he read. These traditions do not mention a platform nor do they provide information as to where the High Priest stood when he did read. It is easy to understand, however, how the similarities between the two ceremonies might lead to the conclusion that they took place at the same spot.

---

[13]TSot 7:13-17 (195 edn Lieberman).

[14]See H.G.M. Williamson, *Word Biblical Commentary 16: Ezra, Nehemiah*, Waco, Texas 1985, 287, 296, 374.

[15]See SifreDeut 145 (200, edn Finkelstein).

[16]See MSot 7:7 and MYoma 7:1.

Whether they did or not, Mishnah Sotah and Yoma make it clear that there was a difference between the King and the High Priest. The King read while sitting and the High Priest read while standing. In fact, the only one who could ever sit in the azarah was the King:

> All the people stand and he (= king) sits. And there was no sitting in the azarah except for kings of the House of David.[17]

The discussions in both PT and BT accepted this principle at face value and considered it to be problematical for the persons mentioned in Mishnah Sotah and Yoma. Thus, for example, PT Sotah 7:7,22a could not imagine how it was possible to conceive of Agrippa sitting at any time in the azarah since he was not of the House of David. BT Sotah 41b understood the statement that he received the Law while standing to mean that he must have been sitting before and could not imagine how he could have been doing this. BT Sotah 40b and BT Yoma 69a asked these same questions regarding the High Priest, since if he too had received the Law while standing, he too must have been sitting before.

All of this led the Babylonian sage Rab Ḥisda to transfer both the *haqhēl* and the reading of the High Priest from the azarah to the Court of Women in which there was no problem regarding sitting. However, since Rab Ḥisda could hardly have ignored the fact that MSot 7:8 explicitly mentions the azarah, the discussions in BT connect his view to the dispute between the Sages and R. Eliezer b. Jacob in TSot 7:13-17 mentioned above, with Rab Ḥisda accepting the view that the platform from the time of Ezra was in the same place as that during the time of *haqhēl* and, therefore, all reading of the Law by King or High Priest would take place outside of the azarah and in the Court of Women.[18] It is interesting to note, however, that Rab Ḥisda did not provide any reasons for his view implicitly dealing with standing or sitting in the azarah.

---

[17]TSanh 4:4 (420, edn Zuckermandel).
[18]See BT Yoma 69a-b and BT Sot 40b.

The traditions in the Palestinian Talmud and in the midrashim do not know of the explicit statement of Rab Ḥisda, but they do mention a view which results in the same conclusions regarding standing and sitting in the azarah. Thus, in PT Sot 7:7,22a and parallels we find a statement attributed to Resh Laqish that:

> Even for Kings of the House of David there was no sitting in the azarah.[19]

No one, therefore, sits in the azarah.[20] The Palestinian Talmud and most parallels do not provide any reason for this. It just seems to be taken for granted that nobody was allowed to sit in the azarah.[21]

By the amoraic period it was already taken for granted that there was no sitting at all in the azarah and a good deal of Temple Mount procedure was interpreted in light of this. Thus, MMid 1:1 stated that the guards of the Temple Mount gates and at the four corners of the gates stood inside the Temple Mount, while those guarding the gates and corners of the azarah stood outside the azarah.[22] According to BT Tam 27a this was obviously because if the guards became tired they would wish to sit and thus they should man positions which would allow them to do this if neces-

---

[19]See the parallels listed in n.7 above. All the traditions then mention the verse in 1 Chr 17:16 that 'David sat before the Lord'. As we saw above (see n.4), sitting before the Lord probably meant bowing or kneeling. The Rabbis in these traditions understood David either to have been leaning against the wall of the azarah, or claimed that the root *yāšab* should be explained in the *pi'el* sense of concentrating and had nothing to do with any type of physical action.

[20]The parallel version of this statement in MidrPss 1:2 (1-2a, edn Buber) has R. Ammi originally quoting Resh Laqish as saying that there is no sitting in the azarah 'except in the place reserved for the Kings of the House of David.' After further deliberations, the statement was changed to agree with the other versions. See our discussion below.

[21]See MidrPss 1:2. In this version alone the following appears: 'But did not R. Huna declare in the name of R. Samuel, that there is no sitting in heaven'. This is clearly a late version. See our comments later on.

[22]Cf. MTam 1:1.

sary. Thus, since they could sit in the Temple Mount, they could guard inside. They could not sit in the azarah, however, so they manned positions outside of it. It apparently did not occur to the author of the discussion in BT Tam that that there could be other reasons such as the strategic placing of the guards to catch those who had no business to be on the Temple Mount or azarah.[23] There were much fewer restrictions regarding entrance to the Temple Mount *per se*; even non-Jews could enter, and, therefore, the guards could be inside. The azarah was a much more serious matter and it made absolutely no sense to place the guards inside the azarah in such a manner that those entering would already be inside when caught and, therefore, they were placed outside. We shall see later on that tannaitic literature was not that concerned with the posture of guards resting, assuming it was a time that they were allowed to rest, or that they were 'off-duty', while by amoraic times, the strict rule of 'no sitting in the azarah' actually determined how the guarding procedures of the Second Temple period were understood.

The same type of thing happened regarding the Chamber of Hewn Stone (*Lishkat ha-Gazit)*. BT Yoma 25a tells us that the Elder of the Sanhedrin sat in the eastern part of the Chamber to officiate in the daily lottery that took place to determine priestly functions. The 4th century CE Babylonian sage Abbaye took it for granted that there was no sitting in the azarah and, therefore, it was taken for granted that the Chamber of Hewn Stone could not be in the azarah itself. Unfortunately, the lottery procedure had to take place in sanctified area of the azarah. This led to the rather clumsy construction that the Chamber of Hewn Stone was partly in a sanctified part of the Temple Mount and partly in unsanctified territory. And all this because the Elder was supposed to sit down, against the rule that there is no sitting in the azarah.

Even biblical history was re-written in light of the 'no sitting' rule. Thus, 1 Sam 3:3 tells us that 'the lamp of God was not yet gone out, and Samuel was laid down to sleep in the Sanctuary of the Lord, where the ark of God was'. This, of course, was the

---

[23]See Philo, *De Spec. Leg.* I.156.

Sanctuary at Shiloh, but it was assumed that the same sitting-standing rules applied. Therefore, the verse was re-interpreted that the lamp in the Sanctuary had not gone out and that Samuel slept somewhere other than in the Sanctuary, since if you could not sit there, you certainly could not sleep there.[24] As we shall see later on, though, sleeping was not an unknown phenomenon in various parts of the Temple Mount during the Second Temple period.

According to one Rabbi, issues of sitting and standing actually determined the entire course of history in the biblical period. The Babylonian Sage Rab Naḥman stated that the schism between Rehoboam the son of Solomon and Jeroboam ben Nebat ultimately revolved around matters of sitting or standing in the azarah, hereby re-interpreting biblical history. Jeroboam was afraid that if the people went up to Jerusalem to sacrifice, since only Rehoboam could sit, as a king of the House of David, Rehoboam would appear kingly while Jeroboam, having to stand like everyone else, would appear servile. If he would sit, mused Jeroboam, he would be accused of rebellion and killed. Therefore, Jeroboam decided to set up the golden calfs at Bethel and Dan.[25] Needless to say, none of this had anything to do with the reality of that time.

Sitting During the Passover Sacrifice

'No sitting in the azarah' was the rule on the Temple Mount as the amoraic Rabbis understood it. The only problem with all of this is that there seem to be traditions which indicate that under certain circumstances it was possible to sit in the azarah. Thus, for example, MPes 5:10 describes the three 'groups' who offered up the Passover Sacrifice. When the first group finished it went out from the azarah and sat in the Temple Mount. As we remember, there was no problem whatsoever regarding sitting in the Temple Mount. The second group, when it finished, sat in the ḥêl, that is

---

[24]Cf. BT Qid 78b.
[25]BT Sanh 101b.

the area between the balustrade and the Court of the Women, and here too one could sit without problem. And the third group, according to the Mishnah, 'stands in its place'. This would have been in the azarah and this is why the third group, unlike the two other ones, did not sit.

However, the Mishnah in the Palestinian tradition, as it appears in the discussion of the Palestinian Talmud apparently did not have the reading 'and stands in its place', but rather 'and the third in its place', meaning that this group, like the others, sits 'in its place' which was the azarah![26] What MPes actually seems to be stating, therefore, is that even within the azarah, if ritual and cult have been concluded, then one can sit. Thus, according to this mishnah, there seems to have been no blanket prohibition against sitting in the azarah for anyone, whether king, High Priest or just plain Israelite. This was apparently too much for R. Eliezer b. Jacob, who, as we saw above, objected to the building of the wooden platform for the *haqhēl* ceremony in the azarah and in TPes 4:12 (p. 164, edn Lieberman) R. Eliezer states that the third group 'went and sat in the Court of Women'.

Regardless of the reasons of R. Eliezer, it seems more likely that the Rabbis of the Mishnah were right and that sitting during periods of cultic or ritual inactivity was not forbidden. Thus, for example, PT Yoma 3:2,40b states that a Priest who fell asleep in the azarah required ritual immersion. One who only dozed off had to sanctify his hands and feet. The discussion in the Talmud, however, immediately raised a number of problems. How could one sleep in the azarah, for instance, when it was not even permitted to sit there. The Talmud then cites the dictum of R. Ḥiyya and the statement of R. Ammi about no sitting in the azarah. Be all this as it may, the very fact that it could be assumed in the first place that a Priest in the azarah, who obviously was not on duty, could fall asleep and need only undergo ritual immersion upon

---

[26] PT Pes 5:10,32d and PT Sot 7:7,22a. The Mishnah in Ms Leiden also omits 'stands' and the phrase was added only by another hand. See J.N. Epstein, 'Me-Diqduqei Yerushalmi', in: J.N. Epstein, *Mehqarim be-Sifrut ha-Talmud u-be-Leshonot Shemiyot*, Jerusalem 1988, II.1, 323-324.

awakening, implies that simple sitting was probably not such a big problem after all.

Sitting on the Temple Mount

A number of other traditions seem to indicate that sitting was permitted in various instances throughout the Temple Mount and azarah. Thus, for example, the Letter of Aristeas 94 tells us that the Priests had for their rest:

> a place set apart for them where those who are relieved from duty take seats.[27]

Aristeas does not add any more details as to the location of this resting place, but the Mishnah does appear to add significant geographic details which might help to identify where the Priests rested.

Thus, MTam 1:1 listed the *bêt hamôqēd* (= Chamber of the Hearth) as one of the places where the Priests did guard duty. It had a vaulted ceiling and no second floor. It was a large chamber and was encircled inside by a terraced landing of stone on which the elders of the priestly watch used to sleep. The younger Priests slept on the floor.[28] The Mishnah adds that other Priests who had been in the *bêt ṭebîlâ* (= Chamber of Immersion), came up to the *bêt hamôqēd*, dried off and warmed up by the hearth there and then such a Priest:

> ... came and sat down by his brethren the Priests
> (= in the *bêt hamôqēd*)
> until the gates were opened.

---

[27]The translation is according to M. Hadas, *Aristeas to Philocrates (Letter of Aristeas)*, New York 1951, 136-137.

[28]See also MMid 1:8.

It would seem likely that this was the resting place mentioned in Aristeas and here, indeed, the Priests, albeit off-duty, not only rested but also slept. It is true that there were four compartments in the *bêt hamôqēd* which faced the main chamber, and that two of these faced the non-consecrated *ḥêl* and indeed one even served as the way to the *bêt ṭebîlâ* just mentioned,[29] but nowhere is there the slightest hint that any of the sleeping or sitting had to be down in the unconsecrated area. Rather one gets the impression that those Priests not on duty were provided with a place to keep warm and rest and bearing in mind that they were to return soon to duty, this could take place even in the azarah. It was only the off-duty Levites who had to sleep at the entrance to the azarah and *bêt hamôqēd* and who were not allowed inside.

Sitting in the azarah, however, was not just a matter of resting from guard duty or waiting in the case of the Passover offering. It could also take place in an official capacity. Thus, it is stated that the Sanhedrin sat in the Chamber of Hewn Stone[30] and, as we saw above, the Chamber of Hewn Stone was in the azarah, in spite of the attempts of later amoraic interpretations to transfer at least part of it to the unconsecrated area of the Temple Mount.[31]

Also, Abot de Rabbi Nathan, usually considered to be a relatively late work, records what seems to be a unique instance of cultic sitting. Among the miracles supposedly taking place on the Temple Mount and in the Temple, it is related that the people, when the High Priest went into the Holy of Holies, used to stand close together, but when they prostrated themselves, an action obviously requiring more space, there was then ample room. The tradition then continues and states:

---

[29]MMid 1:6-7.

[30]MMid 5:4. The verb used in most of the sources is *yāšab*, literally meaning 'to sit'. The members of the court did physically sit (TSanh 6:3, 424 edn Zuckermandel), although certain functionaries like the court scribes had to remain standing (MSanh 4:3). In a wider sense, both in Hebrew and in translation, the phrase 'sitting' took on the meaning of 'to be in session', but ultimately this meaning was dependent on the original actual physical sitting.

[31]See also MSanh 11:2 and BT Sanh 78b.

When (the People) of Israel used to go up to prostrate themselves before their Father in heaven, when they sat they sat pushed together. And no one can put a finger between them. And when they prostrated themselves, they did so with ample room.[32]

The tradition seems to be referring to the area of the azarah, since it is within the greater context of the service of the High Priest on the day of Atonement when the people would be in that sanctified area.[33] In this case, though, the sitting is somewhat problematical since the same tradition also mentions standing (!) close together before the ritual prostration. It is difficult to imagine that the closely packed crowd just sat around in the azarah while waiting. Rather it is likely that sitting here should be interpreted in the biblical sense, as we saw above, meaning that the people sat back on their heals in a kneeling position in preparation for full prostration.[34] This would be a unique instance in which the biblical practice was continued and it is possible that the other traditions which first mention standing and then prostration should be re-interpreted as including the intermediate stage of kneeling. The lateness of the tradition, however, makes it somewhat unlikely that Abot de Rabbi Nathan is actually reflecting cultic reality.[35]

---

[32]ARN, A, 35 (53b, edn Schechter). B, 39 only mentions standing and prostration.

[33]See, for example, MYoma 6:2 and PT Yoma 3:7,40d.

[34]See note 4 above.

[35]A number of other traditions mention sitting in the Temple Mount region, but it is unlikely that they refer to the azarah and we shall deal with them in a different study. See, for example, MSheq 1:3 and MMen 8:7. See also BT Pes 26a on Rabban Yoḥanan b. Zakkai 'who used to sit in the shade of the Sanctuary and teach the whole day.' It is hard to know how far the shade of the sanctuary extended and where he was sitting, if indeed the source is historical or to be taken literally. Cf. Lk 2:46 which has a young Jesus sitting among the teachers in the Temple courts. Here too we have no way of knowing exactly where they were sitting and teaching. Later on, early Christians would meet in the 'hall of Solomon'. However, it is not easy to identify this site. See, for instance, M. Hengel, 'The Geography of Palestine in Acts', in R. Bauckham (ed.), *The Book of Acts in its First Century Setting*, Grand Rapids, Michigan 1995, 37. See also TSanh 2:6 (416-417, edn Zuckermandel) and parallels which mention Rabban Gamaliel and the Elders 'who

Standing in the Azarah

There was nothing unusual about standing in the azarah.[36] In this section we will discuss the different type of 'standing traditions' regarding the azarah and particularly try and determine the reasons for this posture.

Most acts related to sacrifice required that one stood. Thus, for instance, the High Priest used to 'stand and minister at the Altar'.[37] Laying of hands on an offering was done when standing.[38] High Priest or Priest stood while offering sacrifice at the Altar outside the Sanctuary,[39] while dismembering the animal and receiving its limbs[40] and while burning the limbs of the sacrifice on that Altar.[41] Receiving the blood of a sacrifice[42] or pouring it into the base of the Altar[43] was done while standing and the same applied regarding the meal offering.[44] The Priests who blessed the congregation assembled at the Temple and stood on the steps

---

used to sit on top of the steps on the Temple Mount.' This is usually interpreted as those steps leading up to the Double and Triple Gates and this is altogether outside the Temple Mount.

[36] A number of sources also refer to standing in other areas of the Temple Mount outside of the azarah, but these too will be discussed in a different study. See, for instance, MOrlah 2:12, MSuk 5:4, and TBer 3:16 (16, edn Lieberman).

[37] MYeb 7:6.

[38] MYoma 3:8.

[39] MTer 8:1; TYoma 1:19, 21-22 (227-228, edn Lieberman); TSot 2:6 (157, edn Lieberman); TMen 1:13 (513, edn Zuckermandel) and TMiqw 1:18 (653, edn Zuckermandel). See also MTaan 4:2. It was assumed that someone who brought up a sacrifice to the Temple Mount would stand by it while it was being offered by the Priests. It was, of course, also necessary to stand during the actual act of slaughtering. See MTam 4:1.

[40] MTam 4:3; MSheq 8:8.

[41] MTam 7:3. While the High Priest offered up these limbs, two other Priests stood nearby at the Table of the Fat Pieces.

[42] MZeb 2:1; TZeb 1:9 (480); TZeb 3:4 (483-484) and BT Zeb 23b.

[43] TZeb 6:4 (488).

[44] MMen 1:2.

leading up to the porch (*'ûlām*).[45] Everyone stood inside the Temple.[46]

There were also other actions which required standing in the azarah. Thus, for example, the High Priest officiating in the Yom Kippur service sanctified his hands a number of times during the day and that could only be done while standing.[47] Also, the Priests involved in the daily lottery which assigned cultic tasks and which took place in the Chamber of Hewn Stone stood during that lottery process.[48] The Levites used to stand and sing on a platform located between the Court of Priests and the Court of Israelites.[49] The accused woman in the sotah ceremony would stand inside the Nicanor Gate, thus inside the azarah, while all the Priests involved would stand just outside of it.[50] The leper who had been purified would stand in the outer section of the Nicanor Gate while the Priest officiating in the ceremony would stand inside it.[51]

---

[45]TSot 7:7 (193, edn Lieberman). This is not to be confused with the blessing of the Priests before the offering of the Tamid. Cf. MTam 5:1. See also PT MSh 5:6,56c: 'It happened that Rabban Gamaliel and the Elders were sitting on the steps of the *'ûlām* in the Temple Mount etc.', but this is probably a scribal error, since it is hard to imagine anyone sitting here and teaching.

[46]On the High Priest standing in the Sanctuary see MYoma 5:5; TYoma 2:12 (236, edn Lieberman); 3:1 (240, edn Lieberman). The Priest who trimmed the candlestick in the Sanctuary stood on a stone before it (MTam 3:9). The Priest who gave out the Show Bread stood on the terrace of the Porch (TSuk 4:23, 277, edn Lieberman; TMen 11:13, 530, edn Zuckermandel). Cf. MMid 3:6.

[47]On the prohibition against sitting during this see BT Zeb 19b. On the necessary ritual immersions and sanctifications on that day and where they took place in the azarah see MYoma 3:3, 6.

[48]TYoma 1:10 (224, edn Lieberman).

[49]MArak 2:6; TArak 2:1 (544, edn Zuckermandel). On the singing of Hallel there see TPes 4:11 (163).

[50]TSot 1:5 (152); 1:7 (153) and 2:1 (154).

[51]TNeg 8:9 (628).

Why Stand?

Not all of the traditions just mentioned above which require standing explain why this standing was necessary. A few, however, and a number of additional traditions, did attempt to explain the requirement of standing during cultic acts. The Rabbis, particularly in trying to explain the halakhic background of all this, tend to stay clear of religious anthropology and stick to biblical exegesis. Thus, for example, we find in SifreDeut 155 (207, edn Finkelstein) the following teaching:

> 'Unto the Priest that stands to minister (there before the Lord thy God' (Deut 17:12) – This tells us that (Temple) service is not acceptable unless while standing. Thus, if (the Priest) sat and officiated, his act is void.[52]

The reason that Priests and others stood during cultic acts in the Second Temple period, according to the Rabbis, was because the Bible stated that the Priest stood to minister in the Tabernacle. The reason for that, however, was apparently not of concern to SifreDeut.[53]

---

[52] See also SifreDeut 167 (216, edn Finkelstein): "'For the Lord thy God has chosen him out of all thy tribes (to stand to minister in the name of the Lord...)' (Deut 18:5) – This teaches that service is not acceptable regarding him (= Priest) unless while standing. Thus, if (the Priest) sat and officiated, his act is void."

[53] A similar teaching is found in SifreNum 39 (43, edn Horovitz) regarding the priestly benediction: "'Thus you shall bless the children of Israel' (Num 6:23) – This teaches us while standing. While standing or perhaps also while not standing? Thus it is written, 'These shall stand to bless the people' (Deut 27:12). A benediction is mentioned here (= in Num) and a benediction is mentioned later on (= in Deut). Just as the benediction mentioned further on is done while standing, so the benediction mentioned here is done while standing. Rabbi Nathan said: This (teaching from) Deuteronomy is not necessary since it already has been written (earlier in Deut), 'and the Priests the sons of Levi shall come near – for them the Lord thy God has chosen to minister unto Him (and to bless in the name of the Lord...)' (Deut 21:5). (The Bible) compares 'benediction' to service (or ministry). Just as service (or ministry) is done while standing so the (priestly) benediction is done while

The only real attempt to explain the laws mentioned above regarding the cult is found in the amoraic period discussion in BT Zeb 23b-24a on MZeb 2:1.[54] This mishnah, which we cited above (see n. 42) regarding receiving sacrificial blood while standing, actually lists, among other things, the unacceptable postures for this cultic act:

> ... sitting, or while standing on any object, or on the back of a beast or on the feet of his fellow.

In actuality, the mishnah really only lists two unacceptable positions: sitting or standing on anything apart from the ground of the azarah. On this BT Zeb comments:

> How do we know this (= that sitting while receiving the blood invalidates the sacrifice)? Raba said in the name of Rab Naḥman: 'to stand to minister' (Deut 18:5) – for standing I (= God) chose him (= Priest) and not for sitting.

This verse has already been cited above in other teachings that cultic acts required standing (nn. 2, 52), but as we have also already seen, no additional reasons were provided beyond biblical precedent. The BT was apparently also bothered by this and added a more 'personal' touch. Standing was the posture chosen by God for ritual acts associated with sacrifice. God, as it were, demanded standing. This being the case, the discussion in BT went on to point out that standing was obligatory and under no circumstances would a sacrifice be valid if the blood was accepted by a Priest when sitting. In spite of this, however, if the

---

standing." The teaching of R. Nathan is cited anonymously in SifreDeut 208 (243, edn Finkelstein). See also PT Taan 4:1,67c and MidrTannaim on Deut 21:5 (125, edn Hoffmann). Cf. Sifra *Shemini*, Parashah 1:29 (45, edn Weiss). Deut 21:5 is cited to prove that Aaron's benediction mentioned in Lev 9:22 was also done while standing. In none of these traditions or versions is there any attempt to really explain the requirement to stand.

[54]Cf. TZeb 3:4 (483).

Priest did sit he was not guilty of a capital crime and simply caused the sacrifice to be disqualified.

The Talmud then continued to discuss the cases of incorrect or incomplete standing when the Priests' feet were not on the ground and came up with two interconnected reasons for invalidating these postures:

Since the ground (of the azarah) imparts sanctity and the sacrificial utensils impart sanctity. Just as nothing may come between the sacrificial utensils and him (= the Priest), so regarding the ground and nothing may come between him (= the Priest) and the ground.

It was necessary then for the Priest to have two feet on the ground because otherwise he was not really standing and he had to stand because the ground he was standing on imparted sanctity and that ground imparted sanctity because of the cultic or sacrificial act he was undertaking.[55]

Herein lies the key to the understanding of the concepts of sitting and standing in the azarah. The azarah and the area beyond to the Temple were indeed holier than other areas in the Temple Mount, Jerusalem or anything else. But this holiness did not intrinsically require standing as opposed to sitting.[56] What required standing were the cultic acts associated with the azarah and the Temple, as we have seen any number of times. There was never any real attempt to explain this. It was just assumed that this was the correct posture for these acts, whether because the Bible related that Priests 'stood to minister', as was cited in tannaitic and

---

[55]We have explained here in accordance with the view of the Tosaphot on BT Zeb 24a and against the view of Rashi.

[56]See MKel 1:6-9 which list the ten degrees of holiness, culminating in the Holy of Holies. No reference is made to posture. TKel BQ 1:12 likens the area of the azarah to biblical 'camp of the Shekhinah', as opposed to the 'camp of Israel' and 'camp of the Levites', but here too no mention is made of posture. Cf. U. Ehrlich, *Modes of Prayer and Their Significance in the Time of the Mishnah and Talmud* (Hebr.), unpublished doctoral dissertation, Hebrew University of Jerusalem 1994, 19-20, who sees the requirement to stand in the azarah as related the status of the azarah as the 'camp of the Shekhinah', but there are no sources to attest to this.

amoraic sources, or because that was just the way it was supposed to be.[57] As we have seen, when cultic acts were not being undertaken in the azarah, then it was perfectly allowable to sit, sleep or even use the toilet there.

When was this realistic and practical attitude replaced with the view accepted by the amoraic Rabbis that 'there was no sitting in the azarah'? Probably this took place when there was no longer any real problem as to what postures or gestures were acceptable in the azarah, i.e. well after the destruction of the Temple. During the course of the tannaitic period and especially later on during the amoraic period and afterwards, prayer began to be associated with the Temple service. Since, as we have seen above, the Temple ritual was carried out while standing, it was not unusual that comparisons began to be made between standing in prayer and the standing in the Temple ritual.[58] Since, however, the Temple no longer existed, the borrowings did not have to depend on an exact symmetry and a general comparison was probably enough.[59] Indeed, once the initial comparison between sacrifice and prayer had been made, the Sages occasionally began to work backwards

---

[57]Standing is clearly the most common accepted posture for sacrifice and similar ritual acts in the ancient world. See, for instance, J.B. Pritchard, *The Ancient Near East in Pictures: Relating to the Old Testament*, Princeton [2]1969, 197-205. Those participating in the ritual or cultic acts, even kings, stand while the god is occasionally depicted as sitting. See also J.N. Bremmer, *Greek Religion,* Oxford 1994, 39-43 and W. Burkert, *Greek Religion: Archaic and Classic*, Oxford 1985, 56. In the Graeco-Roman world, standing during cultic acts was considered a simple act of respect for the deity. See C. Sittl, *Die Gebaerden der Griechen und Roemer*, Leipzig 1890, 176. Cf. F.J. Doelger, 'Das Niedersitzen nach dem Gebet', *Antike und Christentum* / 5, Muenster 1936 [reprint 1976], 116-137. The Church Father Tertullian (*De Oratione* 16) mentions the custom of some in Christian circles to sit after prayer. He could find no real reason for this custom and, moreover, pagans also occasionally did so, after worshipping idols. This act of sitting represented a formal conclusion to prayer and during the course of time other means, such as chanting 'Amen', were used to represent the conclusion of praying. I should like to thank Dr Marcel Poorthuis for bringing these matters to my attention.
[58]Ehrlich, *Modes of Prayer,* 27.
[59]Ehrlich, *Modes of Prayer,* 20.

from prayer to Temple and thus it was assumed that all Temple
activities in the azarah had to be done standing or that there was
no sitting in the azarah.

There was, however, a major difference between prayer and
Temple ritual. Prayer is an attempt to communicate with a deity
and, thus, prescribes its own set of gestures, postures and body
language appropriate for that purpose. Sacrifice and its attendant
rituals and cultic acts represent an act of offering to the deity and
this clearly required its own set of gestures and postures. Prayer
demanded gestures of supplication; sacrifice demanded respect.[60]

All of this created a number of problems. The comparison, as
we have just seen, was not symmetrical and, moreover, the back-
ward anachronistic elements of the comparison neglected the non-
cultic activities in the azarah. During the Second Temple period,
such a view would have caused a great deal of discomfort for
people who would have had to stand for no real reason. Later on,
however, when there was no Temple, it was all just theoretical
and did not really make any difference.

The last stage in the rabbinic comparison between standing in
the Temple and in prayer introduced the standing of the angels in
the heavens.[61] A number of midrashic sources state that 'there was

---

[60]See Ehrlich, *Modes of Prayer,* 176. Standing in prayer, as opposed to sitting or walking, is an act of self-depreciation and more appropriate to supplication. Prayer also is a much more intimate activity than sacrifice.

[61]This is not to say that the motif in general is late, rather that the Rabbis
seemed to understand it as a late motif. Thus, a correspondence between the
earthly and heavenly cult is found already in the literature of the Second
Temple period and this literature even has angels standing. It would seem,
therefore, that already in this literature of the Second Temple period it was
taken for granted that angels, whether associated with the cult or doing anything else, would stand. On the heavenly cult in general see B. Nitzan, *Qumran Prayer and Poetry* (Hebr.), Jerusalem 1996, 217-218. On angels standing
on the steps of the heavenly Temple see A. Aptowitzer, '*Beth ha-Miqdash
shel Ma'alah al pi ha-Aggadah*', *Tarbiz* 2 (1931), 262-263. The question is
whether the Rabbis were at all familiar with the early motif or if they were,
knew of its correct chronological framework. Thus BT Ḥag 12b has the arch-
angel Michael standing and sacrificing, but it is only the relatively late
midrashic traditions which we shall shortly examine which have the pro-
scription against sitting in the heavenly Temple. Also, although the standing-

no sitting above', i.e. in the heavens. The angels could not or would not dare sit before God.[62] However, only one of these relatively late midrashic sources dealing with the comparison between prayer and the heavens made reference to the Temple. Thus, Midrash Psalms stated that there was also no sitting in the azarah just as there was no sitting in the heavens or during prayer.[63] This represented one of the latest developments in the standing-sitting controversy as described in rabbinic literature and probably only developed in response to the unique statement in Midrash Psalms of R. Ammi quoting Resh Laqish as saying that there was no sitting in the azarah 'except (!) in the place reserved for the kings of the House of David.' Such a lenient attitude would have required a heavenly precedent against it and this is exactly what happened. The statement of R. Ammi was then changed to conform with the other versions of it that there was no sitting at all in the azarah.

All of this brings us back to MSot 7:8 which has the king reading the portion of *haqhēl* while sitting on a platform constructed in the azarah. This is indeed unique. The precedent cannot be the case of Solomon since, as we saw above, he seemed to be sitting only during respites from actual participation in the Temple dedication ceremony and otherwise stood or kneeled. MSot describes the actual reading taking place when the king was sitting.

---

sitting motif also appears in early Christian literature, it is questionable whether the Rabbis knew of this. See, for instance, Acts 7:56. Stephen sees Jesus as the Son of Man standing (and not sitting!) on the right hand of God. Cf., however, C.K. Barret, 'Stephen and the Son of Man', in: *Apophoreta: Festschrift E. Haenchen*, Berlin 1964, 32-38. Jesus is standing because he is about to go to Stephen in his distress; otherwise he would be sitting at God's right hand. I should like to thank Dr Marcel Poorthuis for bringing much of this information to my attention. Ultimately, though, none of this changes the history of the development of the motifs in rabbinic literature.

[62] See, for instance, GenR 65:21 (737-739, edn Theodor-Albeck); ExodR 43:4; DeutR 68; RuthR, Petiḥta 1:1; RuthR 1; TanBuber, *Beshallah* 13 (31a); Tan *Qedoshim* 6.

[63] MidrPss 1:2 (1-2a, edn Buber). See also V. Aptowitzer, *'Beth ha-Miqdash shel Ma'alah'*, 286.

The difference between the dedication ceremony of Solomon and *haqhēl*, as well as what we have seen above, however, might help us in understanding how and why the king could sit during that ceremony. The Temple dedication ceremony was cultic in nature. The ark was brought from the City of David (1 Kgs 8:1-4) and Solomon, after he blessed the people continued the ceremony 'before the altar' (1 Kgs 8:22), praying there and then offering sacrifice. His acts were intrinsically connected with the Temple and cult and his posture was in accordance with this.

The *haqhēl* ceremony, however, was not connected with the Temple. The king, for instance, did not even offer sacrifice. Rather, the Temple Mount area in general was a convenient gathering place for the multitudes who were undoubtedly on hand and holding the ceremony particularly in the azarah was in keeping with the respect that the king commanded.[64] *Haqhēl* revolved around the king and his relationship with the people. God was not absent from the ceremony, but he was not the central player, as it were. Thus, since *haqhēl* was not really cultic or sacrificial, there was no reason why the king should not have been allowed to sit while reading his portions.[65]

One last point remains to be cleared up. All of the talmudic discussions on this Mishnah explained the reference to kings as relating to kings of the House of David and as we saw above, this would have made the Mishnah entirely theoretical, since there were no kings of the House of David in the Second Temple period. In our view, however, the Mishnah, in spite of the talmudic explanations, does not refer to such non-existent kings. The Mishnah states that Agrippa read while standing and the Sages

---

[64]For a good summary of this see Maimonides, *Mishneh Torah, Hilkhot Melakhim* (Hebr.), Chapter 2.

[65]See note 9 above. Josephus, *Ant.* 4.208-210 has the High Priest reading this portion and standing. It should be remembered, though, that in this case the High Priest really should be considered a 'stand in', since the ceremony does relate to the king regardless of who reads it. In addition to that, the High Priest was probably so strongly identified with the Temple cult that it was assumed that any ceremony that he participated in was cultic and it was perhaps, therefore, better for him to stand to avoid confusion.

praised him. If the Mishnah referred only to the House of David then no one would have ever read sitting, every king would have read standing and there would have been no reason to praise Agrippa for doing what was expected and required. If he stood and the Sages praised him, others must have sat, perhaps even Herod. The Sages might have preferred that the king stand, but based on what we have seen above, it would not have been required.

Mishnah Sotah, then, preserves an ancient custom which allowed for non-cultic sitting. Later on, in the wake of prayer–Temple comparisons, it was assumed that sitting was not allowed and if anyone at all, such as a king had been allowed to sit in the azarah, it could only have been a king of the House of David, effectively meaning that no one sat. This, as we have just seen was simply not the case.

POSTBIBLICAL PERIOD:

2. Christianity

THE INSTITUTIONALIZATION OF THE CULT OF SAINTS IN CHRISTIAN SOCIETY

Ze'ev Safrai

Introduction

The culture of sacred sites and the cult of saints in Christian society has been of great interest both to authors in antiquity and to modern research. A short article can hardly hope to encompass all the different aspects of this topic, and therefore the purview of this discussion will be of a more limited nature. The cult of saints has generally been discussed within a wide context, and scholars have raised historical-theological questions regarding the origin of the cult; its theological and sociological foundations; its participants, supporters and opponents, etc. This article will take a slightly different approach, based on the assumption that the culture of sacred sites, each site independently and together as a collective, develops within a social context. The site consecrated to a saint and the cult itself usually becomes known only after the saint in question becomes renowned and accepted by the public. Initially, this phenomenon is limited to a small group of saints, but gradually develops and grows. The process of public recognition is accompanied by the parallel development of cultic practices which take form in clearly-defined rites and public ceremonies, the formulation of a liturgy, the construction of permanent structures, and other such components of the cult.

The culture of sacred sites is known in Jewish society and in pagan society of the Roman Period. The cult of saints is also found in mediaeval and modern Christian society. The many descriptions in historical and sociological literature, and ancient Christian traditions enable us to reconstruct the main phases of this process in the early Christian society of the 2nd-6th centuries. This process may also serve as an interesting test case for examining the characteristics of a similar process in other societies as well. Our basic assumption is that the cult of saints is not inherent to Christianity nor to Judaism, it is not 'natural'. The term 'natural' is not judgmental, nor does it express a qualitative evaluation of the phenomenon, but rather implies a historical-social appraisal. In other words, the cult of saints did not exist inherently in the core of these religions, but rather was created, developed, and formulated in specific circumstances. The concept of sacred locations in which the gods dwelled and from where they direct our world was prevalent in the Hellenistic-Roman pagan culture, and most likely also in other pagan cultures of the period. Humans were connected to them by some sort of physical link which required a physically defined sacred precinct. Christianity opposed such practices and developed within the struggle against them (below).

Furthermore, early Christianity inherited the statements attributed to Jesus which express clear and vigorous opposition to the cult of sacred sites: "Woe to you! for you build the tombs of the prophets whom your fathers killed",[1] an allusion to the prophet Zechariah who, according to Jewish and Christian tradition, was killed by Jews. Matt 23:29 testifies to the existence of this cult in Jewish society: "Woe to you, scribes and Pharisees, hypocrites! for you build the tombs of the prophets and adorn the monuments of the righteous."[2]

Christianity's attitude to Jerusalem was complex and ambivalent. In the second generation the new faith, under the influence of Paul, adopted a stance rejecting the sanctity of the earthly Jerusalem. As time passed, the official position changed. Many scholars have discussed this issue;[3] we shall limit ourselves to noting

---

[1]Luke 11:47; cf. idem, v. 48; v. 51.

[2]Z. Safrai, 'Sacred Tombs and the Holy Sites in the Jewish Tradition' (Hebr.), *Ze'ev Vilnay's Jubilee Volume*, Jerusalem 1987, II.303-13.

[3]E.g. W.D. Davies, *The Gospel and the Land,* Berkley 1974, 222-376; J. Munck, *Paul and the Salvation of Mankind,* Richmond 1959; P.W.L. Walker, *Holy City, Holy Places,* Oxford 1990; F. Cardman, 'The Rhetoric of the Holy Places', *Studia Patristica* 18 (1982) 18-25; J. Prawer, 'Jerusalem in the Jewish and Christian Perspective of the Early Middle Ages', *Settimane di Studio*

that this proves that the culture of sacred sites had to develop, and the phases and components of such a process should be examined.

The process of institutionalization is composed of three components related to one another, though not necessarily connected: (1) the process of emergence, (2) the process of recognition, and (3) the process of fashioning and formulation.

1. The process of emergence

The cult of sacred sites generally begins with a local cult accepted among some type of a local subgroup. It slowly develops, eventually becoming more and more accepted in both local and regional spheres. The 'emergence point' is some imperceptible point of time, which generally cannot be determined with any precision, in which the local cult extends from the bounds of the nearby region and begins to attract believers from afar. An additional emergence point relates to the cultural-social sphere, when the cult location becomes the focal point of a 'sacred rite', or a 'sacred site culture', a culture which reflects the multiplicity of sacred sites. In such cases, the visit to the sacred site also becomes a social event (or series of such events), which concurrently begins to occupy an important place in the religious routine or in the religious and social public calendar. In this phase, the sacred site begins to acquire importance and social standing; the act of pilgrimage there becomes an important event on the calendar and takes on economic significance. The site now becomes important for the religious individual. From this point on, many believers visit the site, or at the very least, the believer feels guilty if he has not visited it during some prescribed time. Though not every believer necessarily visits the holy site, almost everyone believes that it is proper to do so, and such a visit insures a reward. Thus the 'public', as a 'public', visits the site, even if the 'public' is a small fraction of the population.

---

del Centro Italiano di Studi sull'Alto Medieoevo 20 (1980) 739-95; M. Poorthuis & Ch. Safrai (eds), *The Centrality of Jerusalem*, Kampen 1996.

A 'culture of sacred sites' generally requires a large number of sites which will enable the entire public to come and participate in events. Consequently, the emergence process also includes an increase in the number of sacred sites.

The first stages of this process in Christian society can be observed in the 2nd and 3rd centuries. Testimonies regarding these phases have been collected by Taylor[4] and by a number of other scholars.[5]

The earliest information is attributed to the Gospel of the Hebrews. This work has not been preserved, but the Church Fathers cite various passages from it. Origen testifies that this Gospel relate that the miracle of the Temptation occurred on Mount Tabor.[6] If this was indeed written in the vanished Gospel of the Hebrews, then this tradition should be dated to the late 1st or early 2nd century. The extant gospels state that the Temptation took place 'on a very high mountain';[7] the desire to identify even an unnamed mountain reflects the growing attention paid to identifying the site of the miracle. This site has not yet become a sacred site, but rather has undergone precondition and initial stage in the creation of sanctity tradition. The identification already appears as commonly known in *the Narrative by Joseph of Arimathea*,[8] and

---

[4] J.E. Taylor, *Christians and the Holy Places: The Myth of Jewish-Christian Origins,* Oxford 1993, esp. 310-14.

[5] B. Bagatti, *The Church from the Circumcision,* Jerusalem 1971, 17-28; 68-71; H. Windisch, 'Die aeltesten christlichen Palaestinapilger', *ZDPV* 48 (1925) 145-58; C. Kopp, *Die heiligen Staetten der Evangelien,* Regensburg, 1959; J. Wilkinson, 'Jewish Holy Places and the Origin of Christian Pilgrimage', in: R. Ousterhout (ed.), *The Blessing of Pilgrimage,* Illinois 1990, 41-53; idem, 'Christian Pilgrims in Jerusalem during the Byzantine Period', *PEQ* 108 (1976) 74-101; G. Kretschmar, 'Festelender und Memorialstaetten Jerusalem in altkirchlicher Zeit', in: H. Busse & G. Kretschmar, *Jerusalemer Heiligtumstraditionen in altkirchlicher und fruehislamischer Zeit,* Wiesbaden 1987, esp. 62-76; cf. the research of Hunt and Wilken (below).

[6] Origen, *Commentary on John* 2:12; M.R. James, *The Apocryphal New Testament,* Oxford 1955, 2

[7] Matt 4:8; Luke 4:5.

[8] *The Narrative by Joseph of Arimathea,* XI.

later in the hymns of Ephrem the Syrian (mid 4th century).[9] In the writings of Eusebius from the early 4th century, Tabor does not appear yet as a sacred site, even though he alludes to its identity as the location of the miracle.[10] The Bordeaux pilgrim did not visit the mountain, even though he passed through the Jezreel Valley, not far from Mount Tabor, and must have seen the renowned mountain, which was visible from a great distance. This teaches that even if attention and recognition had been given to this place, it had not yet become an active sacred site.[11] Cyril knew already the tradition that the miracle of the Transfiguration had occurred on Tabor,[12] but still refrained from defining it as a Holy Site.

Christian apocryphal literature from the 2nd century contains identifications of sites in which wondrous events of the past had occurred. Thus the tomb of St Mary and the miracles which had taken place around it are located in the Valley of Jehoshaphat.[13] Special emphasis was placed on all the sites on the Mount of Olives. Thus, e.g., this site is mentioned in apocryphal writings such as *The Gospel of Bartholomew* and in other works.[14] The manger stable in which Jesus was born is identified as being three miles from Bethlehem,[15] and the site of the crossing of the Jordan is mentioned in another apocryphal work.[16]

---

[9]A. McVey, *Ephrem the Syrian Hymns,* New York 1989, Hymn 21.

[10]Commentary on Ps 88:13; P.W.L. Walker, *Holy City*, 145-61.

[11]P.W.L Walker, *Holy City*, 145-61. Eusebius' disregard for the sanctity of the mountain in most of the instances in which he discusses it is patently related to his general attitude to geographical problems. Undoubtedly, however, if Tabor had been an active sacred site, this fact would have been reflected to a greater degree in his writings.

[12]*Cathec.*, 12:16.

[13]*The Assumption of the Virgin*, XVII; *The Narrative by Joseph of Arimathea*, XIV.

[14]*The Gospel of Bartholomew*, IV, M.R. James, *The Apocryphal New Testament*, 178; idem, 222; 511.

[15]*Protevangelium or Gospel of James*, XVII, M.R. James, *The Apocryphal New Testament*, 45; J.E. Taylor, *Christians and the Holy Places,* 146 ff., 192-201.

[16]*Gospel of Pseudo-Matthew*, XXXV, M.R. James, *The Apocryphal New Testament*, 78.

The writings of the Church Fathers from the 2nd and 3rd centuries, mainly those by Justin Martyr and Origen, speak of three or four sacred sites: Golgotha, (and) the birthplace or grave of Adam, and the general location of Jesus' empty grave in Jerusalem, the Mount of Olives, and Bethlehem, the site of the birth of Jesus.[17] It is not stated explicitly that these were sacred sites, that pilgrimage should be made to them, or that people do so, but attention was devoted to these locations, and they are clearly regarded as special places.

Origen mentions Rachel's Tomb,[18] the Tombs of the Patriarchs in Hebron,[19] and the Well of Abraham in Hebron.[20] He also devotes a quite lengthy discussion to the identification of the Miracle of the Swine.[21] The problem of identification of this miracle was quite problematic already in the Gospels, which contain different, and even contradictory, descriptions, according to which the miracle occurred in the country of the Gadarenes (Gadara/Gader in Transjordan) or of the Gerasenes (Gerasa/Jerash in Transjordan) or in the country of the Gergasenes, to the east of the Sea of Galilee.[22] Origen's discussion attests to the importance of identifying the site of the miracle, on the one hand, while indicating, on the other hand, that this was not an active and known sacred site. If it had been an accepted pilgrimage site, its location would not have been the subject of controversy.

Somewhat contemporary to these initial testimonies of their recognition as sacred sites, there are also reports of the first visits of pilgrims to them. Thus, Eusebius mentions a number of pilgrims who visited Palestine in the 2nd century: Melitius, Alexander (who would later be appointed Bishop of Jerusalem), and

---

[17]Justin Martyr, *Dialogue with Trypho* 78:12-13; idem, 19; Origen, *Contra Celsum*, 1:51; idem, *Commentary on Matt* 126; see also J.E. Taylor, *Christians and the Holy Places,* 48-294.

[18]Origin, *Catena 34 on Matt 2:18.*

[19]Origin, *De Princ.*, 4:3:20.

[20]Origin, *Contra Celsum*, 4:4.

[21]Origen, *Commentary on John*, 9:24.

[22]Matt 8:28; Mark 5:1; Luke 8:26. For a discussion of the site, see: C. Kopp, *Die heiligen Staetten*, 282-7.

Phirmelinus from Cappadocia.[23] Origen also toured Palestine, and proudly attested to this. The pilgrimage aspect of his visit was, however, overshadowed by, in his words, the 'scientific' aspect of the trip, which was undertaken for the purpose of studying the Scriptures and identifying their sites.[24] Later Christian legends mention the wife of the Emperor Claudius and other important women who came to Palestine.[25] Although these legends are from a later period, they may possibly be combined with testimonies of pilgrimages to Palestine as early as the 2nd century. Thus, for example, Pionius of Smyrna tells of his pilgrimage to the Holy Land. A different source teaches of another Christian visitor from Persia.[26] Eusebius also relates that many pilgrims came to Jerusalem.[27] This work was written before Christianity became the official religion of the Empire.

A graffito, for which various interpretations have been offered, was discovered on an engraved impression of a ship in the lower level of the Church of the Holy Sepulchre. Some scholars regarded it as a pagan inscription addressed to Isis, but it is now clear that this is a Christian inscription in Latin: "...id omini manibus." The ship and the inscription attest to a Christian pilgrim who came to the basement of the temple of Venus that stood on this spot at Aelia Capitolina and expressed his veneration and belief in the sanctity of the site for Christianity.[28] The precise dating of the graffito and inscription cannot be determined. They apparently are from the 2nd century, thus constituting additional

---

[23]See E.D. Hunt, *Holy Land Pilgrims in the Later Roman Empire AD 312-460,* Oxford 1982, 3-4; H. Windisch, 'Die aeltesten', 145-58; B. Bagatti, *The Church From the Gentiles in Palestine,* Jerusalem 1971, 18-22.

[24]Origen, *Commentary on Job,* 6:64; 6:40; *Commentary on John* 9:24; J.E. Taylor, *Christians and the Holy Places,* 105.

[25]*PO* 7:485; *PO* 21: 464-466.

[26]See B. Bagatti, *The Church From the Gentiles,* 20-21.

[27]*Prep. Evan.* 6:10:23.

[28]The primary discussion is by M. Broshi & G. Barkai, 'Excavations in the Chapel of St. Vartan in the Holy Sepulcher', *IEJ* 35 (1985) 108-128; S. Gibson & J.E. Taylor, *Beneath the Church of the Holy Sepulchre,* London 1994, 42-49.

testimony of pilgrimages to the Holy Sepulchre in this century.[29]
Eusebius also mentions a pilgrim who came to the Mount of Olives,[30] but this sentence as well was written after the establishment
of a church there, and may possibly reflect the reality following
the changed attitude of the Church to sacred sites.

Taylor, as well as other scholars, nevertheless errs in concluding that the cult of the saints had already begun in this early
phase. These centuries witnessed the initial formulation of the
traditions of sanctity and the appearance of individual pilgrims.
Almost all the above testimonies attest, at the very most, to the
activities of individuals or to interest in, but nothing beyond this,
in sacred sites. The graffiti of the ship already attests to a 'sacred
site' culture, but its dating is no more than conjecture.

Moreover, despite the interest shown in sacred sites, there is no
clear testimony to the continuous recognition of the sanctity of
sites, or of uninterrupted sacred activity at these sites. To the
contrary, Origen and other writers, including Epiphanius in the
4th century, are undecided regarding the identity of Gergesa, the
location of the Miracle of the Swine. Origen proposes a compro-
mise solution: all three definitions are correct, and the miracle
occurred somewhere between the three territories.[31] The debate
regarding identification was halted, before being decided in the
6th century when the holy place was established. Christian literature contains legends of the finding of remnants of the True
Cross, thereby testifying yet again to the absence of a continued
awareness of the sanctity of the site.

Wilkinson, followed by Taylor,[32] noted that some of the sacred
sites were former pagan temples. Thus, for example, the Church
of the Holy Sepulchre in Jerusalem replaced a temple of Venus-

---

[29]M. Broshi & G. Barkai, 'Excavations'. The Latin inscription may possibly attest to a pilgrim from the West who arrived in a ship. The interpretations that this refers to the symbolic and 'theological' ascent to heaven by
angels and not the journey of flesh-and-blood pilgrims was justifiably rejected in the wake of the cleaning and careful study of the inscription.
[30]*Laud. Con.*, 9:6:7.
[31]Epiphanius, *Panarion*, 6:35:66.
[32]J.E. Taylor, *Christians and the Holy Places,* 318-22.

Aphrodite,[33] and the Manger in Bethlehem was built on and replaced a temple of Adonis-Tammuz.[34] Some authorities doubted this tradition, since the description of the cave's location is neither uniform nor precise,[35] but it is highly improbable that as early as the 2nd century Justin Martyr would have invented such a story without any factual basis. The discrepancies between the descriptions are to be attributed to the indifference of Christian authors to details in Palestine, and possibly also to their distance from the land.[36]

Scholars have naturally been attracted to the connection between pagan temples and Christian sacred sites, which clearly is not coincidental. Either the Christians expropriated existing temples and traditions of sanctity of the vanquished religion, or the Romans built temples on Christian sacred sites. Wilkinson was of the opinion that the Christian traditions were earlier, and that the Roman authorities had appropriated the Christian sacred sites and turned them into temples.[37] The Roman authorities (i.e. Hadrian) indeed acted in such a manner in Jerusalem, Mambre, and the Mount of Olives. These, however, are the most outstanding sites, and it is highly improbable that in the 2nd century the Romans would have acted in such a fashion towards the sacred sites of a marginal religion such as Christianity. Furthermore, the historical veracity of the Christian traditions may be questioned. The Church of the Holy Sepulchre is situated in the suburbs of what was Second Temple Jerusalem, and it is well-known that the Jews buried their dead beyond the bounds of their cities. This location is quite suitable for a Byzantine sacred site, in the heart of Aelia Capitolina, and on the ruins of the central pagan temple of the

---

[33]S. Gibson & J.E. Taylor, *Beneath the Church*, 65-71.

[34]Justin Martyr, *Dialogue with Trypho*, 78:12.

[35]J.E. Taylor, *Christians and the Holy Places*, 96-99.

[36]Taylor's argument, that the tradition is accurate because Jerome of Bethlehem attests to it, is surprising. Jerome was active more than a century after the magnificent church obliterated all traces of the earlier pagan temple, and therefore his independent testimony is of little value.

[37]J. Wilkinson, 'Christian Pilgrims in Jerusalem during the Byzantine Period', *PEQ* 108 (1976) 74-101.

city, but is totally unreasonable for the location of a Jewish grave. The Church of the Holy Sepulchre was situated outside Second Temple Jerusalem, but within the bounds of the populated periphery of the city. The rigorous excavations conducted in the cellars of the church revealed the remains of a cave used as a quarry from the First Temple period,[38] and the foundations of a large structure (probably the temple of Venus),[39] but no remains of a burial cave. In the entire area there are no additional burial caves from the period corresponding to the death of Jesus,[40] with the exception of one small cave within the bounds of the church, which is currently attributed to Joseph of Arimathea. The area in which the church is located therefore seems to have been situated within a suburb of the Second Temple city. The cave it contains was most probably in use only in the early Roman period, because Jews did not bury their dead in populated areas, and such tombs were evacuated when they were enveloped by the built area of a city. Consequently, the probability that this grave was a natural site for the interment of prisoners condemned to death is extremely low.

The same is true of the manger in Bethlehem. The site is located in the center of the ancient settlement, at the top of the hill. Such a location is suitable for the temple of Adonis or for a church, but not for a manger on the fringes of the settlement. There is also another problem. The proto-Gospel of James describes the manger as being located outside the settlement. Such a description is unrealistic, since the church was built in the center of the city. This narrative is therefore unrelated to the testimony of Justin Martyr, who describes the location as being within the settlement itself.[41]

Nor is Mount Tabor a suitable location for the Transfiguration. According to the New Testament, the miracle occurred on a

---

[38]M. Broshi & G. Barkai, , 'Excavations', 108-128; S. Gibson & J.E. Taylor, *Beneath the Church*, 11-17, 51-56.

[39]S. Gibson & J.E. Taylor, *Beneath the Church*, 61-71.

[40]A. Kloner, *The Necropolis of Jerusalem in the Second Temple Period* (Hebr.), Diss. Hebrew University, Jerusalem 1980.

[41]For the sources, see: J.E. Taylor, *Christians and the Holy Places*, 96-112.

desolate mountain, while Tabor was not only settled, but was also an recognized Jewish sacred site.

It therefore is quite likely that the location of Christian sacred sites was influenced by the fact that these spots were already considered to be holy. This is not a transmitted tradition, but rather the identification of a site known from literature mentioning an existing sacred center.

Accordingly, the cult of the saints was still not an extensive and accepted phenomenon in the late 3rd century. The 'emergence' occurred in the first half of the 4th century, with the construction of the four primary churches in Jerusalem, on the Mount of Olives, in Bethlehem, and in Mambre. The seeds of the popular phenomenon, however, were already in evidence in the late 3rd or early 4th centuries. Eusebius mentions pilgrims who visited the Mount of Olives. Since, however, this account as well was written after the construction of the church on the Mount, it may very well reflect the reality after the change in the Church's attitude toward sacred sites.[42] In the Onomasticon Eusebius tells of Bethabra adjoining the Jordan River in which "many of the brothers strive, to this day, to bathe."[43] This composition was written, at the latest, before 305,[44] and therefore it too reflects the reality prior to the adoption of Christianity by the Roman Empire. If such a phenomenon existed then at Bethabra, which occupied a marginal place in the Christian consciousness, this must surely have been the case at more prominent sacred sites.

This enables us to follow the progress of the emergence of the culture of sacred sites in the Christian society. This culture began in the 2nd century; the beginning expressions of its emergence appeared in the late 3rd or early 4th centuries, and the emergence itself took place after the reign of Constantine. The actions of the

---

[42]*Laud. Con.* 9:6:7.

[43]*Onomasticon*, p. 58.

[44]There is a number of proofs for this. Some were cited by T D. Barnes, 'The Composition of Eusebius Onomastikon', *JTS* 26 (1975) 412-15; Y. Tsafrir, 'Why Were the Negev, Southern Transjordan and Sinai Transferred from Provincia Arabia to Provincia Palestina? (Hebr.)' *The Jerusalem Cathedra* 30 (1984), 35-56.

Roman Emperor came in response to the desires of the masses, and were in harmony with the tendencies prevalent among the Christian public.

A similar process was taking place outside Palestine. In Rome, for example, the tomb of Peter was considered a sacred site, and large numbers streamed to the tomb of St John in Ephesus, the tomb of the seven lepers, and dozens of similar centers, all of which exerted decisive influence upon their surroundings.[45] Such a discussion, however, would exceed the purview of the current work.

The emergence of the cult of sacred sites was also expressed in the continuous growth in the number of Christian sacred sites. Constantine established four sacred centers, and his reign also marked the beginning of a number of sacred sites with activities on a smaller scope, such as Bethabra, Tabor, etc. In the 4th-6th centuries the number of sacred sites gradually increased. Wilkinson's book provides a detailed study of this process,[46] and we shall not go into its details.

2. The Process of Recognition

For well-understood reasons, the cult of the saints throughout the world is popular mainly among the lower classes in society, while the intelligentsia is frequently critical of such a phenomenon. It has been argued in scholarship that such a cult is inherently anti-establishment and popular, and therefore earned the disapproval of the establishment.[47] These two assessments are similar, but not

---

[45]The best description is still that by H. Delehaye, *Les origines du culte des martyrs*, Brussels [2]1933; M. Vinson, 'Gregory Nazianzen's Homily 15 and the Genesis of the Christian Cult of Maccabean Martyrs', *Byzantion* 64 (1994) 166-92; for a description of the center in Nola, see: N.K. Chadwick, *Poetry and Letters in Early Christian Gaul,* London 1955, 70-71; P. Brown, *Beneath the Church, Its Rise and Function in Latin Christianity,* Chicago 1991; G. Vikan, *Byzantine Pilgrimage Art,*Washington 1982.

[46]J. Wilkinson, *Jerusalem Pilgrims,* Jerusalem 1977, 173.

[47]V. & A. Turner, *Image and Pilgrimage in Christian Culture, Anthropo-*

identical. The first seems to be generally correct, while the latter is much more problematic. In most instances, the cult of the saints is a popular phenomenon, which gradually develops a relationship with the religious and intellectual establishment. In the first phase, the religious establishment does not afford any recognition to the cult of sacred sites. Its beginnings are popular, and the masses, the believers, and obviously the religious functionaries at these sites promote this cult.

In the second phase, upon its emergence, or even earlier, the economic and political authorities begin to take an interest in this cult. Their interest is economic and social, and is concerned with increasing regional prestige of the cult and its contribution to the process of regional socialization. The religious-intellectual establishment either regards the process with indifference or is opposed to it. We generally do not possess the internal evidence regarding the position of the religious establishment: indifference is self-understood, and latent conflict is not expressed in the written sources. This phase occurred both in Judaism and in Christianity, while the reverse process seemingly occurred in paganism: the local temple establishment was the natural supporter of the local cult, in contrast with the national religious leadership, if it existed at all.

In Christianity, the 'pre-recognition' phases occurred until the 4th century. A paucity of testimonies is characteristic of patristic literature concerning sacred sites and the cult of the saints, until the mid-5th century. A cult of sacred sites already existed to some degree during these centuries, with a prevalent belief in the sanctity of Jerusalem. The canonical literature, however, only marginally reflects such a conception. This phase has been missed by scholars who concluded that the lack of explicit religious literature proved the absence of such a phenomenon. In this phase, an important distinction must be drawn between the popular representatives of the people and its public leaders and intelligentsia, between the masses and the intellectual establishment. The prob-

---

logical Perspective, New York 1978; J. Eade & M. J. Sallow, 'Introduction', in: idem (eds), *Contesting the Sacred,* London 1994, 1-27.

lem faced by scholars is the silence of the masses, which hinders an examination of its beliefs and actions.

To return to our description, the religious establishment slowly associated itself with the cult of sacred sites, which becomes the accepted culture, or one of its major characteristics. This process occurred in Christian society in the late 5th century. The representatives of the civil establishment had been its first open proponents at the beginning of the preceding century. Thus, it is highly improbable that the Emperor Constantine had desired to build pilgrimage centers, or that he built four 'regular' churches, faithfully continuing the tradition of public construction by the emperors of Rome. Eusebius, at any rate, interpreted Constantine's policies as being in sympathy with the cult of the sacred sites. His mother Helena was already a leading representative of the civil establishment that supported and promoted this cult.[48]

During the 4th century the cult of the saints was hardly discussed in patristic literature. In what discussion there was, some authors opposed it while others favored it, albeit with quite modest expressions of praise and encouragement. At the end of that century the cult was still the subject of bitter debate conducted by Jerome. The debate would later wane, but echoes of this controversy resound even to the present. Moreover, at times, the cult of sacred sites found its primary support among the public at large, while the leadership, if not in opposition, nevertheless was not a fervent supporter of this cult. The intellectual leadership was also cool to some elements of the cult of the saints, as can be seen from the following example. Augustine, the most important Church Father in the 5th century, forcefully opposed the holding of religious meals in the tombs of the saints, even though he did not reject their very sanctity nor the existence of their cult.[49] Another expression of the duality between the public and its leaders consisted of the attitude toward Jerusalem. The most widespread and accepted interpretation was that all the biblical verses in

---

[48]E.D. Hunt, *Holy Land Pilgrims*, 28-49.

[49]Augustine, *Confessions* 6:2:2; *Epis.* 29:2; see also: Brown, *Beneath the Church*, 30; Eunapius of Sardis, no. 472.

praise of Jerusalem refer to the heavenly, or allegorical, Jerusalem. The roots of this understanding lie in the New Testament, the Revelation of John, and in additional writings.[50] Jerusalem as a symbol and metaphor for the Church or for some abstract concept repeatedly appears in the works of different authors, and is one of the common literary and theological symbols in the literature of the period.

The Church Fathers did not regard allegorical interpretation as necessarily contradictory to the sanctity attributed to the earthly Holy Land, as is clearly exemplified by Justin Martyr. He explains, for example, that the verse "For out of Zion shall go forth the law" (Isa 2:3) obviously refers to the apostles who went forth from Jerusalem,[51] with the intent being to the earthly, real Zion. In the same sentence in which he speaks of the physical severance of the Jewish people from the Land of Israel, he declares that the Land will be destroyed and the Jews will not be able (or are unable) to enter Jerusalem.[52] We have already mentioned this aspect of his writings. Many times when he speaks of 'Jerusalem', the intent is patently to an actual city: Aelia Capitolina. None of this, however, prevents Justin Martyr from utilizing the Pauline interpretation which understands 'Jerusalem' as an allegory for the renewed Church.[53]

Until the 4th century, the topic of Jerusalem was not central to Christianity, and its attitude towards the city was ambivalent. Irenaeus states that all the churches are of equal status, and all share the same opinion. In the course of his list of churches, however, he also includes the church in 'the center of the world', which is an appellation for Jerusalem. Irenaeus thereby attests that his statement is both a polemic against the supremacy of Jerusalem and an acknowledgement of its preeminence. Furthermore, the polemic by this Church Father indicates that other views were

---

[50]See, e.g., the *Apocalypse of Paul*, chap. 23.
[51]*Dialogue with Trypho*, 39.
[52]*Dialogue with Trypho* 16:2; O. Skarsaune, *The Proof from Prophecy*, Leiden 1987, 334-45.
[53]O. Skarsaune, *The Proof from Prophesy*, 326-74.

also prevalent among the public. Irenaeus also opposed the allegorical interpretation of the heavenly Jerusalem, and he hoped and believed that the day would come when the Christians would actually inherit the earthly city.[54]

The expression 'the center of the world' also appears in the works of other writers.[55] Thus, for example, Salvian stated that if the servant of the Lord from the coenobium of Egypt or from the sacred sites of Jerusalem comes (to Carthage) and enjoys hospitality, he thereby abuses his authority. This is another example of the status of Jerusalem in Christian hierarchy.[56] In his Epistle to the Romans,[57] Clement declares that one need not pray everywhere, just as the sacrifices were not offered in every place, thus expressing once again the sanctity of the earthly Jerusalem. Tertullian mentions the importance of the transmitted and direct testimony from the places in which miracles occurred in the past, such as Corinth or Philippi in Macedonia;[58] Jerusalem is likely to occupy a special place of honor in such a listing.

The understanding of Justin Martyr is quite simple: Jerusalem will in the future be Christian, and its removal from the hands of the Jews is the first step in this direction. Nonetheless, Jerusalem is far from the center of Christian thought at this time.[59]

Another expression of views which were prevalent among the masses, in opposition to the doctrine of the ecclesiastical establishment, is the narrative of Epiphanius regarding the Montanists, a heretical sect in the 2nd century that believed that the new Jerusalem would descend in the Holy City of Peruza in Phrygia.[60] This somewhat strange belief was the first in a series of proposals for the 'second Jerusalem' or the 'other Jerusalem'. It also expressed to some degree the attempt to undermine the supremacy of the

---

[54]Irenaeus, *Adversus Haereses*, 1:10:2.
[55]See W.D. Davies, *The Gospel and the Land*, 222-376.
[56]Salvian, *De Gubernatione Dei*, 8.
[57]Clement, *First Epistle*, 41.
[58]Tertullian, *De Idololatria*, 36.
[59]Skarsaune, *The Proof from Prophecy*, 334-45.
[60]Epiphanius, *Panarion*, 48:14:1.

city, but also proved the power and vitality of the faith in the earthly Holy City.

The debate implicit in the seventh canon of the Council of Nicaea shows that by 325, somewhat more than a decade after Christianity's emergence from its clandestine existence, the Church of Jerusalem already had pretensions to control of the entire Church in the Empire. The Council, which was attended by church leaders from throughout the Empire, while not fully accepting these claims, did not totally deny the importance of Jerusalem. It would seem, therefore, that the standing of Jerusalem in the Christian society was stronger than that expressed in the Christian literature and thought.[61]

Although our discussion has related generally to the cult of sacred sites, a similar process was likely to have taken place for each individual site, or for some of the sites. The sacred site was usually revealed and established upon the initiative of the lower classes. In the characteristic model, an individual dreams of the revelation of a saint, his neighbors in the village believe in this, and the establishment confirms the miraculous event. On occasion this could happen some time later. This was the course of events in the Christian site at Mount Nebo, the Tomb of Zechariah near Eleutheropolis, the tomb of Rabban Gamaliel in Beit Jamal, and other sites. New sacred sites follow this same process at the present time in Israel.

This obviously was not obligatory, but was the common behavioral pattern.[62] The sacred site was known at first to only a few: to a certain subgroup, or only in literary traditions, while the 'revelation' was intended to disseminate to all the sanctity of the site. Thus, for example, the Tomb of Zechariah already appears in the work Vitae Prophetarum at the latest in the 4th century, but is revealed a 'second' time in the 5th century.[63] The general area of the tomb of Moses, (but not the precise location) was known to

---

[61] Epiphanius, *Panarion*, 48:14:1.

[62] Almost all our knowledge about the data is contained in the efficient index in J. Wilkinson, *Jerusalem Pilgrims*.

[63] Sozomenos, *H.E.* 7:29:2.

the Rabbis, and was revealed a second time, on the peak of the mount, to a local Christian villager.[64] There are also present-day examples of such a process, such as the rediscovery of the tomb of Rachel, Rabbi Aqiba's wife, in Tiberias in the 1990s.[65] The order of the different phases discussed and the pace and strength of their development are likely to have varied from one society to another. Nonetheless, they possess an internal sociological logic, and it would seem that similar phases occurred in Jewish society as well.

3. The Process of Fashioning and Formulation

The cult of sacred sites is an aggregate of beliefs, rites, a unique calendar, popular and literary traditions, a literary genre, and formulated prayers, all of which most likely develop slowly. We shall now discuss all the phases included in this process.

In the first phase, the sanctity of these sites is not yet accepted, but traditions of sanctity begin to be woven about them: such-and-such a miracle occurred here; the Children of Israel crossed the Jordan at this spot; or prophet X or the saintly Y was buried here. Such testimonies were collected by Taylor, and some are cited above. This is exemplified by the traditions in the proto-Gospel of James. The valley at the foot of the Mount of Olives had not yet become a sanctified location, but narratives of the burial of Mary are for the first time connected with this site.

A centralization process occurs in the second phase, i.e., additional traditions from the past cluster around the site. Thus, for example, in Jewish tradition, the Tomb of the Patriarchs in Hebron attracted additional traditions: it was the burial place, not only of the three Patriarchs, but also of Adam, the progenitors of the Twelve Tribes, and of Moses.[66] The Tomb of the Holy Sepul-

---

[64]S.J. Saller, *Memorial on Mount Nebo,* Jerusalem 1941, 341-47.

[65]At present, there is no scientific documentation regarding the events around this tomb, and we possess only oral testimonies.

[66]Z. Safrai, *'Sacred Tombs'*, 306.

chre, the resting place of Jesus in Jerusalem, also becomes the repository of the True Cross, and in a wider circle, additional Christian sacred sites are discovered in Jerusalem and consecrated. This process has an interesting parallel vis-à-vis tourism. Tourist sites also undergo a process of development in which additional attractions are established in or near the core site, for the purpose of attracting the tourist and persuading him to spend significantly more time at the site. The tourist will thereby require services on a higher level, not just those directly related to the visit itself, but also food services and lodgings.

In the third phase, the site begins to be 'consecrated', and pilgrims make their initial visits. The location is perceived as 'the gate of heaven', through which prayers can be offered. The site possesses unique qualities, and prayers conducted at it are of special value. The testimonies regarding this phase were presented above, in the discussion of the emergence process. Three substages are characteristic of the pre-emergence phase. In the Christian society, they occurred in the 2nd and 3rd centuries.

Afterwards, when the site emerges, structures are erected around it: tombstones, churches, or other buildings. The structures in these sacred centers constitute the focal point of the site, while also providing services, such as lodging, water, etc. The first such structures were built throughout the Empire in the 3rd century CE, but magnificent edifices could be established only after Christianity had become the official religion of the Empire.

The church at Mount Nebo was built only a considerable period of time after the fashioning of the traditions of sanctity associated with the site. Similarly, Kursi, associated with the Miracle of the Swine, had been recognized as a sacred site by the 2nd century, but the monastery and the holy monument were built only in the 6th century.

This is also marked by the early writings of pilgrim literature which describe the sacred sites and which function both as a mechanism for the marketing and publicizing of the sites, and the promotion of the cult of the site or sites. The number of pilgrims increases, and becomes a movement. The first such book in Christian society, that of the Bordeaux Pilgrim, was written in the first third of the 4th century, and followed by many additional works, not all of which are extant.

This development is paralleled by the initial collection of stories and testimonies relating to the miracles experienced by visitors. These wonders are no longer historical events, but daily occurrences. They are not only the cause of the site's sanctity, but also proof of such, as well as constituting the reward in store for visitors.

In this phase the rites are formulated. Auspicious times are established for mass pilgrimage. Arrangements for reaching the site are made, and rules are set for the processions of pilgrims who undergo a series of ceremonies along the way. Detailed rites are formulated: the direction in which the site is encircled, the itinerary of the visit, the special clothing to be worn by the participants, etc. Specific prayers are formulated, directives are issued for the giving of charity, etc.[67] This is especially evident in the essay by the Piacenza Pilgrim, who devotes much attention to the description of such rites.[68]

The number of sacred sites increases, generally creating a culture of sacred sites which becomes a component of the religious way of life. The number of pilgrims obviously grows, as does the number of works describing them. The plethora of sites leads to the creation of a fixed route for the pilgrim including a maximal number of sites. Christian society experienced this phase in the second half of the 4th century. Not all the details of the process have been established, and the delineation of subdivisions may be in order.

The movement of pilgrims increases, with a symbiotic upgrading of the structures, which become more magnificent. Infrastructure services such as hostels are built, etc. Thus, e.g., hostels intended for pilgrims which apparently were constructed in the 6th century were found in the Monastery of Martyrius in Maaleh Adumim and in the monastery of Kfar Dikhrin, near Antipatris.

[67]E.D. Hunt, *Holy Land Pilgrims*, 202-83.
[68]J. Wilkinson, *Jerusalem Pilgrims*, 79-90.

The amount of pilgrims multiplies and the number of sacred sites continues to increase. The trade in sacred relics begins. In Christianity, this phase occurred in the 5th century. All the testimonies to such commerce and the conveyance of sacred relics throughout the Christian world date from the 5th century or later.[69]

The sale of holy souvenirs begins. Outstanding evidence of this is provided by the lamps and bottles of oil bearing Christian symbols and inscriptions.[70] These bottles carry the explicit message: oil from the sacred sites, or merely 'blessing'. We know of the existence of a number of centers for the production of small glass bottles: in Jerusalem, but also in Antiochia, around the tomb of John the Baptist and the tomb of St Manes.[71] All the archaeological evidence dates from the 6th century or later. There are literary testimonies of the sale of oil from the tombs of the saints from as early as the mid-4th century, and Ephrem the Syrian already speaks of this,[72] but the production of bottles earmarked for such use began only in the 6th century. Once again, this begins as non-

---

[69]E.D. Hunt, *Holy Land Pilgrims*, 48-49, 105-6, 138-35.

[70]J. Magnes, 'Blessings From Jerusalem', *EI* 25 (1996) 37-44; S. Loffreda, *Lucerne Bizantine in Terra Santa con Iscrizione in Greco*, Jerusalem 1989.

[71]M.D. Flowers, 'A Pilgrim's Ampulla from the Shrine of St. John the Evangelist at Ephesus', in: R. Ousterhout (ed*.), The Blessing of Pilgrimage*, Illinois, 1990, 125-39; D. Barag, 'Glass Vessels from Jerusalem', *Journal of Glass Studies* 12 (1970) 35-63; 13 (1971) 45-63; C. Hahn, 'Loca Sancta Souvenirs Sealing the Pilgrims' Experience', in: R. Ousterhout, (ed*.), The Blessing of Pilgrimage,* 85-96.

[72]*PG* 103, 986-87.

institutionalized trade, and only in the second phase is a set procedure established, with an accepted form of bottles designated
for the sale of holy oil.

BETWEEN JERUSALEM AND BETHLEHEM: JEROME AND THE HOLY PLACES OF PALESTINE

Hillel Isaac Newman

T wo sources in particular are conventionally trotted out in most discussions of patristic antagonism towards Holy Land pilgrimage: Letter 2 of Gregory of Nyssa and Letter 58 of Jerome.[1] Writing around the year 381, Gregory emphasizes that the faithful Christian is under no obligation to make a pilgrimage to Jerusalem and warns that various indecencies along the route threaten the modesty of women. In the wake of his own visit there, he reserves his harshest words for Jerusalem itself:

Furthermore, if [God's] grace were greater in the sites of Jerusalem, sin would not be so fashionable among those who live there. Yet today there is no form of depravity which is not undertaken

---

[1] For general treatments of these and other sources regarding the history of Christian pilgrimage to Byzantine Palestine see: B. Kötting, *Peregrinatio religiosa*, Münster 1950; J. Wilkinson, *Jerusalem Pilgrims Before the Crusades*, Jerusalem 1977; H. Donner, *Pilgerfahrt ins Heilige Land: Die ältesten Berichte christlicher Palästinapilger (4.-7. Jahrhundert)*, Stuttgart 1979; E.D. Hunt, *Holy Land Pilgrimage in the Later Roman Empire, AD 312-460*, Oxford 1982; P. Maraval, *Lieux saints et pèlerinages d'Orient*, Paris 1985; R.L. Wilken, *The Land Called Holy*, New Haven/London 1992, 101-125; J. Prawer, 'Christian Attitudes Towards Jerusalem in the Early Middle Ages', in: J. Prawer & H. Ben-Shammai (eds), *The History of Jerusalem: The Early Muslim Period (638-1099)*, Jerusalem 1996, 311-347. On Jerome in particular see: P. Maraval, 'Saint Jérôme et le pèlerinage aux lieux saints de Palestine', in: Y.-M. Duval (ed.), *Jérôme entre l'Occident et l'Orient*, Paris 1988, 345-353. For the chronology of Jerome's writings see: J.N.D. Kelly, *Jerome: His Life, Writings, and Controversies*, London 1975; S. Rebenich, *Hieronymus und sein Kreis. Prosopographische und sozialgeschichtliche Untersuchungen*, Stuttgart 1992 (= *Historia*, Einzelschriften 72). I have touched on some of the issues raised in this paper in *Jerome and the Jews* (Diss., Hebr.), Hebrew University of Jerusalem 1997, 220-232.

among them: fornication, adultery, theft, idolatry, poisoning, envy, murder. Indeed, that evil is so especially common, that nowhere is there such a propensity for killing as in those places, where blood relatives assault each other like wild beasts for the sake of insignificant profit.[2]

Elsewhere – it has been noted – Gregory writes in a more positive vein about pilgrimage, though implying that the truly virtuous pilgrim is only one who succeeds in spiritualizing and internalizing the significance of the holy places.[3]

Letter 58 of Jerome (*CSEL* 54, 527-541), the second source of note, was written to Paulinus of Nola in 395. In it, Jerome does his best to dissuade Paulinus from visiting Palestine and to assure him that he may remain in Italy without impugning his faith. Thus, he argues, it is not praiseworthy simply to have been in Jerusalem, it is necessary to have lived well there. One should, he continues, seek rather the heavenly Jerusalem, for God's omnipotence knows no geographical boundaries, and all earthly things – including Jerusalem – will ultimately pass away. Golgotha and the Holy Sepulchre benefit only those who carry their crosses with them, rising daily in Christ, and since the kingdom of God resides in the believer, it is as accessible in Britain as in Je-

---

[2]Letter 2:9. See P. Maraval, *Grégoire de Nysse, Lettres*, Paris 1990 (= *SC* 363), 116. The precise date of the letter remains uncertain. On the problems of chronology see P. Maraval, 'La lettre 3 de Grégoire de Nysse dans le débat christologique', *Revue des sciences religieuses* 61 (1987), 74-89; idem, *Lettres*, 26, 33-37. Cf. B. Kötting, 'Gregor von Nyssa's Wallfahrtskritik', in: F.L. Cross (ed.), *Studia Patristica*, X, Berlin 1961 (=*TUGAL* 80), 360-367; I. Grego, 'San Gregorio Nisseno pellegrino in Terra Santa', *Salesianum* 38 (1976), 109-125; E. Pietrella, 'I pellegrinaggi ai Luoghi Santi e il culto dei martiri in Gregorio di Nissa', *Augustinianum* 21 (1981), 135-151. We may perhaps learn of a previous journey of Gregory to Jerusalem from a Georgian text purporting to be a translation of a letter by Jerome; see M. van Esbroeck, 'L'histoire de l'église de Lydda dans deux textes géorgiens', *Bedi Kartlisa* 35 (1977), 109-131. On the controversy surrounding Gregory's letter during the Reformation see P. Maraval, 'Une querelle sur les pèlerinages autour d'un texte patristique (Grégoire de Nysse, *Lettre 2*)', *Revue d'Histoire et de Philosophie Religieuses* 66 (1986), 131-146.
[3]See Letter 3:1 (= Maraval, *Lettres*, 124).

rusalem. Numerous saints, in fact, never set foot in Jerusalem, and its holy places were long polluted by the idolatry of pagan captors. Jerome's catalogue of urban blight in Jerusalem is vaguely reminiscent of Gregory's earlier diatribe:

> Were the places of the Cross and the Resurrection not in so populous a city, in which there are a city council, a garrison of soldiers, harlots, mimes, jesters and all things commonly found in other cities, or were it frequented solely by throngs of monks, then such a dwelling place would truly be desirable for all monks. But now it would be the height of foolishness to renounce the world, to forsake your homeland, to abandon cities and to declare yourself a monk and then live abroad among greater multitudes than those among whom you would have lived in your own country. Men flock hither from all over the world; the city is filled with people of every race and with such a congestion of men and women, that here you would be forced to bear in full that from which you fled elsewhere in part (Letter 58:4 [*CSEL* 54, 533]).

Regarding his own decision to tour the Holy Land and settle there, Jerome lamely brushes aside the anticipated charge of inconsistency (Letter 58:3 [*CSEL* 54, 530]). The contradiction between his own behavior and his declared position on pilgrimage would be difficult enough to resolve had Jerome never written another word on the subject, yet he is no less famous for his other writings in praise of pilgrimage and veneration of the holy places than he is for his antithetical critique of the same in Letter 58 to Paulinus. Already around the year 375, writing from the desert of Chalcis to the monk Florentinus in Jerusalem, he expresses his desire to visit that city (Letter 5:1 [*CSEL* 54, 21]), a wish fulfilled only in 385, upon his arrival in Palestine in the company of the nun Paula. While in Rome in 384, he portrays his initial profession of monasticism and his withdrawal to the Syrian desert as a march to Jerusalem for the purpose of serving as a soldier (that is to say, as a soldier of Christ, a monk), suggesting again that he foresaw Jerusalem as his final destination (Letter 22:30 [*CSEL* 54,

189]).[4] Writing en route to Palestine in 385 to Asella of Rome, he describes his travels with Paula as a journey to Jerusalem (Letter 45:2 [*CSEL* 54, 324]). We note the absence of any suggestion in the writings preceding the arrival of the entourage in Palestine that Bethlehem will play a special role in Jerome's future.

Jerome's classic statement on behalf of Holy Land pilgrimage is Letter 46 (*CSEL* 54, 329-344), which purports to be written by Paula and her daughter Eustochium, but is patently Jerome's own handiwork.[5] Sent from Bethlehem to Rome, probably in 386, the letter encourages Marcella, a former member of Jerome's circle of Roman disciples, to rejoin her companions in their new surroundings. This panegyric of Jerusalem and Palestine recalls the numerous miracles and wonders of biblical history; through the eyes of faith, the pious pilgrim may witness and experience these events himself. Furthermore, the biblical education of a Christian is lacking if he has not visited Palestine. "Our entire *mysterium* is native to this province and this city", declares Jerome (Letter 46:3 [*CSEL* 54, 332]), who devotes considerable effort to disposing of anonymous objections to the veneration of Jerusalem and its holy places.[6] Without denying that the kingdom of God is to be sought within one's self, Jerome maintains that the first rank of monks and nuns from all nations is to be found in Jerusalem. There they live in humility and harmony, no one judging his neighbor, lest he find himself judged by the Lord; in contrast to other places, he continues, backbiting is completely unknown in Jerusalem. The Origenist controversy, which exploded in 393 due in no small measure to Jerome's own cantankerousness, would prove this last claim painfully wrong, but for the moment it remained a comfortable illusion. The letter concludes with an idyllic description of Bethlehem and an itinerary of pilgrimage to the holy places of

---

[4]For the argument that this is in fact a reference to the heavenly Jerusalem see S. Rebenich, *Hieronymus,* 40.

[5]See P. Nautin, 'La lettre de Paule et Eustochium à Marcelle (Jérôme, Ep. 46)', *Augustinianum* 24 (1984), 441-449.

[6]On the implied polemic see P. Maraval, 'Saint Jérôme', 346-348.

Palestine. With these and other arguments, Marcella is urged to abandon Rome.

Following a gap of some seven years in Jerome's correspondence, we find him in 393 once again lobbying for pilgrimage. In that year he sent a letter to one Desiderius encouraging him to come with his wife (or sister) to Bethlehem. It is a 'part of faith' (*pars fidei*),[7] he says, to worship where the Lord's feet stood and to observe the traces of his birth, his cross and his passion (Letter 47:2 [*CSEL* 54, 346]). In 394 Jerome implores the aforementioned Paulinus to renounce the world and join him in the study of Scripture in the monastery at Bethlehem (Letter 53:10-11 [*CSEL* 54, 463-465]) – yet a year later, as we have seen, we find him in Letter 58 pressing the same man not to set foot in Palestine. This does not, however, mark the end of Jerome's efforts to induce his correspondents to make the journey. In 397 he consoles a blind pilgrim of Pannonia who was forced by inclement weather and worried friends to turn back from his course; Jerome assures the man that he does not despair of the latter's arrival in the future (Letter 68 [*CSEL* 54, 675-678]). In 398 he writes to Lucinus of Spain, urging him and his wife to part with their worldly possessions and take up residence at the holy places of Palestine (Letter 71:4 [*CSEL* 55, 5]). Jerome's eulogy of Paula of the year 404 is virtually a paean to Holy Land pilgrimage, containing a vivid and detailed description of the pilgrim's itinerary (Letter 108 [*CSEL* 55, 306-351]). In 407 he entreats Rusticus of Gaul to fulfill his promise and join his wife at the holy places; she meanwhile prays on his behalf at the Holy Sepulchre, Golgotha and the Cave of the Nativity (Letter 122:4 [*CSEL* 56, 70]). One of Jerome's last letters contains an appeal to Apronius to come East to the holy places (Letter 139 [*CSEL* 56, 267-268]), and in a letter of uncertain date he exhorts the soldier Exuperantius to forsake his possessions and join him in Bethlehem (Letter 145 [*CSEL* 56, 306-30]).[8] Jerome's

---

[7]Using the equivalent Greek phrase (*en merei eusebeias*), Gregory criticized this notion in Letter 2:2 (=Maraval, *Lettres*, 108-110).

[8]On Exuperantius in Palestine see F. Cavallera, *Saint Jérôme: sa vie et son oeuvre*, I, Louvain/Paris 1922, 170 n.1.

entire career at Bethlehem, in fact, is punctuated by a constant procession of visitors and settlers from the West.

How then do we explain the anomaly of Letter 58 to Paulinus? Abel, Cavallera and others are surely correct in identifying the Origenist controversy raging at the time as the immediate cause for Jerome's abrupt about-face.[9] Instigated in 393 by Epiphanius, the quarrel pitted Jerome against his erstwhile friend Rufinus of Aquileia and John, bishop of Jerusalem. Rufinus and Melania the Elder collaborated at the time in the management of a monastery and convent on the Mount of Olives, and Melania was herself a relation of Paulinus. Because Jerome was placed under the ban by John, he was not in a position to offer Paulinus hospitality in Bethlehem or anywhere else. Jerome foresaw the very real danger that should Paulinus come to Jerusalem, he would find his place among Rufinus and his allies.[10] Against the background of Jerome's vested interest in keeping Paulinus at a safe distance, we may doubt the depth of his conviction and of his identification with the arguments he himself proposes in Letter 58.

It would, however, be misleading to reduce Jerome's critique of pilgrimage and of the holy places to a mere contingency and dismiss it out of hand as an argument designed in self-interest to make a virtue of temporary necessity. Certain elements persist in Jerome's writings in other contexts, and the creeping devaluation of earthly Jerusalem leaves its mark elsewhere. Thus, recalling the years of controversy in a letter to the Roman matron Fabiola, he refers obliquely to Jerusalem as Sodom – that is to say, as a city steeped in sin and facing imminent destruction – and to Bethlehem as the little village of Zoar, the place of refuge (Letter 64:8 [*CSEL* 54, 595-596]; see Gen 19:20-30). In several places

---

[9]See F.M. Abel, 'Saint Jérôme et Jérusalem', in: *Miscellanea Geronimiana*, Roma 1920, 134-135; F. Cavallera, *Saint Jérôme*, I, 171.

[10]See P. Nautin, 'Études de chronologie hiéronymienne', *Revue des études augustiniennes* 19 (1973), 235-236; E.D. Hunt, *Holy Land Pilgrimage*, 192-193. On the place of Paulinus of Nola in the 'social networks' engaged in the Origenist controversy, see E.A. Clark, *The Origenist Controversy*, Princeton 1992, 33-35, 41-42. Cf. P. Maraval, 'Saint Jérôme', 352.

Jerome alludes to Matthew's description of the resurrection of the dead at the moment of the crucifixion:

> There was an earthquake, the rocks split and graves opened, and many of God's people arose from sleep; and coming out of their graves after his resurrection they entered the Holy City, where many saw them. (Matt 27:52-53 [NEB])

Discussing this verse in Letter 46 to Marcella, Jerome argues unequivocally: "The heavenly Jerusalem is not summarily to be understood here, as many ridiculously think, for there could be no sign among men of the Lord's rising, were the bodies of the saints seen in the heavenly Jerusalem" (Letter 46:7 [*CSEL* 54, 337-338]). This, for Jerome, is further proof of the legitimacy of Jerusalem pilgrimage. Yet in 396, a year after sending his letter to Paulinus, he quietly reverses his position in his letter of consolation to Heliodorus, where he writes in passing that it was in the heavenly Jerusalem that these same dead were seen to rise (Letter 60:3 [*CSEL* 54, 551]).[11]

Another example of the diminution of the status of earthly Jerusalem may be found in a homily on Ps 96, delivered during the week of the Encaenia festival, celebrating the dedication of the Church of the Holy Sepulchre. The occasion suggests that Jerome was addressing an audience in Jerusalem, though this is not made explicit in the sermon. Though its precise date is unknown, it apparently postdates the outbreak of the Origenist controversy, probably by several years. The homily is largely an attack on Jewish devotion to the Temple, but Jerome is strikingly silent on the subject of the Holy Sepulchre.[12] Instead, he chooses to elaborate the dichotomy between physical holy places and spiritual ones, giving priority to the latter. The Cross, he says, is to be found

---

[11]See further references in J.H.D. Scourfield, *Consoling Heliodorus: A Commentary on Jerome, Letter 60*, Oxford 1993, 101-102.

[12]On related issues see J. Schwartz, 'The *Encaenia* of the Church of the Holy Sepulchre, the Temple of Solomon and the Jews', *Theologische Zeitschrift* 43 (1987), 265-281.

'in England, in India, in the entire world. Happy is he who carries
in his bosom the Cross, the Resurrection, the place of Christ's nativity and the place of his ascension. Happy is he who has Bethlehem in his heart, in whose heart Christ is born daily ... Happy is
he in whose heart Christ rises daily ... Happy is he who ascends
daily from the Mount of Olives to the kingdom of heaven ... '
(Homily on Psalm XCV [*CCSL* 78, 154-155]).

Radically delocalizing sanctity and remapping it in the heart of
the believer, Jerome alludes to the central triad of holy places: the
Cave of the Nativity, the Holy Sepulchre and the Mount of Olives. Nonetheless, Jerome, the monk of Bethlehem, is addressing
a crowd in or near Jerusalem that has gathered to venerate the
Cross and celebrate the anniversary of the inauguration of the
Church of the Holy Sepulchre. In this light, the homily should be
construed less as a rejection of pilgrimage than as a reminder to
pilgrims to keep their priorities straight. Pilgrimage to the holy
places has meaning, provided it serves as a vehicle to apprehend-
ing higher spiritual values. Such sobriety was nowhere to be
found in the letter to Marcella.

What brought about this change of heart? We have already
stressed the importance of the Origenist controversy, which
caused a breach between Jerome in Bethlehem on the one hand
and Rufinus and company in Jerusalem on the other. To this may
be added other factors. First of all, we may take Jerome at his
word when in his letter to Paulinus he bemoans the evils of city
life that plague Jerusalem. Jerome the wide-eyed pilgrim has undergone a process of disillusionment and woken up to the fact that
Jerusalem is, besides everything else, a real city. While the experience of such a revelation is to be expected in any tourist-turned
resident, for Jerome it is especially discomfiting since a city – any
city – is the antithesis of the monastic life he so cherishes. He
says as much to Paulinus: "I speak not with regard to bishops, nor
presbyters, nor clergy, who have other duties, but rather with regard to a monk" (Letter 58:4 [*CSEL* 54, 532]).

Jerome's monastic antagonism to cities finds expression
throughout his writings. Without exhausting the topic, we may

cite a few examples. In one of his earliest surviving letters, he gushes, prior to his withdrawal to the wilderness of Chalcis: "Would that I could see the desert, the most lovely city of all!" (Letter 2:1 [*CSEL* 54, 10]). While still in Rome he writes to Marcella of his yearning for a rural existence and adds: "Let Rome keep its tumult to itself, let the arena rage, let the circus rave, let the theaters revel" (Letter 43:3 [*CSEL* 54, 321]). In his appeal to Marcella to join the nuns of Bethlehem he says of Rome: "The vain ambition, the power, the size of the city, the seeing and being seen, the greeting and being greeted, the praising and criticizing, the listening and speaking, having to endure reluctantly such crowds of people – all these are foreign to the monks' manner and quietude" (Letter 46:12 [*CSEL* 54, 342]). According to Jerome's biography of the monk Hilarion, it was the saint's custom never to enter a city, nor even a small town (Life of Hilarion 8:6; 23:2).[13] In a letter written in his later years Jerome declares: "For me a town is prison, and the desert is paradise" (Letter 125:8 [*CSEL* 56, 127]). A vivid description of the threats posed by city life for the monks of Palestine is preserved in a homily on Ps 91, in which Jerome warns his listeners: "If you, a lone monk, should go to the city and begin to walk about and hear the clamor in the circus and someone says to you: 'Come and see, it's the circus!' you must say to him: 'It is forbidden, I cannot go' " (Homily on Psalm XC [*CCSL* 78, 129-130]). Small wonder then, that Jerome could scarcely contain his disappointment at the fact that Jerusalem too was a city, with its *curia*, its garrison and its assorted rabble.[14]

Jerome's Encaenia sermon mentioned above suggests a second factor in the devaluation of Jerusalem: Jewish eschatological aspirations. On numerous occasions, Jerome describes the Jews' belief in the future redemption of earthly Jerusalem, together with the restoration of the Temple and its cult. He frequently launches

---

[13]See the edition of A.A.R. Bastiaensen in: C. Mohrmann (ed.), *Vite dei santi*, IV, n.p. 1983, 88-90, 122.

[14]On the distinction between monastic and urban life in Jerome's writings see also S. Rebenich, *Hieronymus*, 91-92.

a two-pronged attack against the Jews and the so-called Christian judaizers, who in context should be identified as Christian millenarians such as Lactantius, Victorinus and Apollinaris of Laodicea.[15] As in the Encaenia homily, Jerome consistently emphasizes the spiritual nature of the prophets' promises of redemption, which in his view have no bearing on Jerusalem of this world. Similarly, he argues at great length in Letter 129 to Dardanus against the literal Jewish belief that Palestine is the Promised Land; he insists upon interpreting the concept as a spiritual category (*CSEL* 56, 162-175).[16] Ironically, Jerome finds that it is precisely the Christian pilgrim in Jerusalem who may best understand this. The pilgrim sees the city in ruins and is confirmed in his faith that the divine promises must surely refer to something else altogether. A favorite proof-text is Ps 87:1-2: "The Lord loves the gates of Zion, His foundation on the holy mountains, more than all the dwellings of Jacob" (NJV). Jerome asks rhetorically: "He loves *these* gates which we see have collapsed? He loves *these* gates and *this* Zion which has been plowed as a field?" (Homily on Psalm LXXXVI [*CCSL* 78, 110]). This argument recurs frequently in Jerome's sermons and writings. It is, incidentally, not completely original and may be found already in the remains of Eusebius' commentary on Psalms and in the writings of Optatus of Mileum.[17]

Between the extremes of the letters to Marcella and Paulinus, Jerusalem emerges in Jerome's writings as a nice place to visit, but a monk would not want to live there. Turning from Jerusalem to Bethlehem, we are now in a better position to understand Jerome's decision to establish his monasteries and hospice where he did. Nowhere in the works written before his immigration to Palestine does Jerome indicate his intention to settle in Bethlehem or display particular fascination with the nativity of Jesus. Of monasticism in Bethlehem before Jerome's arrival we know next to

[15]See M. Dulaey, 'Jérôme, Victorin de Poetovio et le millénarisme', in: Y.-M. Duval (ed.), *Jérôme entre l'Occident et l'Orient*, Paris 1988, 83-98.
[16]See R.L. Wilken, *Land Called Holy*, 126-148.
[17]See in greater detail H.I. Newman, *Jerome and the Jews*, 226-229.

nothing; John Cassian lived there in a monastery for several years before proceeding to Egypt.[18] We may try to surmise the reasons for Jerome's choice. We recall his idyllic fantasy of a rural haven described in a letter to Marcella written before his departure from Rome:

> There coarse bread, greens watered by our own hands, milk and rustic delicacies will furnish simple but harmless fare ... If it be summer, the shade of a tree will provide solitude; if it be autumn, the weather itself and leaves spread on the ground will reveal a place of repose; if it be spring, the fields will be embroidered with flowers, and among chirping birds psalms will be chanted all the more sweetly; if it be cold with winter snows, I shall buy no wood but shall be warmer keeping my vigil or I shall sleep ... (Letter 43:3 [*CSEL* 54, 320-321]).

Compare this to the letter sent from Bethlehem to Marcella a year later, in which we find the following description of Jerome's new home:

> The little farm of Christ is completely rustic, and except for psalms, all is silent. Wherever you turn, the plowman grasping his plow-handle chants Alleluia, the toiling reaper entertains himself with psalms and the vine-dresser sings a song of David while pruning a vine with his curved pruning-hook (Letter 46:12 [*CSEL* 54, 342-343]).

We have noted that Jerome acknowledges in general the need to internalize the pilgrimage experience, yet his greatest reservations about the veneration of the holy places are specific to Jerusalem. In Letter 58 to Paulinus, he advises the new monk to avoid cities even in his own country, but at the same time he prescribes for him to seek out the proximity of holy places (Letter 58:4 [*CSEL* 54, 532]). Not long after his arrival in Palestine, Jerome discovered in Bethlehem the ideal spot to implement his personal dream of Holy Land pilgrimage. Here indeed was one of Christendom's

---

[18]See J.N.D. Kelly, *Jerome*, 129-130.

most holy places, yet it was not in a city but in a small village, one that was decently rustic without being Godforsaken. From his window, Jerome could look out at the desert, but he was close enough to a major urban center to satisfy his cosmopolitan social and intellectual needs. Here he was surrounded by people who spoke civilized languages, not just the barbarous Aramaic gibberish that plagued him during his miserable sojourn in the Syrian desert (Letter 7:2 [*CSEL* 54, 27]).[19] Here he and Paula established the monasteries and hospice that became a bastion of Latin Christianity in the East.

Jerome was not the only panegyrist of Bethlehem in his day, but he was certainly the most important. Sophronius, who translated a number of Jerome's writings into Greek, composed a work in his youth entitled 'Praises of Bethlehem',[20] yet not a trace of it survives. Jerome's adulation of Bethlehem shows none ot the ambivalence that characterizes his attitude towards Jerusalem. Bethlehem is neither a full-fledged city, nor a stronghold of Origenism, nor the focal point of Jewish hopes of restoration. Jerome occasionally refers with pride to his little village as 'more august' (*augustior*) than Rome,[21] and in Letter 58:3 (*CSEL* 54, 532), in the very midst of his negation of the importance of place, he describes it as 'the *most* august spot on earth'.

As in other areas, Jerome has left us a literary legacy on the subject of pilgrimage and holy places that is, at least at first sight, a mass of contradictions. We have tried to untangle his assorted remarks and define their logic according to time and place. In the picture that emerges, we witness the erosion, relatively speaking, of the status of Jerusalem and its holy place in his thought. It is

---

[19]For the correct reading see J.N.D. Kelly, *Jerome*, 49 n.15.

[20]Jerome, *On Illustrious Men* 134 (*TUGAL* 14/1, 55).

[21]Prologue to translation of Didymus' treatise *On the Holy Spirit* (L. Doutreleau [ed.], *Didyme l'Aveugle, Traité du Saint-Esprit*, Paris 1992 [= *SC* 386], 138); prologue to *Commentary on Ecclesiastes* (*CCSL* 72, 249); Letter 54:13 (*CSEL* 54, 481). Note that some scribes have, ironically, corrupted *augustior* to *angustior*, on which see P. Lardet, *L'Apologie de Jérôme contre Rufin*, Leiden [etc.] 1993 (= *Supplements to Vigiliae Christianae* 15), 311.

Bethlehem that remains for him a steadfast and undiminished beacon of sanctity.

POSTBIBLICAL PERIOD:

3. Judaism and Christianity

MOSES' ROD IN ZIPPORAH'S GARDEN

Marcel Poorthuis

1. Introduction

In the first part of this essay, we will investigate the different connotations of the motif of Moses' rod in rabbinic literature[1] (1.1) in
comparison with Christian stories (1.2). The second part will be devoted to the central role of Zipporah in the discovery of the rod and in
Moses' subsequent vocation.

1.1 Moses' Rod in Rabbinic Literature

According to the Rabbis, in the twilight of the last day of creation
before the Sabbath some ten attributes that were to play a significant role in the history of Israel were created. Such attributes can
not but baffle the reader. Thus, for example, there is the *Shamir*,
the worm that was to gnaw the stones for the Temple. Since it was
forbidden to cut these stones with iron, the *Shamir* served to cut
them out in their proper format. Further the different lists mention
the rainbow, the pot with manna, the writing and the ram that
served as a sacrifice in Isaac's place. Generally the sum total of
these attributes is ten.[2] However, the bewildering variety of these
attributes should not obscure what they have in common, i.e. that
these attributes are concrete expressions of God's care and providence and therefore not man-made. This explains the quite bizarre

---

[1]Previous studies on the rod include: I. Abrahams, 'The Rod of Moses and its
Legendary Story', *Jews College Literary Society*, London, 1887, 28-38; and G.
Bienaimé, *Moïse et le don de l'eau dans la tradition juive ancienne; Targum et
Midrash*, Rome 1984.
[2]The earliest source might be *Pirqe Abot* 5:9. A.J. Saldarini, *The Fathers
According to Rabbi Nathan*, Leiden 1975, 306-310, offers a survey of all the lists.

presence of a 'pair' of tongs in some lists: in order to make a tong one needs a tong, and how could the first tong be made without a tong? In addition to their being non man-made they have in common that they remain hidden until the moment that they are to play their decisive role in the history of Israel. Basically, these attributes are history-oriented and in that respect they are widely divergent from the Platonic ideas that presuppose a vertical, supra-historical transcendence.

Most of the lists include the rod of Moses. The vocation of Moses at the burning bush relates the existence of a rod that was to play a significant role in Moses' future career: "This rod, with which you will perform the signs" (Exod 4:17). Moses then went to Egypt and 'took the rod of God with him'. The qualification 'of God' may refer to the supernatural origin of the rod. The Rabbis provide more information: the rod was made of sapphire and its weight was enormous. Sapphires remind us of the heavenly realm (Exod 24:10) and underline the miraculous character of this rod.[3] "Strike the rock" (Exod 17:6), God commands Moses, "and water will issue from it", but literally Scripture says: "Strike with the rock". Rabbi Yose remarks that the rod was made of sapphire and hence can be designated as 'rock'.[4]

This motif of Moses' rod has assimilated many different traditions that, as is often the case in midrash, reflect different concepts and theological views. The student of this literature must unravel and untangle these different traditions. In spite of the use of occasional naive language, the midrash often contains a complex of highly sophisticated ideas. The different traditions may reflect different times and places of origin but the task of decoding the midrash has not yet been completed when this has been assessed. We will undertake this enterprise of decoding the midrash with the rod as an example.

---

[3] See G. Bienaimé, *Moïse et le don de l'eau*, 74-75 and note 61 for references to literature. Cf. I. Abrahams, *The Rod of Moses*, 1, for the high esteem of the sapphire among magical stones.
[4] *Mekhilta de Rabbi Ishmael, Wa-yassa* 7.

The Rod's Origin: Two Approaches to Revelation

The rod that was created at the end of the sixth day, represents the divine authorization of Moses. By the miraculous appearance of this rod, hidden until the proper moment, the history of Israel suddenly takes on another decisive course. But there is another tradition about the rod: this rod was handed over from generation to generation from Adam to Moses! This definitely offers a different view of divine intervention in history.

In ancient oriental thought, the rod symbolizes divine authority and the ability to work wonders. The question then arises: was Moses' divine authorization the result of a sudden divine intervention, 'senkrecht von oben', to use the phrase of the theologian Karl Barth, or was it the fruit of a long process of tradition from one generation to another, a succession, as it were? The midrash of Moses' rod being handed on from one generation to the other contains a sophisticated view of tradition and religious authority in which the balance turns in favour of the institutional and against the charismatic. We cite the midrash in full:[5]

> Rabbi Levi said: the rod that was created in the twilight was delivered to the First Man in Gan Eden and Adam delivered it to Enoch and Enoch delivered it to Noah, and Noah delivered it to Shem and Shem delivered it to Abraham and Abraham delivered it to Isaac and Isaac delivered it to Jacob and Jacob brought it down to Egypt and delivered it to his son Joseph and when Joseph died his household was taken and the rod was placed in the palace of Pharaoh and Jethro[6] [Pharaoh] was one of the magicians of Egypt and he saw the rod and the letters that were on it and he desired it [them] in his heart and he took it and planted it in the middle of his garden [of Jethro]. [And he saw the rod] and nobody could approach the rod anymore. When Moses came to his house

---

[5]*Pirqe de Rabbi Eliezer* (*PRE*, edn Luria) 40, emended after *Yalqut Exodus* (edn Hyman) §170 (traditional edition §173). I put the original reading of *PRE* between brackets. M. Friedmann, *Pseudo-Seder Eliahu Zuta*, Vienna 1904, (reprinted together with *Seder Eliahu Rabba and Zuta*, Jerusalem 1960) p. 53, contains chapter 40 of *PRE* as well, based upon Ms Parma 1240.

[6]Friedmann reads 'Jethro' as well.

he entered the garden of Jethro's house and he saw the rod and read the letters upon it[7] and he put forth his hand and took it.[8] And Jethro saw Moses and said: This one in the future will redeem Israel from Egypt". Therefore he gave him Zipporah his daughter to wife, as it is said: "And Moses was content to dwell with the man; and he gave Moses Zipporah, his daughter" (Exod 2:21).

In this midrash, the rod connects Moses in time with his biblical ancestors. The aim of this story may be to emphasize this chronological continuity as an important issue in view of the fact that Moses grew up at the Egyptian court where there was no knowledge of this tradition. Moreover, in space, there is a connection between the revelation to Moses and Zipporah's house, which makes sense of Moses' flight to Midian and subsequent stay there. Hence this midrash is not prepared to accept the idea that there would be a total rupture between the tradition of biblical ancestors and Moses who would then be steeped in pagan Egyptian wisdom. The transition from the book of Genesis to Exodus is dramatic indeed: Joseph is forgotten, the Israelite people are oppressed, Pharaoh turns out to be a tyrant, 'a king who did not know Joseph' (Exod 1:8). But in spite of that, the midrash searches for continuity within the history of patriarchs and matriarchs. The Israelite people in Egypt could not be the vehicle of that continuity, imbued as they were with idolatry. The people were in need of redemption from slavery and idolatry, as was to be announced by the Voice in the burning bush. But what about Moses, the liberator: did he have an inkling of the Voice's revelation? This midrash emphatically answers this question with a yes.

---

[7] Several texts identify these letters with the Name of God. In Friedmann's version of this story the section about Jethro's planting the rod and Moses' subsequent arrival is missing. Apparently in this version Jethro's earlier seeing and reading the rod is conflated with Moses' seeing and reading the rod.

[8] To see, to put forth the hand, to take; and this taking place in the midst of the garden. The references to the biblical story of Paradise (Gen 3:6,22) are obvious. Moses' acts are a redemptive reversal of Adam's and Eve's transgression.

The rod contained the Name of God. The revelation at the burning bush was new but at the same time it was in harmony with the tradition of the Israelite ancestors. Otherwise, what could have been the meaning of God's revelation as the God of the Fathers to Moses, if Moses was not familiar with his ancestors? Even the Tetragrammaton was known to them (cf. Gen 32:9) in spite of the fact that Exod 6:3 maintains: "with my Name of the Lord I did not make myself known to them". The rod then was 'a revelation before revelation', enabling recognition of the Unknown. The ancestral tradition of the Name of God was preserved by the rod during the tribulations of the slavery in Egypt.

This midrash demonstrates a remarkable tension between revelation as something without precedent and revelation as the re-establishing of the connection with the old-time religion. The rod as revelation to Moses symbolizes the rabbinic re-interpretation of time: the new and the unknown are at the same time authentic tradition.

But the rod also symbolizes a re-interpretation of space. Moses' journey to Jethro was not an aimless roaming in a pagan environment, although Jethro's (pagan) Priesthood remains a moot point. The rod in Jethro's garden is the prerequisite for Moses' vocation as a prophet and as Israel's redeemer. Moses' journey was a search for his vocation. In the midrash, Jethro was clearly aware of the real nature of the rod in his garden. This places Jethro in a curious light: Jethro, a magician at Pharaoh's court and a pagan Priest, is depicted as being aware of Moses' vocation and marries off his daughter to him. Jethro is portrayed as being benevolent to the people of Israel and perhaps even to its God. There is a universalistic tendency in this midrash, but we will soon notice that strongly negative portrayals of Jethro are not lacking in other strands of rabbinic literature. However, these negative portrayals highlight Zipporah's role as redeemer of Moses, as we will see in the second part of this essay.

We have seen that the rod symbolized in mythical narrative form different theological ideas about the relationship between revelation and tradition. Both the hidden rod and the chain of tradition connect Moses' vocation and miraculous working with the past and with Paradise. There is also a Messianic dimension to the rod, although this is not yet developed in *PRE*. Thus, in Midrash *Yalqut Numbers, Ḥuqqat* 20 (edn Hyman §763), Moses' rod is connected with the Messiah: Jacob's rod (Gen 32:10), which became Judah's (Gen 38:18) and which was handed over to Moses and from Moses to Aaron (Exod 7:10) to David (1 Sam 17:40) and from king to king until eventually it will be in the hands of the Messiah to rule the peoples of the world in the future, as it is said: "The Lord will stretch forth from Zion your mighty scepter" (Ps 110:2). Note that this Messianic rod is here conferred from Moses to Aaron.[9] Probably this midrash felt a need to express a priestly element in its view of Messianic expectation. Again, different layers of tradition have been merged in the Messianic interpretation of the rod.

The rod's different origins

Rabbi Levi, in *PRE* 40, connected the rod handed over through the chain of tradition with the motif of the creation of the rod in the twilight of the sixth day. However, there are quite a few texts that perceive the origin of the rod in Paradise in a much different way, such as the rod being a branch from the Tree of Paradise in the possession of Adam. With these texts we leave for the moment the world of the Rabbis.

Samaritan tradition emphasizes Moses' role as God's messenger. In the Samaritan book *Asatir* (about the 11th century CE) it is told that Moses received both Adam's clothes and the rod at Horeb (Asatir 9:2).[10] According to this Samaritan tradition, Moses received these attributes on the mountain of Horeb. Evidently then, Moses received these attributes from non-human hands. It is not clear if this text nevertheless presupposes an ancestral chain; a divine supernatural preservation of the rod is more probable.

---

[9] Likewise in *Yalqut Psalms* §869, while the identity of Moses' rod with Aaron's rod is debated in *NumR* 18:23.

[10] Z. Ben-Hayyim, 'The Book of Asatir with Translation and Commentary' (Hebr.), *Tarbiz* 15 (1944) 75.

Likewise, in the Samaritan *Memar Marqah* that originated in the 4th century CE, the rod is said to be revealed to Moses out of fire.[11] There is no link whatsoever in this Samaritan text with Jethro, nor with the patriarchs. However, according to the Samaritan *Malef* (48-49), the rod was in Adam's possession when he was driven out of Eden, and was handed to Noah, who handed it to Shem's sons and then further on in the holy chain to Jethro, who gave it to Moses.[12] Again, these Samaritan texts contain different traditions concerning the rod, that are still clearly distinguishable. The *Asatir* tells that the rod was Adam's and the *Malef* likewise states that the rod was Adam's when he left Paradise. Does that imply the rod's origin from a tree from Paradise? The text is too succinct to decide. But the *Memar Marqah* relates how the rod was revealed to Moses out of the fire, which seems to refer to a heavenly rod, not to one made of wood nor to one handed down from generation to generation.

1.2 Moses' Rod in Christian Literature

Although patristic literature is replete with the typology of Moses' rod prefiguring the Cross, the actual transmission of the rod through history to become the Cross is considerably later. Christian texts concerning Moses' rod, sometimes demonstrating striking similarities with Jewish material, have forged a synthesis between the stories of Seth's journey to Paradise and the legends concerning the origin of the Holy Rood. The earliest testimonies of this merging of Seth's journey and the Rood-tree legends supposedly date from the 12th century, according to W. Meyer. An

---

[11]See J. MacDonald, *Memar Marqah*, Berlin, 1963, Book I, § 2.

[12]This text, assigned to the 18th century, was not available to me. I quote from J. MacDonald, *The Theology of the Samaritans*, London 1964, 319. The 'Taheb', a Messianic figure, will one day possess this rod. Likewise the rod's Messianic potential may be detected in the way the sectarian Dositheus, who claimed to be a prophet like Moses, wields his rod. Cf. S.J. Isser, *The Dositheans*, Leiden 1976, 134; J. Fossum, 'Sects and Movements', in: A.D. Crown, *The Samaritans*, Tübingen 1989, 379.

interpolation in the Latin *Life of Adam and Eve* relates both the quest of Seth and the connection with the Holy Cross.[13] However, his research should be supplemented by evidence from probably older documents in other languages. Thus, in Armenian texts, the branch from the Tree of Knowledge is connected with Seth.[14] There is debate as to the Jewish or Christian origin of this motif of the rod being from the Tree of Knowledge and brought from Paradise by Seth. True, in a late midrash the name of Seth is connected with the verb *šātal*, to plant, which may suggest a connection between Seth and a branch.[15] But on the other hand, it is striking that all rabbinic chains of ancestors connect Adam to Enoch, skipping over the person of Seth completely.[16] Perhaps Seth's importance as a type of Christ in Christian literature or his central role in Gnostic texts may account for his exclusion from rabbinic chains.[17]

Whereas in rabbinic texts the connection of Moses' rod with Paradise and more specific with a branch from the Tree of

---

[13]W. Meyer, 'Vitae Adae et Evae', Abhandlungen der philosophisch-philologischen Klasse der Königlich Bayerischen Akademie der Wissenschaften (München), XIV (1879) 187-250. Cf. his important study: 'Die Geschichte des Kreuzholzes vor Christus', ibidem, XVI (1882) 103-160.

[14]Cf. M. Stone, *Armenian Apocrypha Relating to the Patriarchs and Prophets*, Jerusalem 1982, 4-13, containing Armenian texts and fragments about Adam and Seth. In 'The Words of Adam to Seth', Seth likewise receives a branch from an angel. In this text the connection with the Cross is not explicit, which may point to a Jewish motif. Note that these texts do not connect the branch with Moses' rod. Cf. E.C. Quinn, *The Quest of Seth for the Oil of Life*, Chicago 1962, 88-101. Apart from these texts, there is an English text from the 11th century that we will quote further on.

[15]L. Ginzberg, *The Legends of the Jews*, Philadelphia 1968, V.148.

[16]Cf. note 5 above and note 49 below for the same chain in midrashic biographies on Moses. The sole exception is the chain in *Midrash Hashkem*, a lost midrash collected from posterior quotations by L. Grünhut, *Sefer Ha-liqutim*, Jerusalem, 1967, I.2b: 'Adam handed it over to Seth and all the generations handed it over to one another until Jacob descended etc.'

[17]Cf. similar observations in A.F.J. Klijn, *Seth in Jewish, Christian and Gnostic Literature*, Leiden 1977, 12. Hence, the absence of Seth in the rabbinic chains may be secondary and due to Christian adaptation of Jewish material.

Knowledge is only marginal,[18] the motif of Seth and the rod, connecting the rod from Paradise with the cross is extremely widespread in Christianity. This would plead for Christian origins of the connection of the rod with the Tree of Life. Likewise, the identity of Moses' rod with the Cross is a constant typological theme in Church Fathers, which should be distinguished from the actual transmission of Moses' rod through history. We focus upon the actual transmission of the rod through history, according to Christian sources.

In terms of time and space, Christian tradition interprets Moses' journey to Midian to be just as significant as the Jewish texts did. By going to Midian, Moses re-established his connection to sacred history, originating in Paradise. The messianic impact of the rod is, of course, stressed to a greater extent in Christianity: the rod is the wood of the Cross and as such strongly connected to subsequent biblical history. But descriptions of this subsequent history in the *Life of Adam and Eve* texts from the 12th century onward, collected by W. Meyer, demonstrate a remarkable tension:

Solomon tried to use the tree for the construction of the Temple, but the tree was always too long or too short. He decided to place it in the Temple and there it remained. The Queen of Sheba (other texts say: the Sibyl) came and prophesied that 'this tree is the blessed tree on which the Saviour of the World shall hang'! She was beaten and put in prison.

Solomon's role as transmitter of the rod is here highly ambiguous: he fails to recognize the true nature of the rod and symbolizes the incredulity of Judaism towards the Christian message. While Moses and David belong to the true believers and are capable of working miracles with the rod, Solomon is not even able to use the tree. Jewish sources know of Solomon's problems with the construction of the Temple due to his arrogant attitude. The

---

[18]Cf. L. Ginzberg, *The Legends,* VI.14. However, there is some fusion between Moses' rod and the wood at Marah, the latter indeed originating from the Tree of Life and inscribed with God's Name. Cf. G. Bienaimé, *Moïse et le don de l'eau,* 31-32, 37, 73-74.

gates of the Temple reduce in size as Solomon wishes to bring in the ark. But note that this Jewish tradition testifies to the holiness of the Temple, whereas the Christian tradition is severely critical of the Temple by not allowing the tree to be part of it. Irrespective of whether Christian stories about the rod have been influenced by Jewish traditions or not, the way it is developed indicates that the motif has undergone a total transformation.

The Sibyl, here identified with the Queen of Sheba, embodies the pagan testimony to the truth of Christianity and is undoubtedly connected to the Sibylline text in the sixth book: "O happy wood, on which God was first stretched out (6:25)". The Queen of Sheba is mentioned in the Gospel as the one to condemn Israel (Luke 11:31). Clearly, by the rod's inability to be adapted for the Temple's construction, the sanctity of this place is radically transformed.

Another curious event demonstrates the quality of the rod to transform time and space. David honored the rod and saw it burning without being consumed. He healed a leper with it and cleansed water with it. David, as the ancestor of Christ, received Moses-like qualities, but not so Solomon. In the Latin *Historia* (dated before 1150), Solomon, upon hearing from the Queen of Sheba that the rod will mean the downfall of Judaism, hurls it into a fishpond. Daily an angel searched for the wood and the movement of the water caused the sick to be healed. In this story the rod is connected to the Bethesda pool of the Gospel of John.[19] The embarrassing idea that this Bethesda pool may have been a pagan healing center or a source of magical healing is countered by this motif: already from the time of Solomon the wood of the Cross was the only source of healing. The quality of the rod to transform is evident: the sanctity of the place of healing is traced back to its only legitimate source: the Cross. And in terms of transformation of sacred time: from Solomon on, biblical history should

---

[19] See M. Parmentier's contribution in this book on Bethesda in patristic thought. The stirring of the water by the angel can be explained as a search for the wood, without intrinsic healing power. Cf. E.C. Quinn, *The Quest of Seth for the Oil of Life*, 66.

be viewed as a history of ignorance. Only the patriarchs Moses and David were the real and conscious bearers of the divine truth embodied in the rod.

However, the most drastic transformation of time by the 'Christian' rod is offered by a very surprising motif: the rod is tripartite! A Rood tree legend from England from the middle of the 11th century, antedating the period of the Crusades,[20] starts with Moses' rod, not with Paradise. In it, Moses' rod is described as threefold, consisting of three trees. Moses realized that these rods prefigured the Trinity. The polemical implications of this text are clear: Moses was already aware of the truth of Christianity. It is not probable that this motif was expressly directed towards Judaism but there may be an anti-Gnostic or anti-dualistic element to it.

Curiously, the oldest known Christian traditions of a tripartite rod are heterodox and of a dualistic nature. The Bogomiles were a dualistic sect living in the Balkans in the 9th and 10th centuries. They attributed creation to the devil. In a Bogomile version of this same story published by Moses Gaster,[21] the tripartite rod in Paradise contained three branches, one belonging to Adam, one belonging to Eve and the third belonging to God. Moses' rod stems from Eve's, clearly to deny to Moses and to the Old Testament as such any authentic divine revelation. The tripartite division may be a reminiscence of the tripartite Gnostic division of mankind into three groups. It was not from Moses' rod, but from God's rod that the cross was made. Possibly this theme is already an orthodox revision of an even more heterodox account. It is well known that Bogomiles abhorred the cross, considering it the work of the devil. They refused to venerate it and refused to make the sign of the cross. It seems that the Cathar *Interrogatio Iohan-*

---

[20]W. Meyer's assumption that his collection of texts from the 12th century onward are the oldest testimonies of the connection between the Cross and the branch from Paradise, should be dismissed. Cf. E.C. Quinn, *The Quest of Seth,* 6. Meyer ignores earlier Jewish, Samaritan and Manichean sources.

[21]M. Gaster, *Ilchester Lectures on Greeko-Slavonic Literature*, London 1887, 23-25, 29, 35-37. This text was allegedly composed about 940 CE by the leader of the Bogomils, Popa Jeremiah. Cf. E.C. Quinn, *The Quest of Seth*, 53-54.

nis has preserved the heterodox elements better. The story is both violently anti-Jewish and anti-Christian. Here tree pieces of wood are taken out of paradise by Sathanas, the fallen angel. He handed them over to Moses in preparation of Christ's crucifixion! Hence both the Law of Moses and the Cross are diabolic in origin.[22] It may be that the English and subsequent versions of the Holy Rood legend are orthodox Trinitarian corrections of this Bogomile account.[23] However, it is more probable that Trinitarian interpretations of the rod preceded the Bogomile account. Chrysostom knows of a Trinitarian interpretation of the cross made of three kinds of wood: the cypress, the pine and the cedar, in fulfillment of Isaiah's prophecy: "The glory of the Lebanon will come unto thee; the cypress tree, the pine tree and the cedar tree together, to beautify the place of my sanctuary" (Isa 60:13 LXX). From this biblical quotation it becomes clear that a tripartite division may even precede a Trinitarian interpretation.[24] The Trinitarian interpretation of the rod transforms biblical history

---

[22]This account, although from Cathar circles, contains Bogomile ideas. Here the cross is attributed to the devil. See E. Bozóky, *Le livre sécret des Cathares. Interrogatio Iohannis. Apocryphe d'origine Bogomile*, Paris 1980, 68-69, commentary on 148-149. See for the Bogomile equation of the Mosaic law with Sathanas, D. Obolensky, *The Bogomils. A Study in Balkan Neo-Manicheism*, Cambridge 1948, 209, 228, who points to Paulician and Marcionic influence. About Bogomile abhorrence of the cross, see index s.v. cross.

[23]See for other heterodox Bogomile accounts of the story of the cross, preserved in Russian Legends of the Cross, Obolensky, *The Bogomiles*, 273. Most of these versions contain the idea that when God created the earth only He and Sathanael were in existence. This heterodox element escaped the notice of many orthodox Christians who perpetuated these stories!

[24]The tripartite division of the Tree may even be of Jewish origin, as a fragment of the Book of the Giants from Qumran (6Q8) shows. Cf. J.T. Milik, *The Books of Enoch. Aramaic Fragments of Qumran Cave 4*, Oxford 1976, 309. This text was used in Manicheism. Manichean iconography knows of a remarkable tripartite tree! Cf. H-J. Klimkeit, 'Manichäische Kunst an der Seidenstrasse', *Vorträge G 338* (Nordrhein-Westfälische Akademie der Wissenschaften) (1996) 17-18. Idem, 'Der dreistammige Baum', *Festschrift W. Perpeet*, Bonn 1980, 245-262. J.C. Reeves, *Jewish Lore in Manichean Cosmogony. Studies in the Book of the Giants Tradition*, Cincinnati 1992, 91 ff.

into Christian history: Adam was the first Christian, believing in the Trinity.

Integration of the Tree, the Chain, the Rod and the Cross

The following Christian text is unaware of a tripartite rod but integrates a variety of different traditions: the rod stemming from the Tree of Knowledge, being handed over from Adam to Seth and then from generation to generation, leading to Jethro in some way and eventually revealing its Messianic significance by serving as wood for the cross. This text is contained in the Syriac *Book of the Bee* (13th century). Here the rod has turned into a full-fledged vision of history in which creation, revelation and redemption are connected. The idea of the continuity of salvation history, expressed in a literal handing over of attributes, played a significant role in the Jewish texts we have reviewed thus far, but no less in Syriac Christianity (and, one may add, in Islam). In this symbolic thought, religious identity is not derived from an event that emerged at a given time in history but is experienced as rooted in Paradise itself. Precisely because of the striking similarity in mythical symbolic thinking, competing claims upon the truth become apparent. The text is replete with Jewish midrashic motifs that may have come to the author directly from Judaism or via earlier Syriac texts.

> When Adam and Eve went forth from Paradise, Adam, as if knowing that he was never to return to his place, cut off a branch from the Tree of Good and Evil – which is the fig-tree – and took it with him and went forth; and it served him as a staff all the days of his life. After the death of Adam, his son Seth took it, for there were no weapons as yet at that time. This rod was passed on from hand to hand unto Noah, and from Noah to Shem; and it was handed down from Shem to Abraham as a blessed thing from the Paradise of God. With this rod Abraham broke the images and graven idols which his father made, and therefore God said to him: "Get thee out of thy father's house, etc". It was in his hand in every country as far as Egypt, and from Egypt to Palestine. Afterwards, Isaac took it and it was handed down from Isaac to Jacob; with it he fed the flocks of Laban the Aramean in Paddam

Aram. After Jacob, Judah, his fourth son, took it; and this is the rod which Judah gave to Tamar, his daughter-in-law, with his signet ring and his napkin, as the hire for what he had done.[25] From him it came to Perez. At that time there were wars everywhere, and an angel took the rod and laid it in the Cave of Treasures in the Mount of Moab, until Midian was built. There was in Midian a man, upright and righteous before God, whose name was Jethro.[26] When he was feeding his flock on the mountain he found the cave and took the rod by divine agency; and with it he fed his sheep until his old age. When he gave his daughter to Moses he said to him: "Go in, my son, take the rod and go forth to thy flock".[27] When Moses had set his foot upon the threshold of the door an angel moved the rod and it came out of its free will to Moses.[28] And Moses took the rod and it was with him until God spoke with him on Mount Sinai. When God said to him: "Cast thy rod upon the ground", he did so and it became a great serpent; and the Lord said: "Take it", and he did so; and it became a rod as at first. This is the rod which God gave him for a help and a deliverance, that it might be a wonder, and that with it he might deliver Israel from the oppression of the Egyptians.

After a description of the miracles that Moses performed with the rod, the story continues that the rod was hidden by Phineas at the gate of Jerusalem. Joseph found it there and handed it over to Jacob, 'the brother of the Lord'. But the thief Judas Iscariot stole the rod and gave it to the Jews when they lacked wood for the cross, 'a judgment and a fall unto them, but an uprising to many'.[29]

---

[25]Note the remarkable inclusion of Judah and Tamar in the chain. But note the allusion to Judah in *Yalqut Numbers, Ḥuqqat* 20 (quoted above. However, instead of the rod's transmission to Joseph, in our text an angel takes care of the rod's transmission.

[26]Here we find Moses' journey to Jethro in combination with the finding of the rod.

[27]Moses' shepherding Jethro's flock is here aptly connected with the rod being a shepherd's crook. Cf. *Book of the Bee* (edn Wallis Budge), Oxford 1886, chapter 29. The *Book of the Bee* utilizes the *Cave of Treasures* (4th-6th century), but adds a lot of material.

[28]Note that the motif of the angel's handing the rod to Moses is preserved.

[29]Cf. Solomon of Bosra, *Book of the Bee*, chapter 30.

In this Christian text, the rod has developed into a full-fledged symbol of salvation history. The finding of the rod is connected with Moses' activity as a shepherd. However, the rod's full significance becomes clear in the typology rod-cross which yields a rich but dangerous symbolism. One should note that this typology in combination with the categorical accusation of 'the Jews' having crucified Christ, turns the rod into a sharp and highly polemical weapon. This weapon serves to stress exclusive Christian claims upon the truth.[30] Jethro's role is highlighted, undoubtedly influenced by midrashic material related to what we summarized before. The finding of the rod and the visit to Jethro to marry Zipporah are much more closely related in this story than in the other Christian texts. Jethro found the rod himself and is part of the divine transmission. His supposedly pagan background completely recedes into the background as he is called 'righteous before God'.

In the continuation of the story the rod is firmly connected to Jerusalem, but note that the rod does not enter the city: it remains outside the gate.

Again it becomes clear that precisely the close affinities between this Christian text and their Jewish counterparts enable a vehement anti-Jewish polemic. The demonization of 'the Jews' reaches its peak in the unholy alliance between Judas and the Jews.

Although it is outside the scope of this article to trace the Jewish influence upon this text, we may safely conclude that Jewish influence upon Christian texts does not warrant a friendly attitude towards Judaism; on the contrary. Both traditions use Moses' rod as a mythical vehicle to express their theological convictions as to sacred tradition. How antagonistic these convictions sometimes are has been shown in our comparison. The motif of the rod being a branch from the Tree of Knowledge is here firmly connected to the chain of ancestors, whereas the idea that the rod existed already in the twilight of the sixth day is wholly lacking. Notewor-

---

[30]V. Flint, 'Anti-Jewish Literature and Attitudes in the Twelfth Century, *JJS* 37 (1986) 49-50, rightly points to the polemical aspect of these 'holy rood' traditions.

thy as well is the combination of two different traditions into one story: Moses took the rod at Jethro's house, and an angel handed over the rod to Moses. In this light, it is interesting that commentators on the Quran (Sura 2:57; 28:28), seem to be acquainted with both these traditions as well and discuss their connection. According to one commentator, Adam broke off a branch from a Tree of Paradise (here: a myrtle tree) that was to become Moses' rod. There is difference of opinion as to the way the rod reached Moses: Moses took the rod in Jethro's[31] house to the dismay of the latter, but seven times it returned into Moses' hand. But others say that after Adam's death the angel Gabriel preserved the rod for Moses. Again others maintain that an angel in human shape handed over the rod to Jethro. Still another is of the opinion that – Moses received the rod at the burning bush.[32]

Here too we see how different traditions such as the rod coming to Moses via Jethro, and the rod being handed over to Moses by an angel, can be found both in a merged form and separately. The question of these traditions' trajectory: are they of Jewish origin and have they reached these Quran commentators directly or via (Syriac) Christianity, must be left undecided. But the issue that is at stake here seems again to focus upon the origin of Moses' authority: is it derived from human tradition or without human intervention?

---

[31]Jethro is called Shuaib in some post-quranic traditions in Islam. Cf. J. Horovitz, 'Jewish Proper Names and Derivatives in the Koran', *HUCA* 2 (1925) 171-172.

[32]See M. Grünbaum, *Neue Beiträge zur Semitischen Sagenkunde*, Leiden 1893, 161. Cf. D. Sidersky, 'La verge divine', in: *Les origines des Légendes Muselmanes dans le Coran et dans les Vies des Prophètes*, Paris 1933, 78-80. There is still another story about an angel as an arbitrator between Jethro and Moses arguing over the staff. The angel says: "place the staff on the ground and whoever can lift it, it is his." Moses is able to uproot it. Cf. Al-Tabari, *Ta'rikh*, 461; translated by W.M. Brinner: *The History of Al-Tabari*, vol. 3: *The Children of Israel*, Albany 1991, 45.

The Motifs and the Texts: A Survey

Quite a few different motifs in different combinations have been attached to Moses' rod. Most of the Christian texts do not deal explicitly with Moses at Jethro's house, except for the *Book of the Bee*. This technique of clustering becomes even more evident when we consider additional Jewish texts. The following survey offers an inventory of motifs from the relevant Jewish texts, including the Christian *Book of the Bee*. The motifs have been listed separately as 'units', without deciding regarding their different affiliations and connections.

1. The rod was created in the twilight of the sixth day
2. The rod stemmed from a branch of the Tree of Knowledge
3. The rod was Adam's
4. The rod was Seth's
5. The rod was been handed down from ancestor to ancestor
6. The rod was handed over to Moses by an angel
7. Moses took the rod himself
8. The rod went via Pharaoh's court to Jethro's garden
9. Moses found the rod at Jethro's house
10. The staff was found at Mount Horeb
11. Moses' rod is that of the Messiah

Next to *PRE* four Jewish text are of importance here. The interrelatedness of these texts will be discussed at the end of this article. Now let us try to arrange the different motifs according to the main texts, some of which we quoted above:

	1	2	3	4	5	6	7	8	9	10	11
Rabbi Levi's midrash in *PRE* 40	1		3		5		7	8	9		
Targum PsJon Exod 2:21	1						7		9		
Chronicles of Moses (Yerahmeel) XLVI[33]	1		3		5		7	8	9		
Chronicles of Moses (printed version)[34]	1						7		9		
Midrash Wa-yosha[35]	1		3		5		7	8	9		
Book of the Bee 30		2	3	4	5	6			9	10	11

Although it is tempting to re-group the motifs into two basic stories: one about the rod created in the twilight and handed over to Moses by an angel at Mount Horeb and another about Adam's branch from the Tree of Knowledge handed over until it came in Jethro's garden, the available texts do not warrant the actual separate existence of these motifs into two basic stories. It is more probable that the motifs summed up above developed gradually into different clusters. Some motifs may actually have existed separately, sometimes indicating an early stage of transmission, like (1) the creation of the rod in the twilight (*Pirqe Abot* and parallels), or (3) Moses' rod being Adam's rod (the Samaritan *Asatir*). Other motifs are combined into a small cluster: (2) branch

---

[33]We will see later on that this text is virtually identical to *Yalqut* §166 (edn Hyman) and *Sefer Ha-yashar*. The Hebrew section of the *Chronicles of Yerahmeel* (translation and commentary by M. Gaster, with a prolegomenon by H. Schwarzbaum, New York 1971), dealing with Moses was printed by A. Shinan, 'Dibre Hayamim shel Moshe Rabbenu', *Hasifrut 24 (1977)* 100-116. Regrettably his critical apparatus fails to identify the different manuscripts and to establish their relation with *Yalqut* and *Sefer Ha-yashar*. All these versions may be called *Chronicles of Moses* and should be distinguished from Jellinek's printed version, that differs from all of them. That version we call *Chronicles of Moses* (printed version).

[34]A. Jellinek, *Beth Hamidrasch* II, Jerusalem 1938, 7. This text is identical to the first printed version of Constantinople 1516, and is widely divergent from the other versions in manuscript (*Yerahmeel* and *Yalqut*), particularly from the episode at Jethro's place onwards.

[35]A. Jellinek, *Beth Hamidrasch* I, Jerusalem 1938, 43.

from the Tree of Knowledge, being (4) Seth's rod (Armenian Pseudepigrapha). This last combination is integrated into the *Book of the Bee* but is totally absent from our rabbinic texts!

Another small cluster may be found in the *Yalqut Numbers, Ḥuqqat* 20, quoted above. This text combines the following motifs: (5) ancestral rod, (7) Moses took it, (10) at Mount Horeb, (11) it is the Messiah's rod.

Sometimes, one gets the impression that a story offers an abbreviated form of a fuller story. Both the *Chronicles of Moses* and *Targum PsJon* state that the rod was created in the twilight, but do not reveal the mystery of how it came into Jethro's garden. However this explanation does not always work. One may point to the fact that certain types of literature, specially the Targums, are bound by their form to have limited space for digressions. On the other hand, it is perfectly possible that some writers were simply not acquainted with the chain of ancestors that explains the rod's presence in Jethro's garden.

The close affinity between *Targum PsJon* and the printed version of *Chronicles of Moses* is obvious in our survey. However, one should note that the identification of the signs of the rod with the Name and with the Ten Plagues is found both in *Targum PsJon* 14:21 and in *Midrash Wa-yosha*. At the end of this article we will deal more fully with the question of these texts' interdependence.

Hence, the existence of full versions that have assimilated different motifs (*PRE* 40; *Book of the Bee* 30) should not lead to the conclusion that these stories actually existed at the time when some of those individual motifs existed. Texts may weave different units into a more or less coherent whole according to the purpose and function of that text. These units may be combined rather freely. The magnetic working of the central symbol, i.c. Moses' rod, may even attract units that are in fact incompatible. This may lead to differences of opinion, as we saw regarding the Quran commentators, or to harmonizing the differences into one version. As we have seen, the rod created in the twilight expresses sudden divine intervention, while the handing over of the rod by the ancestors, expresses continuity on the human level. However, the imaginative power of the storyteller is capable of integrating these heterogeneous elements into a single version.

2. Zipporah and the Rod: the Erotic Motif

We have noticed that the rod has served to crystallize a variety of theological motifs about revelation and tradition. However, there is still another motif that has attached itself to the rod which we may call the erotic motif: the taking of the rod as a condition for marrying Zipporah. This folkloristic motif,[36] the connection between the taking of the rod and the marrying of Zipporah, has been absent in all the texts that have been studied so far. Although some texts do mention the two events side by side, especially the Book of the Bee, no explicit connection was made between them. Zipporah's role until now has been passive: she is given away for marriage conform the biblical account and that is all. But we will now study late midrashic texts in the form of 'rewritten Bible' that confer upon Zipporah a decisive role in the events concerning the rod and the vocation of Moses. All these texts contain the additional motif: the taking of the staff as a precondition for marrying Zipporah. Jethro's role in these texts is strikingly different from what we have seen thus far: his initial treatment of Moses is very hostile indeed!

Two basic versions of Moses' arrival at Jethro's place may be distinguished. One version, dealt with above, depicts Jethro as friendly towards Moses and as a righteous gentile (cf. *PRE* and the Christian *Book of the Bee*).[37] There Moses takes the rod and

---

[36]Cf. I. Abrahams, 'The Rod of Moses', 4, who points to the use of rhabdomancy (prediction with the aid of rods) in arranging marriages.

[37]Of course there are many older midrashic sources that portray Jethro in a positive light. Cf. L. Ginzberg, *The Legends*, V.410, note 82. One rabbinic opinion interprets Jethro being a 'cohen' negatively as a pagan Priest, but another opinion explains this as Jethro's function as a chief (*Mekhilta, Amalek* 3), hereby clearly defending Jethro. See J. Baskin, *Pharaoh's Counselors: Job, Jethro Bileam in Rabbinic and Patristic Tradition*, Chico California 1983. A similar apologetic device is the attempt to trace Jethro's ancestry back to Abraham, as is done by the

marries Zipporah. However, a second and later version, although elaborating upon the first one by absorbing elements of it, views Jethro as initially extremely hostile to Moses and portrays Zipporah in an active role protecting Moses. Jethro imprisons Moses during a number of years, but Zipporah takes care of Moses in secret. After that, Jethro changes his attitude and more or less 'converts' to the God of Israel.

These two basic versions are found in several expanded forms, but obviously both versions end with Jethro recognizing and acknowledging Moses as the redeemer of Israel. Likewise, the subsequent marriage between Moses and Zipporah conforms to the Bible. As we shall see, both Jethro's initial hostility and his later acknowledgment of Moses is rendered plausible in a number of different ways in late midrashim.

These late midrashic texts, often in the form of rewritten Bible, are in some way related to each other. Unfortunately, there is no scholarly consensus as to date and interdependency of these texts. We may safely assume that the redaction of all these texts is post-talmudic and may vary from the 9th to even the 16th century.[38] However, the date of redaction merely offers a terminus ante quem and some texts contain considerably older traditions. From a methodological point of view, it seems recommendable first to concentrate upon each story in its different versions, trying to establish their interdependence and to raise the issue of the different collections' redaction only afterwards.

We will deal with three versions: *Yerahmeel* and parallels (2.1); the *Chronicles of Moses* (printed version) (2.2), and *Midrash Wayosha* (2.3).

Jewish Hellenistic author Demetrios (3rd century BCE).

[38]We assume that all these texts date to a period after *PRE* (7th-8th centuries) which did not hear of Zipporah's active role.

2.1 Yeraḥmeel and Parallels

First of all we have a story of Moses that is virtually identical
in three different collections: *The Chronicles of Yeraḥmeel* XLVI,
Yalqut Shimoni Exodus §166[39] and *Sefer Ha-yashar*, p. 258.[40] The
story in these versions is the following.

> Moses has been king of Cush (Ethiopia)[41] and presently travels to
> Midian. Upon arrival at Jethro's (Reuel's) place, Reuel said to
> himself: "I shall put this man in the guard-house, by which I shall
> please the Cushites from whom he fled". Accordingly he put him
> in prison, where he remained for ten years. But Zipporah, the
> daughter of Reuel, had pity upon him, and fed him with bread and
> water.[42] At the end of the ten years she said to her father: "That
> Hebrew man that you have imprisoned, it has been ten years ago
> now, and nobody seeks or inquires after him. Now, if it seems
> good to thee, father, let us send and see whether he is dead or
> alive." Her father did not know that she had supplied him with
> food. Reuel then answered and said: "Is it possible for a man to be
> imprisoned twelve[43] years without food and yet live?" But Zippor-
> ah replied: "Have you not heard, my lord, that the God of the He-
> brews is great and powerful, and that He works miracles at all
> times? That he delivered Abraham from the furnace of the Chal-
> deans, Isaac from the sword, and Jacob from the angel with whom

---

[39]Edn A. Hyman, Jerusalem 1977. In the traditional edition §168.

[40]Edn L. Goldschmidt, Berlin 1923.

[41]For Moses' 'Ethiopian' wife, see Num 12:1. The development of the motif of
Moses' stay in Ethiopia is extra-biblical. Cf. the Hellenistic Jewish author
Artapanos and the Jewish historian Josephus, *Antiquities* II, 242ff. The literature
on this topic is growing. See T. Rajak, 'Moses in Ethiopia: Legend and Literature',
JJS 29 (1978) 111-122.

[42]Because of chronological considerations *Sefer Ha-yashar* inserts at this point
a digression about the plight of the Israelites in Egypt and picks up our story at p.
262. These considerations and occasional clarifications prove the dependency of
Sefer Ha-yashar upon a version like the less elaborate ones in *Yalqut* and
Yeraḥmeel.

[43]M. Gaster in his *Chronicles of Yeraḥmeel* translates: twelve. However, earlier
the text said 'ten'. *Yalqut* and *Sefer Ha-yashar* read here 'ten' as well. The Hebrew
text in Shinan, 'Dibre hayamim shel Moshe Rabbenu', 112, reads twelve as well,
but the critical apparatus reads 'ten'. Apparently the writer of the *Yeraḥmeel*
manuscript mistook the word 'shanim', years, for 'shnayim', two.

he wrestled by the brook of the Jabbok?[44] That even for this man He does many wonders; that he delivered him from the river of Egypt and from the sword of Pharaoh? He will also be able to deliver him from this place."[45] This word pleased Jethro and he acted as she had asked. He therefore sent to the pit[46] to see what had become of him, and they found him alive, standing erect and praying to the God of his fathers. They brought him forth from the pit, shaved him, changed his clothes and gave him to eat. The man[47] then went to the garden of Reuel behind the house and prayed there to his God Who had wrought so many wonders for him. While he was praying, he looked aside and behold, he beheld a staff of sapphire fixed in the ground in the midst of the garden. When he approached it, he found engraved upon it the Name of the Lord of Hosts, written and clear.[48] He read that Name and pulled up the staff as lightly as a branch is lifted up in a thickly-wooded forest and it was a rod in his hand.

After that an explanation follows about the rod: it was created after the rest of creation and was handed over to Adam, who tilled the ground with it. Adam handed it over to Noah[49] and via Shem,

---

[44]'By the brook of the Jabbok' is lacking in *Yalqut*.

[45]*Sefer Ha-yashar* explains: '(... of Pharaoh) and from the Ethiopians and from the hunger He can save him and keep him alive.' This addition may be seen as a correction: Jethro is surprised about Moses being alive, not of Moses being saved from prison, which is still dependent upon Jethro himself! This eulogy of God from the mouth of a gentile is derived from *BT Sotah* 13a, but strongly elaborated in *Sefer Ha-yashar* (the counselors of king Abimelek, of Pharaoh and of the Amorite kings) and may be meant as religious consolation for the expulsion of the Jews from Spain, as is demonstrated by R.J.A.I. de Leeuw van Weenen in her study on the sources of *Sefer Ha-yashar* (forthcoming).

[46]Note that here the prison has turned into a pit! We will see that other versions of this story speak about a pit from the outset.

[47]This transition is abrupt. *Sefer Ha-yashar* p. 263, harmonizes: 'It happened after that that Moses went ...etc.'

[48]'Clear' ('mephorash'), an expression that may denote the Tetragrammaton. The midrash *The Death of Moses* (Jellinek, *Beth Hamidrasch*, I.121) describes God as creating the world with the heavenly rod inscribed with the *Shem Hamephorash*, Moses' rod being a small copy of it. This is another development of the theme of the heavenly rod.

[49]Note both the absence of Seth (like in *PRE* 40) and of Enoch (unlike *PRE* 40).

Abraham, Isaac and Jacob[50], eventually it came with Joseph to
Egypt, where Jethro took it home with him. This section, containing the explanation about the rod is similar to *PRE* 40, but
more elaborate and with too many divergent readings to warrant
direct dependency. Then the story continues with the information
that whoever can take the rod, will marry Zipporah:

> All the mighty man of Kinkanos[51] who wished to wed his daughter
> tried to uproot it, but without avail, so that it remained there in the
> garden until Moses to whom it rightly belonged, came and took it.
> When Reuel saw that the staff was in Moses' hand he was aston-
> ished. Reuel then gave his daughter Zipporah to Moses. Moses
> was 77 years old when he came out of prison, and took Zipporah
> the Midianite to wife.

The story ends with a remarkable praise of Zipporah:

> And Zipporah went the ways of the women of Israel; she did not
> even in the smallest thing fall short of the righteousness of Sarah,
> Rebecca, Rachel and Leah, the pinnacles of the world.

In this story, the rod is both created in the twilight and handed
over from Adam to Joseph and then to Jethro. In addition to that,
the rod has assimilated a very important folkloristic motif: whoever can take the rod, marries Zipporah.

Zipporah's role is striking indeed: she is acquainted with the
God of Israel and professes her faith in Him. Moreover, she saves
the future saviour of Israel. Without Zipporah there would not
have been an Exodus at all! Eventually she is ranked with the
matriarchs of Israel.

Jethro's role is very different from that in *PRE* 40 and in the
Book of the Bee. Here the initial animosity of Jethro is clear:
Moses is thrown into his prison. Jethro's reason for imprisoning

---

[50]Both *Sefer Ha-yashar* and *Yalqut* have a digression about Esau that is lacking
in *Yeraḥmeel*: Jacob wrested it from Esau.

[51]Both *Sefer Ha-yashar* and *Yalqut* read here 'Kinim', another indication of
their interdependence over against *Yeraḥmeel*.

Moses was to hand him over to the Ethiopians, but this reason is not developed further: Moses remains in prison for ten years! Apparently the storyteller needed a reason to explain Jethro's animosity and tried to fit it into the story but did not completely succeed.

Despite the similarity of the three versions, we noted that *Sefer Ha-yashar* is dependent upon the version in the Yalqut and not vice versa. *Yalqut* and *Yerahmeel* are virtually identical, but in one instance *Yerahmeel* goes its own way. *Yerahmeel* then can not be dependent upon *Sefer Ha-yashar* either.

2.2 Chronicles of Moses (printed version)

The Chronicles of Moses (printed version) is a biography about Moses from his birth to the Exodus. We summarize the relevant passage.[52]

Again, Moses comes from Ethiopia, where he had been king, to Jethro, but here Moses tells what has happened in Egypt.

> Then Jethro said to himself: "This is the man that has stretched out his hand to the crown of the king[53] and now I will catch him and I will hand him over to Pharaoh".

Moses is put on water and bread but Zipporah takes care of him. However, the term of imprisonment is seven years instead of the ten years we saw earlier.[54] After the seven years, Zipporah proposes to her father to inquire after Moses for 'every day he cries

---

[52]A. Jellinek, *Beth Hamidrasch*, II.7. As mentioned before, this printed version differs considerably from the manuscripts.

[53]This refers to an earlier episode when Moses as a child takes Pharaoh's crown and puts it upon his own head to the dismay of the court, including Jethro. A. Jellinek, *Beth Hamidrasch*, II.3.

[54]Curiously the Moslem writer Al-Tabari in his *Ta'rikh*, translated as *The History of Al-Tabari*, III.46, knows a discussion about two different terms of Moses' stay at Jethro's place. However, here is no trace of the story about Moses' imprisonment.

out against you to his God and guilt is upon you'. Jethro (already informed beforehand that Moses lives!), expresses his amazement over this fact. Then 'they went to prison and found Moses standing on his feet and praying to his God and they released him.'

Jethro announces that he will give Zipporah in marriage to anyone who is able to uproot the rod. Kings and warriors fail, but Moses walking in the garden saw the rod fixed to the earth. The rod was made of sapphire and had engraved upon it the Ineffable Name. Moses uproots the rod and an astonished Jethro gives his daughter to Moses. Again the story concludes with a praise of Zipporah but with an extremely interesting addition:

> Zipporah walked in the way of the righteous mothers Sarah, Rebecca, Rachel and Leah *and walked in God's way as Moses her husband had commanded her* (italics, MP).

We summarize the major differences with the Yeraḥmeel version:

* Jethro's reason for putting Moses in prison is not in order to hand him over to the people of Cush. Instead, a link is established with a previous episode wherein Jethro acts as a counselor to Pharaoh.
* Moses remains imprisoned for seven years.
* Jethro knows in advance that Moses lives.
* Again Zipporah's role is decisive for Israel's history: the Exodus cannot take place without her for she redeems the future saviour of Israel. Zipporah is ranked among the matriarchs, but undoubtedly the author of our chronicle could not accept the idea of a gentile woman being a paragon of virtue and belief, equal to the matriarchs of Israel. His addition robs Zipporah of her originality as a righteous woman outside Israel and makes her subordinate for two reasons: on account of her sex ('her husband') and on account of her non-Jewish descent ('Moses'). In everything she is dependent upon Moses.

2.3 Midrash Wa-yosha

The last story, from the *Midrash Wa-yosha*,[55] is an account of the Exodus put into Moses' mouth. This 'first person account' of the episode at Jethro's house is closely related to the themes in the stories we have seen thus far, but the way the themes are incorporated into this account is highly original and justifies a separate treatment. The style of the story is vivid and captivates the reader:

> I fled from Pharaoh (to Jethro) but he too kept me imprisoned in a pit for seven years. I was forty years old when I left Egypt. I stood near the well and met Zipporah, Jethro's daughter and I noticed that she was very modest and I told her that I wanted to marry her. Zipporah told me the habit of her father and told me: "Anyone who wanted to marry one of his daughters my father puts on the test with a tree that he has in his garden. As soon as someone approached the tree it swallows him". I said to her: "Where does that tree come from?" She answered: "It is the staff that was created by God in the evening before Sabbath when God created His world. And God entrusted the staff to the First Man and the First Man entrusted it to Enoch and Enoch entrusted to Noah and Noah entrusted it to Shem and Shem entrusted it to Abraham and Abraham entrusted it to Isaac and Isaac entrusted it to Jacob and Jacob took it with him to Egypt and entrusted it to his son Joseph. And when Joseph died Egyptians plundered his house and brought the rod to Pharaoh's palace. My father Jethro was one of Pharaoh's prominent magicians and he saw the rod and desired it and stole it and brought it into his house. And engraved upon that rod was the Ineffable Name and those ten plagues that God was to bring upon the Egyptians in Egypt in the future. It was written upon it: dalet, tsade, kaf, ayin, dalet, shin, bet, alef, chet, bet.[56] The rod lay in my father's house for many days and years when one day my father took it in his hand and he entered the garden and planted it in the

---

[55]A. Jellinek, *Bet Hamidrasch*, Jerusalem 1938, I.42.

[56]These are the initial letters of the ten plagues, known from the Haggadah of Pesach. Of the different versions, only the Midrash *Wa-yosha* and *Targum PsJon* on Ex 14:21, have the ten plagues engraved upon the rod. Cf. M. McNamara (ed), *The Aramaic Bible*, vol.2. Targum Pseudo-Jonathan: Exodus, translated by M. Maher. Edinburgh 1994, 201. This midrash is attested to in ExodR 5:6 and 8:2 and in *TanB Tazria* § 10.

ground. When he returned to the garden to fetch it he noticed that
the rod had begun to blossom and to sprout. With this rod he puts
to the test anyone who desires to marry one of his daughters". As
soon as I heard her good words and saw how the shepherds drove
them away I saved Zipporah and her sisters from the shepherds. I
drew the bucket and watered the flock and they went to their father Reuel and I went with them.

We interrupt the story for some observations. The creation of the
rod at the sixth day combined with the chain of forefathers that
was brought from Pharaoh's palace to Jethro's garden, is familiar
from *PRE*. In the identification of these letters with the Ineffable
Name of God, *the Midrash Wa-yosha* may be even closer to the
version in the group *Yeraḥmeel/Yalqut/Sefer Ha-yashar* than to
PRE. However, we come across quite a few themes that have no
precedent in any other version:

* Moses asked Zipporah to marry him even before he knew of
  the rod.
* Zipporah informs Moses of the rod's true nature by her confession of faith in Israel's God. Her role is astonishing indeed.
  She, a daughter of a gentile Priest, yet seems to know more
  about salvation history than Moses himself!
* The rod began to bud.
* The rod's frightening ability to swallow any man who fails to
  uproot it.[57]

Undoubtedly, Freudians will recognize in this last folkloristic
motif a hidden fear of castration and male fear of the castrating
woman. The huge rod standing upright in Zipporah's garden,
jealously guarded by her father, is a powerful sexual symbol indeed. Whoever succeeds in identifying that rod as his rod receives
Zipporah in marriage! We continue the account:

---

[57]The detail of the swallowing rod might have been suggested by the biblical
account of the rod swallowing the magician's rods; Exod 7:12.

They entered first while I remained outside. When Jethro saw them he asked: "Why are you so early today?" They said: "An Egyptian has freed us from the hand of the shepherds". And while outside I heard how they testified about me being an Egyptian. And because I did not enter and say: "I am a Hebrew, I was not found worthy to enter the land of Israel".[58]

Zipporah's crucial role is maintained in the whole story and Jethro's wickedness comes to the fore. For when Moses asks for Zipporah and fulfills the condition of taking the rod, Jethro realizes:

This is the prophet about whom all the wise of Israel[59] have prophesied that in the future he will destroy all of Egypt and the Egyptians. Jethro became angry at me and had me thrown into a pit in his house.[60]

Thus instead of being impressed by his future son-in-law's fulfillment of the condition, Jethro, being on Pharaoh's side, throws Moses into the pit![61] Zipporah's saving actions are completely contrary to her fathers wishes. She invents a stratagem to be able to stay at home and takes care of Moses during seven years. After that period, she suggests to her father to see if the stranger is dead or alive. Jethro calls: "Moses", and Moses answers in a prophetic vein: "Here I am!" At that moment Jethro repents of his behavior. He kissed Moses on his head and exclaimed: "Blessed the Eter-

---

[58]This motif is probably derived from earlier midrash: Joseph proclaimed his identity (Gen 40:15) and was granted the burial in the Land, but not so Moses (*DeutR* 2:8).

[59]Here Jethro is well informed. However, L. Ginzberg, *The Legends*, V.412, emendation 'the wise of Egypt', should be rejected.

[60]L. Grünhut, *Midrash Hashkem* 2b, in *Sefer Ha-liqutim* I.2b, Jerusalem 1967, contains a short version of this same event: Moses taking the rod whereupon Jethro throws Moses into the pit.

[61]However, *Midrash Wa-yosha* portrayed Jethro earlier as the one who wanted to protect Moses when the latter as a baby on Pharaoh's lap, took Pharaoh's crown from his head and put it upon his own head. Jethro's portrayal here is far more negative than e.g. in *BT Sotah* 11a, where Jethro flees upon hearing Pharaoh's schemes. A. Jellinek, *Beth Hamidrasch*, I.41.

nal, Who has preserved you those seven years in the pit. I testify about Him, that He takes life and grants it, and I testify about you that you are completely righteous. By your hand Egypt will once be destroyed (...)". And he gave Zipporah to me in marriage.[62]

With this confession of faith, the transition of the pagan Jethro from paganism to biblical religion is sealed. The storyteller's genius is evident. Jethro's change of heart is aptly expressed by the repetition of his exclamation, that Moses will destroy Egypt. However, the second time the exclamation receives a totally different connotation.

Jethro changes, but Zipporah remains a righteous woman all the time. She knows about salvation history and is prepared to save Moses' life against her father's wish. Zipporah and Jethro are in perfect contrast, he being intent to kill Moses both as a child and as an adult.

The Motifs and the Texts: A Survey

In order to get an overview of the different stories we present a list of motifs of which the stories are composed.
1. Moses tells that he had been king in Ethiopia.
2. Jethro intends to hand Moses over to Ethiopia (a)/ to Pharaoh (b).
3. Jethro seizes Moses and throws him in a pit (a)/ in prison (b)
4. Zipporah takes care of Moses in secret during seven years (a)/ ten years (b).
5. Moses appears to be alive and Jethro knows that in advance (a)/ is amazed (b).
6. Jethro finds Moses praying.
7. Moses walks into the garden and takes the rod.
8. Jethro recognizes Moses as the redeemer of Israel.
9. Jethro repents and confesses his faith in the God of Israel.
10. Jethro gives his daughter to Moses in marriage.

---

[62] A. Jellinek, *Beth Hamidrasch*, I.42-43.

11. Apologetic praise of Zipporah ranking her with Israel's matriarchs.
12. Zipporah is virtuous as her husband Moses commanded her.

Now here is a list of the different elements as they appear in the
stories:

Yalqut Exod §166 (edn Hyman)	1	2a	3b	4b	5b	6	7		9	10	11	
Sefer Ha-yashar	1	2a	3b	4b	5b	6	7		9	10	11	
Yerahmeel XLVI (edn Gaster)	1	2a	3b	4b	5b	6	7		9	10	11	
Targum Ps.Jon Exod 2:21[63]:		2b	3a	4b	5		7					
Chronicles of Moses (printed version)		2b	3	4a	5a	6	7			10	11	12

Midrash Wa-yosha	7	8		2b	3a	4a	5b			9	10	

As was noted before, the first three texts are closely related. In
these three texts Moses' departure from the Ethiopians is the reason for Jethro's animosity, not Moses' flight from Egypt. From
the technical narrative point of view, the explanation of Jethro's
animosity by introducing his plan to turn Moses over to the
Ethiopians is not wholly convincing since Moses left Ethiopia
with honour. Besides, we do not hear of this plan any more during
Moses' imprisonment!

---

[63] We noticed already that this Targum on Exod 14:21, contains the motif of the
ten plagues being engraved upon the rod. This motif is attested in *Midrash Wa-
yosha*. But both may have taken it from *ExodR* 5:6 and 8:3.

The interdependency of the versions

Sefer Ha-yashar should be considered the last version of the story of Moses' rod.[64] There is no obstacle then to regard one of the versions of the *Chronicles of Moses* as the source of the *Sefer Ha-yashar*.[65] Our limited investigation of only one section led to this conclusion. Our conclusion can be broadened by circumstantial evidence. A detailed comparison of the *Yerahmeel* version of the *Chronicles of Moses* in its different manuscripts[66] with *Sefer Ha-yashar* shows that sometimes the text of *Sefer Ha-yashar* is parallel to a variant reading of *Yerahmeel* in the critical apparatus. But in other instances (especially in the episode of Pharaoh's dream), *Sefer Ha-yashar* is parallel to the version in the *Yalqut*. This last point was noted already by R. Bloch.[67]

---

[64]We interpret the references in the *Yalqut* and the *Chronicles of* Moses to a *Sefer Ha-yashar* as a poetic reference to the Torah itself. Hence these references do not prove *Sefer Ha-yashar*'s priority as Ginzberg and Schwarzbaum assume. Cf. R.J.A.I. de Leeuw van Weenen, *Sefer Ha-yashar, Herkomst, Bronnen en Tendensen*, Leiden 1992, 49-50 and 152-157 and in her forthcoming book on the same subject.

[65]This is the conclusion of R.J.A.I. de Leeuw van Weenen, after a meticulous analysis of the sources. The use of flashbacks in *Sefer Ha-yashar* as well as certain events that are only to be found in *Sefer Ha-yashar* form the mainstay of her argumentation. In her conclusions she follows such scholars as Flusser, Jellinek, and Shinan. One may note that in the episode of Pharaoh's dream, *Yalqut* and *Yerahmeel* contain closely related versions while *Sefer Ha-yashar* again is more elaborate. Moreover, *Sefer Ha-yashar* often fills in names of persons. It does not seem probable that later versions would remove those names. Hence it does not seem logical to assume that the *Yalqut* used the *Sefer Ha-yashar*, as does R. Bloch, 'Note méthodologique pour l'étude la littérature Rabbinique', *Récherches de Science Réligieuse* 43 (1955) 217. The printed version of the *Chronicles of Moses* shows again major differences in comparison with these three versions and should be dealt with separately.

[66]See A. Shinan, 'Dibre Hayamim'.

[67]However, her conclusion that *Yalqut* used *Sefer Ha-yashar* and another version of the *History of Moses*, should be abandoned. The differences always concern merely small details. Perhaps one should assume the existence of a version of the *History of Moses* being a mixture between the already very similar versions of *Yerahmeel* and of the *Yalqut*. That version then has been used by the author of *Sefer Ha-yashar*.

As the Chronicles of Moses is mentioned in the Arukh, this work should be dated before 1100. D. Flusser maintains that *Sefer Yosippon* (in the year 953) has been used by the *Chronicles of Moses*, which places its origin between 953 and 1100. In addition to that, there are strong arguments to date the *Sefer Ha-yashar* to the 16th century. This fits quite well with our research.[68]

All these texts, including *Targum PsJon*, contain the motif of Zipporah helping Moses, a motif not found in *PRE*. One may assume then that the version of *Targum PsJon* must be later than (the version of) *PRE*. Hence *PRE* should not be regarded as a subsequent elaboration of *Targum PsJon*.[69]

The development of the rod can be described as follows. Tannaitic material about the rod being created on the evening of the sixth day (*Abot*) and being made of sapphire (*Mekhilta*) was combined in a version like that in *PRE* 40, in combination with motifs that may be of later date: the chain of forefathers and Jethro's house. A Christian offshoot of these traditions (chain, Jethro's house) with new developments about Adam's rod can be found in the *Book of the Bee*.

After this initial synthesis in *PRE*, the rod took on the motif of being a precondition for marrying Zipporah. Also the motif of Jethro's animosity and Zipporah's help were introduced. *Yalqut/Sefer Ha-yashar/Yeraḥmeel* represent versions that combine all of this.

Another strand is formed by *Targum PsJon*, the *Chronicles of Moses* (printed version) and *Midrash Wa-yosha*. All three mention Jethro's intention to hand over Moses to Pharaoh. Here *Midrash Wa-yosha* stands at the end of the development. The oc-

---

[68]According to J. Dan, *Hasippur Ha-Ivri*, Jerusalem 1974, 137-145; and idem, 'Matai nitchaber Sefer Ha-yashar?', in: *Sefer Ha-Yovel le-Dov Sadan*, Jerusalem 1977, 105-110.

[69]Occasional expanded motifs in *PRE* in comparison to *Targum PsJon* and 'gaps' in the latter are no proof for the opposite, as a Targum by its nature is necessarily more condensed. Sometimes *Targum PsJon* even presupposes the more elaborate midrash of earlier date. This result may be corroborated by the studies of M. Ohana, M. Perez Fernandez and A. Shinan, who view (against J. Heinemann and R. Hayward) *Targum PsJon* being dependent upon *PRE*.

casional brevity of *Targum PsJon*, although later than *PRE*, does not allow us to make firm conclusions about its relation to these later midrashic texts. The Targum is closely related to the *Chronicles of Moses* (printed version): they both lack the chain of forefathers. Still the Targum agrees with the first group of (three) versions in assuming ten years of imprisonment.

Conclusion

The midrashic texture has woven different ideas about the relation between revelation and tradition (the rod) together with both positive and negative attitudes towards Gentiles (Jethro) and with contrasting female roles, both subservient and independent (Zipporah). By trying to unravel this fabric in its different historical and literary components, the midrash does not appear to us as a hotch-potch. On the contrary, we discovered a multi-layered structure that is characteristic of midrash. The rod appeared as a symbol that radically transformed the significance of biblical time and place. From an aimless roaming in a pagan environment, Moses' journey was developed into a providential connection with the past of patriarchs and even of Paradise, and with a Messianic future. The rod as a precondition for marrying Zipporah transformed her from just another gentile woman to a righteous woman ranked among the matriarchs and indispensable for Israel's liberation.

The Christian interpretations of the rod connected Moses likewise to Paradise and to Messianic connotations, more specifically to the Cross, thereby forging a link between creation, revelation and redemption. Precisely because of the very similar underlying symbolic-mythical thought pattern, these Christian texts' transformation of history appeared highly antagonistic to Jewish ideas of salvation history. Both are radical transformations of biblical time and space.

LITURGICAL TIME AND SPACE IN EARLY
CHRISTIANITY IN LIGHT OF THEIR JEWISH
BACKGROUND

Gerard Rouwhorst

T he question of the origins and the earliest history of Christian
liturgy has long aroused the interest of scholars of liturgy,
especially those with a Christian background. In the numerous
books and articles which have been published and continue to be
published on this issue, much attention is paid to the relationship
between the forms of worship that existed in early Christianity
and the liturgical traditions of Judaism.[1] Which attitude did the
Christians of the first centuries adopt vis-à-vis the Jewish liturgical traditions with which they were familiar? Which elements of
Jewish worship did they give up or even reject and which traditions did they preserve? And as regards the elements they did preserve, to what extent did they transform them and did they Chris-
tianize them?

Generally speaking, one can say that a broad consensus about
the basic outlines of the history of early Christian liturgy has been
achieved. It has become the common conviction of the majority
of the liturgical scholars – be they Jewish or Christian – that
Jewish liturgical traditions have left many marks on the earliest
forms of Christian worship and that indeed the origins of Chris-

---

[1]It is impossible to give a complete overview of the relevant literature. I will
limit myself to the following recent publications: G. Kretschmar, 'Early Christian Liturgy in the Light of Contemporary Historical Research', *SL* 16
(1986/1987) 31-53; P. Bradshaw & L. Hoffman (eds), *The Making of Jewish
and Christian Worship*, Notre Dame/London 1991; S. Wilson, *Related Strangers. Jews and Christians*, Minneapolis 1995, 222-257. One may also refer to P.
Bradshaw's book *The Search for the Origins of Christian Worship*, London
1992, which mentions and discusses many of the theories put forward during
this century.

tian worship are to be searched for in Jewish worship or, more
precisely, in the rituals that were performed and in the prayers
that were said in the synagogue and during meals at home.[2]

However, this does not mean that the final word about the origins, and particularly the Jewish origins, of the early Christian
liturgy has been said. On the contrary, the scholarly discussion
about this issue is still going on, as is proven by the continuing
stream of books and articles on this subject. Several reasons may
be adduced for this phenomenon. First, the number of available
and accessible sources has increased. The discovery of new texts,
the critical editions of important Syriac and Armenian documents[3]
and the growing awareness that not only 'orthodox' writings, but
also 'heterodox' or marginal sources, such as Gnostic texts, apocryphal Gospels and Acts have increased the source material for
the scholar.[4] In the second place, it has to be noted that our image
of the earliest history of Christianity has changed. From historical
research it has become clear that early Christianity was more

---

[2]This view is accepted by recent and influential liturgical handbooks and
reference works such as: C. Jones, G. Wainwright & E. Yarnold (eds), *The
Study of Liturgy*, London 1978; H.B. Meyer et al. (eds), *Gottesdienst der
Kirche* III-VIII, Regensburg 1983-1994; A. Martimort, *L'Eglise en prière*. Edi-
tion nouvelle, I-IV, Paris 1983; H. Schmidt-Lauber, K. Bieritz, *Handbuch der
Liturgik*, Göttingen 1994; H. Wegman, *Riten en mythen. Liturgie in de geschie-
denis van het christendom*, Kampen 1991 (German translation: *Liturgie in der
Geschichte des Christentums*, Regensburg 1994).

[3]See particularly the critical edition of the works of Ephrem the Syrian (preserved partly in Armenian) published by E. Beck & L. Leloir in the series
CSCO (Leuven 1953-1979) and A.Vööbus' new edition of the Syriac Didascalia (*The Didascalia Apostolorum in Syriac, CSCO* 175/176 and 179/180,
Leuven 1979).

[4]In this connection one may, in particular, refer to several publications of
G. Kretschmar, especially to his classical study about baptism in early Christianity: 'Die Geschichte des Taufgottesdienst in der alten Kirche', in: *Leitur-
gia. Handbuch des evangelischen Gottesdienstes* V, Kassel 1970, 1-348 and
to his article about the Eucharist: 'Abendmahlsfeier I. Alte Kirche', *TRE* 1
(1977) 229-278. See particularly for the Apocryphal Acts of the Apostles: G.
Rouwhorst, 'La célébration de l'eucharistie selon les Actes des Apôtres', in;
C. Caspers & M. Schneiders (eds), *Omnes circumadstantes. Contributions
towards a History of the People in the Liturgy Presented to Herman Wegman*, Kampen 1990, 51-77.

variegated and multiform than had been thought for a long time. This pertains in particular to the relationship with Judaism: the distinction between a Gentile, Pauline Christianity on the one hand and a Torah-observing Jewish Christianity on the other hand must be considered as too general and too simple. There appear to have existed all kinds of intermediate forms, such as Christian communities that were for a great part of Gentile origin, but hardly having any affinity with the theology of Paul and in several respects open to influences from Judaism.[5]

Moreover, the parting of the ways between Judaism and Christianity did not occur everywhere at the same time and at the same pace. In this connection, it may be remarked that the Syriac-speaking churches of Syria and Mesopotamia in particular for a long time have preserved a great number of Jewish traditions that had disappeared elsewhere at a very early stage.[6] It will be obvious that this revised view on the origins of early Christianity has implications for the way in which we look at the development of early Christian liturgy. Finally, a third reason why the origins of Christian liturgy remain a subject of scholarly debate has to do with recent developments in the research of the history of Jewish worship, in particular during the period when Christianity emerged and started to develop its own identity.[7] As a result of the work of several specialists in this field our view of Jewish lit-

---

[5]I presume this characterization applies to a considerable part of Syriac-speaking Christianity. See, for example, my article 'Jewish Liturgical Traditions in Early Syriac Christianity', *VigChr* 51 (1997) 72-93.

[6]See, for example: G. Rouwhorst, 'Jewish Liturgical Traditions', and: G. Kretschmar, 'Die Bedeutung der Liturgiegeschichte für die Frage nach der Kontinuität des Judenchristentums in nachapostolischer Zeit', in: *Aspects du judéo-christianisme. Colloque de Strasbourg 23-25 avril 1964*, Paris 1965, 113-137; idem, 'Die Kirche aus Juden und Heiden. Forschungsprobleme der ersten christlichen Jahrhunderte', in: J. van Amersfoort & J. van Oort (eds), *Juden und Christen in der Antike*, Kampen 1990, 9-43.

[7]See, for some convenient overviews of the most important publications in this field: S. Reif, 'Jewish Liturgical Research; Past, Present and Future', *JJS* 34 (1983) 161-170. See further: idem, *Judaism and Hebrew Prayer. New perspectives on Jewish Liturgical History*, Cambridge 1993, especially 1-22; and P. Bradshaw, *The Search for the Origins*, 1-29.

urgy in this period has considerably changed. On the one hand, a number of assumptions that were more or less generally accepted, have been called into question. On the other hand, and this point should be stressed, we gradually get a better insight into the complex development of Jewish worship at the beginning of the Common Era.

The progress made in this field of research sometimes puts the liturgical traditions of early Christianity in a new and surprising light. For one thing, it challenges a number of basic assumptions shared by several Christian liturgical scholars who turn out to have had a wrong idea of Jewish liturgy in the period before and just after the fall of the Temple.[8] In particular, it has become more and more evident that many Christian liturgists wrongly have taken for granted that during the first five centuries of the Common Era, or even during a longer period, Jewish forms of worship had remained more or less unchanged. Starting from that very dubious assumption, they have drawn conclusions about the origins of early Christianity which, to say the least, are highly debatable.[9] On the other side, it is to be expected beforehand that develop-

---

[8]This point has recently been stressed by P. Bradshaw in his book *The Search for the Origins*.

[9]This pertains, generally speaking, to the bulk of the older publications, though, of course, not always to the same degree. In my view, the objection of proceeding from a too static view of the development of Jewish liturgy may be raised in particular against a number of classical studies about the early development of the Christian Eucharist, such as G. Dix. *The Shape of the Liturgy*, London 1945 (many reprints); J. Jeremias, *Die Abenmahlsworte Jesu,* Göttingen [4]1966; L. Bouyer, *Eucharistie*, Paris 1966. Other examples are the detailed reconstructions made by several Christian scholars of reading-cycles, sometimes including the use of Psalms, that would have been followed in the synagogues of the 1st century CE, even before the fall of the Temple, and would have left traces in early Christian liturgy or in the text or the structure of (some of) the Gospels. I shall limit myself to mentioning the influential article of A. Büchler, 'The Reading of the Law and Prophets in a Triennial Cycle', *JQR* 5 (1893) 420-468; 6 (1894) 1-73 and the monograph of A. Arens, *Die Psalmen im Gottesdienst des Alten Bundes*, Trier [2]1968. See for a more comprehensive overview of the different reconstructions and theories: D. Monshouwer, *Markus en de Torah*, Kampen 1987, 16-46 and further: P. Bradshaw, *The Search for the Origins*, 21-24.

ments in Jewish liturgical scholarship will open new perspectives for the reconstruction of early Christian liturgy and will help us to better understand what was happening in early Christian rituals.

With these developments in mind, I will discuss two essential elements of early Christian liturgy: the celebration of the oldest Christian festival, i.e. Passover/Easter and the plan and the interior of the building where Christians met for celebrating liturgy. The choice of these topics is no coincidence; they are indeed of particular relevance for the theme of this book: Sanctity of Time and Space. While dealing with both issues, I will focus on the one hand on recent developments in scientific research and on the other hand upon their relationship with Jewish liturgy as it most probably existed in the same period. To what extent can one speak of continuity between Jewish and early Christian liturgy? To what degree did early Christians preserve Jewish ritual traditions? To what extent did they eventually borrow them from Judaism at a later stage? And if they preserved or adopted these Jewish elements, in what sense did they transform them, did they adapt them to their own specifically Christian ideas and situation? Finally, in doing so I will try to be particularly attentive to the multiformity that existed inside early Christianity.

The Celebration of Passover

We begin with the celebration of Passover. For a long time it was believed by the majority of scholars that already at a very early period in the early Church, two types of Easters existed side by side.[10] One type was celebrated on the fourteenth of Nisan or, to be precise, in the night from the fourteenth to the fifteenth of Ni-

---

[10]See, for a survey of the older publications: B. Lohse, *Das Passafest der Quartodecimaner*, Gütersloh 1953, 20-40. More recent publications that should be mentioned in this connection, are those of R. Cantalamessa (see especially: *La pasqua della salvezza,* Milano 1971, 116-132) and W. Rordorf (see in particular his article: 'Zum Ursprung des Osterfestes am Sonntag', *ThZ* 18 (1962) 167-189 (= W. Rordorf, *Lex orandi – Lex credendi. Gesammelte Aufsätze zum 60. Geburtstag*, Fribourg 1993, 29-51).

san. This Easter was of Jewish-Christian origin and it survived in Asia till the end of the 2nd or the beginning of the 3rd century. The other type was celebrated on the Sunday after the Jewish Passover. This type was considered to be specifically Gentile-Christian, although some scholars assumed influence from the so-called Essene solar calendar that is known, for example, from Jubilees and Qumran.[11] The majority of Christian churches was supposed to have adopted this Sunday celebration in a very early period and at the latest in the first half of the 2nd century.[12]

In the course of this century, our knowledge of Christian celebration of Passover has considerably increased. This is in particular due to the discovery and publication of some important Christian sources, among which I want to mention the discovery of the famous homily of Melito,[13] of Origen's homily 'On Passover' that was found in Toura[14] and the critical editions of the Paschal Hymns of Ephrem the Syrian.[15] To this list may be added a new critical edition of the Didascalia by the Syrologist Arthur Vööbus[16] and the discovery that a Greek homily that in the manuscripts is sometimes ascribed to Hippolytus and sometimes to John Chrysostom,[17] may have a Quartodeciman background.[18]

---

[11] See the publications of Cantalamessa and Rordorf mentioned in note 10.

[12] It should be remarked that this view was challenged by some scholars who argued, mainly on the basis of Eusebius' *Ecclesiastical History* 5, 23-25, that Easter Sunday was the result of a relatively late development and that it was not introduced in Rome until around 165. See especially: K. Holl, 'Ein Bruchstück aus einem bisher unbekannten Brief des Epiphanius', in: idem, *Gesammelte Aufsätze zur Kirchengeschichte II*, Tübingen 1928, 204-224; M. Richard, 'La question pascale au IIe siècle', *OrSyr* 6 (1961) 179-212.

[13] Actually two excellent editions are available: S. Hall, *Melito of Sardes. On Passover and Fragments*, Oxford 1979 and O. Perler, *Méliton de Sardes. Sur la Pâque*, *SC* 121, Paris 1966.

[14] See, for an edition of the text: O. Guéraud & P. Nautin, *Origène. Sur la Pâque. Traité inédit publié d'après un papyrus de Toura*, Paris 1979.

[15] E. Beck, *Des heiligen Ephraem des Syrers Paschahymnen (De Azymis, de Crucifixione, de Resurrectione), CSCO* 249/249 (Syr. 108/109), Louvain 1964.

[16] See note 3.

[17] See the edition of P. Nautin, *Homélies pascales I. Une homélie inspiré du traité sur la Pâque d'Hippolyte*, Paris 1950; G. Visonà, *Pseudo Ippolito.*

Also, quite a lot of research has been done regarding the development of the Jewish Passover in the period between the destruction of the Temple and the redaction of the Mishnah.[19]

As a result of these discoveries, our picture of the earliest history of the Christian Passover has changed considerably.[20] To begin with, it becomes more and more likely that originally there was in Christianity only one type of Passover, the Quartodeciman one that was celebrated on the Jewish date, in the night of the fourteenth to the fifteenth of Nisan. Further, it appears that we can get a quite precise idea of the nature and content of this celebration.[21] It had the character of a vigil that probably began at sunset or possibly a little bit earlier and chronologically coincided more or less with the Jewish Passover meal: the *Seder* meal. The vigil basically consisted of three elements: 1) a fast that probably lasted until midnight 2) the reading of texts from Scripture, among others the twelfth chapter of Exodus which was typologically explained – either by a homily or by a kind of Christian *haggadah* – and most probably a version of the Passion Narratives 3) a meal that must have started after midnight, after the Jewish Passover meal had ended, which was connected with the celebration of the Eucharist and lasted at the latest until dawn.

In sanctum Pascha. Studio, edizione, = *Studia Patristica Mediolensia* 15, Milano 1988.

[18]See R. Cantalamessa, *L'omelia «In S.Pascha» dello Pseudo-Ippolito di Roma. Ricerche sulla teologia dell'Asia Minore nella seconda metà del II secolo,* Milano 1967; G. Visonà, *Pseudo Ippolito,* 55-59; 182-183 and also G. Rouwhorst, 'The Quartodeciman Passover and the Jewish Pesach', *QuLi* 77 (1996) 152-173, especially 156-157.

[19]See, for example: B. Bokser, *The Origins of the Seder. The Passover Rite and Early Rabbinic Judaism,* Berkeley 1984, 3 and 72; J. Tarbory, *Pesah Dorot: Peraqim be-Toldot Leyl ha-Seder* (Hebr), Tel Aviv 1996. See, for references to other important studies, ibid, p. xv.

[20]Cf. for the following my article 'The Quartodeciman Passover and the Jewish Pesach'.

[21]I confine myself to a rash and succinct summary of the reconstruction I have attempted on the basis of the available sources in 'The Quartodeciman Passover'.

If this reconstruction of the original Quartodeciman Passover is correct, it emerges that this celebration was characterized by a very close similarity with the Jewish Passover. True, it cannot be denied that there are some basic differences. As a matter of fact, Jews do not and did not commemorate the death and resurrection of Jesus Christ by reading a version of the Passion Narrative and by the celebration of the Eucharist. Moreover, it is remarkable that form and structure of the vigil have changed: Christians fast while Jews eat and drink. Finally, one cannot overlook the anti-Jewish atmosphere that the Quartodeciman vigil must have had in many places, as we learn from the homily of Melito and in later Syriac sources.[22]

In spite of all these differences, however, one is struck by the analogies with the Jewish Passover, in particular Passover as it was celebrated just after the fall of the Temple when the sacrifice of the Passover lambs had become impossible.[23] Both festivals are celebrated practically simultaneously. Both Christians and Jews commemorate the Exodus from Egypt and explain it in detail, either by the (specifically) Jewish 'midrash' on Deut 26:5-8, or by the Christian reading of the twelfth chapter of Exodus and a typological explanation of its details. Even this difference appears in another light when we take into account the possibility that the midrash did not yet exist at the time that the Quartodeciman celebration took its most early shape, as has been argued by several Jewish scholars.[24] Further, both the Jewish and the Christian celebration culminate in a meal. Finally, the fast of the Christians

---

[22]See G. Rouwhorst, 'The Quartodeciman Passover', 168-169 and especially for the Syriac sources (in particular Ephrem the Syrian): idem, *Les hymnes pascales d'Ephrem de Nisibe. Analyse théologique et recherche sur l'évolution de la fête pascale à Nisibe et Edesse et dans quelques Eglises voisines au quatrième siècle*, Leiden 1989, tome I, esp. 99-105; 124-126.

[23]Cf. for the following 'The Quartodeciman Passover', 169-173.

[24]See B. Bokser, *The Origins of the Seder*, 72; S. Safrai, 'He'erot Historiyot le-Mishnah Pesahim Pereq 'Asiri', in: B. Uffenheimer (ed.), *Ha-Miqra ve-Toldot Yisrael: Mehqarim le-Zichro shel Yaakov Liver*, Tel Aviv 1971, 297-306 (= S. Safrai, *Be-yeme ha-Bayit v-be-yeme ha-Mishnah: Mehqarim be-Toldot Yisrael*, Jerusalem 1996, II:610-619).

might recall the Jewish custom of abstaining from food some hours before the Pesach meal.[25]

Also, apart from the basic structure of the Quartodeciman Easter, in some of the Christian sources related to the Quartodeciman Passover, other more specific elements of the Jewish Pesach have left traces. In this connection particular mention should be made of Melito's homily '*Peri Pascha*' (PP). Some scholars have gone so far as to claim that this homily is 'nothing else than a Christian Paschal Haggadah'.[26] This opinion is certainly untenable, unless one understands the word 'Passchal Haggadah' in a very wide and imprecise sense.[27] It cannot be denied, however, that there is a number of striking affinities between Melito's homily and the Jewish Passover Haggadah, more precisely its oldest nucleus that underlies the oldest available sources, in particular chapter 10 of Mishnah Pesaḥim. These affinities betray some kind of historical connection,[28] and suggest that Melito was quite well informed about the Jewish celebration as it was held in Sardis and reinterpreted some of its ritual elements in a Christian way. First, it is striking that Melito like the Passover Haggadah is preoccupied with explaining the meaning of the basic elements of the Jewish paschal meal, that is the paschal lamb, the bitter herbs and the unleavened bread.[29] Further, several scholars have noted that ch. 68 of PP presents a remarkable parallel with the famous passage of the Jewish Passover Haggadah which in Hebrew begins with the word לפיכך and makes mention of the passage 'from bondage to freedom and from darkness to great light'.[30] Likewise,

---

[25]Cf. MPes 10:1; TPes 10:1.

[26]Thus F. Cross, *The Early Christian Fathers*, London 1960, 107.

[27]Cf. the critical remarks of S. Hall, 'Melito in the Light of the Passover Haggadah', *JTS* NS 22 (1971) 29-46.

[28]See S. Hall, 'Melito in the Light'.

[29]Cf. the answer given to the famous children's questions about the meaning of the rite and the explanation of the Christian festival given in PP from ch. 46 ('What is the Pascha?') onwards. Cf. S. Hall, 'Melito in the Light', 38.

[30]See Melito, *Peri Pascha* ch. 67 and S. Hall, 'Melito in the Light', 31-34 and further: E. Werner, 'Melito of Sardis, the First Poet of Deicide', *HUCA* 37 (1966) 191-210; S. Pines, 'From Darkness into Great Light', *Immanuel* 4 (1974) 47-51; D. Flusser, 'Some Notes on Easter and the Passover Hag-

Eric Werner and David Flusser, among others, have pointed to the
existence of striking parallels between PP ch. 87-89 where Israel
is blamed for returning God's goodness with ingratitude, namely
by murdering Christ (God),[31] and the *Dayyenu*-litany which enu-
merates the benefits that God conferred upon the Jewish people
during the exodus from Egypt and these scholars have argued,
with very good reasons, that the parallels point to a dependence of
Melito upon the Passover rite as it was celebrated in Sardis [32].

It should also be mentioned that one encounters in early
Christianity, though not exclusively in Quartodeciman churches,
traces of other Jewish festivals that are closely related to Pesach.
In a number of Churches the festival of Easter, Quartodeciman or
otherwise, was followed by a joyful celebration of the Pentecost
during fifty days which, in one way or another, must have its origins in the observance of the seven weeks between Pesach and
Shavuot in Judaism.[33] Further, there are strong indications that at
least some of the Syriac-speaking Churches knew of a Christian-
ized version of the Week of Unleavened Bread.[34]

---

gadah', *Immanuel* 7 (1977) 52-60.

[31]This passage may be considered as a forerunner of the so-called *Improperia*, known from the Roman and Byzantine Good Friday liturgy that is
characterized by a juxtaposition of God's benefits and Israel's ingratitude
towards God/Christ.

[32]E. Werner, 'Melito of Sardis, the First Poet of Deicide'; D. Flusser, 'Hebrew Improperia', *Immanuel* 4 (1974) 51-55. See further the response of M.
Brocke: 'On the Jewish Origin of the 'Improperia'', *Immanuel* 7 (1977) 44-
51 and Flusser's reply to Brocke: 'Some Notes on Easter and the Passover
Haggadah', *Immanuel* 7 (1977) 52-60. Cf. also M. Poorthuis, 'De Improperia
en het jodendom', *Jaarboek voor liturgie-onderzoek* 5 (1989) 137-162.

[33]See for the Christian celebration of Pentecost: R. Cabié, *La Pentecôte.
L'évolution de la cinquantaine pascale au cours des cinq premiers siècles*,
Tournai 1964. This fifty-day long festival should be distinguished from the
celebration of the fiftieth day after Easter, either as the commemoration of the
Ascension or of the descent of the Spirit, which is of a somewhat later date,
probably 4th century.

[34]As I have argued elsewhere, these indications are to be found in Aphra-
hat's twelfth demonstration (par.12). See G. Rouwhorst, *Les hymnes pascales
d'Ephrem de Nisibe*, 150-152 and also p. 155, note 20 for further historical
data that may support this hypothesis.

It should, however, be noted that the preservation of these Jewish elements depended to a great extent on local customs and traditions. This seems quite obvious for the ritual elements mentioned in the homily of Melito as well as for the celebration of the Week of Unleavened Bread in some Syriac Churches. But even the celebration of the Pentecost appears not to have been as common in early Christianity as is usually suggested. In fact, we find clear traces of it in several areas, especially in Egypt and Africa and most probably in some parts of Asia Minor and Rome,[35] but it is very surprising that not even the slightest allusion to its existence is made either in Melito or in the Syriac sources,[36] which in my opinion can mean only one thing: in the areas where these writings originated, the celebration of the Pentecost either did not exist at all or it was celebrated only very locally and on a very small scale.

That this multiformity was characteristic of the way Christians celebrated their Passover in the period prior to Constantine, finally also emerges from the process during which the Christians gave up the Jewish date and transferred the festival from the 14th/15th of Nisan to the Sunday of Easter, or rather to the Paschal Triduum that lasted from Friday until Sunday morning. This important change did not occur everywhere at the same time and at the same pace.[37] In fact, we know that a number of Christians

---

[35]See, for a survey of the references in early Christian literature to the Pentecost: R. Cabié, *La Pentecôte*, esp. 37-45; 61-76.

[36]I want to leave here out of consideration the custom of celebrating the Ascension of Christ on the fiftieth day after Easter, as attested by some Syriac sources of the 4th and 5th century, in particular the Doctrina Apostolorum and the list of pericopes preserved in ms. 14528 of the British Library (see. G. Kretschmar, 'Himmelfahrt und Pfingsten', *ZKG,* 4° Folge IV, 64 (1954-55) 209-253). Neither Aphraates, nor Ephrem or the Didascalia do make the slightest allusion to its existence. In my view, this means that this usage cannot have its roots in a 2th or 3th century tradition as is argued by Kretschmar who traces back this custom to the Jewish festival of Shavuot, as it was celebrated in some Jewish circles (book of Jubilees; Qumran) who commemorated on this day the conclusion of the Covenant at Sinai and, as a part of it, also Moses' ascension of the Mount.

[37]See for the following: G. Rouwhorst, 'The Quartodeciman Passover',

began very early to celebrate Passover on the first day of the Christian week, i.e. on Sunday. However, in spite of the pressure exerted by the bishop of Rome and several synods that were held about this question,[38] a large number of churches did not follow their example. The Christians of Asia remained faithful to the Quartodeciman practice till the end of the second century and the Christians of Syria and Mesopotamia remained so even till the Council of Nicea and even then they did not all adapt themselves immediately and whole-heartedly to the traditions of the majority.[39]

Church Buildings and Synagogues

The picture we have regarding the development of early Christian worship in relation to its Jewish background will be corroborated. At the same time it will become more differentiated when we take into account another element of early Christianity: its architectural setting or the building in which it was celebrated, and the development of the synagogue building in the same period.

For a long time, books about early Christian Church building hardly took into account the architecture of the synagogue. Usually they passed directly from so-called house-churches or church-houses to early Christian basilicas constructed according to 'pagan' models. I presume this is for the most part due to the defective and poor knowledge most scholars had of the development of synagogue architecture. In general, one seemed to assume that synagogues of the 1st and 2nd centuries resembled those of the 5th or 6th centuries or even later periods, with a fixed Torah shrine and a *bema*. This leads to the conclusion that there was not any continuity between the plan of the synagogues and that of the buildings where the early Christians met.

---

esp. 157-160.
      [38]Eusebius, *Hist. Eccl.*, V, 23.
      [39]See G. Rouwhorst, *Les hymnes pascales* I, 128-193.

In the last few decades our understanding of the history of synagogue building has changed drastically, thanks to a great number of excavations in the Diaspora and in the Land of Israel and also due to many important publications that have been devoted to them.[40] It is quite difficult to obtain an overview of the results of the research, but there is at least one thing that becomes clear: the emergence of synagogues as they are known from the 5th or 6th centuries is the result of a long and gradual process. As far as I can see on the basis of the available literature, the earliest synagogues, let us say of the 1st century CE, before or just after the fall of the Temple, were, on the basis of their plan and interior, very difficult to distinguish from other civic buildings.[41] It is only gradually that their 'sanctity' increased, that, for example, impressive and permanent Torah shrines were construed that the use of religious symbols increased and that, to put it briefly, the synagogue became a replacement for the lost Temple.[42]

If this is true, its relationship to the early Christian church building appears in a different perspective. In effect, it seems that

---

[40]I confine myself to mentioning here: F. Hüttenmeister and G. Reeg, *Die antiken Synagogen in Israel*, 2 vols, Wiesbaden 1977; L.I. Levine, *Ancient Synagogues Revealed*, Jerusalem 1981; R. Hachlili, *Ancient Jewish Art and Archaeology in the Land of Israel*, Leiden 1988; and the essays collected in D. Urman & P. Flesher, *Ancient Synagogues. Historical Analysis & Archaeological Discovery*, 2 vols., Leiden 1995.

[41]Cf. for example: R. Hachlili, *Ancient Jewish Art*, 84-88; 135-233; L. Grabbe, 'Synagogues in pre-70 Palestine: a Re-assessment', in: D. Urman & P. Flesher, *Ancient Synagogues,* 17-26; P. Flesher, 'Palestinian Synagogues before 70 CE A Review of the Evidence', ibid, 27-39.

[42]Ibid. See further: D. Groh, 'The Stratigraphic Chronology of the Galilean Synagogue from the Early Roman Period Through the Early Byzantine Period (Ca 420 C.E.)', in: D. Urman, P. Flesher, *Ancient Synagogues*, 51-69 and A. Kraabel, 'The Diaspora Synagogue: Archaeological and Epigraphic Evidence since Sukenik', ibid, 95-126 (= H. Temporini and W. Haase (eds), *ANRW* 19,1, Berlin/New York 1979, 477-510).

To prevent any misunderstandings, this is not meant to deny the fact that even before the fall of the Temple, synagogues, as places where the Torah was read, had to a certain extent a sacred character. The only point I want to stress is that this sacredness did not become apparent in architecture, at least not as clearly as in later periods.

as far as the concept of sanctity is concerned, church and synagogue went almost simultaneously through a very similar process
of sacralization.[43] Whereas in the earlier synagogues the Torah
scrolls were preserved in moveable receptacles,[44] from the 2nd
century onward these were replaced by permanent Torah shrines
located either in an aedicula or in a niche or apse.[45] A more or less
comparable development took place in Christian churches where
moveable altars were replaced by permanent ones. Furthermore,
in both synagogues and church buildings we find a tendency to
restrict 'secular' functions to side rooms.[46] Finally, it would be
interesting and rewarding to compare the use of curtains both in
the synagogues such as of Beth Alpha and in Christian churches
and in particular in the Syrian and the Syriac-speaking area.[47]

However, maybe there is more to say about the relationship
between church building and synagogue. I would like to suggest
that apart from the remarkable analogies as regards the increasing
sacralization, mutual influences also could have existed. I think
we have to seriously reckon with the possibility that at least in
certain regions, the plan and/or the interior of church buildings
were influenced by synagogue architecture. Whether there was

---

[43]See in this connection also: L. White, *Building God's House in the Roman World. Architectural Adaptation among Pagans, Jews, and Christians*,
Baltimore/London 1990.

[44]See for example S. Safrai, 'The Synagogue', in: *CRINT* 2, As-
sen/Amsterdam 1976, 908-944, esp. 938-939. This 'accepted explanation' is,
however, called into question by R. Hachlili (*Ancient Jewish Art*, 166) who
points to the fact that nearly every excavated synagogue yields traces of a
Torah shrine or at least of the place where it might have been located. It
seems, however, very probable that at least the earliest synagogues had no
fixed structure for Torah Scrolls (see also L. Grabbe, 'Synagogues in Pre-70
Palestine', and: D. Groh, 'The Stratigraphic Chronology').

[45] See for the different types of Torah-shrines: R. Hachlili, *Ancient Jewish
Art*, 166-182.

[46]Cf. A. Kraabel, 'The Diaspora Synagogue', 120.

[47]See, for the Syriac churches, for example: G. Khouri-Sarkis, 'Notes sur
l'anaphore syriaque de saint Jacques. Note 14, suite: Prière du voile', in: *Or-
Syr* 7 (1962) 277-296; See for Antioch: F. van de Paverd, *Zur Geschichte der
Messliturgie in Antiocheia und Konstantinopel gegen Ende des vierten
Jahrhunderts*, Roma 1970, 42-47.

also traffic in the other direction, that is whether synagogues underwent influences from church buildings, is a question that I do not want to discuss here. I want to suggest that there is at least one element of early Christian church architecture which might have been borrowed from the synagogue, i.e. the presence of a special place intended for the reading of the Bible during the first part of the Eucharist, usually in the form of a kind of platform or podium located somewhere in the middle of the church.[48]

The shape and the precise location of these reading-platforms have considerably varied in the different Christian liturgical traditions.[49] The largest and most impressive ones are the so-called *bemas* found in Mesopotamia and in north and northeast Syria where they fill a large part of the nave and even contain seats for the bishop and the clergy.[50] Elsewhere, in some other parts of Syria, we find constructions, which are sometimes designated as bemas and at other times as 'ambos' but are of a more modest size.[51] Finally, there are the lecterns and pulpits, usually called 'ambos' and mostly located in the front part of the nave near the sanctuary and often connected with it. This is a type found in Syria, as well as in Palestine, Asia and Greece.[52] These lecterns and pulpits became common in the Byzantine liturgy and from

---

[48]For the sake of clarity, by '*bema*' we do not mean the sanctuary in front of the apse, as is the case in later Byzantine sources and equally, it seems, in the writings of John Chrysostom (F. van de Paverd, *Zur Geschichte der Messliturgie*, 33-42).

[49]See for an overview: G. Vrins, 'De ambon. Oorsprong en verspreiding tot 600', in: *Feestbundel F. van der Meer. Opstellen aangeboden aan prof. dr. F.G.L. van der Meer ter gelegenheid van zijn zestigste verjaardag op 16 november 1964*, Amsterdam/Brussel 1964, 11-55.

[50]See for example: A. Schneider, *Liturgie und Kirchenbau in Syrien, Nachrichten der Akad. der Wiss. in Göttingen*, Phil.- hist. Klasse, 3, 1949, 45-68; J. Lassus and G. Tchalenko, 'Ambons syriens', *Cahiers archéologiques* 5 (1951) 75-122; J. Dauvillier, 'L'ambon ou bêmâ dans les textes de l'Eglise chaldéenne ou syrienne au moyen âge', *Cahiers archéologiques* 6 (1952), 11-30; R. Coquin, 'Le «bîma» des Eglises syriennes', *OrSyr* 10 (1965) 443-474 and especially: R. Taft, 'Some Notes on the Bema in the East and West Syrian Traditions', *OCP* 34 (1968) 326-359, esp. 330ff.

[51]Ibid.

[52]G. Vrins, 'De ambon', 30-34.

Byzantium seem to have spread to Rome and further to the West.[53]

Not only the form, but also the liturgical function varied.[54] In the Mesopotamian area, which later on became Nestorian, and in the region north and northeast of Antioch, the whole first part of the Eucharist of the Word was held on the large podium that was common there.[55] The smaller reading-platforms and the ambos/lecterns, on the other hand, were exclusively used for some parts of the Liturgy of the Word, in particular for the reading of the Bible pericopes and the Psalms. The members of the clergy who had no special task to fulfil, remained in the apse.

The question arises as to where these different types of bemas and ambos originated. Were they a purely Christian creation? Or did they go back to a pre-Christian tradition? If the latter is the case, the first possibility that immediately comes to mind is that of Jewish influence and more precisely from synagogue architecture.

Before we go on, however, it should be pointed out that it is impossible to rule out the possibility that the different types of reading-platforms were invented by the Christians independently from Judaism and the synagogue. We can, however, adduce several arguments that make this solution highly unlikely and point rather in the direction of an historical influence from Judaism.

1. There are strong indications that the phenomenon of a place exclusively designed for the reading of the Bible first emerged in one very specific area, i.e. the region east of Antioch, in the Syriac-speaking churches where the later East Syrian rite had its principal roots. As far as I know the earliest source reflecting the existence of such a special place for the liturgy of the Word, designated as a 'bema' and located in the centre of the church is a

---

[53]G. Vrins, 'De ambon', 43.

[54]See G. Vrins, 'De ambon', 23-24 and also R. Taft, 'Some Notes on the Bema'.

[55] See in particular: J. Dauvillier, 'L'ambon ou bêmâ', and: R. Taft, 'Some Notes on the Bema', 335-337.

memra of Ephrem the Syrian, preserved in Armenian and held at the occasion of a devastating earthquake in Nicomedia (358 CE).[56] Another early, 4th century document that refers to the existence of a reading place in the middle of the Church, the Apostolic Constitutions,[57] derives from this region as well. Moreover, the earliest archeological evidence that is relevant in this connection also derives from the same geographical area.[58] It is therefore very likely that the phenomenon of the reading-platform located more or less in the centre of the church first appeared in the Syrian-Mesopotamian region and eventually spread to the Byzantine area and afterwards to the West, where in the first five centuries there is hardly any evidence of the existence of podiums or pulpits apart from the Episcopal throne in the apse, and probably none at all.[59] If this conclusion is correct, it means that podiums intended for the liturgy of the Word or the reading of the Bible originated in the region that for a long time had preserved a number of Jewish liturgical traditions that had disappeared much earlier elsewhere. Thus, the example of the Quartodeciman Passover celebration mentioned above, should be remembered here. Still more remarkable, though, seems to me the fact, at least in this connection, that it is only in this area that a regular reading from the Torah and the Prophets has been preserved during the celebration of the Eucharist.[60]

---

[56]See *Memra on Nicomedia VIII* (edn C. Renoux, *Ephrem de Nisibe. Memre sur Nicomédie*, Turnhout 1975, 151-153.

[57]Ch. II, 57, 2-4 (edn M. Metzger, *SC* 329, Paris 1986).

[58]The oldest example of a church that has been excavated and contains a podium in the middle is that of Fafertin (372 CE) (cf. M. Schneider, *Liturgie und Kirchenbau in Syrien*, esp. 56.

[59]Cf. in this connection once again: G. Vrins, 'De ambon'.

[60]Cf. G. Rouwhorst, 'Jewish Liturgical Traditions', 77-78; idem, 'Continuity and Discontinuity Between Jewish and Christian Liturgy', *Bijdragen* 54 (1993) 72-83. One may also note a very interesting passage of the so-called Doctrine of the Apostles, a Syriac document dating most probably from the 4th century which emphasizes that according to the Apostles from the bema nothing should be read other than the 'Old Testament, the Prophets, the Gospel and the Acts of the triumphs of the Apostles' (W. Cureton, *Ancient Syriac Documents*, Edinburgh 1864, 27; cf. A. Vööbus, *The Didascalia Apostolorum*

2. There are very good reasons to believe that at quite an early
date and in any case before the earliest Christian churches were
built, synagogues had some special provisions designed for the
reading of the Bible, in particular that the pericopes from the Torah and the Prophets were read from some kind of dais or podium.
This is what one might expect beforehand, at least in synagogues
that could accommodate a large number of people. Moreover,
some more specific arguments may be advanced to substantiate
this presumption. First, a well-known passage of the Tosefta,[61]
according to which the great synagogue of Alexandria, the Dip-
lostoon destroyed under Trajan, had a wooden podium that was
located in the centre. Even if the historical reliability of this passage is not accepted, it should at least be admitted that it reflects a
tradition dating back to the tannaitic period which was acquainted
with a platform designed for the reading of the Bible. Furthermore, the existence of some kind of podium seems to be corroborated by archaeological data, though these are very scarce.[62]

---

in Syriac, CSCO 401/402, 44 (38). It is extremely likely that in this case the
'Old Testament' is the Pentateuch.

[61]TSuk 4:6. See also S. Safrai, 'The Synagogue', 940.

[62]One of the very few synagogues where possibly traces of a reading-
platform in the centre may have been preserved, is that of Sardis (cf. A. Sea-
ger, 'The Building History of the Sardis Synagogue', *AJA* 76 (1972), 425-
435, esp. 426; A. Kraabel, 'The Diaspora Synagogue', 104; R. Hachlili, *Ancient Jewish Art*, 182). It should, however, be admitted that the identification
of these remains is quite hypothetical. The question is, of course, why so few
vestiges of a reading-podium have turned up, assuming that it existed. It is
conceivable that such a platform was not common everywhere and, for example, did not exist in the synagogues excavated in the Land of Israel. A solution that seems more likely is that these podiums were made of wood and
therefore did not survive. This possibility has already been suggested by several scholars, such as S. Safrai ('The Synagogue', 940). Another question is
raised by the stone bases and aediculae found on the Jerusalem-oriented walls
of some Galilean synagogues, for example in Nabratein, that in the literature
usually are designed as 'bemahs'. Some scholars have suggested that these
would have been used for Torah reading. In that case a podium in the middle
would have been superfluous. It seems, however, more likely that these bases
and aediculae contained the Torah shrine or served as supports for holding

3. The presumption that the Christian podiums in one way or another were borrowed from the Jewish synagogue, is confirmed by a linguistic argument. In fact, it is very striking that in both Jewish and Christian sources, in different languages, the same term *bema* is used for the place from which the Bible is read. This term, indeed, is used by the Tosefta, but also very frequently by Christian literary sources, whether they are written in Syriac, Greek or even in Armenian.[63] In my view, this can mean only one thing: the Greek word 'bema' had become a technical liturgical term in Judaism and as such it was adopted by the Christians who, for that reason, did not translate it in Syriac and Armenian, but just transliterated it.

As a matter of fact, I am aware that the last word on this subject has not yet been said. On the contrary, it is a theme that lends itself to further research, preferably in collaboration with Jewish and Christian scholars. It is, indeed, conceivable that this research would lead to a different conclusion. But as long as no further research had been done, the most plausible hypothesis seems to me that Christians living in the surroundings of Antioch and in the more eastern region took over the *bema* from the Jewish synagogue.[64]

---

certain ritual objects, such as the *menorot* (cf. R. Hachlili, *Ancient Jewish Art*, 182 and 198).

[63]See Ephrem, *Memra on Nicomedia*, ch. VIII where the Armenian word 'bem' is used.

[64]I want to stress here that this thesis itself is not new. It has already been suggested by several scholars and amply developed by D. Hickley in his article 'The Ambo in Early Liturgical Planning – A Study with Special Reference to the Syrian Bema', *HeyJ* VII (1968) 325-359. This author, however, bases himself on outdated material and from the methodological point of view, his article is on rather shaky grounds (see my critical remarks in: 'Jewish Liturgical Traditions', 75-76).

Conclusion

It is undeniable that during the last decades our picture of the earliest development of Christian liturgy has changed. This does, however, not mean that the hypothesis of the Jewish origin of early Christian liturgy has been refuted. Quite the contrary, the features that Jewish post-Temple liturgy and early Christian forms of worship had in common, seem to become rather more obvious.

This implies that it remains necessary to look at the earliest history of Christian liturgy from a double perspective. On the hand, it remains legitimate to be eager to the differences between both liturgical traditions and to search for what is original in early Christian liturgy and the same holds also true for the study of Jewish liturgy. Nobody will benefit from a kind of ecumenism that irons out all the embarrassing points of difference. At the same time this approach need to be complemented by a more positive one which looks rather for elements that both liturgical traditions have in common, for the Jewish origins and background of Christian rituals, for mutual influences between both, for similarity and symmetry in both traditions and finally for common human patterns, such as the need for structuring and sacralizing time and space.

HOLY CITY AND HOLY LAND AS VIEWED BY JEWS AND CHRISTIANS IN THE BYZANTINE PERIOD: A CONCEPTUAL APPROACH TO SACRED SPACE

Aaron Demsky

In the Byzantine period, both Judaism and Christianity had well developed ideologies of sacred space, whether it be in terms of the Holy City or of the Holy Land, which was perceived as a distinct area in the former religion or as the totality of many holy sites in the latter religion.[1] We are fortunate in having two extraordinary archaeological finds that illustrate how these competing faiths viewed the Land as the medium for experiencing the holy. The first artifact is the famous Madaba Map,[2] generally

---

[1] See R.J.Z. Werblowsky, 'The Meaning of Jerusalem to Jews, Christians and Muslims', *Jaarbericht Ex Orient Lux* 23 (1973-4) 1-15; W.D. Davies, *The Gospel and the Land: Early Christianity and Jewish Territorial Doctrine,* Berkeley 1974; idem, *The Territorial Dimension of Judaism*, Berkeley,1982; E.D. Hunt, *Holy Land Pilgrimage in the Later Roman Empire AD 312-460,* Oxford 1982; L. Hoffman (ed.), *The Land of Israel: Jewish Perspectives,* Notre Dame 1986, especially his Introduction, 1-23 and Pt. II 'The Land in the Tannaitic Period', 95-136; see now the collection of essays in M. Poorthuis & Ch. Safrai (eds), *The Centrality of Jerusalem – Historical Perspectives,* Kampen 1996. Early Christianity developed the idea of pilgrimage to specific holy sites where miracles were to have occurred or where biblical and Christian saints were supposedly buried. The reliance on the Bible and the ongoing contact with the Jewish community shaped Christianity's idea of the 'Holy Land', which is a biblical term (Zech 2:16). While in the Madaba Map the notations emphasize the sacred localities, the overall work is that of the entire Land within maximalist borders, at least to the south.

[2] M. Avi-Yonah, *The Madaba Map – Translation and Commentary* (Hebr.), Jerusalem 1954 (reprinted from *Eretz-Israel* 2 [1953] 129-156); H. Donner, *The Mosaic Map of Madaba – An Introductory Guide,* Kampen 1992; G. Barkai & E. Schiller (eds), *Eretz-Israel in the Madaba Map* (Hebr.), Jerusalem 1996.

dated to the late 6th century CE.[3] It was discovered in 1884 during local church renovations where it was found to be part of the ancient floor. It was brought to the attention of the scholarly world a hundred years ago in 1897. The second find is the 6th or 7th century Reḥob mosaic discovered in 1973 in the ruins of a synagogue now in the fields of kibbutz Ein Hanaziv in the Beth Shean valley.[4] It was placed at the main entrance at the northern side of the building. [see illustration 1]

A comparison of the two mosaics is in order and long overdue for they have much in common. They are roughly contemporary from the end of the Byzantine period; their sites are about 100 kms distant from each other, though on opposite sides of the Jordan river; and of course, both were fashioned similarly as mosaics.[5] In each case, the artifact before us is the end product of a combination of different sources composed over hundreds of years. On the basis of their location in a house of worship and of their subject matter, they must be considered as having primarily a religious message. Moreover, since they were so prominently

---

[3]The date is certainly after the Nea church was constructed by Justinian in 543, see M. Avi-Yonah, *Madaba Map*, 5. However, recently D. Bahat has suggested that since the Byzantine 'Gate of Mercy' is depicted and according to him it was constructed probably for the visit of Heraclius in 629 on the eve of the Muslim conquest, the Madaba Map now should be redated to the second half of the 7th century, see D. Bahat, 'A New Suggestion for the Date of the Madaba Map' (Hebr.), in: G. Barkai & E. Schiller, *Eretz-Israel*, 74-75. On the unabated local tradition of church mosaics in the Madaba area that continued to be produced into the 8th century, see M. Piccirillo, 'The Mosaics at Umm-er-Rasas in Jordan', *Biblical Archaeologist* (1988) 208-213; idem, 'Umm er-Rasas', *The Oxford Encyclopedia of Archaeology in the Near East*, Vol. 5 (1997) 279-281.

[4]J. Sussmann, 'An Halakhic Inscription from the Beisan Valley' (Hebr.), *Tarbiz* 43 (1974) 88-158; 44 (1975) 193-195, cf. esp. 94 n.38 where Sussmann compared *en passant* the paragraph describing the halakhic 'Borders of Eretz Israel' and the Madaba Map; idem, 'The Inscription in the Synagogue at Rehob', in: L.I. Levine (ed.), *Ancient Synagogues Revealed*, Jerusalem 1981, 146-151; S. Lieberman, 'Regarding the Halakhic Inscription from the Beisan Valley' (Hebr.), *Tarbiz* 45 (1976) 54-63, 331.

[5]J. Naveh, *On Stone and Mosaic – the Aramaic and Hebrew Inscriptions from Ancient Synagogues* (Hebr.), Jerusalem 1978.

displayed, I can only assume that their *Sitz im Leben* was to serve the same pedagogic purpose of visually imparting to their coreligionists the essence of the value concept of the 'Holy Land' as perceived in their respective faiths. Because of the many external similarities, it is imperative that both of these great finds are compared. Hopefully, the juxtaposition of these mosaics also will clarify the conceptual aspects of Christian land theology as reflected in the Madaba Map and especially the idea of sacred space expressed in the Reḥob inscription, representing rabbinic Judaism.

The Madaba Map

The originally rectangular Madaba Map measured about twenty by seven meters and included some two million cubes.[6] M. Avi-Yonah assumed that the mapmaker, following Eusebius, reached Byblos on the Phoenician coast in what is now the missing northwestern corner of the mosaic. In the south-west corner the map reaches beyond the Delta up the Nile valley. Naturally, the Transjordan to the east is prominently displayed. The orientation of the map is biblical, that is, the upper part is toward the east, the lower part is toward the west, the south is toward the right, and the north is toward the left. The basic biblical source is the description of the promised Land of Canaan in Num 34:1-12. The Christian mapmaker displays some maximalist tendencies by including 1) the Nile, which he seems to imply should be identified with the elusive 'Brook of Egypt' and 2) the Transjordan, because of the presence of a significant Christian community [see Map 1].

The scale is uneven: 1:16000 for central Judea and 1:1613 for Jerusalem, enhancing the importance of the latter.[7] This is the oldest map of Jerusalem and our primary source for knowing the

---

[6]M. Avi-Yonah, *Madaba Map*, 3.

[7]For a discussion of the scale of the map, see N. Kadmon, 'Mapat Madaba, Cartographic Aspects' (Hebr.), in: G. Barkai & E. Schiller, *Eretz-Israel*, 89-96.

city in the Byzantine period. [see Map 2] The city is portrayed realistically, so much so that it can be followed even today as a guide in locating the various churches. Surprisingly, there is no reference either in iconography or in biblical quotation to Jerusalem's former glory, especially in noting the Temple. One might say that it is the 'New Jerusalem'. The city's early history, both biblical and Jewish, has been erased. 'The Holy City of Jerusalem' is filled with churches, monuments of Christianity's historical triumph and theological vindication.[8]

Similarly, the mapmaker depicts realistically the relative size of the various contemporary cities and towns and their internal plan. It is worth noting that not since Shishaq's list of conquests (ca. 925 BCE) do we have such details regarding the settlements in the Negeb.

The decorative aspect also cannot be ignored. The great care for topographic detail and for city plans as well as the delightful use of eight different hues for the landscape, fauna and flora are evidence of the genuine love and interest the mapmaker had for his subject.

We might say that the map in most of its biblical details is a polychrome illumination of Eusebius' *Onomasticon* written about 325 CE, which was the main source of the mapmaker's text. One should also note that he included details found in the *Onomasticon* that were based on a few Jewish midrashim, probably taught in Caesarea, regarding sites in or near the Jordan Valley like Beth Agla, Beth Hammarzeah-Baal Peor and the anti-Samaritan polemical location of Mts. Ebal and Gerizim opposite Gilgal.[9] Be-

---

[8]M. Avi-Yonah, *Madaba Map*, no. 52, 17-20; G. Barkai, 'A Tour of Jerusalem According to the Madaba Map' (Hebr.), in: G. Barkai & E. Schiller, *Eretz-Israel*, 112-125. In this context, note especially H. Amitzur, 'Justinian's Solomon's Temple in Jerusalem', in: M. Poorthuis & Ch. Safrai (eds), *The Centrality of Jerusalem*, 160-175.

[9]See M. Avi-Yonah, *Madaba Map*, 14f. It should be noted that Eusebius' identification of *gôren hâ ʾâṭâd* in Gen 50:10-11 with Beth Agla was probably stimulated by the homily of Rabbi Abbahu, his contemporary and neighbor in Caesarea (BT Sotah 13a); on the biblical site and its location, see A. Demsky, 'The Route of Jacob's Funeral Cortege and the Problem of ʿEber

cause of their proximity, these sites were no doubt of interest to the neighboring Christian communities in Transjordan. Eusebius wrote his work as a guide for literate Christian pilgrims who were seeking the numinous in the Holy Land. It seems that more than a decorative element on the church floor, the map was conceived as an illustrated guidebook for the local and the itinerant believer.[10] Its pictorial form was well suited for those who might not have known Greek or who had limited reading skills in that language. The final product is an idealized picture of the Christian view of the Holy Land, indeed a 'mosaic' of biblical, Roman and contemporary Byzantine sites.

From a conceptual point of view, early Christianity saw the Holy Land in terms of holy sites where biblical events occurred. The Land was the great stage of miraculous acts of revelation and redemption and where later-day churches displayed relics of the early saints and martyrs. It was a place to visit and relive the great moments of religious history or – as E.D. Hunt has put it – to be 'in search of the biblical past'.[11] In fact, it was Christianity that gave renewed meaning to pilgrimage as a religious act. By visiting the sites of the Holy Land, one could sense or witness, albeit vicariously, a bygone biblical event or divine revelation and in so doing, the individual could draw spiritual strength or even experience mystical communion. The devout Christian pilgrim might have expressed his inner joy on his religious journey by quoting from the *Liturgy of St. James*: "We give Thee thanks, O Lord, for Thy holy places, which thou hast glorified ... by the visitation of Thy Holy Spirit ...".[12]

Hayyarden', in: M. Brettler & M. Fishbane (eds), *Minhah LeNahum*, Sheffield 1993, 54-64.

[10]See also B. Rahmalevitch, '"Holy Geography" and the Mosaics of Madaba and its Environs' (Hebr.), in: G. Barkai & E. Schiller, *Eretz-Israel*, 76-81. However D. Bahat, (above, n.3) has suggested that the Madaba map was composed after the Islamic conquest and was intended to serve a polemic purpose emphasizing Christianity's claim on the Holy Land.

[11]E.D. Hunt, *Holy Land*, 4, 83.

[12]E.D. Hunt, *Holy Land*, 118.

With Constantine's becoming emperor and subsequently patron
of Christianity in the early 4th century, we find the emergence of
the related literature of Christian pilgrimage. At first, Eusebius'
classic *Onomasticon*,[13] composed to aid the Christian pilgrim, and
shortly afterward the account of the pilgrim from Bordeaux[14] and
somewhat later the travel records and letters of Jerome and his
disciples[15] and of course the most public expression of Christian
land theology in antiquity the Madaba Map, an illuminated con-
cretization of the religious concept of the 'Holy Land'.

The Reḥob Mosaic

The roughly contemporary Reḥob Mosaic is strikingly different in
appearance for it lacks the decorative and colorful elements found
in the Madaba Map. [see illustration 2] One can say that it even
stands apart from most synagogue mosaics which contain illustrated biblical themes, zodiac motifs or votive notices.[16] For the
most part, the mosaic is a collection of passages from the Mishnah and Palestinian Talmud, dating from the 2nd to the 4th centuries. In fact, it is the oldest version, by some five hundred years of
these texts. What is more, they were formulated only some 35
kms away in the rabbinic academies of Tiberias.[17] Shortly after it
was discovered, the late Prof. Saul Lieberman proclaimed that
this was the most important archaeological find for the clarifica-

---

[13]E. Klostermann (ed.), *Onomastikon,* Hildesheim 1904, repr. 1966; see
also E.Z. Melamed, *The Onomastikon of Eusebius* (Hebr.)*,* Jerusalem 1956.

[14]P. Geyer & O. Cuntz (eds), *Itinerarium Burdigalense,* in: *CCSL* Series
Vol 175, 1965, 1-26; see also S. Klein, 'Itinerarium Burdigalense (The Pilgrim of Bordeaux)' (Hebr.), *Zion* 6 (1934) 1-18.

[15]See J. Wilkinson, *Jerusalem Pilgrims Before the Crusades,* Jerusalem
1977, 47-52; also see in this book the article by H.I. Newman, 'Between Jerusalem and Bethlehem – Jerome and the Sanctity of the Holy Land', 215-27.

[16]See J. Naveh, *Stone and Mosaic, passim.*

[17]J. Sussmann, 'Inscription', 93.

tion of rabbinic literature, especially the Palestinian Talmud, composed in the Land of Israel.[18]

The twenty-nine line inscription is an halakhic compilation of 'the commandments relating to the agricultural produce incumbent upon a Jew living in the Holy Land' or in Hebrew – מצוות התלויות בארץ [see Appendix for the full text in translation]. This includes matters of first fruits, sabbatical years, heave-offerings and tithes.[19] These were not theoretical issues from biblical times long past, but rather they were of a practical, contemporary nature.

Indicative of the contemporary nature of the text is the fact that there is no reference to Jerusalem. From the Bar Kokhba revolt to the end of the Byzantine period, the city was probably not inhabited for any length of time by a significant community of Jews, although some would come to gaze at and mourn the Holy Mountain plowed over and left in ruin.[20] The place of Jerusalem or its absence is another point of comparison between the Madaba map and the Reḥob inscription. While Jerusalem is not mentioned explicitly in the inscription, it is not forgotten, for it is implicit in the orientation of the mosaic, placed at the entrance of the synagogue constructed on a north-south axis facing toward the Holy City.

---

[18]S. Lieberman, 'Inscription', 54.

[19]There were other categories as well not mentioned in our text like the rules for giving the Priests portions of the dough-offering; giving the poor the corner of the field or the harvest leftovers; not eating of the fruits of the tree until it reaches its maturity; or eating the fruit of its fourth year in Jerusalem or redeeming it; not planting diverse seeds of grain and of the vine; bringing the new cereal crop. For these *mitzvot* and the differences between them, especially their applicability outside the Land as well, see the discussion in BT Qidd 36b -37b. Regarding this last point, see C. Primus, 'The Borders of Judaism: The Land of Israel in Early Rabbinic Judaism', in: L. Hoffman, *The Land of Israel*, 97-108; on the different categories see R.S. Sarason, 'The Significance of the Land of Israel in the Mishnah', in: L. Hoffman, *The Land of Israel*, 109-136, esp. 112ff.

[20]See J. Schwartz, *Jewish Settlement in Judaea After the Bar-Kochba War Until the Arab Conquest* (Hebr.), Jerusalem 1986, 183-194.

Of particular interest for our study is the precise geographic limitation of areas in which it was permitted or not permitted to eat of the produce grown there, like the city limits of Beth Shean or the district of Caesarea Maritima or the lists of Jewish villages in the gentile provinces of Sussita (Hippos) and Tyre.[21] In general, the definition of borders and the fixing of limitations of all types is central to *halakhah* in its attempt to concretize aspects of spirituality.

Further evidence of the synchronic nature of the text can be found in the addendum in lines 26-29 presenting a post-talmudic list of the nineteen minuscule gentile villages in the province of Sebaste in which it was permitted to eat untithed fruit as well as produce grown in the sabbatical year.[22] One gets the impression that this addition was specifically made to instruct the Jews of the adjacent Beth Shean Valley of the 6th and 7th centuries who would travel through these towns in Samaria on their way to the coastal cities.

What makes the Land holy for Jews? Obviously the Land was sacred because of the biblical experience. It is the Promised Land, chosen by God, conquered by Joshua and united under David. It was the place of prophetic revelation. It is the space sanctified by God's blessing and the indwelling of the *Shekhinah*. "It is a land which the Lord your God looks after, on which the Lord your God always keeps His eye, from year's beginning to year's end" (Deut 11:12). From the Patriarchal period it was chosen as the only land where one wanted to be interred (Gen 23; 49:29-31; 50:25).

It is in the early Second Temple period that these terms of geographic sanctity become current. The term 'Holy Land' appears in Zech 2:16: "The Lord will take (the territory of) Judah to Himself

---

[21]See I. Finkelstein & R. Frankel, 'The North-west Corner of Eretz-Israel in the *baraita detehummin*' (Hebr.), *Cathedra* 27 (1983) 39-46; I. Finkelstein, 'The Shephelah of Israel', *Tel Aviv* 8 (1981) 84-94.

[22]J. Sussmann, 'The "Boundaries of Eretz-Israel"' (Hebr.), *Tarbiz* 45 (1976) 213-257; Z. Safrai, 'Marginal Notes on the Rehob Inscription' (Hebr.), *Zion* 42 (1977) 1-23, esp. 1-12; A. Demsky, 'The Permitted Villages of Sebaste in the Rehob Mosaic', *IEJ* 29 (1979) 182-193.

as his portion in the Holy Land and He will choose Jerusalem once more". In this second vision of the prophet (ca. 520 BCE), Zechariah sees the return of the exiles, the renewal of the covenant, and particularly the indwelling of the *Shekhinah*, signs of God's choice of the territory of Judah and Jerusalem within the larger confines of the Holy Land, termed here אדמת הקדש (*ʾadĕmat haqōdeš*).

Jerusalem is called עיר הקדש (*ʿîr haqōdeš*), i.e. 'the Holy City', for the first time in the description of Nehemiah's repopulation of the city (Neh 11:1,18), probably during the year 443 BCE. Note also the undated Second Temple prophesy in Joel 4:17 – "... Dwell in Zion, My holy Mount. And Jerusalem shall be holy; nevermore shall strangers pass through it" and Ps 20:3 – "May He send you help from *Qodesh,* and sustain you from Zion". Jerusalem the sacred housed the *Miqdash,* the holy Temple, entered only by the ritually pure. Furthermore, it is in Second Temple times that we begin to find a distinction between the two precincts of Jerusalem, i.e., the Temple Mount and the City confines (see Neh 7:2; Dan 9:26). In the Mishnah, their respective degrees of holiness were expressed in terms of the sacrificial cult, in particular in the two general categories of offerings, the קדשי קדשים (*qōdĕšê qĕdošîm*) the 'most sacred sacrifices' and the קדשים קלים (*qĕdošîm qalîm*) the 'less sacred sacrifices', each permitted to be eaten in the different parts of Jerusalem according to their respective degrees of holiness (M Zeb, ch. 5).[23]

---

[23]The exact boundaries of the Holy City followed the lines of the restored city wall and were probably sanctified soon after it was completed under Nehemiah's direction, which I have dated to the last week of Elul, 443 BCE. The description of the ceremony is found in Neh 12:27ff. Following rabbinic interpretation, the purpose of the festivities was cultic, i.e., to delineate the extent of the sacred or purified area in which the 'less holy sacrifices' (קדשים קלים and the second tithe could be eaten (MZeb 5:6-8). Another example of how the sanctity of Jerusalem was observed is found in an old *halakhah*, with obvious parallel to the Sinai tradition, calling for a three day ritual cleansing period for those about to alight to the Temple Mount (11Q Temple Scroll, col. 45, lines 7-12). I have suggested that this tradition is first found in the three day waiting period noted for both Ezra and Nehemiah upon their respective arrivals to Jerusalem (Ezra 8:32f; Neh 2:11) see A. Demsky, 'Who

In Judaism, the Land of Israel is therefore the center stage of religious history. In post-Second Temple times, most of these categories, e.g., prophesy and sacrifice, were recognized as belonging to a former historic period and had ceased to exist, although it was believed that if merited they might be renewed at a later time. As such, the concept of the Holy Land as shaped and as deriving its sanctity from divine presence as witnessed in past biblical events, is the basis of the shared tradition of historical monotheism as we have noted for the Madaba Map.

What then is the intent of the Reḥob mosaic? This inscription points to another dimension of land-theology, a particularly Jewish concept of sacred space. In this case, sanctification is through the continued and constant observance of those *mitzvot* relating to the produce of the Land. It is a this-worldly approach, essentially rationalistic and geographically defined, which places the full responsibility of maintaining the holiness of the Land upon man, i.e. the Jew.

In order to understand Judaism's conception of the Holy Land, one must note that this second form of sanctity is based on Israel's initiative and physical presence in the Land, either through conquest or through settlement. It is distinct from the other form of holiness based on the belief in God's everlasting spiritual presence in the Land. Therefore, the rabbis formulated this second concept in terms of two historic periods of sanctification of the Land (BT Ḥul 7a; BT Yeb 82b):

1) ארץ ישראל של עולי מצרים, i.e. 'The Land of Israel *conquered by Joshua and those who came out of Egypt*', as described in the Book of Joshua – that is, the biblical Holy Land.[24] This Land was sacred in its own time and with the destruction of the First Temple and exile of the tribes of Israel, it ceased to be holy. However,

Came First – Ezra or Nehemiah? The Synchronistic Approach', *HUCA* 65 (1994) 1-19, esp. 16, n. 55.

[24]See A. Demsky, '"From Kziv unto The River *Near* Amanah" (MShebi 6:1; MHal 4:8): A Clarification of the Northern Border of the Returnees from Egypt' (Hebr.), *Shnaton* 10 (1986-89) 71-81.

it did retain some partial status, i.e. from which one could eat but not work in the sabbatical year (see MShebi 6:1; MHal 4:8).

2) ארץ ישראל של עולי בבל, i.e. 'The Land of Israel as *settled* by those who came up with Ezra out of Babylon'. While attributed to the renewal of Jewish presence in early Second Temple times, this term probably reflects the contemporary pattern of Jewish settlement and demography in the Roman period.[25] The majority opinion is that 'this second (later) sanctity prevailed in its own day and continues unabated into the future' (BT Hul 7a; BT Arak 32b).

The fulfillment of these *mitzvot* was not a purely spiritual or theoretical matter, but rather a practical, daily issue, one could say that it was 'a down to earth' issue, which had to be defined geographically since one had to know the extent and limits of the Holy Land.[26] It is within the geo-halakhic borders of the above second period of 'those who returned from Babylon' that the Jew is obligated to observe the *mitzvot* that are derived from the produce of the Land, i.e. first fruits, heave-offerings, tithes and sabbatical year growths. The oldest version of the tannaitic formulation of the halakhic borders of the Holy Land,[27] is found in lines 13-18 of the Rehob Mosaic. For the sake of comparison with the

---

[25]A case in point is the listing of sites in Transjordan, that Sussmann and others have taken as schematic references, like Nahal Zered which probably reflects Jewish presence around the south-eastern end of the Dead Sea as we find in the Bar-Kochba Letters from the early 2nd cent CE (Beth 'Agaltain) and in talmudic sources (Zoar).

[26]For another formulation of spacial holiness, compare MKel 1:6, which begins – "There are ten degrees of spatial sanctity: (The first) The Land of Israel is holier than all other lands, and what makes its holiness? It is the only place from where one brings the barley offering and the first fruits and the two loaves of bread (on Shavuot, Lev 23:17)". These ten degrees of holiness are formulated in relation to the Temple service, moving concentrically from the outer space of the lands of the Gentiles (which in other sources is referred to as impure and defiling, in Hebrew – טומאה ארץ העמים) to the Holy of Holies in Jerusalem at the very center. In particular, see Serason's treatment of this mishnah, (above n. 19), 115f.

[27]Other versions of the *baraita detehumin* are found in TShebi 4:11; PT Shebi 6:1,36g; and *SifreDeut* 51.

Madaba Map, one can draw a fairly precise map based on this text, especially regarding the western and northern borders. [See Map 3] However, one must keep in mind that this map is a *religious* statement and not a political one.

Conclusion

In summing up, in our comparison of the Madaba Map and the Reḥob mosaic, we find that each artifact reflects a different concept of sacred space as understood by their respective faiths. For Christianity, holiness was to be found in visiting places, identified with specific biblical sites and in reliving their story of past divine grace. For rabbinic Jewry, holiness was to be found in the reality of working the whole Land and the eating of its produce. It was the difference between the Christian pilgrim's vicarious witnessing to the divine beneficence recorded in the Bible and the native Jew's sense of responsibility and adherence to an operative approach of maintaining the ongoing holiness of the Land.

PART THREE

MODERN PERIOD

POST-MODERN PILGRIMAGE: CHRISTIAN RITUAL BETWEEN LITURGY AND 'TOPOLATRY' [1]

Paul Post

1. Introduction

S acred space and time come together in a special and direct way in the ritual of pilgrimage. One could also argue that in an anthropological and phenomenological sense, the essence of the ritual of pilgrimage is determined by them. At certain times marked as full of potential, on both the axis of life and in the year, the pilgrim breaks through the course of daily events, the rhythm of life, leaves, goes to and returns again from a *locus sacer*, a place or a site marked out as sacred. As may be seen in the working definition of the large-scale Dutch pilgrimage project, for instance, it is principally the element of the sacred place which is rather generally regarded as distinctive and characteristic of pilgrimage ritual.[2]

---

[1] Translated by D. Mader, M.Div.

[2] P.J. Margry & P. Post, 'Het project "Bedevaartplaatsen in Nederland": een plaatsbepaling', *Volkskundig Bulletin. Tijdschrift voor Nederlandse cultuurwetenschap* 20 (1994) 19-59; cf. P.J. Margry & P. Post, 'Wallfahrt zwischen Inventarisierung und Analyse. Ein niederländisches Forschunsprojekt in historiographischem und methodologischem Kontext', *Rheinisch-westfälische Zeitschrift für Volkskunde* 39 (1994 [1995]) 27-65. On sacred places and sites: A. Dupront, *Du Sacré. Croisades et Pèlerinages, Images et Langages,* Paris 1987; B.C. Lane, *Landscapes of the Sacred. Geography and Narrative in American Spirituality,* Mahwah/New York 1988; P. Post, 'Raum und Ritus. Perspektiven für die Analyse des liturgischen Raumes', *Jaarboek voor liturgie-onderzoek* 5 (1989) 301-331; J. Scott & P. Simpson-Housley (eds), *Sacred Places and Profane Spaces. Essays in the Geographics of Judaism, Christianity, and Islam,* New York [etc.]; B. Bender (ed.), *Landscape: Politics and Perspectives,* Providence/Oxford 1993; U. Tworuschka, (ed.),

In regard to the analysis and characterization of modern and post-modern pilgrimage, from the Christian and European perspective, it is productive to openly take stock of the ritual and liturgical market. It is only then, for instance, that one really catches sight of ritual in the process of transformation that from the perspective of Christian liturgy, can be seen as a fanning out of the Christian ritual repertoire. The originally rather homogeneous Christian ritual now broadens out over ecclesiastical, general religious, and secular profane paths. In ritual[3] and liturgical studies, attention is now being given to the interaction between these three distinctive patterns of shifts in post-modern ritual repertoires.[4] These shifts are certainly to be found in the exploration of the sacralizing tendencies associated with post-modern pilgrimage ritual.

Heilige Stätten, Darmstadt 1994; D. Carmichael, J. Hubert, B. Reeves & A. Schanche (eds), *Sacred Sites, Sacred Places*, London 1994; H.-J. Auf der Maur, in: P. Harnoncourt, H.-J. Auf der Maur, *Feiern im Rhythmus der Zeit II,1,* Regensburg 1994, 237-242; C. Park, *Sacred Worlds. An Introduction to Geography and Religion*, London 1994, esp. Ch. 7: Religion and Landscape, 197-244 and Ch. 8: Sacred Places and Pilgrimage, 245-285.

[3]See for the so called ritual studies: R.L. Grimes, *Beginnings in Ritual Studies*, Washington DC 1982; R.L. Grimes, *Ritual Criticism: Case Studies in its Practice, Essays on its Theory*, Columbia 1990; R.L. Grimes, *Reading, Writing, and Ritualizing. Ritual in Fictive, Liturgical, and Public Places*, Washington DC 1993; C. Bell, *Ritual Theory, Ritual Practice*, Oxford/New York 1992; M.B. Aune & V. De Marinis (eds), *Religious and Social Ritual: Interdisciplinary Explorations*, Albany/New York 1996.

[4]See for the changing ritual market: P. Post, 'Het verleden in het spel? Volksreligieuze rituelen tussen cultus en cultuur', *Jaarboek voor Liturgieonderzoek* 7 (1991) 79-124; P. Post, 'Goede tijden, slechte tijden: devotionele rituelen tussen traditie en moderniteit', in: P.J. Margry (ed.), *Goede en slechte tijden: het Amsterdamse Mirakel van Sacrament in historisch perspectief*, Aerdenhout 1995, 62-80; P. Post, 'Zeven notities over rituele verandering, traditie en (vergelijkende) liturgiewetenschap', in: *Jaarboek voor liturgieonderzoek* 11 (1995) 1-30; A. Schilson, 'Das neue Religiöse und der Gottesdienst. Liturgie vor einer neuen Herausforderung?', *Liturgisches Jahrbuch* 46,2 (1996) 94-109. A very striking diagnosis on the rise of the culture of feast and festival offers: O. Marquard, 'Kleine Philosophie des Festes', in: U. Schultz (ed.), *Das Fest: eine Kulturgeschichte von der Antike bis zur Gegenwart*, München 1988, 413-420.

The design of this paper is as follows: in the context of modern ritual changes and transformations, several currents in the field of pilgrimage will be briefly described in terms of their form and experience. A change in the way in which the past is dealt with is central to these. The question of the quality and identity of the religious ritual of pilgrimage is raised in a closing note.

2. Form

2.1 Four Forms of Pilgrimage Undergoing Chance

It is impossible here to give an detailed and differentiated de-scription of the present very complex situation in the field of pil-grimage.[5] Without reopening the debate about the definition of pilgrimage,[6] I only wish to draw attention to four types, distin-

---

[5]See for recent studies on pilgrimage the survey: P. Post, 'Thema's, theo-rieën en trends in bedevaartonderzoek', in: J. Pieper, P. Post & M. van Uden (eds). *Bedevaart en pelgrimage. Tussen traditie en moderniteit*, Baarn 1994 , 253-301. Some important recent studies are: M. Nolan & S. Nolan, *Christian Pilgrimages in Modern Western Europe*, Chapel Hill 1989 (cf. my review in: *Volkskundig Bulletin. Tijdschrift voor Nederlandse cultuurwetenschap* 17 (1991) 84f.); J. Eade & M.J. Sallnow (eds), *Contesting the Sacred. The An-thropology of Christian Pilgrimage*, London-New York 1991; A. Morinis (ed.), *Sacred Journeys. The Anthropology of Pilgrimage*, Westport/London; I. Reader & T. Walter (eds), *Pilgrimage in Popular Culture*, Hound-mills/London 1993. From the large-scale Dutch research project 'Christian pilgrimages' we mention: M. van Uden & P. Post (eds), *Christelijke bede-vaarten: op weg naar heil en heling*. Nijmegen 1988; P. Post, 'Bedevaart zonder grenzen', *Tijdschrift voor Liturgie* 73 (1989) 135-156; M. van Uden, J. Pieper & P. Post (eds), *Oude sporen, nieuwe wegen. Ontwikkelingen in bedevaartonderzoek*. Baarn 1995; P. Post, 'The Modern Pilgrim. A Study of Contemporary Pilgrims' Accounts', *Ethnologia Europaea* 24 (1994 [1995]) 85-100.

[6]See for the definition-problem especially the German discussion in the context of modern European ethnology. Here I only mention: P. Berbée, '"Bedevaart" en "pelgrimstocht" in Nederland. Over oude termen en nieuwe methoden in bedevaartonderzoek', in: N. Lettinck & J. Molenbroek (eds), *In de schaduw van de eeuwigheid. Tien studies over religie en samenleving in laatmiddeleeuws Nederland*, Utrecht 1986, 167-199; P. Berbée, 'Zur Klärung

guishing among them and characterizing them by their contemporary, post-modern shape and context.

2.1.1. Traditional International Mass Pilgrimage
The first form is represented by the traditional mass pilgrimages to great, international sacred places. In addition to Jerusalem and Rome, one must here think particularly of the great sites identified with Mary, such as Lourdes, Fatima, Banneux, La Salette and Beauraing.[7] The otherwise scanty figures available demonstrate how, even through the years of what has been termed seculariza-

---

von Sprache und Sache in der Wallfahrtsforschung. Begriffsgeschichtlicher Beitrag zur Diskussion', *Bayerische Blätter für Volkskunde* 14 (1987) 65-82; P.J. Margry & P. Post, 'Het project "Bedevaartplaatsen in Nederland": een plaatsbepaling', *Volkskundig Bulletin. Tijdschrift voor Nederlandse cultuurwetenschap* 20,1 (1994) 19-59, esp. 40-45; P.J. Margry, P. Post, 'Wallfahrt zwischen Inventarisierung und Analyse. Ein niederländisches Forschunsprojekt in historiographischem und methodologischem Kontext', *Rheinischwestfälische Zeitschrift für Volkskunde* 39 (1994 [1995]) 27-65, esp. 55-61.

Important in this context is the relation between pilgrimage and tourism and pilgrimage and other forms of popular culture: P. Assion, 'Der soziale Gehalt aktueller Frömmigkeitsformen. Zur religiösen Volkskunde in der Gegenwart', *Hessische Blätter für Volks- und Kulturforschung Bd. 14/15*, Gießen 1982/83, 5-17; W. Brückner, 'Gemeinschaft Utopie Communio. Vom Sinn und Unsinn "sozialer" Interpretation gegenwärtiger Frömmigkeitsformen und ihre empirischen Erfaßbarkeit', *Bayerische Blätter für Volkskunde* 10 (1983) 181-201; M. Scharfe, M. Schmolze & G. Schubert (eds), *Wallfahrt Tradition und Mode. Empirische Untersuchungen zur Aktualität von Volksfrömmigkeit*, Tübingen 1985; E. Cohen, 'Pilgrimage and Tourism: Convergence and Divergence', in: A. Morinis (ed.), *Sacred Journeys. The Anthropology of Pilgrimage*, Westport/London 1992, 47-61; A. Mulder, 'Op zoek naar de ware pelgrim. Over pelgrimage en toerisme', in: M. van Uden a.o. (eds), *Oude sporen, nieuwe wegen*, 15-51. See also n.12.

[7]Cf. the survey in: P. Post, 'Thema's, theorieën en trends'; for Jerusalem: G. Bowman, 'Christian Ideology and the Image of a Holy Land: the Place of Jerusalem Pilgrimage in the Various Christianities', in: J. Eade & M.J. Sallnow (eds), *Contesting the Sacred*, 98-121; G. Bowman, 'Contemporary Christian Pilgrimage to the Holy Land', in: A. O'Mahony, G. Gunner & K. Hintlian (eds), *The Christian Heritage in the Holy Land*, London 1995, 288-310; for the Marian sites: Ch. 8 'Sacred Places and Pilgrimage', in: C. Park, *Sacred Worlds*, 245-285; W. Beinert & H. Petri (eds), *Handbuch der Marienkunde*, Regensburg 1984, esp. chapters XIII and XV.

tion – that is, the period since the 1960's – these 'traditional' locations have continued to attract pilgrims, and there has even
been a constant growth.

2.1.2. National, Regional, Local Pilgrimage

A second form is that of national, regional and local pilgrimage.
A precise delineation between these and our first group can not
always be made, particularly when we consider what are thought
of as 'national' sacred places, such as Czestogowa in Poland,
Kevelaer and Vierzehnheiligen in Germany or Scherpenheuvel in
Belgium,[8] and new sacred places that often have a certain contesting or conservative character, such as the Southern Italian
centre of Padre Pio, San Giovanni Rotondo,[9] and the Eastern
European Marian location of Medjugorje[10]. Focusing on the regional and local places, this second group includes sacred places
which at a certain time of the year, generally the feast of the patron saint, exercise a certain power of attraction in their immediate local or regional environment as is evident from the many
processions. It is now interesting to note how since the 1980's,
both these smaller local or larger regional sites all over Europe,
which in the 1960's often went into decline, are again flourishing.
Clearly one can say there has been a revitalization.[11]

---

[8]See the literature mentioned in n.5 and n.7 above. For Kevelaer there is
now the outstanding study of R. Schulte Staade (ed.), *Kevelaer-Wallfahrt
1642-1992: 350 Jahre Kevelaer-Wallfahrt*, Bd. I en II, Kevelaer 1992.

[9]C. McKevitt, 'San Giovanni Rotondo and the Shrine of Padre Pio', in: J.
Eade & M.J. Sallnow (eds), *Contesting the Sacred*, 77-97.

[10]M. Bax, *Medjugorje: Religion, Politics and Violence in Rural Bosnia*,
Amsterdam 1995.

[11]Dokkum, the place in North Friesland, The Netherlands, where St. Boni-
face was murdered in the 8th century CE, is a striking example of this. See
for the Dokkum revitalization: P. Post, 'De pastor aan de bron. Over de op-
bloei van Dokkum als Bonifatius-stad', in: E. Henau & F. Jespers (eds), *Liturgie en kerkopbouw. Opstellen aangeboden aan Ad Blijlevens...*, Baarn
1993, 239-267; P. Post, 'Het wonder van Dokkum en andere verhalen van
afstand en betrokkenheid; lokale pastorale interactie op heilige plaatsen ver-
geleken', in: P. Post, M. van Uden & J. Pieper (eds), *Oude sporen, nieuwe
wegen: ontwikkelingen in het bedevaartonderzoek*, Baarn 1995, 107-132; P.

2.1.3. Individual Pilgrimage to Classical Sacred Sites
A third form of pilgrimage representing a striking development
around Christian sacred places, is the post-modern phenomenon
of individual pilgrimage to classical sacred sites from Christian
tradition. The old pilgrimage routes in Europe are busy these
days: thousands upon thousands of usually single and unaffiliated
pilgrims spend weeks, even months, on their way to traditional
goals of pilgrimage such as Rome, Assisi, Chartres and the Holy
Land. The old mediaeval routes to Santiago de Compostela in
Spain are far and away the most popular. From all corners of
Europe people walk and cycle to the tomb of St. James. Here one
could speak not just of a process of revitalization, but even of a
European 'pilgrimage boom'.[12]

Post, *Ritueel landschap: over liturgie-buiten,* Heeswijk-Dinther [etc.] 1995,
23-27 sub 4.1.; P. Post, '"God kijkt niet op een vierkante meter..." of Hobsbawm herlezen', in: C. van der Borgt a.o. (eds), *Constructie van het eigene.
Culturele vormen van regionale identiteit in Nederland*, Amsterdam 1996,
175-200. See for the context of ritual revitalization in general: P. Post, 'Het
verleden in het spel? Volksreligieuze rituelen tussen cultus en cultuur', *Jaarboek voor Liturgie-onderzoek* 7 (1991) 79-124; P. Post, 'Volksreligieuze rituelen tussen cultus en cultuur', in: M. van Uden & J. Pieper (eds): *Bedevaart
als volksreligieus ritueel,* Heerlen 1991, 47-76; J. Boissevain (ed.), *Feestelijke vernieuwing in Nederland?*, Amsterdam 1991; J. Boissevain (ed.), *Revita-
lizing European Rituals*, London 1992.
[12]A. de Jong, 'Meegaan met pelgrims naar Santiago de Compostela. Ver-
slag van een onderzoeksproject in wording', in: Pieper a.o. (eds), *Bedevaart
en pelgrimage*, 59-79; A. Mulder, 'Op zoek naar de ware pelgrim. Over pelgrimage en toerisme', in: M. van Uden a.o. (eds), *Oude sporen, nieuwe wegen*, 15-51; J. Pieper & M. van Uden, 'Op weg naar Santiago de Compostela.
Ervaringen van pelgrim', in: Van Uden a.o. (eds), *Oude sporen, nieuwe wegen*, 53-84; P. Post, 'Pelgrimsverslagen: verkenning van een genre', *Jaarboek
voor Liturgie-onderzoek* 8 (1992) 285-331; P. Post, 'Pelgrims tussen traditie
en moderniteit. Een verkenning van hedendaagse pelgrimsverslagen', in: J.
Pieper, P. Post & M. van Uden (eds). *Bedevaart en pelgrimage*, 7-37; P. Post,
'The Modern Pilgrim. A Study of Contemporary Pilgrims' Accounts', *Ethnologia Europaea* 24 (1994 [1995]) 85-100; B. Haab, 'Weg und Wandlung.
Ethnologische Feldforschung zur Spiritualität heutiger Jakobs-Pilger und -
Pilgerinnen', in: P. Michel (ed.), *Symbolik von Weg und Reise*, Bern [etc.]
1992, 137-162.

2.1.4. 'Topolatry'

With this renaissance of traditional pilgrimage in a post-modern setting, we touch upon a fourth, more general form and development with regard to sacred locations. In the form under consideration here, developments around pilgrimage such as were briefly described above, are connected to broader, more diffuse developments surrounding sacred space and time in Western culture. On the one hand this takes the form of what an essay by Gottfried Korff, a prominent representative of European ethnology, recently termed 'topolatry',[13] and on the other hand there is the context of an unmistakable rise of a culture of public and private celebrations.[14] I want to further discuss and illustrate this fourth form.

2.2. Impressions of Post-Modern Lieux de Mémoire and 'Topolatry'

Only a few impressions can be given here with regard to this current of 'topolatry', which in my mind has a good deal to do with post-modern developments surrounding pilgrimage. This category involves a more general religious, or even chiefly secular and profane form of pilgrimage. Ritual change here is closely connected with a specific form of dealing with the past.

In a general sense, I would first of all want to point to the interest in what have been termed, since Nora's prestigious French project, *lieux de mémoire*.[15] All around post-modern Europe,

---

[13]G. Korff, 'Musealisierung total? Notizen zu einem Trend, der die Institution, nach der er beannt ist, hinter sich gelassen hat', in: K. Füßmann, H. Grütter & J. Rüsen (eds), *Historische Faszination. Geschichtskultur Heute*, Köln 1994, 129-144, esp. 130-139; see also: E. Jonker, 'De betrekkelijkheid van het moderne historische besef', *Bijdragen en Mededelingen betreffende de Geschiedenis der Nederlanden* 111 (1996) 30-46. On Korff: 39ff..

[14]See the revitalization-literature mentioned in n.11.

[15]P. Nora a.o. (eds), *Les Lieux de Mémoire*, t. I: *La République*, Paris 1984, repr. 1992; t. II: *La Nation*, 1986, repr. 1992; see also: H. Lübbe, *Geschichtsbegriff und Geschichtsinteresse. Analytik und Pragmatik der Historie*,

places are being set apart, declared 'sacred' and cherished as sites for the celebration of bygone culture in a variety of ways. Many researchers see these *lieux de mémoire* as post-modern centres of pilgrimage where rites of remembrance are performed. They are sacred spots where historical memories in cultural inheritance are acknowledged, fixed, isolated and celebrated. The ritual component is unmistakably present, and is also emphasized by people like Nora. These are sacred places which can be termed more or less 'anamnestic', in the sense that 'present, past and future are caught up in one understandable and meaningful chronological framework'.[16] For many, these places of remembrance where one's history can be celebrated as *mémoire* are coupled to an altered consciousness of history itself.

A culture in which people have lost their connection with the past and where they diligently search for something to hold on to, for continuity and identity in a fast-changing society, has need of new sacred places. In the meantime, these post-modern 'sacred places' take the form of a true 'topolatry', and appear to be connected with an inclination toward a culture of celebration which could be labeled 'chronolatry' as is evident for instance from the revitalization of rituals of feasts and festivals in Europe.

What is taking place here at the level of content, and more particularly experience, is yet to be discussed. For now we are concerned with the phenomenon itself. The rise of *lieux de mémoire*, which once again is connected with the rise of a specific culture of celebration, a public culture of feast and festival, demands our

---

Basel/Stuttgart 1977; D. Lowenthal, *The Past is a Foreign Country*, Cambridge 1985; S. Bann, *The Inventions of History. Essays on the Representation of the Past*, Manchester [etc.] 1990; P. de Boer & W. Frijhoff (eds), *Lieux de Mémoire et Identitées Nationales*, Amsterdam 1993; Füßmann, Grütter & Rüsen (eds), *Historische Faszination*; R. Samuel, *Theatres and Memory*, London/New York 1994; N. van Sas (ed.), *Waar de blanke top der duinen en andere vaderlandse herinneringen*, Amsterdam/Antwerpen 1995; E. Jonker, 'De betrekkelijkheid'; P. Post, 'Het verleden in het spel?' and W. Frijhoff, 'Traditie en verleden. Kritische reflecties over het gebruik van verwijzingen naar vroeger', *Jaarboek voor liturgie-onderzoek* 7 (1991) 125-136.

[16]E. Jonker, 'De betrekkelijkheid', 32.

attention precisely because it appears to be closely connected with the changes in Christian pilgrimage.

In order to bring some order to the chaos surrounding this 'to-polatry', I wish to point to some forms taken by these post-modern sacred places.

2.2.1. Memorials to War and Shoah

First of all, there are memorials to war in general, and to the *Shoah* in particular. Thus, for some time now, pilgrimage studies have included such memorial sites, chiefly for the First and Second World Wars, and books and brochures about these sites speak generally about pilgrimage in a way which clearly goes beyond the level of a purely metaphorical use of the word.[17] In terms of spatial and ritual design, the similarities are indeed striking. The battlefield at Verdun (France), the bridge at Arnhem (The Netherlands), the honor cemetery for executed resistance members at Overveen (The Netherlands), local, regional, national and international war memorials, the European network of war cemeteries and concentration camps: these are all sacred places which attract post-modern pilgrims and where, at fitting times, rites of remembrance are celebrated.

Here, however, we are already able to detect a certain tension surrounding the sacred status of these places. Although we shall treat the post-modern museum as a new form of sacred place, the rites of the museum are inadequate for these sacred places, and are often even considered inappropriate. They never 'just' function as museums for remembrance; there are often ritual (in the sense of religious or anamnestic ritual) or liturgical spaces, sometimes oriented to specific religious traditions, as, for example, Christian churches or chapels, as in the case of the Church of

---

[17]J. van der Heijden, *Don't Forget Us; We Shall Not Forget You. The Fiftieth Commemoration of the Battle of Arnhem; a Meaningful Commemoration*, Arnhem 1994 (esp. 87, n.5-7; Introduction: 13-19; Symbolism and Ritual of a Commemoration: 65-73; Conclusion: 75-81); T. Walter, 'War Grave Pilgrimage', in: J. Reader & T. Walter (eds), *Pilgrimage in Popular Culture*, 63-91; J. Winter, *Sites of Memory, Sites of Mourning. The Great War in European Cultural History*, Cambridge 1996.

Reconciliation at Dachau. But often they are general post-modern
memoriae where it is the ritual of silence and the ever-burning
fire which dominates all else. Because of the 'anamnestic' content, *lieux de mémoire* of this sort seldom confine themselves to
distant 'museal' or museum-oriented rites, but there is always a
ritual component of engaged celebration, generally in the form of
memorial rituals such as the silent procession, laying flowers,
chimes, going there and coming back. Thus Dachau, as a *lieu de
mémoire*, has both the character of a ritual/liturgical place and
that of a museum.

2.2.2. All Possible Segments of Past Culture
Subsequently, not only the focal points of our history come into
consideration as *lieux de mémoire*, but people discover and cher-
ish more broadly all possible segments of past culture. The spectrum appears inexhaustible: archaeological sites, houses, villages
and cities with their *centro storico*, industrial monuments: everything can potentially come into consideration for the rites of topolatry. Naturally, and without any difficulty, Christian pilgrimage sites, particularly local and regional ones, are included in this
process.

2.2.3. Museum
The museum is a very specific form of post-modern sacred place.
In many respects, museums – both museums dealing with (cultural) history and art museums – are the temples or cathedrals of
the post-modern era. Museum culture has blossomed remarkably.
The Netherlands has one of the highest concentrations of museums in Europe: there are at present more than 1000 museums in
our country. It is here that a striking shift in sacralizing tendencies
is apparent: while church buildings are often stripped of their
character as 'houses of God' (motto: from temple to meeting
house!), new museums take on the aura of the sacred. The planning principles of pilgrimage architecture return there.[18] A striking

---

[18]P. Post, 'Raum und Ritus. Perspektiven für die Analyse des liturgischen
Raumes', *Jaarboek voor Liturgie-onderzoek* 5 (1989) 301-331; H.-J. Auf der

example is the Shrine of the Book in the Israel Museum, Jerusalem.

On the other hand, the post-modern pilgrimage sites take on the character of a museum. More and more they become places where a cultural inheritance is cherished, their venerated relics displayed in museums, admission fees are paid, and there is a conscious or unconscious conflict between ritual and museum-oriented design.

There is a constant tension in post-modern sacred places, as we noted above. Thus, the often strong reactions which arise when churches or synagogues are threatened with demolition or secular alternative uses are also telling in this regard. The discussion which has been going on for some time now over a second life for the restored Dutch synagogue building in Weesp is one illustration. A proposal to use it as a clothing store unleashed powerful emotions, while it appears acceptable to use it as a museum.

2.2.4. Nature and Landscape

Finally there is nature and landscape. In an recent book, Simon Schama rightly connected landscape and memory.[19] As a place of collective memory, the landscape shares in the general process of sacralization. Forms of topolatry in the open air can be very closely bound up with traditional forms of Christian sacred places. Placing markers in the landscape is closely connected with the first form of memorial sites for war and Shoah. There are also more individually oriented new ritual marking tendencies along highways.[20] Sudden deaths in traffic – in The Netherlands more

---

Maur, in: P. Harnoncourt & H.-J. Auf der Maur, *Feiern im Rhythmus der Zeit II/1, Der Kalender; Feste und Gedenktage der Heiligen*, 240 f.

[19] S. Schama, *Landscape and Memory*, New York 1995; see for landscape and nature the literature mentioned in: P. Post, *Ritueel landschap*, 52f n.24; esp. I mention here: B. Bender, 'Stonehenge Contested Landscapes (Medieval to Present-Day)', in: B. Bender (ed.), *Landscape: Politics and Perspectives*, Providence Oxford 1993, 245-280; see also the literature cited in n.2 above.

[20] P. Post, *Ritueel landschap*, 42-46 sub 4.4.; A. Franke, U. Friedrichs & H. Mehl, 'Unfallkreuze an Schleswig-Holsteins Autostraßen', *Kieler Blätter zur Volkskunde* 26 (1994) 189-212.

than 1300 people die every year in the battle to get somewhere quickly – are marked by post-modern highway-side crosses, and by flowers, stones and little gardens. On a global scale we encounter these markings in special places where attacks, airplane crashes, stadium disasters and the like have occurred. Rituals surrounding disasters seem to be very much connected with places, and are related to pilgrimage rites. The spots where Olaf Palme and Yizhak Rabin were killed are being shaped as sacred places, marked and ritualized.[21]

But in addition to these specific memorial locations, there is the sanctity peculiar to nature and landscape itself. Thus the qualities that the goals of Christian pilgrimage have as landscapes – idyllic spots often with a park, a spring and a hill – are being rediscovered, or what can be termed ancient, 'pre-Christian' landscape elements are rediscovered as ritual places. In Great Britain Glastonbury[22] and Stonehenge[23] are striking examples, in France Carnac.

But the process is broader. The perspective can expand to include the whole landscape, to 'nature'. Nature becomes sacred and is seen as a lieu de mémoire, a monument, acquired by the government, protected.

These are only impressions, but they are to my mind certainly unmistakable signals of remarkable shifts in the sphere of the sacred and space.

3. Content and Experience: the Musealization Process

As we have already seen, a very dominant substantive component of developments on the field of pilgrimage, is the past. In pilgrimage ritual in its post-modern forms, people are specifically

---

[21]M. Scharfe, 'Totengedenken. Zur Historizität von Brauchtraditionen. Das Beispiel Olof Palme 1986', *Ethnologia Scandinavica* 19 (1989) 142-153.

[22]M. Bowman, 'Drawn to Glastonbury', in: I. Reader & T. Walter (eds), *Pilgrimage in Popular Culture*, 29-62.

[23]B. Bender, 'Stonehenge Contested Landscapes'.

occupied with the past. It is striking how we can follow this aspect when reading accounts of the experiences of the post-modern pilgrims themselves.[24] In the pilgrimage accounts of individual pilgrims to the old, classic sacred places of Europe, involvement with the past is a very dominant theme. This has been demonstrated in the analysis of these unique sources. The experience of modern pilgrimage is defined to an important degree by cherishing the past. It is very fruitful for an exploration of the level of experience, to follow the thread of the past, and proceed further along it.

The experience of ritual is hard to describe or measure, but to a certain degree it can be categorized, for instance, on the conceptual scale of (a) myth, (b) folklore, (c) theatre or museum and (d) commerce or decoration. At one end of the scale there is the 'mythic phase' of a ritual, the phase of the ideal ritual, a mythic, collective celebration, as for example it is experienced by monks performing the divine office in a monastic liturgy. The key concepts are participation and community. Then there is the phase of 'folklore'. The celebration becomes more of a performance, staged and viewed. The collective mythic form is partially eroded by having an audience. Sacred dance becomes folk dance, performed at local festivals. There is an audience to hear and watch the liturgical choir. The gap opens further in the phase of 'theatre' or 'museum'. Here there is complete distancing: a gospel choir on TV, the Mass or vespers performed by ensembles specializing in old music. For what was originally a liturgical celebration, there is an admission charge, and the performance is followed by applause. Commerce and decoration is the last phase. Here the original mythic content evaporates or is changed into an entirely new kind of sacredness.[25]

---

[24]See n.11.

[25]For this musealization process (and the related concepts of historization, theatralization, folklorization) see: P. Post, 'Het verleden in het spel'; P. Post, *Ritueel landschap*; P. Post, 'Goede tijden, slechte tijden' (esp. 74 n.24). Furthermore I mention only: P. Assion, 'Historismus, Traditionalismus, Folklorismus. Zur musealisierenden Tendenz der Gegenwartskultur', in: U. Jeggle a.o. (eds): *Volkskultur der Moderne. Probleme und Perspektiven empirischer*

Devotional images offer a good example. A liturgi-
cal/devotional image of Mary or Christ can begin in a private or
public setting and it is now possible to follow it then down the
path of folklorization, such as the nostalgic image cherished in a
rural chapel, to musealization, such as Mary or Christ as 'art' or
'cultural inheritance' in a museum, to the level of commerce, such
as the devotional image in the antique shop and finally to decoration, as seen in the fact that large department stores now include
statues of Mary among their selection of all sorts of decorative
figurines.

To an increasing degree, it is now being acknowledged that
with the aid of this scale, the level of experience and degree of
contextual shift surrounding rituals can also be categorized.[26]

I see the traditional pilgrimage goals such as Jerusalem, Rome
and Santiago de Compostela, our first category, and many other
forms of traditional Christian liturgical repertoire, as being in-
creasingly taken over in this manner.[27]

On the other hand, as we have seen previously, at the very
same time and place there is sometimes a counter-movement with
a certain 'mythic' calibre. The memorial rites at sites which
commemorate war and the *Shoah* are to a great extent characterized by a struggle between engaged mythic celebration and de-
tached regard of a piece of the past. There is a search for ritual

---

Kulturforschung. Reinbeck bei Hamburg 1986, 351-362; K. Köstlin, 'Folklorismus und Modernisierung', *Sweizerisches Archiv für Volkskunde* 87 (1991)
46-66; Korff, 'Musealisierung total?'; H. Lübbe, 'Erfahrungsverluste und
Kompensationen. Zum philosophischen Problem der Erfahrung in der Ge-
genwärtigen Welt', *Giessener Universitätsblätter* 12 (1979) 42-53; H. Lübbe,
'Der Fortschritt und das Museum', in: *Dilthey Jahrbuch* I, Göttingen 1983,
39-56; W. Zacharias (ed.), *Zeitphänomen Musealisierung; das Verschwinden
der Gegenwart und die Konstruktion der Erinnerung.* Essen 1990, esp.: E.
Sturm, 'Museifizierung und Realitätsverlust', 99-113.
    [26]See the literature in n.12 and n.25 above. A summary is given in: P. Post,
'The modern pilgrim. A Study of Contemporary Pilgrims' Accounts', *Ethnologia Europaea* 24 (1994 [1995]) 85-100, esp. 92f.
    [27]Illustrative is the recent CD-Rom production: *Jerusalem an Interactive
Pilgrimage to the Holy City*: motto: 'Experience the sacred landmarks and the
glorious heritage of this timeless city'.

repertoires that can construct anamnestic bridges touching down in the past, present and future. This is rarely achieved through mythic celebration, though often through the rites of the theatre such as musical performance, recitation of a poem, dance, the rites of the museum such as exhibition, documentary, the rites of nurturing the idyll of nature or landscape, or by the rite of formulae of admonition as is seen by the recurrent sounding of the formula 'never again' in the speeches.[28]

I am here simplifying an extremely complex process, which in time and space operates in most diverse and contingent ways, and a process which appears to have taken place in all times, although for the past the signals are more difficult to interpret. In contemporary ritual and liturgical situations, people are becoming more aware of these changes of context which touch so deeply upon the nature of experience. Therefore, it is not by chance that in current cultural studies, including theology and religious studies, themes such as ritual, landscape, theatre and museum are at present quite numerous.[29]

At the close of this sketch of the musealization process, I must yet explicitly emphasize that it may come across as somewhat static and mechanical. It equally must be emphasized that the shifts of context here labeled as musealization is always a matter

---

[28]Cf. M. de Vries, 'Twee minuten lang stilstaan bij de doden. De betekenis van de Overveense Stille Tocht in de jaren tachtig', in: J. Boissevain (ed.), *Feestelijke vernieuwing in Nederland?*, 15-26.

[29]Literature on the themes of ritual, landscape and museum is already given in sections and notes above; I here only mention some examples of the theme of 'theatre': P. Post & J. Pieper, *De palmzondagviering: een landelijke verkenning*, Amsterdam/Kampen 1992, 59-63, sub 6.2.5.; W.M. Speelman, 'The Plays of Our Culture. A Formal Differentiation Between Theatre and Liturgy', *Jaarboek voor liturgie-onderzoek* 9 (1993) 65-81; W. Früwald, 'Zwischen Märtyrerdrama und politischem Theater. Vom spannungsvollen Verhältnis der Kirche zur Theaterkultur', *Theologie und Glaube* 85 (1995) 35-46; K. Koch, 'Liturgie und Theater. Theologische Fragmente zu einem vernachlässigten Thema', *Stimmen der Zeit* Bd. 213, Jg. 120 H.1 (1995) 3-16; J. Bärsch, 'Das Dramatische im Gottesdient. Liturgiewissenschaftliche Aspekte der Osterfeiern und Osterspiele im Mittelalter', *Liturgisches Jahrbuch* 46 (1996) 41-66.

of an extremely dynamic process which, for individual pilgrims or groups of pilgrims in various situations, can run at a very uneven rate. Indeed, within a single pilgrimage, the experiential dimension can vary. A museal appropriation and experience can suddenly turn into a mythic liturgical ritual – or vice versa.

4. Conclusion: 'Anamnestic Loss'

In closing, I would like to make one final evaluative and interpretative remark about the quality of this liturgical/ritual innovation, principally from the perspective of the identity of a religious ritual.[30]

In my opinion, in connection with the description above on the field of pilgrimage regarding form, content and experience, particular reference must be made to what can be characterized as 'anamnestic loss'. Religious rites and myths, including those surrounding sacred places, are borne by a delicate balance among the three dimensions of anamnesis: in the present, the past is celebrated in ritual with an eye to the future. The Greek, originally Semetic concept of the anamnesis is untranslatable into English. Memorial, commemoration, remembrance, all these suggest that a person, deed, time or place commemorated is past and absent, whereas anamnesis signifies exactly the opposite: it is an act, in and by which the person or event commemorated, is brought into the realm of the here and now, as Grisbrooke puts it.[31] That refined tension is now under pressure from the shifts taking place in post-modern ritual. As we have described it, the evolving shape of our relation with the past disrupts this tension and enervates the anamnestic tension. In the rites of the museum and com-

---

[30]This note on 'anamnestic proportion' deals *in fondo* of course with the so-called liturgical inculturation theme: cf. G. Lukken, *Inculturatie en de toekomst van de liturgie*, Heeswijk-Dinther 1994; G. Lukken, 'Inculturation de la Liturgie: Théorie et Pratique', *Questions Liturgiques* 77 (1996) 10-39.

[31]W.J. Grisbrooke, s.v. 'Anaphora': sub 7 *Anamnesis*, in: J.G. Davies (ed.), *A New Dictionary of Liturgy and Worship*, London 1994, 18.

memorations at post-modern *lieux de mémoire*, the past is stripped of its dangerous dimensions, becomes safe, offering a temporary refuge from everyday life. Essentially the 'here and now' are central, and that is made bearable by a selected, and often indeed a created past or invented tradition.[32] Korff is sharp and sometimes derisory on this: in 'topolatry' nothing is problematized any more, all the sharp corners are rounded off in the version of the past which we encounter, and it is put on display and commemorated.[33]

That also appears to be the case for the anamnestic content of religious rites such as Christian pilgrimage: despite processes of new sacralizing and liturgizing, the danger is often eliminated from the play, and the liturgy ceases to be relevant because the past is enervated and the tension of past, present and future is not maintained. The mythic process of going and returning, the play of devotion around the sacred place, is tamed, reduced to a quaint old tradition, a form of 'living history'. The pilgrimage of an initially dangerous commitment through folklore, museum and theatre to the pseudo-sacredness of commerce and decoration is well under way.

---

[32]Cf. P. Post, 'Rituals and the Function of the Past: Rereading Eric Hobsbawm', *Journal of Ritual Studies* 10 (1996), 85-107.

[33]G. Korff, 'Musealisierung total?', 137-139; cf. also: E. Jonker, 'De betrekkelijkheid', 42f.

THE SANCTITY OF MOUNT HERZL
AND INDEPENDENCE DAY IN
ISRAEL'S CIVIL RELIGION

Ophir Yarden

Introduction

If one were to recall an episode in the history of the Jewish people in which a political leader by the name of David had the box containing a certain national relic loaded on a wagon or vehicle and brought through the Judean hills to Jerusalem, where it was placed at the crest of a hill so as to enhance the 'spiritual centrality' of the new capital city, one could equally well be imagining either of two stories separated by nearly 3,000 years.

Such, of course, was the case in the days of (King) David ben Yishay and the Ark of the Covenant, and so too was the episode of (Prime Minister) David Ben-Gurion and the bones of Theodore Herzl, which were brought from Vienna to Jerusalem for re-interment in the summer of 1949.

The parallel is particularly striking both in terms of the acts themselves and in terms of the reasoning and motivations which lay behind them. While the goals of David's conversion of Jebus to the City of David, a national religious center and his capital, are well known,[1] the latter story is less familiar. Regarding the decision to rebury Herzl in Jerusalem we find sentiments expressed which are similar to those ascribed to King David. When Minister of Police Bekhor Shitrit suggested burying Herzl in

---

[1] In bringing the Ark to Jerusalem David 'transformed his new capital into a religious center'. H. Tadmor in: H.H. Ben-Sasson (ed.), *A History of the Jewish People*, Cambridge 1976, 97.

Haifa – as some thought was his request[2] – Minister of the Interior
Yizhak Gruenbaum replied:

> "I think that specifically now, when our intention is to strengthen
> Jerusalem and to make it into a *spiritual center...* the most appro-
> priate place for Herzl's tomb is in Jerusalem."[3]

This paper will explore the centrality of Mt. Herzl and the ceremonies which take place there in the context of the sacred time
and space of the civil religion of Israel. While most of our attention will be focused on the early years of the state when these
phenomena came into existence, some examples will be taken
from more recent times as our interest lies in how these have
evolved in Israel's civil religion.

Mount Herzl

While David Ben-Gurion was unenthusiastic regarding the choice
of Mt. Herzl,[4] a hill then on the outskirts of western Jerusalem and
far from the city's inaccessible historical center, the site rapidly
became a national shrine.[5] Indeed this mountain, distant from the
traditionally sanctified sites of Jerusalem's history but relatively
near the region destined to house the complex of institutions rep-

---

[2] The recommendation of the committee to implement the decisions of the
Zionist Congresses to bring Herzl's body for burial in Israel concluded with
the phrase, 'Jerusalem bleibt Jerusalem, auch ohne die Grabstätte Herzls, aber
Herzl verdient, daß man seinen Willen befolgt.' (Jerusalem remains Jerusalem, even without Herzl's grave, but Herzl deserves to have his wish fulfilled.), *Die Frage der Überführung der Gebeine Herzl's nach Erez-Israel*,
Vienna, 1935, 15 Central Zionist Archives (CZA), J 95/24.

[3] Protocols of the 14th meeting of the first elected government of Israel, 11
Iyyar 5709 (10.5.49), 26 Israel State Archives (ISA) (Hebr., emphasis mine).

[4] Ibid., 30.

[5] The term 'shrine' was used almost immediately. In a letter to the editor of
the Jerusalem Post (21.5.51), Aryeh Geismar complained that Mt. Herzl was
closed to the public for the Independence Day ceremony and refers to 'this national shrine'.

resenting the State of Israel (the Knesset, government offices and the Shrine of the Book at the Israel Museum), was to become the locus of ritual for the new state.

We may better understand the evolution of this secular alternative by recalling the initial hostility and ambivalence felt by leaders of the *yishuv* (the Jewish settlement in pre-State Palestine) toward the 'Holy City' of Jerusalem. Motti Golani has shown that the Zionist leadership harbored reservations regarding the role of Jerusalem in the state-to-be, as had Herzl himself.[6] As an example we may note that David Ben-Gurion did not visit the city during his first two years in Palestine, and others waited far longer.[7]

Popular Acclamation of Holiness

Theodore Herzl is buried at the peak of the hill which now bears his name. This is the venue of the annual Independence Day ceremony, at which time right of entry to the 'holy' precinct is limited. Not only is the public at large not allowed access to the site, but the ceremony itself was required to take place at some distance. A letter from the World Zionist Organization to the government's Independence Day committee reminded the committee members that, in accordance with Herzl's will, eulogies are not to be recited at his graveside, and hence that nothing was to be done within several meters of the tomb itself.[8]

A special sense of civil propriety was demonstrated regarding this sacred site. It became clear that there were dictates of decorum which applied to Herzl's tomb. A letter sent to the Prime Minister's office in August 1949 complained of the selling of ice cream and soft drinks close to the tomb and protested the site's

---

[6] M. Golani, *Zion in Zionism: The Zionist Policy and the Question of Jerusalem 1937-1949* (Hebr.), Israel Ministry of Defense 1992, 10 -14.

[7] M. Golani, *Zion in Zionism,* 10-14. Berl Katznelson, quoted below (see note 27), waited nine years from his arrival in Israel until his first visit to Jerusalem.

[8] The conducting of ceremonies was limited as well, as is seen from the draft of by-laws for Herzl's tomb (4.6.50) CZA, S5/11330.

accessibility by vehicle. In likening the shrine to the Western
Wall, the writer said 'you can't make a pilgrimage in a vehicle'.[9]
This critic's disappointment reflects the distinction which Pierre
Nora expresses regarding solemn ceremonies: 'One attends them
rather than visits them'.[10] In a similar vein, Yizhak Gruenbaum
(the same Minister of the Interior who advocated Herzl's reburial
in Jerusalem) noted the profanation of the grave-site and called
upon Ben-Gurion to have the government guard קדושי האומה, the
sacred of the nation.[11] This idea of restricted access is similar to
that expressed in many Jewish sources which discuss controlled
access as a characteristic of the holy.[12]

Independence Day

Having introduced Herzl's tomb as the central shrine of Israel's
civil religion, we can examine the evolution of the date for Independence Day. In spite of the fact that the date of Israel's celebration of independence has been established for nearly 50
years,[13] there was a degree of ambiguity on this issue during the
first year of the state's existence. Even after it became clear that

---

[9]The writer was from the Public Council for the Sabbath of the Ministry of
Religion. While representing a religious body, the concerns expressed tran-
scend the dictates of the halakhah. ISA, G 5595 file 4717. The writer was also
concerned that visitors (pilgrims?) would content themselves with a view
through the windows of their vehicles. Correspondence between the government and the Jewish Agency ensued dealing with the need to establish by-
laws for the site.

[10]P. Nora, 'Between Memory and History: *Les Lieux de Memoire*', *Repre-
sentations* 26 (1989), 23.

[11]ISA, G 5595 file 4714. This term could be understood in many ways.
Rather than denoting 'martyrs', or venerated national treasures, it conveys the
sense of holy deceased, like 'saint'.

[12]MKel 1:6-9 regarding the Temple and Nachmanides' introduction to
Num regarding the Tabernacle.

[13]Though it may be noted that in 1997 the government decided to postpone
Memorial Day and Independence Day so that they would not fall on Sunday
and Monday so as to avoid desecration of the Sabbath in the preparations.

the national day was to be celebrated as the anniversary of the declaration of independence, it remained to be determined according to which calendar. Was the holiday to be celebrated according to the non-Jewish Gregorian reckoning or according to the Hebrew calendar?[14] The centrality of the calendar to culture is clear; Nora has referred to calendar – not only to sites – as *lieu de memoire*.[15] In this case the determination of a holiday by Israel for the Jewish Diaspora as well is highly indicative of a (civil) religious framework.

Lively communications between local Zionist Federations worldwide and the government of the young state provide the story of the weeks leading up to the decision that Independence Day would be celebrated on the Hebrew anniversary of independence, 5 Iyyar.[16] Figure 1 is an urgent telegram from the Zionist Federation of Great Britain inquiring as to the determination of the date of the holiday.

---

[14]The date was 5 Iyyar 5708 which had fallen on 14 May 1948. Member of Knesset (henceforward MK) Y. Idelson (Mapam) and others suggested that the date be according to the Gregorian calendar. *Proceedings of the First Knesset*, Session 22, 12 Nisan 5709 (11.4.49), 350 ff. He and P. Lubianiker, who consented, claimed that the issue was that of recognition in the international sphere and not an attack on the use of the Hebrew calendar. Following the decision that the Hebrew calendar was to be used, it remained to be determined when the holiday's observance would be scheduled if the date fell on Saturday, so as to avoid profanation of the Sabbath (though some in the Knesset erroneously believed this to be a calendrical impossibility).

[15]P. Nora, 'Between Memory and History', 19.

[16]The Executive of the Zionist Organization, which was responsible for Mt. Herzl, served as liaison between these Diaspora groups and the government. Beyond the telegram reproduced here, the communications included several letters: On 1 March 1949 Dr. Lauterbach (of the Zionist Executive) and Dr. Schafler (of the Zionist Federation of Gt. Britain) wrote each other. Dr. Schlafler described the time for arranging celebrations as 'precariously short', while Dr. Lauterbach opined that the government was 'busy with affairs which ... are still more urgent'. CZA, S5/10214. The Knesset confirmed the decision only on 12 April (13 Nisan), less than one month before the 5th of Iyyar. *Knesset Proceedings*, 357.

Fig. 1. Telegram From the Zionist Federation of Great Britain
to the Zionist Executive in Jerusalem (CZA S5 10214)

Sent on 25 February 1949, its text reads:

> "Thanks Yours received 21 february – stop – urgently request
> definite reply concerning official date first anniversary establish-
> ment Israel."

A subsequent telegram of 9 March explicitly demands 'clarification of date 14 May or 5 Iyyar' and the government's response on
17 March reads:

> Regarding your telegram of 9.3.49 the government has decided to
> fix 5 Iyyar the date of the state's declaration as 'the Day of Up-
> right Standing'[17] in the State of Israel. This year the Day of Up-
> right Standing will fall on Wednesday 5 Iyyar 4 May [18]

---

[17]The Knesset changed this to 'Day of Independence'. יום הקוממיות (upright standing) was the choice of Ben-Gurion. *Knesset Proceedings*, 357. The
meaning of this name is discussed in note 69.

[18]All three telegrams are from CZA, S5/10214.

An agreed upon calendar is a fundamental characteristic of any religion and conversely, disagreement regarding calendrical issues is typical of sectarian schism. The evolution of Independence Day, its place in the Israeli calendar and the nature of its celebration are important parameters to be examined in the study of Israel's civil religion.

Civil Religion versus Traditional Judaism

While the inaccessibility from 1948 until 1967 of traditional holy sites including the Western Wall in the Old City of Jerusalem and the ancient Jewish cemetery on the Mount of Olives, may certainly have played a role in the evolution of Mt. Herzl as alternative sacred space, other factors were at work as well.

Charles S. Liebman and Eliezer Don-Yehiya have shown that, in the process of reconciling of the tradition with the needs of the state, the traditional symbols 'must be reformulated through a process of transformation and transvaluation'.[19] The founders of the state were well aware that 'Zionism ... had a special need for values and *symbols of a sanctified character* which would attract Jews to its ranks, integrate them into its new society, and mobilize them in the pursuit of Zionist goals'.[20]

Sanctified symbols have played a role in secular Zionist thinking from its earliest stages. Labor, עבודה, was the symbol, esteemed value and common term for socialist Labor Zionism. The use of this expression, which not insignificantly coincided with the term denoting the Temple service, was not mere coincidence; manual

---

[19]C.S. Liebman and E. Don-Yehiya, *Civil Religion in Israel: Traditional Judaism and the Political Culture in the Jewish State*, Los Angeles 1983, 19 (emphasis mine). The authors define transformation as 'retaining certain structurally recognizable features of the symbol but changing other aspects of its form', and transvaluation as 'retaining the form of the symbol but interpreting it to have meaning other that the traditional meaning'.

[20]C. Liebman and E. Don-Yehiya, *Civil Religion in Israel*, 28 (emphasis mine).

labor was consecrated and hallowed. The sanctification of labor
was that much more significant since the land being worked was
the Holy Land. Pioneer ideologue Aaron David Gordon wrote of
the need to have 'zealots of labor'.[21] The phrase 'religion of labor'
is often used to describe his thinking which included the idea that
redemption, certainly a religious concept, is to be attained only
through physical labor.[22] Gordon went so far as to make the parallel
between national life and religion explicit:
Religion knows how to impose duties, to assert its rightful place
and to be intrinsically important.... Is national life ... [not] valuable
enough to require the same effort made by the religious Jew on behalf of religion?[23]

In describing leaders of the history of Zionism it is common to
speak of Aḥad Ha-Am as Zionism's 'secular Rabbi', of A.D.
Gordon as it's 'secular mystic'[24] and of Herzl himself as 'messiah'.[25] Indeed, Herzl's original funeral in Vienna was a crowded
affair 'swamped by a kind of elemental and ecstatic mourning'[26] of
the type which might be expected for a saint or Rebbe.

The ambivalence and hostility of the state's Socialist-Zionist
founders toward many of the elements of the Jewish religious tradition is well known. But, for the most part, their attitude was not
one of total rejection. As Berl Katznelson, a central figure in So-
cialist-Zionism wrote:
A renewing and creative generation *does not* throw the cultural
heritage of ages into the dustbin. It examines and scrutinizes, *ac-
cepts and rejects.* At times it may keep and add to an accepted
tradition. At times it descends into ruined grottoes to excavate
and remove the dust from that which had lain in forgetfulness, in

---

[21] A.D. Gordon, 'People and Labor (1911)', in: A. Hertzberg (ed.), *The Zionist Idea,* New York 1982, 374.
[22] A. Hertzberg, *The Zionist Idea*, 369-70.
[23] A.D. Gordon, *The Nation and Labor* (Hebr.), Haifa/Jerusalem 1952, 126.
[24] A. Hertzberg, *The Zionist Idea*, 369, 251.
[25] A. Bein, *Theodore Herzl: A Biography of the Founder of Modern Zionism*, New York 1970, 506.
[26] E. Pawel, *The Labyrinth of Exile: A Life of Theodor Herzl*, London 1990,
531.

order to resuscitate old traditions which have the power to stimulate the spirit of the generation of renewal.[27]

One of the great ideals of the Zionist movement was not only to redeem the Jewish people but also to rehabilitate the individual and evolve a 'new Jew'.[28] Similarly, many strove to create new forms of Jewish life, a new Judaism. This Zionist vision of Judaism stressed a combination of modern values and concepts derived from post-enlightenment Europe, such as humanism and equality, along with elements of the Jewish tradition which emphasized heroism and the freedom of pre-exilic Jewish life in the ancient Land of Israel. The most outstanding examples of these phenomena would be the emphasis on agricultural elements of biblical festivals, and the transvaluation of historical holidays such as Hanukkah or Passover so as to highlight human activism at the expense of miracles and Divine intervention.[29]

These were the first steps in the evolution of what we can today call the *civil religion* of Israel. This term, originated by Jean J. Rousseau and applied in contemporary research by Robert Bellah,[30] was clarified for the Israeli context by Liebman and Don-Yehiya in their seminal work by that name as: 'the ceremonials, myths, and creeds which legitimate the social order, unite the population, and mobilize the society's members in pursuit of its dominant political goals. Civil religion is that which is most holy and sacred in the political culture. It forges its adherents into a moral community'.[31]

Regarding civil religion in America, Bellah has written 'though much is selectively derived from Christianity, this religion is

---

[27]B. Katznelson, 'Revolution and Tradition (1934)', in: A. Hertzberg (ed.), *The Zionist Idea*, 392-93, (emphasis mine).

[28]M. Rosenstein, 'The New Jew: The Ideal of the Zionist Education Enterprise in the Land of Israel before the Establishment of the State' (Hebr.), in: *Studies in Jewish Education* 3 (1988) 69-81.

[29]E. Don-Yehiya, 'Hanukkah and the Myth of the Maccabees in Zionist Ideology and in Israeli Society', *The Jewish Journal of Sociology* 34 (1992) 5-23.

[30]R. Bellah, 'Civil Religion in America', *Daedalus* 96 (1967), 1-21.

[31]C. Liebman and E. Don Yihiya, *Civil Religion*, ix.

clearly not itself Christianity'.[32] If this distinction between civil religion and Christian religion is delicate in the United States, a more
or less Christian country maintaining a slim separation of religion
and state,[33] then certainly it will be delicate for Israel, a state defined as Jewish. The relationship between civil religion and traditional Judaism is multi-dimensional. It maintains a dynamic dialogue with the tradition, creating an 'alloy of religious and patri-
otic elements'.[34]

The complex attitude of Israeli civil religion toward traditional
Judaism has been schematized by Liebman and Don-Yehiya as
being comprised of three approaches: confrontation, selective
adoption and reinterpretation.[35] To these we shall add selectively
inspired innovation in which new forms are created which borrow
from elements of the traditional religion. We shall see that all four
of these are operative regarding the innovation of sacred time and
sacred space in the case of Independence Day and Mt. Herzl.

Sacred Time – The Civil Religious Calendar

In many ways, the forms of Independence Day adhere to the para-
digms of traditional Jewish holidays. Here we shall examine aspects of Independence Day which were suggested to achieve this
adherence.

Independence Day (Yom Ha'Atsmaut) as a Jewish Holiday

---

[32]R. Bellah, 'Civil Religion in America', 7.

[33]Christmas, for example, is a national holiday. As W. Lloyd Warner has
said of American Memorial Day, 'Being both sacred and secular, it is a holy
day as well as a holiday and is accordingly celebrated.' W.L. Warner. 'An
American Sacred Ceremony', in: R.E. Richey & D. Jones (eds), *American
Civil Religion*, New York 1974, 89.

[34]R. Braun, *Sozialer und kultureller Wandel in einem ländlichen Indus-
triegebiet im 19. und 20. Jahrhundert*, Erlenbach-Zürich 1965, 337.

[35]C. Liebman and E. Don Yihiya, *Civil Religion*, 19-21 Their term for 'selective adoption' is dissolution.

In the Knesset debate regarding the nature of Independence Day, Mapai (Labor) MK Shlomo Lavie called for an evening-to-evening celebration 'like all holidays of Israel', and for the holiday (חג) to share the characteristics of other Jewish holidays by including 'a decorative dinner-table, illumination and holiday candles'. Two weeks before this Knesset debate, Lavie had published a call to stress the sanctity (קדושה) of the day. He said that Independence Day is no less a festival of liberation than Passover, while expressing doubt as to the possibility of creating such a holiday in the circumstances of his time.[36]

One of the major personalities involved in setting the tone for Independence Day was historian MK Ben-Zion Dinaburg. Dinaburg believed that Independence Day shared the characteristics of all Jewish holidays: a historical element, an idea and a symbol. He announced his agreement with Lavie that the holiday should be included among the 'sanctified' days of Israel which would be observed in the home. He advocated decoration of homes with greenery and flowers and called for legislating the use of festive lights. Dinaburg quoted Josephus to make the point that the Hanukkah lights symbolized the transition from enslavement to liberation, and from darkness to great light. Perhaps most tellingly, he called for writing a neo-canonical *Megillah* (scroll) of the Liberation of Israel.[37]

There were those in the Knesset and in the press who used the terminology of conventional Jewish holidays, referring to Independence Day not only as *ḥag* (holiday) but specifically as *Yom Tov*, a term traditionally reserved for the three biblical pilgrimage festivals. They also used the term *qedusha* (sanctity).[38] Shlomo Lavie was concerned that the day be proclaimed a 'day of rest', using the positive terminology of *Shabbaton*, replete with the as-

---

[36]*Knesset Proceedings* I:22, 12 Nisan 5709 (11.4.49), 349.

[37]The extent of his intention can be inferred from his attempt to parry the inevitable question regarding the role of God and the mentioning of His name in the document. Dinaburg pre-emptively pointed out that the canonical Scroll of Esther did not contain the name of God. *Knesset Proceedings* I:22, 12 Nisan 5709 (11.4.49), 350-51.

[38]*Knesset Proceedings* I:22, 12 Nisan 5709 (11.4.49), 350-51.

sociations of Yom Kippur, Sabbath and the Sabbatical Year, rather than by means of the negative bureaucratic phrase 'cessation from work'. He felt that this would remove the holiday from its 'profane' sense and place it in the realm of the sanctified.[39]

Both the religious and secular poles of the political spectrum promoted their own visions of the appropriate character for Independence Day. Some Knesset members sought a more clearly religious character for the holiday[40] and in that vein the Chief Rabbinate called for the distribution of gifts to the poor based on the model of Purim.[41] Representing the secular position, Knesset members of the Mapam party advocated the use of the Gregorian date for the holiday, as we have noted above.[42] The reservations expressed by the secular mainstream were of a practical nature. In addition to Lavie's doubt about the possibility of creating the new holiday, we may add Herut party MK Esther Raziel-Naor's admonition 'to be a bit careful so that it not be perceived as artificial ... and capriciously invented'.[43]

The symbolic significance of the consecration of this date is apparent from the Knesset debate held three weeks in advance of the first Independence Day. In response to the proposal that the Prime Minister be entrusted with determining and proclaiming the celebrations of Independence Day, MK Lavie said:

> "In my opinion this matter belongs to the Knesset. The government is an executive body but a holiday for the Jews doesn't depend upon an executive body, it demands the authority of the

---

[39] *Knesset Proceedings* I:23, 13 Nisan 5709 (12.4.49), 356.

[40] MK D.Z. Pinkas, *Knesset Proceedings* I:22, 12 Nisan 5709 (11.4.49), 351.

[41] Communique, CZA, S5/10214. The attitudes of the religious minority are beyond the scope of this paper.

[42] See note 14.

[43] *Knesset Proceedings* I:22, 12 Nisan 5709 (11.4.49), 352. MK Raziel-Naor's use of 'invented' is negative. Presumably she would not have objected to the definition of 'invented' tradition as 'responses to novel situations which take the form of reference to old situations ... [and] ... attempt to establish continuity with a suitable historic past'. E. Hobsbawm and T. Ranger, *Invention of Tradition*, 1-2.

Knesset of Israel. This authority is far greater and stronger than the authority of the government. This very much expresses the sanctification of the holiday, and its cultural content."[44]

Lavie's concern with the authority by which the holiday is declared introduces a parameter in which traditional religion and civil religion differ. Traditional religion finds authority in God, the Sovereign of the Universe, while for civil religion authority rests with the people and stresses their sovereignty. Lavie's preference for the authority of the Knesset over that of the Prime Minister[45] recognized that there had never before been a central Jewish civil polity which consecrated a holiday for the Jewish people outside the biblical and rabbinic traditions. Seeking the highest possible level of authority, he demanded that the holiday be ordained through the due proceedings of the relevant sovereign, which for the corporate entity of Israel, is the Knesset.[46]

Popular Celebration

In the context of sacred time, we now turn our attention to the structuring of Independence Day for the public at large. Here we shall examine issues regarding the public celebrations in the street and family observance in the home. We shall return to examine the ceremonies at Mt. Herzl in our discussion of sacred space.

The celebration in the public space was perceived as essential. For example, Rabbi Sh.Z. Cahana, who felt that in the Diaspora Jews had been forced to celebrate their holidays at home since

---

[44]A correction accepted at the time of voting determined that the Knesset, rather than the Prime Minister, was invested with he authority to proclaim a day of rest for Independence Day. *Knesset Proceedings* 1:23 13 Nissan 5709 (12.4.49), 356-7.

[45]The draft legislation before the Knesset read: 'The *Prime Minister* is authorized to give instructions regarding the flying of flags and the carrying out of public celebrations on Yom Ha'Atsmaut.' *Knesset Proceedings* 1:23 13 Nissan 5709 (12.4.49), 357 (emphasis mine).

[46]In the press Lavie argued that the Knesset could 'impose the holiday on all of Israel'. CZA, S5/10214.

public space was not within their realm, saw public celebrations in the street as representative of sovereign statehood.[47]

Regarding the nature of the public celebrations, there was tension between two different models. Some leaders expressed a desire for spontaneity. Their ideal was visualized as similar to the unplanned outbursts of joy which accompanied the United Nations partition vote on 29 November 1949, announcing the end of the British mandate and the creation of the Jewish State.[48] Others called for more direction, offering two arguments. First was the development that an increasing percentage of Israelis – new immigrants – had not shared the excitement of the partition vote. Nor were they brought up on the singing and dancing common in the cultural reality of the native Israelis and those who had arrived earlier. Second was their desire, as part of the striving to create a neo-traditional Jewish festival, to develop ritual and to have the holiday celebrated in the home as well as on the streets.

In fact, much direction was given from above. In addition to the 1949 law which gave 'instructions regarding the flying of flags and the carrying out of public celebrations on Yom HaᶜAtsmaut',[49] in 1950 the government orchestrated celebrations which included free screenings of films and planned gatherings for children.[50] The striving for ritual and the suggested celebration in the home can be seen as expressions of a tendency to legislate behavior for the occasion. MK Dinaburg had recognized this decision as the Knesset's first step in shaping the cultural image of the State of Israel, a challenge which he was later to take up as Minister of Education.[51] The selection and authorization of symbols by the civil authorities progressed: For example, the government established fixed prices for pictures of Theodore Herzl. In 1951, the government Independence Day Committee issued what Azaryahu

---

[47]M. Azaryahu, *State Cults: Celebrating Independence and Commemorating the Fallen in Israel, 1948-1956* (Hebr.), Sde Boqer 1995, 102.

[48]M. Azaryahu, *State Cults*, 48.

[49]*Knesset Proceedings* 1:23 13 Nissan 5709 (12.4.49), 357.

[50]'On the Holiday of Independence Torches will be raised on Mountain-Tops', *Al HaMishmar*, 27 March 1950, 1, 4.

[51]*Knesset Proceedings* I:22 12 Nisan 5709 (11.4.49), 350.

has called 'a catechism' of uniform slogans to be displayed in public.[52] Similarly, there were discussions regarding the coining of a
unique greeting and response according to the pattern of traditional
greetings for Jewish holidays.[53] The suggestions included: 'Peace to
Israel!' and 'To complete redemption!' To the latter greeting one
was to respond 'Amen. For all Israel'.[54] The most far-reaching proposal came in 1952 when the committee discussed a plan to legislate a requirement to fly the national flag.[55]

It can be easily understood that there was a call amongst some
religious Zionist circles to apply a quasi-*halakhic* approach based
on existing Jewish models which would lay down procedures for
celebrating the holiday at home, in the synagogue and in public.
We have already noted the Chief Rabbinate's suggestion to model
Independence Day on Purim.[56] The adoption by the non-religious
civil authorities of such a traditional model in which specific observances are structured and mandated for the individual is surprising. Nonetheless, there are many examples of ceremonial behavior prescribed by the political, cultural and educational leadership for Independence Day.

These attempts took two inter-connected forms. First we find
menus for the new festival. The idea was first suggested by writer
and folklorist Yom Tov Lewinsky and was based on the model that
each Jewish holiday had its traditional delicacies.[57] Hence, in order
to be accepted into the culinary pattern of the Jewish holidays,
there was a need to create dishes and menus for Independence Day.

---

[52]M. Azaryahu, *State Cults*, 44 The six slogans stressed the national challenges of immigration, absorption and security.

[53]'Greetings and Congratulations', in: *Encyclopaedia Judaica*, VII, Jerusalem 1971, 914-918 includes a table which lists 30 different formulae for
various occasions.

[54]M. Azaryahu, *State Cults*, 98.

[55]M. Azaryahu, *State Cults*, 47. There were voices in the Knesset which
objected to such measures. MK Cohen had complained that it was difficult to
make an Israeli flag and called upon the house to insure that ready-made flags
would be available and inexpensive. *Knesset Proceedings* I:22 12 Nisan 5709
(11.4.49), 352.

[56]See note 41.

[57]M. Azaryahu, *State Cults*, 99.

Some amusing examples include use of the 'Jaffa' orange for which Israeli agriculture was well known, and a seven-species cake which was to be cut into four pieces representing the ingathering of the exiles from the four corners of the earth.[58]

The second element prescribed for home use complements the culinary suggestions. Independence Day *haggadot* were composed for use according to the model of the Passover *seder*. The first, in 1952, was prepared for the army. A second *haggadah* was commissioned by the Independence Day Committee. The intention was that through the combination of newly-traditional foods and an appropriate text, a *seder* ritual like that for Passover would be observed in homes. The committee even sought to coordinate public events so as to leave a free time slot for family celebrations. Among the arrangements intended to strengthen this new tradition was the use of the state radio to broadcast appropriate background music for the dinner-service.[59]

From the above we have seen that the nature of Independence Day was intentionally structured according to reinterpreted motifs of Jewish holidays and practices so as to fit into the Jewish religious calendar in a natural way. Now we shall turn from the examination of Independence Day's celebration to the manner in which it fits into the calendar's underlying conception of time.

Cyclical Time: The Civil High Holidays and Zionist Cosmology

The most intense period in the calendar of Israel's civil religion is that which immediately follows Passover. This season includes the two days of commemoration; Memorial Day for the Holocaust and Heroism (*Yom HaShoah ve-HaGevurah*) and Memorial Day for the Fallen in the Battles of Israel (*Yom HaZikkaron*), and the holiday Independence Day (*Yom Ha'Atsmaut*).

This period comprises what we shall term the 'high holidays' of Israel's civil religious calendar. Passover, the traditional festival of freedom, introduces the entire period. Indeed, as civil re-

---

[58]Made from the seven fruits for which the Land of Israel is praised in Deut 8:8. These examples are taken from M. Azaryahu, *State Cults*, 99-105.

[59]M. Azaryahu, *State Cults*, 105-108.

ligion depends upon traditional religion, the civil period of high
holidays depends upon and emerges out of Passover, the most
widely observed of the traditional Jewish holidays.[60] Whether
transvalued or not, its message serves as a powerful background
to the days which ensue, and to their themes of suffering, liberation and the sacrifice of a transitional generation. This role of
Passover, in the context of the civil religion, is not at all strange if
we recall the strategy of selective adoption in which some elements of tradition are embraced while others passed over.

Memorial Day for the Holocaust and Heroism falls on the 27th
of Nissan, the sixth day following Passover. With this date commences the unfolding of Zionist cosmology.[61] We employ the
long and cumbersome official name, 'Memorial Day for the
Holocaust and Heroism', rather than the popular, shorter 'Holocaust Day', for it is heroism which reveals the day's significance
in terms of the values and symbols venerated in Israel's civil religion. Elaboration would be beyond the scope of the present paper but we may simply note that the very choice of the 27th of
Nissan, a date connected to the Warsaw ghetto uprising, was significant. It was chosen over the 10th of Tevet, a traditional fast
day mourning catastrophe.[62] This choice demonstrates a rejection
of tradition in favor of the Zionist values of activism and heroism.
It is an expression of historical discontinuity and confrontation
between the pre-Zionist era and the present.

---

[60]S. Levy, H. Levinsohn and E. Katz, *Beliefs, Observances and Social Interaction Among Israeli Jews*, Jerusalem 1993, 39-41.

[61]J.E. Young, 'When a Day Remembers: A Performative History of Yom
Hashoah', in: *The Texture of Memory: Holocaust Memorials and Meaning* ,
New Haven/London 1993, 269. See D. Handelman, 'State Ceremonies in
Israel-Remembrance Day and Independence Day', in: *Models and Mirrors:
Towards an Anthropology of Public Events*, Cambridge/New York 1990,
194-199.

[62]Though this date, in addition, is observed and recognized by the state.
Official state posters announce 'יום הקדיש הכללי' (The Day of General Kad-
dish): 'A Time of Remembrance and Communion with the Souls of the
Martyrs of the Shoa' which include a ceremony attended by the President.
See D. Golinkin, 'Yom HaShoah: A Program of Observance', *Conservative
Judaism* 37/4 (1984), 52-3.

Memorial Day for the fallen soldiers and Independence Day which complete this high holiday season[63] fall one week after Memorial Day for the Holocaust and Heroism. The seven day period between two Memorial days corresponds to the traditional Jewish mourning period, the *shivah*, meaning seven. It has often been observed that the bittersweet juxtaposition of the sadness of Memorial Day for fallen soldiers with the euphoria of Independence Day is a common Jewish combination. It is reminiscent of elements such as the remembrance of Jerusalem's destruction at happy occasions or the custom of visiting the cemetery to invite the souls of the departed to participate in a wedding celebration.[64]

In exploring the relationship between the traditional Jewish calendar and that of civil religion, we find that Memorial Day for the fallen soldiers and Independence Day correspond in different ways to both Rosh HaShanah and Yom Kippur. This accord between the civil and traditional calendars does not exhibit a strict one-to-one equivalence, but rather an intertwining of motifs. We shall demonstrate that Independence Day possesses elements akin to both Rosh HaShanah and Yom Kippur. The interconnection of themes is not surprising as until 1951 there was no separate Memorial Day.[65]

Independence Day and Yom Kippur are similar in their central characteristic. Each is the pinnacle of its ritual year and high holi-

---

[63]There are additional dates on the traditional calendar which, like Passover, play significant roles in the civil religion. In addition to Hanukkah which has been mentioned, these include Lag Ba-Omer and, recently, Jerusalem Day. Other minor dates on the calendar of civil religion include commemorations which are not derived from Jewish tradition. These include Tel Ḥai Day (11 Adar, celebrated as Haganah Day in 1948 and 1949) and 20 Tammuz which was Herzl Day for the Zionist movement in the pre-state era and was noted by Israel as State Day (1948) and as Army Day (1949). M. Azaryahu, *State Cults*, 34, 71-3 We shall return to this date below, on page 342.

[64]BT BB 60b. The custom linking the cemetery visit to the wedding festivity was mentioned by MK Shmuel Dayan (Mapai) in the Knesset discussion regarding the first Independence Day. He was calling for including an element of memorial in the program for Independence Day. *Proceedings* I:22, (11 April/12 Nissan 1949), 353.

[65]M. Azaryahu, *State Cults*, 64.

day season. Yom Kippur and Independence Day are the dates when the paramount ceremony associated with the relevant central mountain-top shrine is conducted. For Yom Kippur this is the sacrificial order and scapegoat ritual at the Temple, and for Independence Day it is the torch lighting ceremony at Mt. Herzl, to which we shall return. In both cases the figure at the apex of protocol presides over the ceremony, the High Priest in the Temple or the Chairman of the Knesset at Mt. Herzl, each as representative of the people.[66]

On the symbolic and spiritual level there were those who thought other parallels ought to be introduced. In the discussions of the Knesset preceding the first Independence Day, Yizhar Harari, chairman of the Knesset Committee, said 'This holiday should be a day of soul searching'.[67] This term applies equally well to Rosh HaShanah, as it does to Yom Kippur, but the point of comparison is the similarity of theme to be found in the tradition and in civil religion.

Several additional analogies may be noted regarding the two pairs of days: Rosh HaShanah / Yom Kippur and Memorial Day / Independence Day. First in terms of nomenclature: Both Rosh HaShanah and Independence Day have multiple names. For Rosh HaShanah we find יום תרועה (*Yom Teru'ah,* day of shofar sounding) as well as יום הזיכרון (*Yom HaZikkaron,* Memorial Day). [68] Hence, in both calendars the penultimate date bears the name *Yom HaZik-*

---

[66]The Chairman of the Knesset is not actually at the peak of protocol. The President is, of course, Head of State. Nonetheless the Chairman, as head of the legislature, represents the people via a more directly democratic process. This may be likened to that of the High Priest in the late Second Temple period whose role was to represent the people. In the context of Yom Kippur, the High Priest 'makes expiation for himself and his household, and for the whole congregation of Israel' (Lev 16:17). Handelman and Katz have referred to the Chairman ('Speaker') as 'the first citizen of [the] democratically elected parliament'. D. Handelman and E. Katz, 'State Ceremonies of Israel-Remembrance Day and Independence Day', in: D. *Handelman, Models and Mirrors: Towards an Anthropology of Public Events*, Cambridge, 1990, 215. See also page 206.

[67]*Knesset Proceedings* I : 23, 13 Nisan 5709 (12.4.49), 357.

[68]Num 29:1, Lev 23:24.

karon. Not only does the name Memorial Day yield a parallel, *Yom Teru'ah* does as well. As the name indicates, the sounding of the shofar is one of the major characteristics of Rosh HaShanah. Similarly, the sounding of the siren (evening and morning) is the telltale sign of Memorial Day. As is the case with many Jewish holidays, different names stress different aspects, whether historical or agricultural. Independence Day was also referred to by different names by those stressing different aspects. We have already noted that יום העצמאות (Independence Day) was referred to as יום הקוממיות (Day of Upright Standing) in the original draft of the Knesset Law.[69] The first celebrations of independence, albeit not yet on the 5th of Iyyar but on the 20th of Tammuz in 1948, were called יום המדינה (State Day). MK Y. Gil suggested that Independence Day itself be called by that name and MK B. Dinaburg referred to it as חג השחרור (Holiday of Liberation).[70]

Lastly we may point out that before the establishment of a regular Memorial Day for fallen soldiers, the commemorative element was subsumed into the rituals of Independence Day. This is reminiscent of the *Yizkor* (remembrance service), which is one of the trademarks of Yom Kippur, as well as of the pilgrimage festivals.

---

[69]*Knesset Proceedings* I:22 12 Nisan 5709 (11.4.49), 349. The term קוממיות (erect, upright standing) is based on the biblical usage 'I am the Lord your God who brought you out from the land of the Egyptians to be their slaves no more, who broke the bars of your yoke and made you walk erect'. (Lev 26:13 emphasis mine). Ben-Gurion preferred this name as its resonance from the prayer book indicated an end to the exile: '... and break our yoke [of Diaspora] from our necks and speedily bring us, *standing erect*, to our land.'

[70]*Knesset Proceedings* I:22, 12 Nisan 5709 (11.4.49), 350.

Linear Time: The Creation Motif

Both Independence Day and Rosh HaShanah mark beginning points. Rosh HaShanah is the anniversary of the creation of the world, as stated several times in the liturgy of the day: היום הרת עולם (the world was born today). The Jewish calendar symbolically measures time from this point. Likewise, Independence Day marks the creation of the state. As Azaryahu has pointed out, the establishment of the state was a transition *ex nihilo* from a state of chaos to a state of order,[71] to both a 'state' of sovereignty and to a geo-political state.

The creation of the state marked a discontinuity in history, the beginning of a new epoch which dictated a new reckoning of time. From independence, a new linear calendar began with its absolute zero anchored at the declaration of the state on the 5th of Iyyar 5708 (May 15 1948). A strong sense of this new era is conveyed by a newspaper headline which accompanied the declaration of independence proclaiming the event as: 'zero-hour in Tel Aviv'.[72]

While the use of the reinterpreted creation motif links Independence Day and Rosh Hashanah, this same theme was the subject of confrontation with the tradition. The gap between the approach of traditional Judaism and that of the civil religion can be seen in the distinction between the model of creation by Divine fiat and that of human action in the creation of the state. The Zionist cosmogony which saw in the establishment of the State of Israel the creation of a new Jewish world emphasized that this was achieved through the work of flesh and blood. The choice of the 5th of Iyyar as Independence Day accentuated the role of human action in the attainment of independence.

Several alternative dates might have become the national day for the State of Israel. These included the 2nd of November, the anniversary of the Balfour declaration, the 29th of November, the United Nation's 1947 decision to create the state, Hanukkah, the

---

[71]M. Azaryahu, *State Cults*, 22, 59.
[72]M. Azaryahu, *State Cults*, 22, n.5. From this point of reckoning commences the era of the State of Israel which, on occasion, it is to be found in parallel use to other systems of numbering the years.

thematically appropriate festival of liberation which fell nine days later in 1947, Tel Ḥai Day, the 11th of Adar which, since 1920, commemorated Zionist heroism and the 20th of Tammuz, the date of Herzl's death and pre-State holiday of the Zionist movement.[73] Adoption of this last date as the national day would have offered the greatest degree of continuity with the then current practice. But rather than any of these dates, the 5th of Iyyar was chosen – the anniversary of the declaration of the state. This act, in distinction to all of those commemorated by the other days, was an exclusively positive symbol which stressed the activism of the Zionist movement.[74] The symbol chosen for the national day was not one of heroism, with the attendant reminder of vulnerability (as in the incident at Tel Ḥai) nor one of passivity (the receiving of a charter by the global powers), but rather purely positive action by the People's Assembly – the declaration of independence.

Sacred Space – Mount Herzl and Its Rituals

As Charles S. Kamen has noted, 'new rituals are often introduced to mark the establishment of the new order ...'.[75] From the perspective of the calendar of Israel's civil religion, it is appropriate to turn not only to Mt. Herzl – the site – but first and foremost to that which transpires there: ritual.[76]

The Torch Lighting Ceremony

Since the early years of the state, the major ceremony for Independence Day was the torch-lighting at Mt. Herzl. This came to

---

[73] D. Handelman & E. Katz, 'State Ceremonies of Israel', 195; M. Azaryahu, *State Cults*, 20-21.

[74] M. Azaryahu, *State Cults*, 22.

[75] C.S. Kamen, 'Affirmation or Enjoyment? The Commemoration of Independence in Israel', *Jewish Journal of Sociology* 19/1 (1977) 5.

[76] See D. Handelman & E. Katz, 'State Ceremonies in Israel' for a discussion of this ceremony in great anthropological detail. Here I shall concentrate on analysis of religious symbolism.

include commemoration of fallen soldiers, cannon fire, a speech, a marathon run culminating in Jerusalem and military parades and displays.[77] The torch lighting ceremony which takes place at Mt. Herzl is both the oldest (dating from the very first Independence Day celebration at Mt. Herzl in 1950) and the most widely known. Indeed today, the ceremonies at Mt. Herzl which include many of the elements enumerated above are commonly referred to as 'the ceremony of the lighting of the torches on Mt. Herzl'. Special attention to the central, formal ceremony at Mt. Herzl is justified, for as Kamen's sociological research regarding the public's attitude toward Independence Day has shown: 'Only the ceremony proclaiming the holiday [at Mt. Herzl] is perceived as being part of the tradition'.[78]

The elemental use of light and fire signifies redemption, heroism and power as well as creation.[79] The commencement of a national holiday with the kindling of a torch is clearly similar to the candles with which the Sabbath and traditional holidays are welcomed. The traditional blessing is, of course, replaced with a secular formula.[80]

Until 1952, the torch-lighting consisted of the Knesset Chairman's igniting of a single torch. Recalling Shlomo Lavie's call for the ordination of Independence Day by the Knesset we are reminded that this ritual act signifies the sovereignty of the Knesset. This act, performed at the central shrine of Zionism and the State of Israel, drives home the characteristics of civil religion observed by

---

[77]Letter from Y. Sternber, secretary of the Yom Ha'Atsmaut Committee to Dr. Lauterbach, President of the Executive of the World Zionist Organisation (1.3.51) with details of celebrations.

CZA, S5/10216. Other non-ritual conventions observed on Independence Day include the World Bible Quiz and the awarding of the Israel Prize for outstanding achievements.

[78]C.S. Kamen, 'Commemoration of Independence in Israel', 18 n.15.

[79]D. Handelman and E. Katz refer to the 'polysemic qualities of fire'. 'State Ceremonies in Israel', 223.

[80]The formula is of the form: 'I [name] representing [biographical details] ... light this beacon for the glory of the state of Israel.' The replacement of a blessing with such a formula is an excellent example of selective adoption while the entire ceremony embodies reinterpretation.

Liebman and Don-Yehiya namely that 'at the core stands a corporate entity rather than a transcendent power', which involves 'the
transfer of ultimate authority from God to society'.[81] With Chairman Yosef Sprinzak's lighting of the torch at Mt. Herzl on Independence Day 1950, the sovereign people consecrated its temple.

Hanukkah and the Symbol of Light

The popularly perceived themes and symbols of Hanukkah – a
military struggle, freedom, rededication and light – were to be of
great significance in the development of the Independence Day
rituals. The torch lighting had evolved out of spontaneous popular
custom observed already on Independence Day of May 1949, even
before Mt. Herzl was inaugurated with Theodore Herzl's re-
interment on 17 August 1949.[82] The early use of torches continued
on Hanukkah of 1949 when Gadna members (the army youth
movement) ran with torches from sites of Israel's heroism, past and
present, to Mt. Herzl where a giant Hanukkah lamp was lit. This
was conceived as part of the 'central celebrations of [Jerusalem as]
the renewed capital',[83] a motif quite close to that of the *Hanukkah*
(rededication) of the Temple. Independence Day of 1950 was the
first to be celebrated at Mt. Herzl. Its torch-lighting ritual was
something of a mirror image of the Hanukkah observance. While
runners continued the custom of the marathon run to Jerusalem,[84]
the torch element was changed in a way which introduced new
symbolism. After the Chairman of the Knesset lit the central torch
on Mt. Herzl, the signal was given for the Gadna youth to light
torches in settlements throughout the State.[85] In this way the lights

---

[81]C. Liebman & E. Don-Yehiya, *Civil Religion in Israel*, 4-5. See D. Handelman & E. Katz, 'State Ceremonies in Israel', 216.

[82]M. Azaryahu, *State Cults*, 57.

[83]M. Azaryahu, *State Cults*, 58.

[84]The race commenced in Jaffa. ISA, G 5367 file 204. While the marathon
run may have been similar to the ancient Greek practice, in the Israeli case
the torches were not carried from point to point in a linear fashion but dis-
persed from a central locus.

[85]Letter from Mordekhai Maklef, Deputy Chief of Staff, 5.3.50. ISA, G

did not arrive at Mt. Herzl but emanated from it. The press noted the parallel to an ancient custom inherent in the signaling for nation-wide torch lighting being given from Mt. Herzl.[86] This is the practice of Second Temple times in which, following the arrival of witnesses of the new moon to give testimony in Jerusalem, the word of the court sanctifying the month emanated from the Temple, to the Mount of Olives, to Sartaba and from there towards the Diaspora.[87]

The Ingathering of the Exiles

The nation-wide torch lighting was discontinued after 1955,[88] having been eclipsed by a 1952 innovation which modified the ceremony. The ceremony was expanded beyond the lighting of a single flame by the Chairman of the Knesset with the addition of the lighting of twelve torches by citizens representing various elements of society. Here too we see the symbolism of the collective body politic as the expression of sovereignty, but there is an additional symbol which has been introduced, that of the ingathering of the exiles. By 1952, the population of the five year old state had doubled. Mass immigration was one of the strongest characteristics of the period and its encouragement was a highly cherished value. The twelve torches – symbols representing the twelve tribes – and those who lit them as they stood in front of the tribes' emblems, symbolized the re-gathered tribes of Israel.[89]

5367 file 204 and letter from Independence Day Committee to World Zionist Organisation, CZA, S5/10215.

[86]*Al HaMishmar* 27.3.50 (and *HaAretz* of the same date) described the torches as being 'according to the tradition of the days of the Second Temple ... harbingers of the sanctification of the holiday of Independence (Ḥag Ha-ʿAtsmaut).' CZA, S5/10215. Many government documents mention this comparison as well ISA, G 5367 file 204.

[87]MRH 2:4. We have noted the Diaspora's dependence upon Israel for the fixing of Independence Day. Had the pantheon been erected on Mt. Scopus (according to the wishes of Menahem Ussishkin – see note 98) then this torch ceremony might actually have taken place on Mt. Scopus as well.

[88]M. Azaryahu, *State Cults*, 60.

[89]Symbolizing connection to the 'mythic collective', according to

On the 20th of Tammuz (Herzl's *Jahrzeit*) of 1948 and 1949 an additional holiday was celebrated, The Day of the Ingathering of the Exiles.[90] On this date in 1950, the Knesset passed the Law of Return guaranteeing free immigration and citizenship for Jews coming to Israel.[91] These special celebrations lasted only three years. Subsequently, the theme of mass immigration was introduced into Independence Day.[92] In 1950, an official holiday leaflet included the text of the Declaration of Independence, symbols of the state and the army and various texts amongst which was: 'The Ingathering of the Exiles is as great as the day upon which the heavens and earth were created'.[93] The use of this phrase sought to unite the ingathering of the exiles with the theme of creation.

Music and Marching

During the lighting of the twelve torches, a choir sings a medley of background music. The theme song has often been: *We Are Carrying Torches*. This is a Hanukkah song, praising light, which proudly proclaims in its chorus 'There was no miracle; we found no cruise of oil!' Its inclusion clearly emphasizes the rejection of Divinely wrought miracles and embraces the concept of human activism. More than a song, this piece is really a military march and that is precisely what ensues.

Azaryahu, *State Cults*, 60. See D. Handelman & E. Katz, 'State Ceremonies in Israel', 219-220.

[90] in addition to State Day and Army Day. See note 64.

[91] M. Azaryahu, *State Cults*, 34.

[92] From 1950 the calendar of events was pared down. These additional holidays disappeared (and others became extremely minor; see note 63) and Independence Day, along with Holocaust Day and Memorial Day, became the only widely noted non traditionally religious dates on the civil calendar. See Azaryahu, *State Cults,* 34.

[93] ISA, G 5367 file 204. The text itself is from BT Pes 88a. The ingathering of the exiles has remained a prominent theme of the ceremony. D. Handelman & E. Katz, 'State Ceremonies in Israel', 216.

The military parade through the streets, which had been a feature of the day-time festivities of Independence Day until 1969,[94]
did not continue into the 1970s. At that time, an exercise of military formation marching was added to the ceremony at Mt. Herzl.
This march, in full dress uniform and with the flags of the army's
various units, adds pageantry to the ceremony and provides what
is perceived as a link to the military legacy of the Maccabees.[95] In
these elements of Hanukkah, we have observed the selective
adoption of the elements of light, dedication and military heroism
and the rejection of the miraculous.

The Glory of the Military and the Sanctification of Death

Two aspects of the Mt. Herzl complex and the ceremony there
might seem to detract from the aptness of the civil religion model.
These are the military and death. We shall see that when understood in context they prove to be consonant with this perception.

One of the most outstanding aspects of the ceremonies of Independence Day, and the very essence of Memorial Day, is the
military. As we have noted, the army is a prominent feature in the
ceremony. While the marching dates only from the 1970s, it was
preceded, as early as 1951, by cannon fire.[96] In the context of
Jewish tradition, the military and instruments of war would be out
of place at a holy shrine. The disparity is illustrated by a passage
in the Mekhilta on the verse from Exod 20:25: 'And if you make
for Me an altar of stones, do not build it of hewn stones; for by
wielding your tool upon them you have profaned them'. In the
Midrash we read:

> In this connection Rabbi Simeon b. Eleazar used to say, "The altar
> is made to prolong the years of man and iron is made to shorten

[94]In the first years of the state the military march took place on 20 Tammuz. See note 63.

[95]This association was certainly in keeping with Herzl's statement with
which he concluded *The Jewish State*: 'The Maccabees shall rise again'. See
also note 29.

[96]M. Azaryahu, *State Cults*, 58.

the years of man. It is not right for that which shortens life to be lifted against that which prolongs life."[97]

The parallel to Herzl's tomb is persuasive, as the appearance of the tombstone – a low, black obelisk – is indeed that of a rectangular altar.

The second seemingly incongruous element is death. One of the most serious considerations pertaining to entry into the Temple precincts is that of ritual impurity derived from contact with the dead. As opposed to the absolute taboo on contact with death at the Temple, death is ubiquitous at the mount of Herzl's grave. In addition to Herzl, leaders of the state and the Zionist movement and thousands of soldiers are buried on this mountain.

The presence of both the military and death at Mt. Herzl and in its rituals can be understood when seen in the context of the values system of Israel's civil religion which stresses the pivotal role of people rather than of God. The key themes and values of heroism, bravery and the attainment and preservation of independence demand the prominent presence of the instrument of much of this: the army. The carrying of arms or the fire of cannons, and their presence at this grave-shrine, indicate their centrality.

We can best understand Mt. Herzl in this sense by seeing it as a pantheon.[98] With the human-centered, activist ideologies of

---

[97] *Mekhilta de R. Ishmael, Baḥodesh* 11, (Translation Lauterbach, 290).

[98] The concept of a national pantheon was articulated by Menahem Ussishkin in the 1930s and abortively implemented with the reburial of Dr. Y.L. Pinsker in Nicanor's cave on Mt. Scopus in 1934. See B.Z. Michaeli, 'The Pantheon which Never Arose' (Hebr.), *Et-mol: Journal of the History of the Land and People of Israel*, 15 (1989) 14-15. The term 'pantheon' is mentioned in the memorandum of the committee to implement the decisions of the Zionist Congresses to bring Herzl's body for burial in Israel. *Die Frage der Überführung der Gebeine Herzl's nach Erez-Israel*, CZA, J95/249. The association with the Roman Pantheon is strengthened by considering the design for the dome which was to be built over the tomb. Joseph Klarwein's winning 1951 plan was cited for 'the excellent use made of the *light penetrating into the Tomb from above*'. Joseph Weitz, Mount Herzl, Jerusalem 1968, in CZA, 30.608, n.p. (emphasis mine). The 'light penetrating ... from above' is reminiscent of the oculus of Hadrian's Pantheon in Rome. It seems that the

Zionism having blurred the distinction between man's and God's role in history, the Greek term *pantheon*, all gods, can reasonably be understood to encompass Herzl and all the political and military heroes honorably buried nearby.

Even more important than explaining the presence of death is understanding its elevation to a higher level, that of sacrifice. The Temple was of course the site to which Jews brought their sacrifices. Mt. Herzl, this time actually its northern slope which comprises the military cemetery, is the resting place of those who are themselves often regarded as sacrifices.[99] President Shazar, on Memorial Day 1969, spoke of 'those who *gave their life for* our freedom and [the] release of *our souls* ... their *pure sacrifice* will be accepted, forever and ever'.[100] We may note that his use of the term sacrifice through death – which he associates with purity, not impurity – goes so far as to include the idea of substitution. Just as a sacrifice stands in lieu of and redeems the one who brings it so those who fell 'gave their life for ... our souls'.

The 'Temple' in Political Service

Since the 1950s it has occasionally been the custom for foreign dignitaries on state visits to Israel to pay their respects at Herzl's tomb. At times, as part of these visits, the ceremonies included the planting of a cedar tree near the plaza surrounding Herzl's grave. This ceremony, which is not a necessary element of the

---

irony of this shrine of independence resonating with the image of a structure ascribed to the emperor who put an end to the Jewish dreams of independence was not noted.

[99]Hobsbawm has noted that 'temples for offerings' are part of the 'powerful ritual complex formed round these occasions'. E. Hobsbawm & T. Ranger (eds), *The Invention of Tradition*, 6. W.L. Warner has noted the role of sacrifice in American civil religion as well. 'An American Sacred Ceremony', 93.

[100]D. Handelman and E. Katz, 'State Ceremonies in Israel', 205 (emphasis mine). Handelman and Katz suggest that while Shazar used the term הטהור קרבנם (their pure sacrifice) his association was with קרבן עולה (the wholly consumed sacrifice which 'ascends'), n.26.

Foreign Ministry's protocol,[101] is not unlike other nations' ceremonies in which diplomatic visitors pay their respects at the
Tomb of the Unknown Soldier. As Israel has no such tomb, it
may be posited that Herzl's grave functions in this capacity. The
bringing of Herzl for re-burial in Jerusalem is not unlike 'the idea
of bringing home an unknown soldier from the battlefield to the
capital to bury him in its *most important national shrine'*.[102] Of
course Herzl was not unknown – quite the contrary – and he was
brought in accordance with his own last testament. Herzl was not
brought *to* the shrine but rather *brought about* the shrine by his
presence. Despite the differences, Herzl's tomb indeed constitutes
Israel's 'most important national [civil] shrine'. As for the tree-
planting ceremony by representatives of foreign nations, this may
be seen as corresponding to the 'well attested fact ... [of the way]
Gentiles participated in Temple worship at Jerusalem ... [as] ... *an
act of courtesy towards the nation* or city'.[103] While the paying of
respects or tree planting is not similar to the Gentile participation
in Temple worship, it does demonstrate the recognition of this
site's significance, even by those outside Israel. The role of the
tomb-side ceremony in Israel's protocol does function as 'an act
of courtesy towards the nation'. Protocol, like ceremony, is part
of the cult of the civil religion.

Conclusion

The above evidence demonstrates that the forms advocated and
the religious motifs and mechanisms adopted were the result of
purposeful intention on the part of those responsible for legislating and implementing national symbols and rituals. Our best

---

[101]Personal communication from Ambassador Yakov Aviad, former Head
of Protocol of the Foreign Ministry, 14.8.96.

[102]G. Mosse, *Fallen Soldiers: Reshaping the Memory of the World Wars*,
Oxford 1990, 94 (emphasis mine).

[103]E. Schürer, *The History of the Jewish People in the Age of Jesus Christ*,
G. Vermes and F. Millar (eds), Edinburgh 1973, II.309 (emphasis mine).

sources for the thoughts and goals chosen as the elements of Independence Day are the debates in the Knesset in which the government ministers and members of the parliament expressed their visions. The many examples and high degree of correlation between elements of the civil religion and expressions of traditional Judaism are neither coincidental nor trivial.

Civil religion develops in a complex and nuanced dialogue of deliberation which yields a dynamic tradition with a force of its own. The political and cultural elites were unsuccessful in dictating the character of the observance of Independence Day. Many of the elements which were suggested or presented to the people were rejected, including the foods, greetings, slogans and the *seder* ritual. The prerogative of the corporate entity to decide – to express its sovereignty in the cultural realm – is characteristic of the system in which the civil religion operates: democracy. This very sovereignty thwarted the plans of some of the leadership to control and shape new ritual.

Examination of those elements accepted as against those rejected indicates that those in the public-ceremonial realm became established. Conversely, despite the attempts to create Independence Day in the mold of traditional Jewish holidays, practice in the home was not successfully inculcated. The window of opportunity was too small and the diversity of the population too great for all-encompassing acceptance of a ramified set of holiday rituals to take hold throughout the nation.

Not all that was desired remained unattained. While government officials of the 1950s complained of their failure to see the country draped in blue and white flags, their fears proved to be unwarranted. Today the approach of the high holiday season of the civil religious calendar can be perceived by the appearance of flags on homes and automobiles.

Observance of Independence Day is diverse. Only a small fraction of the population attends the ceremony at Mt. Herzl, though many more watch it on television. Some pray in synagogues and others celebrate with festive meals and parties (though most without the *haggadah*). A great many young Israelis walk the crowded streets for hours. Walking in the streets has been described as 'aimless wandering by people who don't know what to do, but *feel they have to* be out doing it'.[104] The broad consensus that Independence Day must be noted and celebrated indicates its acceptance as a festival as 'it is only a collective sense of ritual and meaning – a shared norm – which makes a holiday more than just a day off ...'.[105]

In conclusion we may say that when David Wolffsohn, the second president of the World Zionist Organization and Herzl's scion, eulogized Herzl in Vienna in 1904, with the words: '... we swear to you that we will keep your name *sacred* and that it will remain unforgotten...',[106] he could not have known how right he would prove to be.

---

[104]C.S. Kamen, 'The Commemoration of Independence in Israel', 18 n.13 (emphasis mine).

[105]C.S. Kamen, 'The Commemoration', 19 n.26.

[106]E. Pawel, *The Labyrinth of Exile: A Life of Theodor Herzl*, London 1990, 531 (emphasis mine).

A RACHEL FOR EVERYONE:
THE KINNERET CEMETERY
AS A SITE OF CIVIL PILGRIMAGE[1]

Amos Ron

Introduction

The focus of this article is on the making and the using of symbolic landscapes of modern Zionism in the Sea of Galilee region, and especially the Kinneret cemetery. During the period known in Jewish historiography as the Second Aliyah (1904-1914), small groups of young Jewish immigrants established agricultural settlements at the south-west corner of the Sea of Galilee. Among these settlements was Degania A (established in 1910), later known to be the first kibbutz in the world. Many of these immigrants (more known as 'the pioneers') were buried, when their time came, at the Kinneret cemetery, and are now frequently visited by those who regard them as 'founding fathers' (and mothers) of contemporary Israeli society.

Theoretical Background

The term 'symbolic landscapes' is widely used by cultural geographers and other social scientists; such landscapes are places, or sites where ideologies, values, emotions and other subjective aspects of our lives, are manifested.[2]

---

[1] This article is based mainly on my Ph.D. dissertation in Cultural Geography on the spatial commemoration of pioneers in the Sea of Galilee region.

[2] Erik Cohen, for example, claims that the symbolic orientation to the landscape "...relates to the environment in terms of its symbolic significance for an individual, a group, or a society." E. Cohen, 'Environmental Orientations:

Donald Meinig was one of the first geographers to realize that these landscapes are usually ordinary everyday places that share a common meaning and symbolism for a particular group of people.[3] According to Meinig, 'Every mature nation has its symbolic landscapes. They are part of the iconography of nationhood, part of the shared set of ideas and memories and feelings which bind a people together.'[4]

There are times when these sites are intentionally established as symbolic, or representational landscapes – as is the case with most monuments and memorials; but quite commonly, these representational landscapes are ordinary rural homes which were later restored, and have become small, local historical museums narrating a history of a group of people. I am deliberately using here the words 'a history', and not 'the history', because research shows that quite often these museums present and re-present different narratives, or versions of what 'really' happened.

The renowned American geographer, J.B. Jackson, calls such landscapes 'born-again landscapes'.[5] This term is of prime significance and interest, because of its double meaning. On the one hand it is a restored, or renovated landscape, but the term 'born-again' is used for describing a person (usually a Christian) experiencing for the first time 'real' salvation, and thus adopting some of his/her collective past. The term 'born-again landscape' thus designates a bridge between the past and the future; the context of a born-again landscape is that of a return to the previously taken-for-granted sources and roots. In a born-again landscape a person re-lives his/her past and heritage – even if he or she is there for the first time – and at the same time attributes new and more updated and relevant meanings to this heritage.

A Multidimensional Approach to Social Ecology', *Current Anthropology* 17 (1976) 49-70, at 56.

[3]D. Meinig, 'Symbolic Landscapes – Models of American Community', in: D. Meinig, (ed.), *The Interpretation of Ordinary Landscapes*, New York/Oxford 1979, 164-192.

[4]D. Meinig, 'Symbolic Landscapes', 164.

[5]J.B. Jackson, 'The Necessity for Ruins', in: J.B. Jackson, *The Necessity for Ruins and other Topics*, Amherst 1980, 89-102.

The symbolic meanings of landscapes are often hidden to us, the observers; in order to understand these underlying layers of significance, we should employ qualitative methods as well; the method suggested here is known as 'the interpretation of landscape'. One of the basic axioms of this method is that landscapes can be regarded as texts as well, and thus, can be interpreted by using methods that are more common in academic disciplines such as theology and history.

The Kinneret Cemetery

The Kinneret cemetery is one of the most pivotal representational landscapes in Israel. Officially, the cemetery serves as a burial site for the inhabitants of the two Kinneret settlements – the kibbutz (founded in 1914) and the moshava (founded in 1908).[6] However, many other Jewish pioneers and non-pioneers are buried there as well, and the place is unofficially named 'The Pantheon of the Labour Party'. Despite its secular appearance and origin, and despite the relatively non-religious background of the majority of the pioneers buried there, as well as those who visit them, the cemetery functions as a holy site and as a central place of pilgrimage in contemporary Israeli civil religion.

A visit to this cemetery can be a powerful way to link up to these founding figures. On a visual-descriptive level, the visitor can learn while visiting about the sequence of the events in the lives of the pioneers. But on a different and deeper level the Kinneret cemetery can teach us (both readers and visitors) a great deal about those buried there, and those visiting them. The relative location of the tombstones, their outer appearance and inscriptions are important in the process of decoding the site and its hidden meanings. The experiences of the visitors at the site – as expressed through questionnaires and personal interviews – are

---

[6]Both are agricultural settlements, but the kibbutz is a communal way of life, whereas the moshava consists of several privately owned small farms.

also a true and deep reflection of the symbolic meanings of this cemetery.

The Cemetery as Text: Burial Customs and the Pioneers

A close look at the cemetery, and especially the earlier tomb-stones, suggests that the pioneers did not follow many of the normative Jewish burial customs:

* The orientation of the graves: In a traditional Jewish cemetery the graves face Jerusalem. In the Kinneret cemetery the early graves face all directions.
* Open top: In a traditional Jewish cemetery the top of the tomb-stones is always closed. Some of the early tombstones at the Kin-neret cemetery have an open top.
* The writing on the tombstones: The traditional Jewish cemetery is not very liberal with the formulas of writing on the tombstones, and variations are few. In the early tombstones of the Kinneret cemetery the common writing formulas[7] hardly exist.
* Vegetation: Traditional Jewish cemeteries have no vegetation be-cause of potential impurity. The Kinneret cemetery is in a lovely tropical garden setting.
* Suicide: Since Judaism forbids the act of suicide, those who commit suicide are buried outside the cemetery. In the Kinneret cemetery there is no such distinction until this day.
* Relative location of graves: In a traditional Jewish cemetery the graves are arranged according to the chronological order of the burial; the only exceptions are family relatives who expressed their desire to be buried near their beloved ones when the time will come. In the Kinneret cemetery there is no such chronological order, and in certain cases the adjacent graves indicate a time dif-ference of several years.

---

[7] תנצב"ה (may his soul be bound among the bundle of the living), פ"נ (here lies …).

* Burial in a coffin: Burial customs in Judaism do not include the use of coffins, in accordance with the verse 'for dust thou art, and unto dust shalt thou return' (Gen 3:19). According to Ram Nissan, some of the earlier burials were in coffins.[8]
* The ceremony: The traditional Jewish burial ceremony includes eulogies and prayers ('Kaddish' and 'El Male Rahamim'). According to Nissan, the burial ceremonies in the early years of the settlements included eulogies and long silences. [9]

The Cemetery as Text: Spatial Order and the Pioneers

As mentioned above, in a traditional cemetery the location of the graves is determined according to a chronological order. In the Kinneret cemetery the reasons for the location of the graves seems to be of a completely different order. The time difference between adjacent graves can reach half a century; possibly, the relative location reflects the inner social order of the two communities.

As an example, the graves of three pioneers, Leah Meron (died 1976), Sarah Shmuckler (died 1919) and Berl Katzanelson (died 1944), are placed in a separate group, one next to the other.[10] Berl Katzanelson became in later years a political leader and a founder and editor of an influential (then) daily newspaper (Davar). From various historical sources we learn that choosing between the two women, Sarah and Leah, was indeed a very difficult task for him, and only Sarah's death (from malaria, while draining a swamp) enabled him to marry Leah.[11] With Berl's grave in the middle, surrounded by the two women, the relative position of the three graves reflects the dramas of their lives.

---

[8]R. Nissan, *The Sanctification of Space: How is the Holy Represented in the Kinneret Cemetery, a seminar paper presented to Dr. Yoram Bilu & Dr. Eyal Ben-Ari*, Dep. of Sociology & Social Anthropology, the Hebrew University of Jerusalem, Unpublished Manuscript (Hebr).

[9]Ibid.

[10]Nissan lists four other examples (ibid.).

[11]A. Shapira, *Berl – A Biography* (Hebr), Tel Aviv 1980.

Photograph No. 1: the graves of Berl Katzanelson,
Leah Meron & Sarah Shmuckler

The Visitors

During field work that took place at the cemetery (and in two other nearby heritage sites) in the spring of 1995, questionnaires were handed out to 104 visitors.[12] The social profile of these visitors includes only Israeli Jews. The main categories observed were: non-religious school children, members of youth movements, Jews of Yemenite origin, and settlers from the West Bank and the Gaza Strip. The youth movement members and the school children were there in the framework of educational activities very common in the Jewish-Israeli society, i.e. tours to heritage sites;[13] the Yemenite Jews were there because some of their an-

---

[12] Thirty four questionnaires were circulated among visitors to the cemetery; the remaining questionnaires were circulated among visitors to the Kinneret Courtyard and the historical museum at Moshavat Kinneret.

[13] See for example: S. Katz, 'The Israeli Teacher-Guide: The Emergence and Perpetuation of a Role', *Annals of Tourism Research* 12 (1985) 49-72; T.

cestors, who made an unsuccessful attempt to settle there at the
beginning of the century, are buried there.[14] The social categories
missing from the cemetery include foreign tourists (both Jews and
non-Jews), Arabs and ultra-orthodox Jews.

The Visit as Pilgrimage

One of the ways to decipher the sacred nature of this civil cemetery is by relating to the experiences of the visitors at the site. The
results of our research indicate that in most cases a visit to the
modern heritage sites in the region includes a visit to the cemetery
as well;[15] this is where many of them reach a highly-emotional
reaction. Many save the visit to the end of the day. An analysis of
questionnaires filled out by visitors suggests that the visit is perceived as an uplifting emotional and spiritual experience, or in the
words of one visitor: "The combination of a cemetery, the poetry
of Rachel, the exotic vegetation, the Kinneret lake and the mountains across – creates a very special and enchanted microcosmos."

In analyzing the questionnaires – a distinction was made between those that came to seek a personal refuge, and those that
stated collective-ideological reasons for their visit. For example,
one visitor claims that she comes to the cemetery every week to
visit her mother, who is buried there. The mother was not a pioneer at all; she was a city woman of a Swiss origin that lived in
the nearby city of Tiberias. According to the daughter, her mother
used to come to the cemetery from Tiberias whenever 'things got
too rough' in her life, and the place itself had a calming effect on
her.

Katriel, 'Touring The Land: Trips and Hiking as Secular Pilgrimages in Israeli Culture', *Jewish Folklore & Ethnology Review* 17 (1995) 6-13.

[14]The most detailed and most recent account of the Yemenites' settling
was written by Y. Nini, *The Yemenites of Kinneret – The Story of their Settling and Deportation 1912-1930* (Hebr), Tel Aviv 1996.

[15]Out of 70 questionnaires that were circulated among visitors to the other
two sites – 56 (80%) answered that their visit includes a visit to the cemetery.

The second category, those that come for a collective-ideological reason, includes Jewish settlers from the West Bank and the Gaza Strip. One of them, about forty years of age, wrote in his questionnaire of April 1995: "We, the inhabitants of Net-zarim, in the middle of the Gaza strip, are in the midst of the po-litical storm. To me, the graves with the inscriptions on them cry from the ground to us:[16] continue our works, make roots and sprouts everywhere in this land, even when difficult. Do not let certain words or phrases like Zionism, Judaism, 'Love of the Land' and Hebrew fade. We will try, in our own way, to do the utmost, in this direction. And even if nowadays there are some that do not understand it, a day will come when they will under-stand, just as once upon a time the Tel-Ḥai settlers were asked to desert their settlement,[17] and later it became a symbol and an ex-ample." Later I heard this settler explain to his seven children by the grave of Berl Katzanelson: "He was a great man that was di-verted from the straight and right path". Here we hear echoes of the biblical language used in the Old Testament to refer to the wicked kings of the Northern Kingdom of Israel.

Rachel the Poet

But undoubtedly, the key figure in this site of civil pilgrimage, and the most venerated heroine, is the poet Rachel. Almost every visit to the cemetery includes a visit to her grave, and almost all the other heritage sites in the area refer to her as well, and claim some sort of relation to her. Her book of poems, chained to the tomb, enables the visitors-pilgrims to read and sing from the 'sa-cred text', as indeed, they do.

Another important aspect of the encounter with Rachel is her informality. At the edge of the cemetery there is a Palm tree

---

[16]God says to Cain in Gen 4:10: "... the voice of thy brother's blood crieth unto me from the ground".

[17]Tel-Ḥai was a small Jewish settlement in Upper Galilee. In March of 1920 the place was attacked, and consequently deserted.

which (according to some) is mentioned and described in her poem 'Kinneret':

> ...There by the lakeside stands a lowly palm tree,
> Tousled is its hair as a naughty child...

The words of this poem are inscribed on a nearby stone (see photograph No. 2), but the inscription is in her own Hebrew handwriting and includes her signature. One of the more popular editions of her book of poems sets side-by-side the printed version of her poems, and photocopies of her original handwritten version. The result is that most readers are familiarized with Rachel's handwriting, but very few will know her last name (Bluwstein). This creates a feeling of familiarization and collective intimacy. One wonders, by comparison, how many English people would know Lord Byron's first name, and are familiar with his handwriting and signature. In a society where informality of speech and clothing are both a characteristic and a virtue[18] – such observations are significant because one can learn from them not only about the life of the poet, but about the very nature of contemporary Jewish-Israeli society.

Rachel's life in Israel was not easy. Many pioneers were attracted to her, both as a woman and as a human being, but despite her great beauty and charming personality she did not marry nor raise a family. The place that she loved so much, Kibbutz Degania, rejected her because of her illness (tuberculosis), and consequently she left rural Galilee and lived in the 'exile' of cities like Jerusalem and Tel Aviv. She died at the age of 41 after great suffering, and her funeral was a day of great distress for the emerging nation.

---

[18]Many scholars and others have commented upon the phenomenon of informality in contemporary Israeli society. See for example T. Katriel, *Talking Straight: 'Dugri' Speech in Israeli Sabra Culture*, Cambridge 1986.

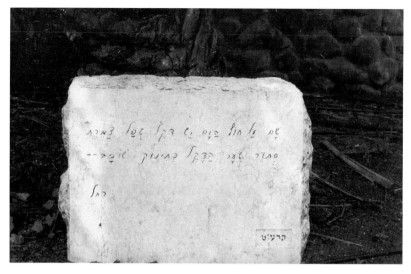

Photograph No. 2: the Palm tree & the inscription

Her romantic personality and tragic biography, as a pioneer and as a woman, is known to many and is reflected in her writing. Her presence at the cemetery enriches and encourages the visitors, and many feel there a spiritual climax that transforms the cemetery into a hallowed and meaningful place.

Conclusion

The Kinneret cemetery is made up of several graves which function as individual memorials. James Young observed that by themselves these memorials "... remain inert and amnesiac, mere stones in the landscape without life or meaning. For their memory, these memorials depend completely on the visitor. Only we can animate the stone figures and fill the empty spaces of the memorial ..."[19]

---

[19]J. Young, *The Art of Memory: Holocaust Memorials in History*, Prestel-Verlag & the Jewish Museum 1994.

On the surface it seems that visiting these memorials is not an essential part of human life, and one can survive physically quite well without paying a visit to these pioneers. However, the frequent visits and the emotional reaction of the visitors at the cemetery suggest that for a large number of Israeli Jews, these founding fathers and mothers fulfil a strong emotional need.

The Kinneret cemetery is a landscape text, rich with meanings that were once given by the makers of the cemetery, the 'writers' of the text, and by the visitors, the 'readers' of the text. The civil pilgrimage to the pioneers at the Kinneret cemetery, turns the 'mere stones in the landscape' into powerful and significant memorials that contribute to the shaping of the individual and collective identity of several Jews in Israel.

Appendix 1: Translation of the 29 line Reḥob Inscription[1]

1. *Shalom!* {Ia} These fruits are forbidden at Beth-Shean in the Seventh Year, and in the other sabbatical cycle years they are tithed (as) *demai* (i.e., produce about which there is uncertainty whether they were properly tithed or not): the marrows,

2. and the melons and the cucumbers and the parsnips and the mint which is bound by itself and Egyptian beans which are bound

3. in shavings and leeks from the Holiday (Sukkoth) to Hanukkah and seeds and dried figs and sesame and mustard and rice and cummin and dry lupine,

4. and large peas which are sold by measure and garlic and village onions sold by measure and onions

5. and pressed dates and wine and oil; in the Seventh Year (they are considered) Seventh Year (produce) and the other years of the sabbatical cycle (they are tithed as) *demai* and the bread for *hallah* (dough offering) is eternally (due). /{Ib}These are the places

6. which are permitted around Beth-Shean: on the south which is the Campus Gate till the 'white (i.e., wheat) field'; on the west

7. which is the Gate of the (oil-) Press till the end of the pavement; on the north which is the Gate of Sukota till Kefar Qarnos and Kefar Qarnos

---

[1] For an earlier English translation, see L.I. Levine, *Ancient Synagogues,* 152-153. In our translation, we have indicated not only the lines of the inscription but also the composite structure of the text made up of eight sources, each introduced by a Roman numeral. Other than the last paragraph, which is outside the original framework indicated by the double greeting "*Shalom!*", all the other sources are found in the rabbinic literature formulated in the academies of the Galilee. The geographic lists are found in both the tannaitic sources TShebi 4:8-11; *SifreDeut* 51 and in the later amoraic sources PT Demai 2:1,22d; PT Shebi 6:1,36g. However, the lists of agricultural products are found only in the amoraic formulation, PT Demai 2:1,22b.

8. is as Beth-Shean; and on the east which is the Dung Gate till the tomb of *pnwqtyyh* and the gate of Kefar Zimrin and the Meadow Gate.

9. Before the gate it is allowed and beyond it it is forbidden. // {II} The forbidden towns in the territory of Sussita: Ayyanosh and Ein-*hrh* and *dmbr*,

10. Iyyon and Yaarut and Kefar Yahrib and Nob and Hasafiya and Kefar Zemah; and Rabbi (Judah the Prince) permitted Kefar Zemah. // {III} The towns which are doubtful within the territory of Naveh:

11. Sir and Sayyer and Gasimei and Zeizun and Raneb and Harbata and *ʿygry hwtm*
and the town of Bar-*Hrg*. // {IV} The forbidden towns in the territory of Tyre: Shezet

12. Bezeth and Pi Masoba and Upper Hanotha and Lower Hanotha and *bybrh* and Rosh Mayah and *ʿmwn* and *mzh* which is Castella; and all (the lands) which Jews have purchased,

13. is forbidden. // {V} The borders of the Land of Israel, the district settled by those who returned from Babylon: (Starting from) the Crossroad of Ashkelon, Straton's Tower (Caesarea Maritima), Dor, the city wall of Acco,

14. and source of the waters of the Gaato(n), and Gaato(n) itself, and Kubrata (Cabri) and Beth-Zanita (Kh. Zanitha) and *castrum* of the Galil (Kh. Galil) and Qebaiya de ʾAiita (ʾAita-ash-shʾab) and from Masyah (the source?) of Yarkata

15. and the watering trough(?) of Kuraim (Kh. Kur) and Saharta de-Yatir (Surrounding area of Yaʾtir) and the Brook of Bezal and Beth-ʾAit and Barshata (Birʾashit) and the greater Auli and the Valley

16. of Iyyon and the Sefanhah incline/slope (?) (Sefinah-north-east of Hasabiyeh) and the town of Bar-Sangorah and Upper Tarnagolah of Caesarion (Paneas) and Beth-Sebel and Keneth

17. and Reqem of Trachonitis, Zimra in the district of Bosra, Jabbok and Heshbon and the Brook of Zered (Wadi Hasa), ʾIgar Sahaduta, Nimrin

18. and the Salt (lake) of Ziza(?), Reqem de-Gaya (Petra?) to the Gardens of Ashkelon and the highway to the Desert. // {VI} These fruits

19. are forbidden in Paneas in the Seventh Year and in the other years of the sabbatical cycle they are tithed as full(?) *demai:*

20. the rice and the nuts and the sesame and Egyptian beans. Some say even choice plums

21. for these in the Seventh Year are (considered) Seventh Year (produce) and in the other years of the sabbatical cycle they are tithed as *demai* and even

22. from upper Tarnagolah and beyond. // {VIIa} These fruits are tithed (as) *demai* at Caesarea (Maritima): the wheat and the bread

23. for *hallah* (which is) eternally (due) and the wine and the oil and the dates and the rice and the cummin for these are permitted in the Seventh Year at Caesarea

24. and in the other years of the sabbatical cycle they are due (as) *demai* and there are some who forbid white onions from

25. the King's Mountain. / {VIIb} And until where is the region of Caesarea? Till Soran and the inn of Tabithah (perhaps the name of the hostess) and the Column,

26. and Dor and Kefar Sabah; and if there is a place which was purchased by Jews our rabbis are suspicious of it. // *Shalom!* // {VIII} The towns

27. permi[tt]ed within the territory of Sebaste: ʿIqabin and Kefar Kasdayah and Sir and ʿzylyn and Shafirin and Einanin and Upper Yibleam and Mu(!)haru

28. and Dothan and Kefar-[Ra]mayah and Shelata and Pentakomia, Liviah and Upper Paradise and Yazit and ʿrbwnwryn and Kefar

29. Yehudit and *mwnryt* and half of Shelaf.

PLATES

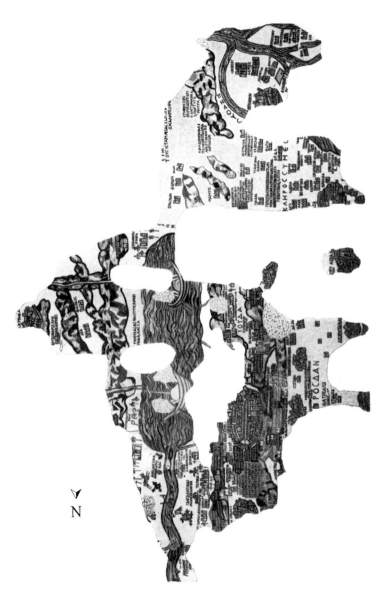

Map 1. The Madaba mosaic

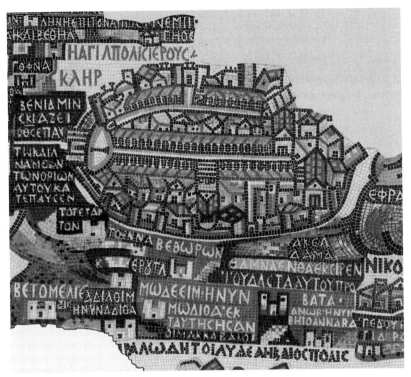

Map 2. Jerusalem in the Madaba mosaic (detail)

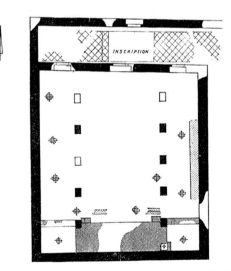

Illustration 1. Plan of the synagogue at Reḥob

Illustration 2. The Reḥob mosaic

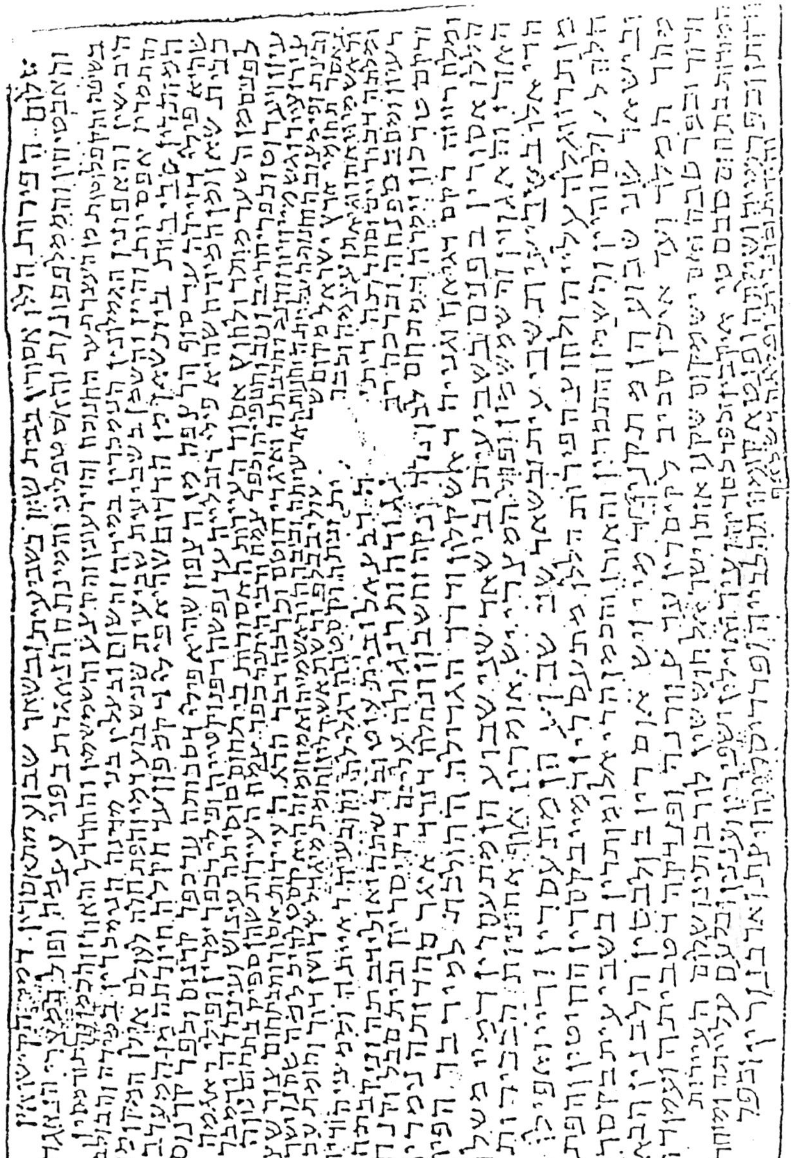

Illustration 2. The Reḥob mosaic (text)

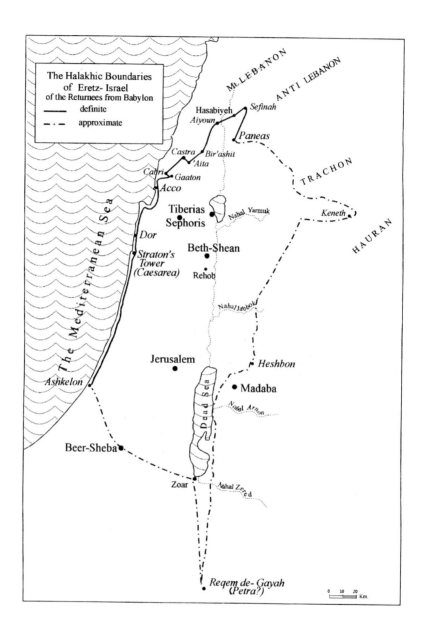

Map 3. The halakhic borders according to the Reḥob mosaic

INDEX OF NAMES AND SUBJECTS

INDEX OF ANCIENT SOURCES

Numbers Rabbah
18:23   236n.9

Pirqe de Rabbi Eliezer
40   233n.5,236,248,249
            254

Pesiqta Rabbati
33   159,160

Pesiqta de Rab Kahana
12   133
12:11   125
12:21   123
12:22   119,121,122,127-129

Ruth Rabbah
1   187n.62

Sefer Ha-yashar
–   252,253n.47,261

Sifre Numbers
8   146n.29
39   182n.53
75   148n.37
116   145n.24

Sifre Deuteronomy
29   159,160
51   295n.27,361n.1
145   171n.15
155   182n.52
208   183n.53

Song of Songs Rabbah
1:12   130n.38
4:4   159,160

Tanḥuma
Bemidbar
22   140n.11

Lekh Lekha
20   150n.42
Qedoshim
6   187n.62

Tanḥuma (Buber)
Bemidbar
27   140n.11
Beshallah
13   187n.62
Wa-yishlaḥ
21   159,160
Yitro
14   122n.24

Targum Jonathan to Samuel
2:2-5   56n.28
2:5   58n.34

Targum Jonathan to Isaiah
42   57n.31

Targum Ps.-Jonathan to Exodus
2:21   248,261
14:21   249,261

Yalqut Shimoni
Exodus
166   248n.33,252,261
Numbers
20   236,244n.25
Psalms
869   236n.9

Yelamdenu
Ginzê Schechter
1:99   159